EXPERIENCES WITH GOD

Experiences with God

A DICTIONARY OF SPIRITUALITY

Columba Cary-Elwes

Sheed & Ward
London

ISBN 0–7220–3495–4

Cum permissu superiorum, OSB
Nihil obstat Anton Cowan, Censor
Imprimatur Mgr John Crowley, VG, Westminster, 20 August 1986

Published in Great Britain in 1986 by
Sheed & Ward Limited,
2, Creechurch Lane,
London, EC3A 5AQ

Book production by Bill Ireson

Filmset by Fakenham Photosetting Limited, Fakenham, Norfolk
Printed and bound by A. Wheaton & Company Limited, Exeter, Devon

Introduction

Introduction

This unpretentious little book began as a personal ABC or Alphabet of Catholic spirituality; but in order not to give the impression of a learned dictionary on the lines of the incomparable and still incomplete *Dictionnaire de Spiritualité*, I have called it something else, leaving the sub-title as a memorial to its simple origins.

Naturally over the years of its emergence it has grown, but still remaining a collection of my own personal choice, from the highways and the byways, hoping that as these topics have interested and helped me, they might be of interest and of use to others on the way to God.

For those who are in search of something more extensive and more profound, there are now a number of learned publications. Compared to them, this is more an appetizer than the long drink. The great traditional works, of an Augustine, a Thomas, a Gregory, a Bernard, of Teresa and John of the Cross, quite apart from the valuable translations of the Bible, they are on every shelf – or should be. So I say with regard to them, and to this work, what Augustine heard in that Garden in the voice of a child at the moment of crisis: *Tolle lege, tolle lege* – 'Take up and read, take up and read'.

COLUMBA CARY ELWES
July 1986

Abbreviations

A.C.W.	Ancient Christian Writers, The Works of the Fathers in translation, J. Quasten (ed.) and others (Westminster, Maryland and London, 1946 ff).
A.N.C.L.	Ante-Nicene Christian Library (Edinburgh, 1864 ff).
B.A.C.	Biblioteca de autores cristianos (Madrid).
Bettenson	H. Bettenson (ed.), *Documents of the Christian Church*, (London, 1943; New York, 1947).
Bremond	H. Brémond, *Histoire litteraire du sentiment religieux en France depuis la fin des guerres de religion jusqu'à nos jours,* 11 vols (Paris, 1916–33, Index 1936).
C.E.	*Catholic Encyclopedia,* 15 vols and Index (New York, 1907–14).
C.R.S.	Catholic Records Society (London, 1905 ff).
D.A.C.L.	*Dictionnaire d'archéologie Chrétienne et de Liturgie,* F. Cabrol (ed.), OSB, and H. Leclercq OSB, 15 vols (1907–53).
D.B.T.	*Dictionary of Biblical Theology,* Xavier Leon-Dufour (ed.), London, 1978.
D.H.G.E.	*Dictionnaire d'histoire et de géographié ecclesiastique.*
D.N.B.	*Dictionary of National Biography,* 1885–1960 (various volumes).
D.T.C.	*Dictionnaire de Théologie Catholique,* A. Vacant (ed.), E. Mangenot and E. Amann, 15 vols (1903–50).
E.C.	*Enciclopedia Cattolica,* P. Paschini (ed.) and others, 12 vols (1949–54).
D. Spir.	*Dictionnaire de Spiritualité.*
E.E.T.S.	Early English Texts Society (London, 1894 ff).
H.C.S.	*History of Christian Spirituality,* Louis Bouyer (ed.) and others, 4 vols (English translation, London and New York, 1963).
N.C.E.	*New Catholic Encyclopedia,* 14 vols and Index (New York, 1967).
O.D.C.C.	*The Oxford Dictionary of the Christian Church,* 2nd edition, F. L. Cross (ed.) and E. A. Livingstone, (Oxford, 1974).
S. Th.	*Summa Theologica* of St Thomas Aquinas.
↗	before a word refers to an entry in the Dictionary under that word or a cognate one.

EXPERIENCES WITH GOD

A

Abandonment

Christian, Jewish, ↗Sufist, Hindu and ↗Zen Buddhist seekers after the absolute proclaim the need, as a preliminary, to abandon all else for the pearl of great price. The Gospel's 'go sell all . . .' is an echo of one of the world's oldest pieces of wisdom. However, 'abandonment' and 'abandoning all' are not exactly the same thing. Abandonment could mean a readiness to give up all if God so requires it. Thus Job expressed it when he said, 'God has given, God has taken away, blessed be the name of the Lord' (1:21).

Some would prefer a more positive concept such as acceptance, conformity to the divine will, one that comes from a spirit of love rather than resignation. Indeed Christian abandonment is shown by a cheerful acceptance of God's providence, a grasping of the teaching of Christ, of his Church, obedience to lawful authority, an acceptance of whatever befalls in the ups and downs of everyday life. Jesus' own words express this perfectly, 'Father, into your hands I commend my spirit' (Lk 23:46) or, 'not my will but thine be done' (Mt 26:39), or we have Mary's words, 'May it be done to me according to thy word' (Lk 1:38). In these cases we find an active acceptance. The Quietist error was to be so negative that even sin was accepted with an excess of abandonment, in which resistance to temptation was nil, resulting in the collapse of morality. Molinos (d. 1697) was condemned for this amoral stance. He is recorded as having said, 'We must not resist temptation' (cf. Proposition 17, Denzinger 2217).

↗John of the Cross wrote: 'To attain to joy in the All, reach out for joy in nothing' (*Ascent*, Bk. 1, ch. 13). Thomas More on the other hand accepted with gratitude all the joys God granted him, and, when finally stripped of all, even of his liberty, he was at peace.

The world in which we live today provides ample opportunities for the practice of abandonment to the divine will, not least the world situation as such with the threat of nuclear war. Besides, we appear to be in the hands of merciless scientific means of destruction and of uncontrollable economic systems. Modern Christians should take a stand against what is evil in these tyrannies, and at the same time accept whatever cannot be changed.

J.-P. de Caussade, SJ, in *Self-Abandonment to Divine Providence* has given us the classic statement of the true doctrine of abandonment, and provided a practical way of applying it: 'The sacrament of the present moment.' We need to say 'yes' to God now.

I.S. Alphonsus, *On Conformity to the Will of God*. Pamphlet.

J.-P. de Caussade, *Self-Abandonment to Divine Providence*, (London, 1962).

J.-P. de Caussade, *The Sacrament of the Present Moment*, (London, 1981). As above, different translation and title.

Abba

The name used by Jesus when speaking of his own father in heaven (Mk 14:36). It was not the ordinary word in use for 'Father' in Aramaic but originally the child equivalent such as 'papa' might be in our world, almost a pet name like 'daddy', though by the time of Christ not quite so familiar.

Before Jesus this name was never used of God, and it is noticeable that the evangelists retained it. Prof Jeremias considers it to be one of the most authentic 'sayings' of Jesus. It signifies the intimate closeness between Jesus and his father, also delineating the character of the father as not remote but compassionate, gentle, merciful and loving. It is a word that expresses the verse of Isaiah (49:15) and recalls God's own description of himself in Exodus (34:6): 'A God of tenderness and compassion, slow to anger, rich in kindness and faithfulness.' It is the style of the father in the parable of the Prodigal Son, in which the father outdoes the wayward son in generosity by going out to meet him and taking him in his arms (Lk 15:11 ff).

The word used in the prayer that Jesus told his disciples to use, when turning to God, is 'Father'. We share Jesus' sonship and therefore the same relationship with our father (Mt 18:3). Three times in the Greek New Testament the Aramaic word *abba* is given (Mk 14:36; Rom 8:15; Gal 4:6).

J. Jeremias, *The Prayers of Jesus*, (London, 1977), especially pp. 94–8.

Abnegation

Its root is to negate, to deny oneself, never a popular idea, but present at the heart of all the great religions of the world. It has degrees: renouncing of sin, of imperfections, then the stripping of self-love in order to share in the passion and death of Christ. In the words of Charles de Foucauld: 'Is it conceivable that we should see you (Christ) poor and remain ourselves voluntarily rich?' (*D. Spir.* Vol 1, col. 108).

In Christian thought abnegation is grounded on such sayings as, 'He who would come with me, let him deny himself and take up his cross and follow me', and, 'He who would save his life, must lose it' (Mt 16:24). All the saints from Paul to Soeur Thérèse follow Christ's example: even Francis of Sales, the humanist, insists on the need for self denial; but none of them for the reason that the things of this world are bad, quite the contrary. It is rather because they are good and become rivals to God in men's hearts. Abnegation is not an end in itself, but a means of liberating the self from self, people and things, to be free for God. St John of the Cross is the doctor of the 'Nothing', *nada*, but we must remember he was writing specifically for enclosed contemplatives. People in the world have to use the world, even to the extent of the saying 'with this body I thee worship'. We are expected to love people. It is a matter of degree, of balance, of subordination of one love to another. So we are led to ask, how does a person in the world practise this essential asceticism? We reply: 'By accepting the rough with the smooth (what God has given, God takes away); by a curb on extravagance; by a sharing of this world's goods with those who are in want; by not clinging to them, or being over-anxious. Without abnegation true prayer is impossible.'

Acarie, Madame Barbe (1566–1618)

Bl Marie de l'Incarnation was an outstanding example of sanctity in a worldly situation. Most of her life was spent as a lay woman, married to an eager but politically inept husband. In spite of exacting work as mother of six children and with anxieties as chatelaine of a large household, with the family fortunes temporarily shattered, she experienced continuous intimate converse with Jesus, yet it was she who restored the family fortunes. The incident that provoked her 'conversion' in her early married life was a sentence of St Augustine: 'Indeed he is a miser for whom God is not enough.' Her chief guide was the English Franciscan, ↗Benet of Canfield whose work on the *Will of God* was put on the Index as part of the Quietist scare. Its theme – and her spirituality – was to resign oneself absolutely to the Divine Will. Partly through her inspiration and energy the Spanish Carmelites of the Teresian Reform were introduced into France. She ended her life as one of them.

She was the heart and soul of the spiritual revival in Paris after the Wars of Religion. At her house gathered Vincent de Paul, ↗Bérulle, ↗Francis of Sales, Descartes; and linked with her were the Carthusians of the Paris Charterhouse in the Faubourg St Jacques, especially Dom Richard Beaucousin. She is an excellent example of a busy lay woman of considerable gifts being used by the Spirit of God, and yet with deep humility, to gather for God's work an élite of the time. She was never without a director and remained always devoted to the authority of the Church.

Bremond, Vol. 2, pp. 193–263.

C. Sheppard, *Barbe Acarie, Wife and Mystic*, (London, 1953).

Accidie

From Greek *akedia*: carelessness, indifference. Cassian brought this vice into prominence (*Institutes* Bk. 10, 2) and claimed it attacked hermits particularly. He suspected it was the same as the noonday devil mentioned in Psalms (90:6 [Vg]), since the height of the 'fever' comes at midday. According to him it is a fever both of heart and mind for the monk finds no longer any savour in his solitude, no delight in his prayer, but rather irksomeness; which all leads to a clamorous desire for change – to go visiting, to receive the brethren, to leave his cell. Reasons abound: his life is meaningless, unprofitable to others; the active ministry would be more useful. The response Cassian suggests is a greater devotion to prayer.

If accidie only attacked hermits, this notice could be cut short. But in many forms it attacks today the active Christian too, especially in middle life, when the romantic mood has dissolved. The chosen vocation – the life of a barrister, merchant, civil servant, physician – and still more the factory or office job, unaccountably seem empty and meaningless, the very faith a mere dream. Our practice of religion seems a mere external ritual. Why continue? This is the noonday devil of the 20th century. He is slain by faith and courage and doggedness, in practice, especially by prayer. If one begins to slacken off, what had been perhaps only difficult, will become positively distasteful: 'Now is the acceptable time' (Ps 69:13).

Active Life

For the Fathers of the Desert, it was that first part of the monastic life, which consisted in the struggle to overcome vice and acquire virtue. That achieved, the contemplative life followed. Already with ↗Augustine we find our modern use of the terms. He would make three styles of Christian living: the active, the mixed, the leisured (or as often called, contemplative). As for the three kinds of life, the life of leisure, the life of action, and the combination of the two, anyone might spend his life in any of these ways without detriment to his faith, and might thus attain to the everlasting rewards (*City of God*, 19:19). He goes on that it must be the love for truth that seeks out leisure and the urge to love that undertakes active work in the affairs of men. But neither should those seeking leisure utterly abandon good works, nor those in the active life abandon the search for truth, and the leisure it demands. So for St Augustine the 'active' is the Christian life of good works and this is its usual meaning in our day. But he insists on prayer as well in the active life.

In our time the Spirit is moving vast numbers to pray; the West is becoming fascinated with the prayerful traditions of the East. But another strand is claiming that the active life is prayer. Augustine we see above does not agree: the active people need prayer, if only to clarify their motives, but more to slake their innate desire for ultimate truth and love which are God. Yet the active life is all engrossing; it tends to make the things of the spirit seem unreal because unseen, and we appear to be doing all the work, not God. Prayer then is all the more important, yet the prayer life for the active has still to be worked out: e.g. times for it, kinds of prayer; perhaps short shafts of prayer, emphasizing abandonment, acceptance, petition for prudence, wisdom, courage, for love and compassion and understanding of others.

Field Marshal Foch in the First World War gave an hour to prayer every day. Thomas More, Chancellor of England, took part in the Eucharist every day, and once a week spent a whole day in prayer.

Adoration

When ↗Francis of Assisi composed his ↗Canticle to the sun he was adoring the creator of all; when Mary sang her Magnificat she was adoring the mysterious ways of God's providence. According to Matthew (4:10) we must worship the Lord our God by reason of his infinite greatness and of the submission we owe him, we his creatures. He can be adored in his infinity, immensity, immutability, eternity, as Three in One, for his unbounded mercy and love, his all-powerfulness, wisdom, perfection, holiness; his goodness, sovereignty, providence and justice. We may adore the Word made Man in the Eucharistic mystery, his love as symbolized in the Sacred Heart; adore him in our mind and will, with a reverential fear. We may adore the Spirit who guides all in his Truth and Love.

Man also worships in act, by ritual or symbolic signs; typical ways would be kneeling or prostrations. Man is the mouthpiece of creation as the adorer. Monks have a special task of adoring the Divine Majesty through the liturgy.

Aelred of Rievaulx, St (1109–67)

He was the son of a priest in a period when this was common; he became a monk at Rievaulx in Yorkshire under its first abbot St William, 1133, and was soon made novice master, then Abbot of Revesby, and finally Abbot of Rievaulx in 1147 till his death. Friend and disciple of St Bernard – founding Abbot of Rievaulx – yet he had his own spiritual contribution to make. He believed that we go through spiritual human friendship to that with God, (*cf. de Spirituali amicitia* where he writes that true friendship never concerns only two, it always involves Christ, the source of true friendship, its framework, its end). He preached on the humanity of Christ, his childhood as well as his Passion. His spirituality was affective. He wrote a rule for hermits at the request of his sister (*de Institutione inclusarum*). He is undoubtedly the most influential spiritual writer of his age in England; his immense sensibility is unlike the supposed characteristic of the modern Englishman.

F.M. Powicke (ed.), *Life of Ailred, Walter Daniel, monk of Rievaulx*, (1950).

A. Squire, *Aelred of Rievaulx: A Study*, (London, 1981).

H. Talbot (tr.), *On Spiritual Friendship*, (London, 1942).

G. Webb and H. Talbot (tr.), *On Jesus at twelve years old*, (London, 1956).

See *D. Spir.*, Vol. 1, pp. 225–34. Also *N.C.E.*, Vol. 1.

Agape
A Greek word signifying love, or in primitive Christian society a love feast. It became associated in apostolic times with the Eucharist; indeed it was the origin of unseemly behaviour which Paul condemns (1 Cor 11:17–34). The faithful brought wine and got drunk; some came with little food and were not fed from the plenty of others. Today a revival of interest has occurred in the symbolism of the meal; sign of friendship, union, love. To be noticed is the frequency of the meal motif in the New Testament and the miracles of the multiplication of the loaves. An *agape*, or love feast is common again among Christians, particularly in ecumenical circles, as a temporary substitute for a sharing of the Eucharist proper.

Agape was not used as a noun in classical Greek; but much so used in the New Testament for altruistic love, God's love for us, ours for him and for one another. *Eros*, another Greek word for love, stands for a love which loves another for one's own sake. It is scarcely possible or right to love others without any associated joy, except loving our enemies and those who in some way revolt us. Jesus loved those who killed him; St Francis embraced the leper. Once the love we have for another has become centred on the pleasure received, it is no longer *agape* but *eros*, and can become an idolatry.

G. Quell and E. Stauffer, *Love*, (Kittel's Bible Key Words series), (London, 1949).

Spicq, *Agapè dans le Nouveau Testament, Analyse des textes*, 3 vols., (Paris, 1959–66).

Albert the Great, OP, St (*1200–80*)
In the story of spirituality his importance is two-fold and profound, first as the teacher and defender of his great disciple ↗Thomas Aquinas, but less known perhaps for his studies on ↗Denis the Pseudo-Areopagite, which he did when teaching his Dominican pupils at Cologne. Thomas was one of them and the latter's works, especially the *Summa Theologica*, in spiritual matters are frequently supported by quotations from Denis. In this way the neo-Platonic stream entered late medieval spirituality. This was particularly true of the Rhineland mystics who derive from Denis, not only through Thomas but also through another disciple of Albert, namely Dietrich of Freiberg, who was himself the inspiration of Eckhart; and, as is

generally known, he is the main source for the neo-Platonic vein both in ↗Tauler and ↗Suso, later in ↗Ruysbroeck and finally in the Spanish mystics. Of course none of these are exclusively either Dionysian or Eckhartian.

See 'Albert the Great' in *N.C.E.*

Al-Ghazali (444H/1058 AD– 497H/1111 AD)

Born at Tus in Khorasan, Persia. A philosopher. He is the Descartes of Islam who reached universal doubt except for immediate experience, and in religious mystical experience. 'I learned with certainty that it is, above all, the mystics who walk on the road to God; their life is the best life, their method the soundest method.' ('Confessions of a Troubled Believer', p. 190 in *An Anthology of Islamic Literature* by James Kritzech, Harmondsworth, 1964).

'I realized that I was caught in a veritable thicket of attachments . . . the voice of faith was calling. "To the road! to the road! What is left of life is but little and the journey before you is long."' (W. Montgomery Watt [tr.], *Faith and Practice of Al-Ghazali*, London, 1953, p. 57.) He became a Sufi and experienced the mystical life. His greatest work, *The Revival of Religious Sciences*, made Sufism respectable in Islam. But towards the end of his life he left the contemplative life in order to help others. 'Now I am calling men to the knowledge whereby worldly success is given up.' (Kritzech, *op. cit.*, p. 191.)

cf. M. Asín-Palacios, *La espiritualidad de Algazel y su sentido cristiano*, 4 vols., (Madrid, 1934–41).

Al-Hallaj (244H/858 AD–309H/922 AD)

Born at Fars in Persia. The supreme example of the ecstatic Sufi mystic. The heroism of his death and the details of its execution invite comparison with the crucifixion of Jesus. His last days were recorded by a faithful disciple: he was scourged, crucified and finally beheaded. The accusation was that he had claimed to be God. At his trial he protested, 'God forbid that I should pretend to Divinity or to Prophecy. I am a mere man who worships God and practises prayer and fasting; that is all.' (Kritzeck, *op. cit.* p. 108.) Other utterances are both profound and startling, e.g., 'Hide me from God, you people! Hide me from God! . . . He took me from myself and has not given me back; and I cannot perform the service I should do in his Presence for fear of His leaving me alone again. He will leave me deserted, abandoned . . .' (*ibid.* p. 104). He was faced with this experience of 'naughting', of *nada*, that we find in the English mystics and in St John of the Cross: 'For me in this moment there is no veil, not so much as a wink, between me and Him – a time for quiet, that my humanity die into his Deity while my body burns in the fire of his power.' (*ibid* p. 105). The sense of the indwelling of God is overwhelming in his sayings: 'Thou it was didst will my beginning, Thou who didst seize my being to use it for thy symbol, Thou who didst proclaim it, as my last and highest, as my Divine Being. Thou didst cause me to speak the BE of my own creation.' (*ibid* p. 110). And as he was dying he expresses a duality in unity: 'All who have known ecstasy long for this . . . the loneliness of the Only One . . . alone with the Alone.' (*ibid* p. 112).

Al-Hallaj remained faithful to the Islamic belief in creation, but he, like many mystics, saw the image of his own creation in the mind of God. We must not be surprised that he could only stammer the insight he saw.

J. Kritzech, *An Anthology of Islamic Literature*, (Harmondsworth, 1964).

Alumbrados
See ↗Illuminism.

Ambrose, St (*circa 339–97*)
Bishop of Milan and Father of the Church. While still a catechumen he was acclaimed bishop by both the Catholics and Arians of Milan (374). By his knowledge of Greek he could introduce into the West the allegorical interpretation of the Old Testament used by Origen. This helped St Augustine to appreciate the sacred text. Ambrose befriended him and was largely instrumental in his conversion. Ambrose also introduced into the Western church the singing of hymns, some of which he composed. His Christian courage and sense of justice were manifested in his resisting the imperial power. He condemned the Emperor Theodosius for having thousands of citizens massacred at Thessalonica in revenge for the killing of its governor. In Milan he fostered the groups of virgins for whom he wrote a treatise. He had become the chief spokesman for the Church in the West, by the sheer power of his holiness and intelligence.

Bernard Botte (ed.), *Des Sacraments; Des Mystères*, (Paris, 1950).

E. Cazzaniga (ed.), 376 'De Virginibus', in *Corpus Scriptorum Latinorum Paravianum*, (Turin, 1948).

E. Cazzaniga (ed.), 377 'De Virginitate' in *Corpus Scriptorum Latinorum Paravianum*, (Turin, 1952).

F.H. Dudden, *Life and Times of St Ambrose*, 2 vols., (Oxford, 1935).

A. Paredi, *St Ambrose, his Life and Times*, (London, 1964).

See also, for his relations with St Augustine, *Confessions*, Bks. 5, 6 and 9.

Ancren Rule
Written for three noble sisters living the eremitical life together in, as the author wrote, 'as it were, the mother house'. Its date is probably early 13th century. The author was probably a secular priest; and the kind of English points to the West Country or Marches of Wales. Though the recipients are hermitesses, the main body of this early medieval classic is mostly concerned with the seven deadly sins, entitled, for example, 'the lion of pride', 'the sow of gluttony', 'the fox of envy'. The style is homely and direct. Nevertheless the writer clearly expects the sisters to be practising contemplative prayer, from his use of the *Song of Songs* (e.g. Part 2.14) and from his use of the traditional contrast between the lives of Martha and Mary (Part 7).

M.B. Salu (tr.), G. Sitwell (intro.), *The Ancrene Riwle*, (London and New York, 1955).

Annihilation
The root of the word, *nihil*, means nothing, therefore making nothing. In some Buddhist literature and mysticism/meditation this word may literally mean the self ceasing to be, in order to reach Nirvana, though Northern Buddhism (*Mahayana*), which seems to have

some affinities with Christianity, would not so state the case. Hinduism would be for eliminating – annihilating – the superficial self and recognizing the identity of the real self with the all. (To put all this so succinctly is to be misleading.)

The Christian use of the word is guarded, because according to Christian belief the human element is not annihilated by union with God, though mystics and poets use the word or its equivalents – naughting, extinction and so on – to express absorption in God. But its use is hyperbolic. St John of the Cross in the *Dark Night* (stanza 5), writes: 'The Loved One with his beloved, the beloved transformed into the Loved One.' (*Amado con amada, / amada en el Amado transformada!*)

According to Abbé Cognet, (*Post-Reformation Spirituality*, p. 16, n. 2), in the technical prayer-language of Christians, particularly among northern writers of the 14th–16th centuries, its meaning was 'absorption without destruction'.

Drug experimenters, especially with LSD, would recognize an experience of void and apparent annihilation of self, but as something not permanent, an in-out experience: (*cf.* T. Leary, *The Politics of Ecstasy*, London, 1972). In any case this is only at the level of experience not at the philosophical or ontological level. The effect on the brain can be devastating.

Anselm, St (*1033–1109*)
Became Abbot of the Benedictine abbey of Bec (1078) in Normandy and Archbishop of Canterbury (1093); but he was neither English nor Norman, being born at Aosta in Northern Italy and of Lombard ancestry. He represents what was best in the Western Christendom of his time and, though spiritually medieval, intellectually he was modern. He represented the Western Church at the Dialogue with the Orthodox at Bari in Southern Italy. In his writings he set out to prove what he believed not so much by Scripture texts but by reason: yet he would begin with belief: *credo ut intelligam* – 'I believe that I may understand'. He applied this approach (in his early *Monologion* [1078]) to the very existence of God and more penetratingly in the *Proslogion* (1079) where his onto-logical argument is to be found. Six years later he explored the mystery of the Incarnation in *De Incarnatione Verbi*; then in 1098 he published *Cur Deus Homo*, or *Why God became man*. This was the first formal study of the Redemption or the Atonement, but done from a reasoning point of view. We can exaggerate the legalistic atmosphere of his argument. We are fortunate in having a contemporary life by his monk chaplain Eadmer and in possessing more than 300 of his letters, personal and tender, sensible and deeply pious, together with a collection of prayers and meditations he wrote for others. For Anselm the truths of the faith were the springs of his spiritual life, they were also the source and stimulation to his intellectual life. He was at ease with his faith and his reason, each supporting and nourishing the other. As archbishop, Anselm defended the right of the Church to free herself from too great a dependence on the State, for which cause he suffered two bouts of virtual exile during 1098–1100 and 1103–7 mostly in Rome.

F.S. Schmitt, OSB, *Opera Omnia*, 6 vols., (Edinburgh, 1946–61). See also his article, 'Anselm', in *N.C.E.*

R.W. Southern (ed. and tr.), *The Life of Saint Anselm ... by Eadmer*, (Oxford, 1972).

R.W. Southern, *Saint Anselm and his Biographer*, (Cambridge, 1963).

Sr Benedicta Ward, SLG, (tr.), *The Prayers and Meditations of Saint Anselm*, (Harmondsworth, 1979).

Apatheia

Stoic impassivity, impassiveness, freedom from all the passions, it was a Stoic 'must', in order to be calm in judgement. Besides, life, they thought, is a painful business, and passionlessness would reduce pain to a minimum. The Fathers of the Desert use *apatheia* in a Christian sense central to the spiritual life, following first Clement and Origen of Alexandria. But it was ↗Evagrius (who died among them in 399) who claimed there could be no contemplation without *apatheia*. He was not denying love of God and neighbour but any disordinate love that would interfere with these two. This rather negative attitude was turned by St Maximus, Evagrius's friend, into peace of soul. First we must turn from vice, then from all thoughts that could lead us astray, then cut off all appetites of reason or sense, in order to be in one's soul the mirror of God. Is impassiveness truly Christian?

↗Augustine was not quite happy with all this, and in the *City of God* he analyses the concept closely (*cf.* Bk. 14.9): 'If apatheia is the name of that state in which the mind cannot be touched by any emotion whatsoever, who would not judge this insensitivity to be the worst of all moral defects?' Augustine is a useful antidote to a resurgence of this theory in our day in certain Buddhist schools of thought. He goes on to say that Jesus felt angry grief at the hardness of heart of the Jews (Mk 3:5); shed tears before awakening Lazarus (Jn 11:35); and as the Passion approached his soul grieved (Mt 26:38).

↗Cassian, the main spiritual reading, apart from the Bible, of monks in the West up to the later Middle Ages, sums it up by saying that not all passions are evil; some are good. Therefore only evil ones should be suppressed, others should be controlled by reason and the grace of God. In Latin he changes *apatheia* to purity of heart (*cf.* Conference 22); see also (*S. Th.*, Ia, IIae, q. 24, aa. 2 and 3) where St Thomas considers all passions are good except where disordered.

Today, when the slings and arrows are more outrageous than ever, the Christian needs help in this matter. The emotions are part of God's creation and there to help. They must not be suppressed but restrained. The Stoic's impassivity is only the first step to victory; the second is acceptance. God has given, God has taken away. The third step is a loving grasping of all that God sends. Christ himself in his passion found the third hard. 'Thy will be done' is the perfect expression of willing acceptance and goes far beyond stoic *apatheia*.

Apophatic, and Kataphatic

These are Greek derivatives: *apophatic* means Negative and *kataphatic* means Positive. They are used with reference to ways of knowing God, and in particular to ways of praying: (i) The positive or *kataphatic* way – sometimes also called the way of causation – would be: God is love because he causes love; (ii) the negative way or the *apophatic* way would be expressed: God is not love (what we mean by love) because that concept is limited, and God in all respects is limitless; (iii) There is a third way, the way of the mystics and called sometimes (by

St Thomas Aquinas) the more eminent way, or by others the way of transcendence. Whatever of being, of goodness, of perfection is in created beings, is in a more eminent way in God (*S. Th.*, Ia pars, q. 4, a. 2). ↗Nicholas of Cusa has emphasized this third way; and the pseudo-↗Denis and ↗Eckhart the first. But none of these denies the possibility of the positive way. They do not forget that Jesus said, 'He who sees me sees the Father' (Jn 14:9). The negative way is much favoured by Eastern religions: '*neti, neti*', 'not this, not that'. In prayer there is a time for all these ways, according as the Spirit leads.

Apophthegmata of the Fathers

Sayings of the Fathers of the Desert, gathered together by an unknown editor probably at the end of the 5th century. The collection is arranged in alphabetical order according to authors. It also includes accounts of the virtues of the Fathers. Altaner in his *Patrology* (p. 256) compares the *Apophthegmata Patrum* in this to the *Lausiac History* of Palladius.

These sayings of the elders or acknowledged holy monks or hermits of the desert were treasured by the disciples and pilgrims. It was customary for the disciple to ask for a saying, for him to meditate upon it for a week, a month, or more, until the deeper meaning was borne in on him. This reminds us of the Hindu mantras and the Zen ↗koan: pithy, enigmatic, always profound sayings, thought on, puzzled over and over again.

This method is still useful. Some modern Christian movements make use of this technique (e.g. Focolari) providing a saying from the Gospel for the members to be chewed over for a month, e.g. 'Where two or three are gathered together in my name, there am I in the midst of them.' (Mt 18:20).

Sr Benedicta Ward, SLG, *The Wisdom of the Desert Fathers*, (Oxford, 1975).

Aridity

A common condition among prayerful people, in which one is unable or able only with difficulty to pray. It is not revulsion but inability; not tepidity but perhaps even over-zeal. Prayer seems nothing, and this is distressing. Possible causes are: bad health, since physical condition affects the spirit; physical weariness, likewise; lack of skill at praying (a guide useful); excess of business; a basic moral fault, especially pride or sensuality, both of which put up high barriers; or negligence. On the other hand the cause could be, if it appears to be none of the above, a divine cleansing of the soul, preparing it for closer union with God; a desert of the senses or of the spirit, of which there is much in the works of St John of the Cross. St Teresa pointed out that it could last months or years, and that it was important to have a wise guide or director. (*cf.* 'John of the Cross', *The Ascent of Mount Carmel*, Bk. 2, ch. 13, in E. Allison Peers [ed. and tr.], *The Complete Works of St John of the Cross*, 3 vols. in 1 London and New York, 1964, pp. 108–11, see especially n. 2, p. 109.)

Asceticism

From Greek *askesis*: exercise, and for Stoics the exercise of virtue and elimination of vice. The word and idea are taken over and transformed by the Alexandrine church, especially ↗Origen. By itself this is too self-centred for the Christian who would live by faith in God and loving obedience. The Christian *askesis* is to denude oneself of self in order to live by and in God. This is the way of Abraham, who left all and his own ideas to follow the call of God (*cf.* Heb 11:8). The New Testament is clear: take up your cross and follow me (Mk 8:34); he who loves his life must lose it (Jn 12:25); go sell all ... and follow me (Mt 19:21); eunuchs for the kingdom (Mt 19:12). Paul is no different: he preaches only Christ crucified (1 Cor 2:2).

The asceticism of the Fathers of the Desert was a literal giving up of all, as a substitute it seems, for martyrdom, which had ceased to be a possibility. St ↗Benedict, himself at one time a hermit of the old style, moved away from this extreme to moderation. Asceticism he saw as only a means, and excess could hinder, not help, the movement of the spirit towards God. With the advent of ↗Francis of Assisi a new aspect emerged, from his intense relationship to the person of the historical Jesus, especially his passion, and Francis's desire to imitate his sufferings, to share them. He was granted the stigmata or marks of the Passion on his hands and feet. But with the advent of the Renaissance a shift in emphasis again occurred, with more consideration for the body and a greater interiorization ˙ of asceticism, in which the control of the will rather than macerations or fasts for the body were favoured. The chief exponent of the modern approach is undoubtedly ↗Francis of Sales, the supreme Christian humanist and saint. The strand of extreme austerity however continued in, among others, Abbot de Rancy and St Paul of the Cross. The form asceticism should take depends on the personality of the individual. For some, expiation for sin looms very large, with a possibility of sharing in the sufferings of Christ. No

Christian indeed can escape the obligation of love, to share in the Cross, if only by sharing in his death by one's own.

See 'Asceticisme' in *D. Spir.*, Vol. 1, cols. 936–1010.

See also *H.C.S.*

Athanasius, St (*circa 296–373*)
Small in stature, a giant in faith, Archbishop of Alexandria, Father of the Church, the outstanding defender of orthodox Christianity at the Council of Nicaea (325) and after. But his outstanding contribution to the spirituality of the Church was his support of the emerging monastic movement in Egypt, culminating in his writing of the life of Saint Antony of the Desert, the model for innumerable other lives of saints. He himself, exiled for the faith, carried the monastic ideal to Rome and as far as Trier. His *de Incarnatione*, besides being theologically lucid, is a treatise to be read for devotion.

Athos, Mount
A peninsula on the north-east coast of Greece. It has been the centre for monastic life in the Orthodox Church for over a thousand years. The first monastery was founded there by St Athanasius in 962 AD. There are twenty main monasteries which between them govern this 'City of God'. At the height of its glory as many as 40,000 monks lived within the confines of this small area. For Christians of the East it stands for all that is most spiritual in religion, as a mighty icon or sacrament or sign of the Kingdom, the other-worldliness of the Christian religion. It is nothing else, unlike Rome which is both sacred and profane. Over the centuries it

has been the goal of pilgrims from all over the Orthodox world.

In practice the Greek Church controls Mount Athos though there are monasteries for Russians, Rumanians, Yugoslavs and others. In 1903 on the peninsula there were 3,496 Russian monks and 3,276 Greek ones. The Russians have dwindled to a handful, less than 50.

Every form of monastic life can be found on Mount Athos from the eremitical (*hermits*) and the hermits grouped together (*laura* or *lavra*). Though the great first monastery of St Athanasius is called the Lavra, it is in fact a *cenobium* or *monastery* with the monks living a common life and governed by an abbot. Besides these are many smaller monasteries but dependent, at least financially (they pay tribute to one of the twenty). These are sometimes called *sketes* (or skites).

No women are allowed on the island nor female animals nor beardless youths. The novitiate is for two to three years at which time the novice is clothed as a monk (*rasophore*) but he can leave or change monasteries. Only when he takes the Little Habit, after many years, is he a full monk with all rights and duties. He is a *stavrophore*. The Great Habit is only granted after long years as a *stavrophore* or on his death bed.

There are peculiarities, especially among the Greek monks of Mount Athos: (i) They may have '*peculium*', i.e. private property, especially money and the profit from whatever work they do; (ii) The individual monk is not 'bound' to perform the Divine Office, only the community as such. The monks live within their monasteries in 'families', i.e. sharing together their wealth under the president of a senior. This system of private property is called '*idiorrythmia*'.

Besides these larger monasteries

there have always been innumerable hermits or groups of hermits living very prayerful and austere lives. These monks are usually in small groups. They too depend on one or other of the great monasteries.

See *D.H.G.E.*, Vol. 5 and under *Athos*, col. 54–123.

Atman

Hindu word for Self. Hindu religion has for centuries been vitally concerned to discover the relationship between the self and the all. In the Upanishads (those writings of the Hindu desert dwellers of the 8th to the 6th century BC), we find accounts of contemplative souls discovering the meaning of reality (*Brahman*) and of the self (*Atman*). The first conclusion come to was the identity of *Atman* and *Brahman*, 'I am that'. But the later Upanishads tended more to a dualism, seeing Brahman as a Personal Ultimate Reality which loves us and for whom we can have devotion (*bakti*).

This later tendency reached its culmination of expression in the *Bhagavad ↗Gita*, which proclaims the possibility of liberation not only through meditation but also by action; and it at one point even speaks of the ultimate reality as a loving personal God. The two greatest theologians of Hinduism, Sankara (*circa* 800 AD) and Ramanuja (*circa* 1100 AD) each propounds with great subtlety one of these approaches; Sankara, the oneness of reality; Ramanuja, dualism, though this, of course, is too simple a statement of their divergence.

R. de Smet, *Religious Hinduism*, (Bombay, 1964).

R.C. Zaehner (tr.), *Hindu Scriptures*, (London, 1966).

R.C. Zaehner, *Concordant Discord*, (Oxford, 1970).

Augustine of Hippo, St (*354–430*)

Born at Tagaste in North Africa. He died at Hippo as the Vandals were besieging the city whose bishop he was. He is acclaimed for the vast treatise, *City of God*, for the *Homilies* on the Psalms and St John, for the *de Trinitate* and most of all for the profoundly personal yet God-directed *Confessions*. In these great works there is everything from anecdote through psychology to theology and beyond to contemplation. This last is our main concern. Chiefly this is to be found in the *Confessions* and the *Homilies* on the Psalms. (*Confessions* Bk. 7:10–21; Bk. 9:10; Bk. 10:23–9, 43; and *Psalms* 41 [42].)

Probably the nearest to an accurate description of Augustine's mysticism is to say that it is a Christian experience dressed in neo-Platonic words. He speaks of the Ultimate Reality, Absolute Being – That which Is – the Unchangeable Good, the Unchangeable Truth, Light Unchangeable. These titles are partly Biblical (Mosaic and Johannine) partly Platonic. He describes how, to reach this Ultimate, one has to go beyond all sense things, all images, all earthly thought, though not beyond mind, and there, with great desire (love) receive a touch (*ictus*) of God (*cf. Confessions* Bk. 9:10). His mysticism is a vision of truth, but truth *loved*, which provides indescribable delight. He exclaims, in despair of saying what he has experienced, 'What do I love, when I love you? It is a certain light that I love when I love my God – a light, a melody, a fragrance and food, which *space does not contain*, an embrace of the inner man, where that light shines for my soul, and where that embrace is close which brings no satiety. That it is that I love when I love my God.' (Bk. 10:6.)

Augustine's great realization after years of search was that God, whom he thought distant, was within: 'You were within me, and I far away, and there I searched for you. You were with me, but I not with you.' (*Confessions* Bk. 10:27): 'You were more inward to me than my most inmost part, and higher than my highest.' (*Confessions* Bk. 3:6.)

At first sight one might mistake Augustine's prayer as more Platonic than Christian, but if we remember the famous passage in *Confessions* (Bk. 3), we are left in no doubt as to where his heart lay. He had just read Cicero's now lost *Hortensius*: 'The book excited and inflamed me; in my ardour the only thing I found lacking was that the name of Christ was not there.' For he had drunk in with his mother's milk that name, 'and whatever lacked that name, no matter how learned, and excellently written, could not win me wholly' (ch. 4). When he was reading the Platonists, he wrote that he found in those writings much concerning the Word of God, 'But I did not find that the Word became flesh.' (Bk. 7:9.)

Like that of Paul, Augustine's spirituality was based in his conversion experience which gave him the conviction that God's grace is the source of good action, not our own powers, yet in some mysterious way it leaves us free: 'Grant what thou dost command, and command what Thou wilt.' (*Confessions* Bk. 10:29.) It is not difficult to see how his expressions might lead the unwary to determinism, yet he himself was the most independent in thought and action.

H. Bettensen (tr.), D. Knowles (tr.), *The City of God*, (Harmondsworth, 1972).

P. Brown, *Augustine of Hippo, A biography*, (London, 1967).

C. Butler, *Western Mysticism*, (London, 1922).

E. Gilson, *The Christian Philosophy of Augustine*, (London, 1967).

E. Portalie, *A Guide to the Thought of St Augustine*, (London, 1960). Translated from *D.T.C.*

F.J. Sheed (tr.), *The Confessions*, (London, 1943).

F. Van der Meer, *Augustine the Bishop*, (London, 1961).

Authority

Those who wield it are as often the problem as those who obey. This applies not only in religious life but between husband and wife and between parents and children.

Today we recognize more readily that the 'subject', the one who should obey, also has a right to be heard. Furthermore, the authority does not always have the competence of the one who obeys. Certainly both parties are rational beings, including children, and they too should be treated as such, if only to train them to be responsible as time goes on. Therefore discussion should normally precede a decision and usually a 'consensus' should be sought. The one who has the authority to decide should also normally not go against the solid opinion after a group discussion has taken place, except in unusual circumstances.

Sometimes the structure is at fault, i.e. the limits of the authority have not been clearly stated, especially for those in minor posts – an outstation. Likewise the right of appeal to a higher authority is sometimes not clearly indicated as a normal and reasonable procedure.

In active groups, teachers, medical people, social workers and the like, the obligations of religious life and the obligations of their profession can often be in opposition. As the authority is sometimes less knowledgeable in the professional area than his or her 'subjects', this can create a serious tension, since the latter can rightly claim that the superior is not fully aware of the problems involved. This is a case where joint discussion within the whole group becomes important and also the appeal mentioned above.

At a deeper level, religious obedience is an effort to find the will of God in a particular situation; therefore the one in authority should be the 'mediator' of this search. Further, this search is a community effort. If we refer to the early Church (*cf.* especially Acts chs. 14 and 15) we find: (i) It is the community that finds the answer even if the decision is made by the Apostles and presbyters; and (ii) That it is done after prayer and fasting and an appeal to the Holy Spirit, who will guide and lead the Church to the decision needed. In this charismatic age we rightly return to the attitude, methods and Spirit-directed action of the early Church. It no longer is a matter simply of authority and subjects, but members of Christ's body seeking his will in their common lives under the guiding hand of the ever-living Spirit in their midst.

See ↗Obedience.

Avarice, Spiritual

People are greedy for spiritual experiences; warmth, response, locutions, visions, tongues, ecstasies. Not one of these is God. To seek them in prayer is, then, a form of idolatry and comes from spiritual avarice or greed. It is not surprising that this is a common complaint, since God, who is our true goal in prayer, hides himself from us, often for long stretches of time. We clamour for reassurance, we hunger for some pleasure in the desert of our prayer. But it is fatal to grasp at a substitute for God himself. Besides, he will give himself in his own good time.

John of the Cross makes special mention of beginners who attach excessive importance to special devotions: Agnus Deis, rosaries, relics. He would have them seek perfection by being ready to throw overboard all their treasure, to find God (*Dark Night*, Bk. 1, ch. 3).

Relics perhaps are no longer our 'treasure'; but since Vatican II we may have recognized other substitutes: Latin Mass, private Masses, old devotions. One may pine for these – good in themselves – but we must not forget St John's advice to beginners, that they are not God. Perhaps if it were possible to let them go, God might show himself more surely, just as he might to those excessively attached to guitars and folk music and all the little idiosyncrasies of the 'moderns'.

B

Baker, Augustine (*1575–1641*)
A Welshman, born at Abergavenny and died in London. After studying and practising law he became a Catholic and monk, making his profession at the reformed monastery of St Justina of Padua. Later he helped revive the English Benedictine congregation and himself went on the 'English Mission' to help rally the Recusants, but he also spent 1624–33 as spiritual director to the English Benedictine

nuns at Cambrai (among whom was Gertrude ↗More), where he wrote many little treatises on prayer. These were synthesized by Fr Serenus Cressy, one of his disciples, and published after Baker's death under the title of *Sancta Sophia* or *Holy Wisdom* (1657), a book beloved of English-speaking people with a taste for contemplative prayer. Its special merits are: its clarity of exposition of the various states of prayer; its solid justification for the contemplative life; the defence of private inspiration in an age when authoritarianism quite understandably was in the ascendant in the Catholic Church; its description of the prayer of acts. Today we find his style heavy but his matter sound. In a liturgical age, such as ours, his emphasis on private prayer is salutary; whilst in his own time, when complex systems of meditation were all the rage, Baker's reaction towards a return to the more ancient method of *custodia cordis* or the presence of God was also salutary. Baker is the link between the important English medieval tradition of ↗*The Cloud of Unknowing*, *The Scale of Perfection*, etc., and modern times, as he had a strong hold on the teaching of his predecessors. A notable emphasis in his thought is his stress on personal guidance by the Holy Spirit. At a time when the authorities were anxious to assert external authority, he was encouraging private inspiration, though not excessively (*cf.* *Holy Wisdom*, 1, section 2, chs. 1–9).

The best edition of *Sancta Sophia – Holy Wisdom* is that of Dom Gerard Sitwell (London, 1972). David Knowles writes of Baker in *The English Mystical Tradition* (London and New York, 1961). The experts do not agree as to whether Baker himself reached the highest point of mystical prayer – he does not claim to have done so. Justin McCann edited the two *Lives* of Augustine Baker, by P. Salvin and S. Cressy (London, 1933); *cf.* also his chapter on Baker in *Ampleforth and its Origins* (London, 1952).

Memorials of Fr Augustine Baker and other Documents relating to the English Benedictines (C.R.S., 1933), pp. 1–154, was edited by J. McCann and H. Connolly and includes Baker's *Autobiography* and the *Life* by Fr Leander Prichard.

Baptism

Ritual cleansing and washings occur in the Qumran documents. But these were frequently repeated. John the Baptist gave his disciples *one* baptism, or sign of penance. The baptism of Jesus, he told them, would be a baptism of the Holy Spirit (Jn 1:33). Jesus allowed himself to be baptized by John in order to show his solidarity with all mankind under sin, though he never sinned, but took all sin upon himself.

The visible action in baptism is the washing or *dipping* in water. Water, as a universal symbol, has three elements: water the destroyer (the devastation of the Flood); water the giver of life; and water the cleanser. Christian baptism makes use of all three elements. It destroys sin, the old dispensation, the Old Man; it brings to life in us the New Man, Christ; it cleanses from past sins. By bringing us to the new birth (*cf.* Nicodemus in Jn 3) we become children of God, and can truly call him our Father. We become brothers of Christ; more, we are 'oned' with Christ. 'Now not I live but Christ lives in me', as St Paul wrote (Gal 2:20). As it is Christ who lives in us, we share all the ↗Gifts of the Spirit (Is 11:1 ff and also 1 Cor 12–14), thus sharing the Life of Christ. More, we share in the very life of

God, because we share his nature (2 Pet 1:4). Our life is hid with Christ in the Holy Trinity; this is true Trinitarian spirituality. For we share in the knowledge and love of the Persons of the Blessed Trinity for one another, already darkly in this life, and in the next we shall see God as he is (1 Jn 3:2).

Baptism brings us also into the Communion of the Faithful, makes us members of his Church and so fit to share in the Mysteries, especially the mysteries of the Eucharist.

St Paul in Chapter 6 of the Epistle to the Romans brings much of the above out clearly: 'When we were baptized we went into the tomb with him (i.e. Christ) and joined him in his death, that as Christ was raised from the dead by the Father's glory (i.e. power), we too might live a new life' (v. 4), and so we are 'alive for God in Christ Jesus' (v. 11).

Baptism is a 'once and for all' but it should not be 'A done and done with', for baptism continues through life just as our very life does, transforming it into the life of Christ, and so a mighty source of strength.

Baptism of the Spirit

Considered by Pentecostal groups to be another Baptism over and above the sacramental one. It is administered by prayer over the person and the laying-on of hands. The gift of tongues is often claimed to be a sign that the rite has 'taken'. It is maintained that all this is in line with the New Testament (*cf.* Acts 1:5; 8:14; 9:18–19) and also that experience shows that the Spirit does come. Traditional theologians are not happy with this interpretation of the New Testament nor of the interpretation of the experience. The references to Acts (above) could refer to sacramental Baptism or Confirmation. The experience of the

Spirit could as well be the 'freeing' of the Spirit already received. It must be admitted that in a vast number of cases baptized persons do not seem to have the 'experience' of the Spirit that Pentecostals speak of. Why is this? The possible explanation may be that, in our relations with God, he always leaves us free to accept or reject, develop or restrict the relationship, because the very essence of our human nature is to be *free*, and therefore free to accept God's advances or not. The Pentecostalists repeat at their prayer meetings: 'Let go, let the Spirit work.' In this they are right, provided we are prepared to do our part. We are not designed by God as automata.

Basic Communities

A name given in the Catholic Church to groupings of Christians, smaller than parishes, who pray together for the sake of building up the Christian life within the group and which normally have no resident priest. This occurs very frequently in missionary countries such as Nigeria and Tanzania but also in old Christian countries, such as Brazil and Argentina in South America and also France. One priest might be in nominal charge of 100,000 Christians. This is common in Africa, since a missionary could have 100 outstations. The heart of the matter seems to be that almost by 'spontaneous generation', or movement of the Spirit, this nucleus of Christians comes to life, choosing its own leader, dividing up the work of the Christian ministry: catechizing the young and preparing the neophites for baptism, preparing couples for marriage, visiting the sick, caring for the aged and the lonely; there are those who are in charge of and execute the liturgy, which of course cannot be the full Eucharist; those who distribute communion, those who evangelize and so on. It is as though many of the 'ministries', that for centuries have been enclosed within the episcopate and the priesthood, have come back to life as they had existed in the early Church. Some difficulties arise; for instance these basic communities sometimes find themselves at loggerheads with their clergy, as in Hungary where the groups think that the episcopate is too subservient to the Communist regime, or as in south-east Nigeria where the bishops considered that the para-liturgy of these groups was becoming entangled in pagan rites. The latter were finally excommunicated, only to form a widespread sprinkling of sects that exist to this day. It would seem that a paramount need is close contact between the basic communities and the hierarchy. To achieve this is not easy, on account of distances and lack of personnel.

Basil the Great, St (*circa 329–79*)

Of Caesaria in Pontus, Asia Minor; born in Pontus. An aristocrat, an intellectual, an administrator, he abandoned all to withdraw into ascetical retirement at Annesi. The ascetical movement in Pontus was not derived from Egypt but from Eustatius of Sebaste – part of an enthusiastic movement with a tendency to create a separate elitist sect. Basil reacted against this. He was ordained priest in 365 and bishop in 390. After an exploratory journey to Mesopotamia, Syria, Palestine and Egypt, to visit the monks, he concluded that monks should also practise the love of neighbour by corporal works of mercy, thus fulfilling their obligation with regard to Jesus' second commandment. St Benedict in his *Rule* (*circa 540*) mentions Basil, perhaps especially because of his flexible understanding of monastic life. Unlike the Fathers of the Desert, Basil legislated for strong links with the world around, while still maintaining an area of withdrawal. He would establish hospitals, orphanages, hostels for the poor and pilgrims, which he would have cared for by the monks. Basil also wrote two 'Rules' but these are no more than long and short answers to questions on the spiritual life put before him by his monks; hence the titles: *The Longer Rule* and *The Shorter Rule*.

He had little sympathy for the 'inwardness' of his friend Gregory of Nazianzus but emphasized rather the objective element of prayer, and the mingling of prayer and work. 'Prayer was for Basil more a song than a silence' (*cf.* G. Gribomont, 'Basil' in *N.C.E.*).

W.K.L. Clarke (tr.), *The Ascetical Works of Saint Basil*, (London, 1925).

Beatrice of Nazareth
See ↗Beguines

Beginners
Called by Thomas Aquinas *principientes*, taking their first steps in prayer and the spiritual life. Their condition is one of struggling against temptations and towards virtue – what in the Patristic Age was called 'the active life'. Their prayer is full of distractions from the imagination; it will be meditative rather than contemplative. Discursive meditation is most suitable, such as described by St Ignatius in the *Exercises*. Beginners often have plenty of warm sense (sensible) devotion in prayer, which however will vanish; a condition which can lead to despondency and tepidity. At

this point one should simply hold on like a limpet, change the form of prayer, experiment to find the one that holds the heart. But as no two persons are alike, each must seek his own way. A beginner has to be like a man sailing a small boat, alert to catch the slightest breeze no matter from which quarter it may blow. The aim, ever, is to love God, do his will and love those around, indeed all men.

T. Merton, *Seeds of Contemplation*, (New York and London, 1949).

Beguines, Beghards
Beguines (women) and Beghards (men) lived a devout life as Christians *in* the world. They first emerge indistinctly in the late 12th century, in Liège and its vicinity (in Brabant) and then in Cologne and neighbouring towns, to spread later across northern Europe. Their emergence coincided with the deep concern of the Church over the Albigensian heresy with which they were often unjustly confused. Their name is a folk-corruption of the name Albigensian, invented as a nickname, its origin soon to be forgotten. The Church found these spontaneous gatherings difficult to classify and control, this upsurge of the Spirit among the laity claiming the possibility of holiness without becoming monks, nuns or friars. Thus the Beguines took no real vows but rather a statement of intent to live poorly and chastely and be obedient to the one (the Mistress) they had chosen, but only for so long as they remained in the Beguinage. If they left, they were free to marry. They followed none of the recognized 'Rules' written by some saint of the past. They had no enclosure, though they lived to-

gether in a private house or in a cluster of little houses with an encircling wall (one such is still used at Ghent). Poverty for them did not mean begging but working for their own livelihood. The Beghards were often weavers and related traders, while the women often looked after the sick, made vestments and even ran schools for girls. But essentially they wanted to dedicate themselves to God *in the world*, praying, sharing and walking humbly before the Lord. Matthew Paris, the English chronicler, wrote in 1243 that 2,000 lived in Cologne and the surrounding cities. This was a women's movement under the local bishop or prior of the Friars. Eckhart in Cologne would preach to them.

In Cologne they became suspect and efforts were made to suppress them. The fourth Lateran Council (1215) forbade starting new religious Orders. The Council of Lyons (1274) ordered any new Order, founded after 1215, to be suppressed. The Council of Vienne (1312) both condemned the Beguines by name at the beginning and then at the end encouraged those who lived humbly. In the Low Countries the Beguines seem to have survived these attacks better than their Rhineland neighbours, even surviving to our day. This is an interesting example of the need for balance between liberty of the Spirit and the guardianship of the Church.

Among the Beguines were some remarkable writers and mystics. The fact that they were in Cistercian convents does not deprive them of being part of the movement, as these convents were a spontaneous growth which the early Cistercian monks even refused to recognize. They were part of the Beguine movement.

ST MECHTILD OF MAGDEBURG (*circa* 1210–*circa* 1280) She began as a Beguine and in 1270 entered the convent of Helfta. She wrote down her visions, concerning the Sacred Heart.

BLESSED MARY OF OIGNIES (1177–1213) Married at 14, she later persuaded her husband to make a vow of continence, to abandon wealth and help to nurse lepers in her own house. In the contemporary *Life* (1215), James of Vitry tells of her devotion to the Passion and the Eucharist.

BLESSED HADEWIJCH OF ANTWERP (*floruit circa* 1200) Wrote of 11 visions, 31 discerning letters of 'direction' and 45 poems on mystical love. Her message was that the aim of contemplation is deification.

BEATRICE OF NAZARETH (*circa* 1200–68) She wrote *There are Seven Manners of Divine Loving*, a description of the soul's ascent to God. She became abbess of Notre Dame de Nazareth and died there.

MARY OF NYMEGHEN She lived at the same period and wrote the *Story of my Life* in the form of a play.

E.W. McDonnell, *Beguines and Beghards in Medieval Culture with Special Emphasis on the Belgian Scene*, (New Brunswick, N.J., 1954).

R.W. Southern, *Western Society and the Church in the Middle Ages*, (Harmondsworth, 1970).

See 'Beghards and Beguines' in *D.H.G.E.*, and 'Beguine' – the more important – in *D. Spir.* See also *N.C.E.* and E. Colleges (ed.), *Medieval Netherlands Religious Literature*, (London, 1965).

Benedict, St (*circa* 480–*circa* 547) Born at Nursia, a small town in the vicinity of Rome, and died at Monte Cassino. On prayer he is reticent – let it be short, he writes in his *Rule*, and done with a pure heart. He claimed that his *Rule* was for beginners (ch. 73) and refers to the writings of the Fathers for more advanced teaching (ch. 73). The *Rule* provides a complete plan for public prayer (chs. 8–18). Benedict would have the minds and hearts of his monks in tune with their voices as they recite the Divine Office, and have them remember that they are in the presence of almighty God (ch. 20). Nothing is to be put before it (ch. 43). Though he says little on prayer, there is much on humility, obedience and a habit of silence, all of which are closely linked with prayer – humility being an attitude of spirit in which we recognize our wretchedness due to sin and our dependence on God (ch. 7); obedience being the readiness to subject our whole being and life, in love, to the will of God (ch. 5); silence being the openness to God's leadings (ch. 6). The three vows of the *Rule* (ch. 50) provide the basis of a life of prayer: obedience (mentioned above); stability, which means a commitment to this way of life in this place under this abbot; conversion of manners, or a dedication to the monastic way of self-surrender to God's will, which is a life of prayer in act. Benedict, though he himself had been a hermit in his youth, was not in favour of his monks being hermits, at least at first, but rather living in community so as to help each other in obedient love, shoulder to shoulder along the way. A characteristic of his *Rule* is his compassion and consideration not only for his monks but also for the poor and pilgrims at the gate.

The community in the *Rule* is strong. The superior is *Abbas*, father, the members brothers, who must have mutual respect and love, despite each other's physical or psychological limitations (ch. 72).

Though the abbot makes the final decision, Benedict insists that all should be called to Council (ch. 3) and that often the youngest are moved by the Spirit to provide the best solutions to problems.

Benedict's chapters on the abbot (chs. 2 and 64) and on the cellarer (ch. 31) are justly famous for their analysis of spiritual leadership, which should be compassionate yet firm; considerate of the weak yet leaving the strong something to strive for. They should be careful to arrange all in such a way as to avoid providing a legitimate grievance.

C. Butler, OSB, *Benedictine Monasticism*, (London, 1919).

J. McCann, OSB, *Life of St Benedict*, (New York, 1937).

J. McCann, OSB, (ed.), *The Rule of St Benedict*, (London, 1952).

T. Fry, OSB, (ed.), *The Rule of St Benedict, in Latin and English with Notes*, (Collegeville, Min., 1981). This is by far the most comprehensive study in English to date.

E. de Waal, *Seeking God: The Way of St Benedict*, (London, 1984).

See ↗Asceticism.

Benet of Canfield (*1562–circa 1610*) He became a Recollect Franciscan after a strange and wonderful conversion which he recalls in his autobiography; after which he went to France where his spiritual teaching was most felt. In Paris he met Mme ↗Acarie, the centre of the Catholic renewal in the capital. She followed his spirituality, especially on 'the naked will', subjecting the whole of life to conformity to the will of God. His book of that name was put on the Index as being infected with Quietism; it at least pointed in that direction. His teaching on conformity to the Divine Will is commendable so long as it is combined with a strong desire for virtue and acknowledgement of the need for grace, especially through the sacraments.

Bremond, Vol. 2, pp. 136–59.

J. Brousse, *The Lives of Ange de Joyeuse and Benet Canfield*, (London, 1959). The *Life* of Benet is partly autobiographical (chs. 2–13), that is, the account of his conversion.

L. Cognet, *Post-Reformation Spirituality*, (London, 1959).

W. Fitch, D.M. Rogers (ed.), *The Rule of Perfection, 1609*, (1970). Fitch was Benet Canfield's name in the world before joining the Capuchins.

Bernard, St (*1090–1153*)
Born at Fontaine near Dijon in Burgundy, and died at the Cistercian abbey of Clairvaux of which he was founder. Though Bernard was not one of the founder-members of the original Cistercian abbey of Cîteaux, his arrival there (1112) with his brothers and friends to become monks probably saved it from a premature extinction. His warm sincerity, ascetical life, his brilliant and winning eloquence, drew hundreds of recruits to the Order. Besides being the most forceful personality of his century he was also one of the greatest exponents of mystical prayer in the history of the Church. The *Sermons* he gave to his monks on the *Song of Songs* are the chief source for Bernard's teaching on prayer. The book discusses, he says, not only the union between Christ and his Church, but also between God and the individual soul. This union is one of love. He denies the possibility of *unity* between God and man, because the plurality of natures persists – God's nature and human nature. It is a union not of nature but of one spirit if they adhere to one another with 'the glue of love'; it is a union of wills. (Sermon 71:5–10) Elsewhere (in his *de Gratia et libero arbitrio*, 15) he says that the happiness of contemplation is only rare and momentary. (See also *Sermons on the Song of Songs* 85:12–24.)

Though Bernard is at home in the heights of prayer he often speaks of the humanity of Christ, his childhood, his Passion and Death, preparing, as it were, for the coming of ↗Francis of Assisi and his school. However, the experience of contemplation itself for Bernard, as for ↗Gregory the Great and ↗Augustine before him is beyond thought and sense experience.

C. Butler, *Western Mysticism*, (London, 1922).

T.L. Connolly, SJ, (tr.), *On the Love of God*, (London, 1937).

E. Gilson, *The Mystical Theology of St Bernard*, 2nd ed., (New York, 1955).

B. Scott-James (tr.), *Letters of St Bernard of Clairvaux*, (London, 1953).

B. Scott-James, *St Bernard of Clairvaux*, (London, 1957).

E. Vacandard, *Vie de St Bernard*, 2 vols., (Paris, 1920).

K. Walsh (tr.), *Sermons on the Song of Songs by St Bernard*, Vols. 1 and 2, (Spencer, Mass., 1971). See especially, Vol. 2, 26, for the lament on his brother Gerard's death.

See also 'Bernard' in *D. Spir., D.T.C.,* and *D.H.G.E.*

Bernardino of Siena, St (*1380–1444*)
The outstanding preacher of the first half of the 15th century in Italy. Born

in Massa di Carrera – his father was its governor – in 1402 he became a Franciscan. Three years later the Master General of the Order designated him to preach and nothing else. In 1438 he became Provincial of the Franciscans of the Strict Observance. The following year he took a prominent part in the Council of Florence. But his great work was preaching to huge crowds throughout Italy, from Bergamo and Milan to Ferrara and Rome. He was called the apostle of the Holy Name. He would preach against blasphemy, on faith, on the dangers of bad books, on immorality and homo-sexuality, on peace, almsgiving, usury. False relics roused him to ridicule: not a hundred cows, he claimed, could equal all the milk of the Mother of God around.

Each sermon might last several hours. The proceedings would begin with Mass, with everyone coming to the square in procession with much blowing of trumpets and ringing of bells. He used bonfires as the climax of his preachings. In Florence, in 1424, the bonfire – the Devil's Castle – was piled high with 400 back-gammon tables, baskets full of dice, over 4,000 packs of cards, vast supplies of false hair, rouge, pots, high-heeled shoes, mirrors. (J. Moorman, *A History of the Franciscan Order*, Oxford, 1968, p. 462.)

I. Ongo, *The World of San Bernardino*, (London, 1963).

Bérulle, Pierre de (*1575–1629*)
The founder of the French Oratorians and finally a cardinal. As a disciple of Mme ↗Acarie he took part in the renewal of French spirituality in the French Church, and with her had a hand in introducing the Spanish Carmelites of St ↗Teresa's reform into France.

He was a leader in the spiritual life, going somewhat contrary to a trend of extreme voluntarism of which ↗Benet of Canfield was the chief exponent together with ↗Harphius. Bérulle leaned rather towards a strong Christo-centric prayer life. The Incarnation was for him the centre of prayerful wonder. (*cf. Grandeurs de Jésus*, 1623.) This was a valuable corrective. The Logos did not become man to be side-stepped but as a help to man, as a means to God, since man is by nature not only spirit but material. On the sacramental plane Jesus, God made man, is of the essence, since the sacraments, especially baptism and the Eucharist, are signs of Christ's death and resurrection. As St Paul wrote, 'in baptism we die and rise again in Christ's death and resurrection'. While, as for the Eucharist, Christ himself said, 'this is my body . . .'

Bremond, Vol. 3, 1–256.

A. Mollien, *Le Cardinal de Bérulle*, 2 vols., (Paris, 1947).

See also 'Bérulle' in *D. Spir.*

Bhakti (Sanskrit)
Love or devotion (*bhaj*, verb, to love, to honour). In Hindu literature an early form of *bhakti* is in the *Katha-Upanishad*, but the most important is in the *Bhagavad* ↗*Gita* (variously dated 100 BC–200 AD), where we are given at its end, the summit, the way of Love. The God Krishna speaks to Arjuna the young prince. This is the great climax: 'And now again give ear to my highest Word, of all the most mysterious, "*I love you well*"' (ch. 18).

This goes contrary to a whole other school of Hindu tradition that holds the highest form of prayer to be, not *bhakti* or love between two, but the realization of the One, in which the dualism of love ceases. *Bhakti* would also seem to go counter to southern Buddhism which in this matter resembles the Hinduism referred to above. Northern Buddhism (sometimes called Mahayana) has a *bhakti* approach to religion. The Bodhisattva, the enlightened one, out of love or compassion renounces Nirvana to go to the help of his fellow men. The *bhakti* element in Eastern religions may prove to be the link with Christianity through which some mutual enrichment may occur in the future. The Jewish, Christian and some Islamic tradition is prayer of love between God and man, even if at times the union is blurred and expressed as unity.

Klaus K. Klostermaier, *Hindu and Christian theology of Love.*

Journal of Ecumenical Studies (Winter, 1973), pp. 750–76.

R.C. Zaehner, *The Bhagavad-Gita commentary and translation,* (Oxford, 1973).

Bodhisattva (Sanskrit)
In southern Buddhism (or Theravada) he is one who is striving towards enlightenment and Buddhahood. In Mahayana (northern) Buddhism, a Bodhisattva is one who, having reached the threshold of Nirvana, and therefore attained enlightenment, yet draws back out of compassion, to help his fellow men to aspire to this end. Such are called Compassionate Buddhas. It is a sublime form of love and comparable to that of the Son leaving, as it were, the bosom of the Father to come upon earth to save mankind. Thomas Aquinas would have approved of these men, since he also thought that the highest form of

life was that of a contemplative who having found God returned to the world to tell others and encourage them on the way.

Bonaventure, St (*1217–74*)
Born at Bagnoregio near Viterbo, Italy. As a young man he attended (*circa* 1234), the great university of Paris, but the direction of his life was changed by the attraction of the new Franciscan movement which he joined in 1243. In spite of its early unintellectual leanings, he was encouraged to take his Doctorate in Theology at Paris in 1253. Four years later he became head of the whole Order, by then spread throughout Europe, as its Minister General. At the end of his life he was raised to the episcopate and made cardinal. He wrote much on the spiritual life, the most famous of his works being the official *Life of St Francis of Assisi.* All earlier lives were to be destroyed. God and the friars saw to it that they were not, fortunately, as they have a more intimate atmosphere than Bonaventure's own. His legacy to the Church on prayer is *The Journey of the Mind to God* (1259). In it he gives the Augustinian approach: *per viam splendoris*, through intellectual contemplation of God; the Dionysian one, *per viam amoris*, by love, and experimental knowledge, tasting that the Lord is sweet, ending with affections of the will. But this knowledge is a darkness of the mind, a learned ignorance. In his *Apologia pauperum* he expounds the nature of the religious life. At Lyons during the great Church Council there in 1274 he died.

Opera Omnia Quarrachi (1882–1902). *cf.* especially Vol. 5.

See 'Bonaventure' in *N.C.E.*, Vol. 2.

See also 'obras de S. Bonaventura', 6 vols. (bilingual ed. Latin, Spanish, nos. 6, 9, 19, 28, 36 and 40) in B.A.C.

Bossuet, Jacques Bénigne (1627–1704)

Preacher, apologist, controversialist (Histoire des variations des Eglises protestantes, 1688), ecumenist (correspondence with Leibniz), writer of spiritual works, he became first nominated Bishop of Condom (1669) consecrated the following year, then Bishop of Meaux (1681). He was educated by the Jesuits, prepared for his ordination under ↗Vincent de Paul, was a protégé of ↗Bérulle and, on account of his oratorical gifts as a preacher, soon became a figure of importance at the court of Louis XIV. His Oraisons funèbres are both noble and moving. The Discours sur l'histoire universelle is a theology of universal history, somewhat in the spirit of Augustine's City of God. From the point of view of the spiritual life his importance lies in his two works that are in line with Bérulle's christocentric school of spirituality, his Méditations sur l'Évangile (posthumously published, 1731) and the Elevations sur les mystères (ditto, 1727). More important for the history of the life of prayer in the Church was his brush with ↗Fénelon connected with the latter's defence of Mme ↗Guyon. It was Bossuet who worked for the condemnation of Mme Guyon in 1695, and when Fénelon published his Explication des maximes des saints this gave Bossuet further opportunity to harry his rival. The Holy See condemned 23 propositions from Fénelon's book without mentioning Fénelon by name. But he was banished from the court of Louis XIV and mystical prayer remained under a cloud for nearly two centuries. On the subject of ↗Quietism, Bossuet wrote two works at this time, Instructions sur les états d'oraison (1696) and Relations sur le Quiétisme (1698). In his early days he had something of the suavity of ↗Francis of Sales but latterly his style became more acid.

A. Thorold (tr.), On Prayer: Spiritual Instructions on the Various States of Prayer according to the Doctrine of Bossnet, (London).

Brahman

A name used in the Upanishads – those writings of the Hindu 'Desert Fathers' of the 8th to the 6th century BC – to express that Ultimate Reality which lies behind all nature. This Reality, it was claimed, is one and absolute and beyond all knowing and expressing. It was said of Brahman: 'Not this, not that', (neti, neti). The earlier Upanishads identified what was ultimate in consciousness, what was deeper than one's reasoning, or sense or thought i.e. the ↗Atman, with Brahman. Atman and Brahman are one: 'I am that'. Some later Upanishads maintain a dualism between the Atman and Brahman. It could therefore, perhaps, be reasonably claimed that, expressed differently, this apparent unity of Atman with Brahman was an experience by the soul of the immanence of God.

Breathing

Christians, Hindus and Buddhists all encourage the practice of calm, deep, rhythmical breathing during meditation. The Philocalia of the Eastern Orthodox tradition encourages the monk to breathe in and hold the breath while saying the Jesus Prayer. The Buddhists encourage a posture with the back straight, especially the lotus position, deep breathing inward, counting or repeating a prayer (for example the word *Om*) at every intake of breath. All this helps to relax the body, to keep out other thoughts and to quiet the imagination, allowing for deep, wordless contemplation.

Bridal Spirituality

The theme of God's love for his people is often expressed in terms of human love and marriage, of human infidelity and divine forgiveness and the theme of union as in human relationships. The Prophets, supremely Hosea (ch. 2 especially) and Ezekiel with even more realism describe how God 'picked out of the gutter' a new born child, nourished her, clothed and bejewelled her, took her to wife (the People of God), but how then she went awhoring, and when abandoned by her lovers, was with magnanimous love received back by God (Ezek. ch. 16), God being always faithful. This has been applied to the relationship between God and the individual soul. In the *Song of Songs* we find human love described in all its stages, the fears and hopes, the search, the finding. Though in Jewish thought this was often applied to God and the Chosen People, early (Origen) in Christian times it was applied to God and the individual.

In the New Testament Jesus calls himself the Bridegroom (Mt 9:15, also 25:1–13), while John the Baptist implies the same (John 3:29). In Ephesians (5:21–33) Christ is the Bridegroom, the Church, the Bride, without spot or wrinkle. Inevitably Christian writers would enlarge on this, for human love is the only true love we know. It is not surprising that in the 12th century, when love was everywhere being analysed, the

saints should use human love to describe God's love for us and ours for him.

The greatest exponent was St Bernard in his *Homilies on the Song of Songs*. John Ruysbroeck brought this theme to its perfection in his *Spiritual Espousals*, while St John of the Cross used it for two of his most celebrated poems, *In a Dark Night* and the *Spiritual Canticle*. St Teresa also commented on the *Song of Songs*. But St John was cautious that this should not get out of hand. He says the Bride must bid the aspirations and motions of her lower part be stilled (see *The Spiritual Canticle*, xxxl, (tr.), E. A. Peers Vol. II, p. 145). This was not altogether unnecessary when one remembers Margery ↗Kempe's unsuitable descriptions. St Francis of Sales, in his masterpiece *The Love of God*, does not hesitate to use the same general symbolism.

Bruno, St (*1032–1101*)

Born at Cologne, died at St Mary of the Tower in Calabria, Italy. Brilliant student, favoured master of his time, in 1075 he was nominated Chancellor of Rheims. In 1082–3, when on the point of being nominated archbishop of that see, he fled, first to St Robert of Molesmes, then to St Hugh, Bishop of Grenoble, who gave him the site of la Grande Chartreuse (1084). Pope Urban II, a Cluniac monk and friend of Bruno, called him to Rome in *circa* 1089–90. Bruno with some of his followers, who had stayed with him in Rome, founded St Mary's in Calabria.

We can exaggerate the detachment of the saints, including Bruno's, who loved the beauty of nature, and not only the grandeur of mountains but also the joy of orange trees. Bruno's chief spiritual characteristic was his complete simplicity of outlook. Free from all in this world, he sought only God. His companions claimed that his face was always radiant, as if on festival. On his lips came repeatedly the one phrase, '*O beata Bonitas*'. His *Commentary on the Epistle to the Romans* begins, '*Divinitas, id est Bonitas*' ('The Divinity, that is Goodness').

See 'Chartreux' in *D. Spir.*, col. 705–10.

Buddhist Terms

Buddhism began in India some 500 years before Christ and spread across much of Asia where it still has millions of adherents.

The four holy truths of Buddhism are: (i) The truth that birth is ill; (ii) That decay is ill; (iii) That sickness is ill; (iv) That death is ill. The Buddha then asks: in order to be rid of these ills, what is the source of these ills? And his answer is: desire, or better, craving, craving for anything – to exist, for rebirth, even extinction.

How then can these ills be made to cease? The answer is: by cessation of all desire, by non-attachment to anything.

The eightfold path of Buddhism, which leads to Nirvana (enlightenment) are as follows: (i) Right views; (ii) Right intentions; (iii) Right speech; (iv) Right conduct; (v) Right livelihood; (vi) Right effort; (vii) Right mindfulness; (viii) Right concentration.

E. Conze (tr.), *Buddhist Scriptures: The Diamond Sutra and The Heart Sutra*, (Harmondsworth, 1975). Contains text of the scriptures.

D. Goddard (ed.), *A Buddhist Bible*, (Boston, 1966).

The paths to enlightenment, and the terms used to describe them, are many but we look at some below:

DHYANA   A Buddhist term signifying the practice of mind control, by which we stop thinking and try to realize truth by intuition. This is the road to enlightenment. Ten conditions are required for this, which include external setting to interior right behaviour.

SAMADHI   The last step or stage along the Buddhist Eightfold Path, before the arrival at Nirvana; a form of wordless contemplation, deeper than reasoning in which the dualism of thought or images and ultimate Reality ceases and is dissolved into One. As it is a common opinion among Buddhists that the reality we are normally conscious of, through our mind and senses, in ultimate analysis, has no true reality, it follows that those 'Ten Thousand Things' of ordinary life, are the Void, Sunyata. As mind is the only reality, the rest can vanish away. The All is the ultimate reality of which individual minds, infinite in number, each is a part without being dissolved into one. 'The parts are parts within the whole, not merged in it' (Christmas Humphreys, *Buddhism*, Harmondsworth, 1967, p. 17).

We are not here concerned with the validity of the analysis given above of the nature of our cosmos; it is however important to understand that this particular experience of it, which undoubtedly is very powerful, is not the experience of the Christian mystics, who warn that there are many delights along the way, which are not God, and though good in themselves, must be transcended.

Irenic attempts at showing the unity of the mystical experience are not always helpful; we should faithfully recognize the differences. The objective seems to be different, the means are very similar, up to a certain stage. The Christians pass beyond the 'natural'.

The above is written, not in disparagement of a very real experience, but to affirm, as do most serious students of this delicate matter, that we are here confronted with two distinct experiences not one.

SATORI Japanese for Enlightenment, used by Zen Buddhists; an awareness of self, or reality or Nirvana, beyond analysis or description, sometimes described as a falling over a precipice or a break-through or no-mind; at first a momentary flash of insight; and all schools of Zen say that this is but the first step. The disciple has to make his whole life in tune with it; or rather this insight will gradually pervade his whole life. Satori is the grasp of one's real Self, and can be realized in everyday things. A Zen Buddhist is not one to spend his whole life in contemplation; he sees Satori everywhere. Satori is not a supernatural state; it can be acquired by natural means needing no grace or freedom from sin, or faith, or God, or future life.

The Zen enlightenment discloses the absolute unity of Reality, it has no place for dualism; a realization by intuition of the oneness of all; thus no distinction between God and the soul as in Western thought and mysticism. Zen writers point out the similarity between Zen expressions on this point and those of Meister ↗Eckhart. At first sight their expressions seem to run very close. On further research however it is generally admitted among scholars that, in view of Eckhart's own clarifications, he never abandoned the Christian dualistic approach: the soul and God.

D.T. Suzuki, W. Barrett (ed.), *Zen Buddhism, Selected Writings*, (New York, 1959), p. 146, n. 1.

D.T. Suzuki, *An Introduction to Zen Buddhism*, (London, 1970).

See also ↗Deification.

Bunyan, John (*1628–88*)
Prolific writer, the most famous of his works being *The Pilgrim's Progress* (1678), *Holy War* (1682), posthumously *Antichrist and her Ruin* (1692) and *Grace Abounding to the Chief of Sinners* (1666), in which we have one of the great Christian spiritual autobiographies.

Bunyan's family had been in the neighbourhood of Elston, Bedford since the 12th century; his father was a glazier or tinker, and so too was John. He claims that he had the education of the poor, learnt to read and write, but nothing more, as he was a bad student, and even as a young man was only interested in dancing, bell-ringing, sport and being a mighty blasphemer. At 16 he joined in the Civil War. About that time he married a girl poorer than himself. They had, he wrote, between them neither dish nor spoon. But she was a devout Christian, and she brought as her only dowry two books which were to have a profound influence on John, Dent's *The Plain Man's Pathway to Heaven*, and *The Practice of Piety* by Bishop Lewis Bayly.

John began to read the Bible and also Foxe's *Book of Martyrs* (1563). In 1653 he was received into the Independent Congregation in Bedford which soon appointed him preacher (1657). This was during the Protectorate when dissenters were tolerated. Hundreds began to assemble to listen to 'this blaspheming tinker' turned preacher.

At the restoration of the Stuarts, as the old laws against dissenters were revived, he was gaoled for unlawful preaching; and, though the judges were loath to enforce the law, he, John Bunyan, flouted it, thus remaining, off and on, in Bedford county gaol from 1660 to 1672, during which time he poured out pamphlets and polemics. *The Pilgrim's Progress*, however, must have been written during a second gaol term in 1676 and published in 1678. A sequel came out in 1684. This minor masterpiece answered a tremendous Christian need for something to take the place of the medieval morality plays, the murals, the stained glass windows. These had gone, but now the printed word could take their place. The book was an immense success and has remained so ever since. Its characters and situations have become household words: the Slough of Despond, Mr Worldly Wiseman, Vanity Fair. Its vivid portrayal, its simplicity and zest, shine in contrast to the turgid theological controversies of the period.

cf. A most sympathetic biographical sketch is that by E. Venables in the *D.N.B.*

C

Carmelites
See St ↗Teresa of Avila, St ↗John of the Cross, St ↗Thérèse of Lisieux.

ELIZABETH OF THE HOLY TRINITY (1880–1906) A Carmelite mystic, entered the Carmel of Dijon in 1901. From St Paul she learned to praise the Holy Trinity, from St Teresa that the Trinity is always there in her soul. Her vocation was to praise the blessed Trinity in the 'cell of her heart, so that her life became one continuous prayer of union with God'. But to reach that union, an inner silence was necessary together with faith and love. Her special devotion to Mary concentrated on the time between the Annunciation and the birth of Jesus.

EDITH STEIN (1891–1942) A philosopher of standing in the School of Phenomenology at Göttingen University. In 1922, helped by reading St Teresa's *Autobiography*, she was received into the Catholic Church. She taught for a time but the Nazis made that impossible (1933) because she was of Jewish origin.

In 1933 she became a Carmelite in Cologne and was now called Sister Teresa Benedicta of the Cross. But, in 1938, she was transferred to a Dutch Carmel at Echt. After the invasion of Holland, the Nazis took her to Auschwitz where she died in the gas chamber.

Edith Stein (Sr Teresa Benedicta), L. Gelber and R. Leuven (eds.), *The Science of the Cross*, (London and Chicago, 1960).

Sr Elizabeth of the Holy Trinity, M.M. Philipon (ed.), *Spiritual Writings*, (New York, 1962).

Cappadocian Fathers
See St ↗Basil the Great, ↗Gregory of Nyssa, ↗Gregory Nazianzen.

Caroline Divines
The title given to those eminent members of the Anglican Church of the 17th century who, by their writings and their lives and sometimes by their violent death, bore witness to the Catholic element in the Elizabethan Settlement. Bishop Richard Hooker (d. 1600) for all his learning and judicious defence

of Christian values cannot belong here, not only because he is previous in time but because of his 'Protestant' attitude to the episcopate. We must begin with Bishop Lancelot Andrewes (1555–1626), attractive in personality and holy in his life, London born and Cambridge bred. He was learned in modern and ancient languages. The private devotions which he wrote in Latin and Greek remain a monument to his piety; the most moving are those on Death. On the subject of the episcopate and on the Eucharist his thought was very close to the traditional Catholic teaching. In his day his sermons were much praised, as he was (according to the title page to the early edition of his works) 'a Learned Prelate and painful divine', by which was meant painstaking. As with Hooker the style is too ponderous for today. His spirituality was expressed in his care of prisoners and the poor as much as in his diligence at private devotions – five hours he prayed each day. When death approached 'and sickness deprived him of his voice, yet his eyes and hands prayed, and when both failed, his heart still prayed, till it pleased God to accept it as his last sacrifice' (*Minor Works*, Oxford, 1854, p. 226). It was right that the ↗Oxford Movement two centuries later should look back to Andrewes with veneration.

William Laud (1573–1645) fellow of St John's College, Oxford, Archbishop of Canterbury, also stood firm against the Calvinist influences abroad. Once in power he used new laws to reverse the Puritan trends, even in Scotland requiring the Eucharistic table to be set up in the centre of the church in place of the pulpit. He, like Andrewes, set that character on Anglican services of simplicity and reverence. The Divine Right of Kings was pivotal to his theology and his political system. The Long Parliament impeached him and in 1645, he, having been judged guilty without due trial, was executed on Tower Hill.

Thomas Ken (1637–1711), who belongs to the next generation was, at first, fellow of Hart Hall, Oxford, then Bishop of Bath and Wells. He stood out against the Romanizing efforts of King James II but believed nevertheless that he had a divine right to remain king and no one had a right to depose him. He therefore refused allegiance to William III and lived as a celibate in devout seclusion until his death. His dying words express the sentiments of the Caroline divines: 'I die in the Holy, Catholic and Apostolic Faith, professed by the whole Church before the disunion of East and West. More particularly I die in the Communion of the Church of England as it stands distinguished from all Papal and Puritan Innovations . . .'

These, together with George ↗Herbert, Nicholas ↗Ferrar, Jeremy ↗Taylor and others, preserved what they considered to have been the Faith of the Church of the early centuries. The 18th century witnessed a decline in religion in England, as elsewhere, and the threads of their thought were picked up in the 19th century by the Oxford divines of the ↗Oxford Movement.

F.A. Clarke, *Life of Thomas Kenn*, (1896), p. 223.

P. More and F. Cross, *Anglicanism*, (London, 1957). Contemporary documents and lives of Andrewes, Herbert, Ferrar, Taylor and others in the 17th century.

J.R.H. Moorman, *A History of the Church in England*, (London, 1953). A general picture of Anglicanism.

See also *D.N.B.*

Carthusians

Solitaries who share a chapel, kitchen, library and once a week a refectory. They are governed by a prior. Their little three-roomed houses stand round a cloister garth. Each monk has a small garden at the back of his house. In his house he prays, eats, sleeps, studies and works. They foregather in the church for Divine Office and Mass, but much of their prayer life is in their houses. On Sundays and great feasts they eat together.

Carthusian prayer consists of three hours recitation in choir, which is all sung, also offices of Our Lady and of the Dead, in their cell. The aim is continual prayer, even at work. The communal Divine Office is oriented towards greater personal prayer. ↗Bruno (1032–1101), the Carthusians' founder, in an age of increasing complexity in the liturgy, simplified his; for example the Office is taken entirely from the Bible. 'We rarely sing Mass, because our principal care is solitude and silence . . . we put nothing above silence. (*Customary of Prior Guignes* in 1127, ch. 14, no. 5.) The ceremonial preserves a rustic simplicity; the day dress is their choir dress; their music without organ. They sing '*viva voce et rotunda*', but slowly and gravely. The lay brothers until recently recited *paters* and *aves* instead of the Latin Office.

For a Carthusian there is only one primary end – it is union with God in love. Their role in the Church is to support it by their prayers and austerities, and be a reminder to all of the primary purpose of all men, namely to love God above all.

Cassian, John (*360–435*)

Born in, perhaps, Rumania. In his youth he was linked with the monks of Bethlehem but *circa* 385 he visited the Egyptian monks and hermits and from there went on to the Thebaid (*circa* 386–92). In *circa* 415 he founded a monastery for men near Marseilles and another for women. He wrote two books to help monks in the West: *The Institutes* (417–8) which describes the monastic way of life (Bks. 1–4) and the struggle against vices (Bks. 5–12); the *Collations* or *Conferences* (419–29), in three parts, which describe various problems of the monastic life. Thus he provided the Western Church with many of its basic principles on the ascetical and contemplative life, such as he had found among the Desert Fathers of Egypt. The two great works were the staple food for monks all during the Middle Ages and beyond. In them, perhaps by a literary device, he recounts stories and conversations of famous abbots and Fathers of the Desert, thus giving the traditional teaching on a great variety of subjects: on *custodia cordis*, or non-attachment, on prayer, asceticism, humility, obedience. He was undoubtedly influenced by the 'passive' teaching of ↗Evagrius, whom he knew, but avoided seeming to approve of pure passivity (↗*apatheia*) by translating it, rather, into a loving conformity to God's will. Jerome had already attacked Evagrius, so Cassian is careful not to mention his name. Already in Cassian's writings – but here he is echoing ↗Origen – are the three ways of prayer – purgative, illuminative and unitive (*cf. Conference* 10:11). Pure prayer, for Cassian, is the soul bathed in light, and 'it says so many things in so short a time that it cannot readily express them' (*Conference* 9:25). In *Conference* 10:10 we seem to hear the first stirrings of the technique of the Jesus Prayer with Cassian's insistence on the repetition of 'O God come to my assistance . . .'

The influence of Cassian on the

Rule of St Benedict, and therefore on the whole history of monasticism in the West, is immense.

O. Chadwick, *John Cassian, a Study in Primitive Monasticism*, (Cambridge, 1950).

E.C.S. Gibson (tr.), 'Works of Cassian' in *Nicene and Post-Nicene Fathers*, (1894). Vol. xi, pp. 161–641.

Catherine of Genoa, St (*1447–1510*)
Born, lived and died in Genoa. As a member of the powerful noble family of Fieschi, she was married off (1463) for political reasons to a spendthrift rake of a rival family. After ten years of a mixture of misery and frivolity she underwent a sudden conversion (1473) and soon the husband too was drawn by her to God. For years – indeed till her death – they both gave themselves to caring for the sick in a great hospital which from 1490 she ran in every detail; yet at the same time she was one of the profoundest mystics the Church has ever nurtured. Soon a group of disciples gathered round her, laymen for the most part, chief among them Ettore Vernazza, whose zeal became the example for the founding of the Oratory of Divine Love in Rome and other cities of Italy. The Roman Oratory of Divine Love was central to the renewal of the Church as the Reformation broke. She is the patron saint of the active laity, of those with broken marriages, of those thousands helping the sick and dying.

Baron von Hügel in his monumental two-volume work on her spirituality, *The Mystical Element of Religion* (latest edition 1961), casts doubt on parts of the '*Life and Doctrine*' as being later additions. But, in view of the discovery recently of a very early manuscript of the whole text, it must now be admitted that in all probability though produced by her confessor P. Marabote and her friend Ettore Vernazza, yet it is her words and experiences that are its core. Her spirituality was lay, she had no desire to be a religious; her outlook was simple and concentrated, though not exclusively, *on conformity to the will of God*. From 1475 she received Holy Communion daily. In her *Treatise on Purgatory* she expresses, again, a very modern attitude to Purgatory and to the spiritual life. That state, she says, is a continuation, but joyful and willing, of the denuding of one's selfishness. It is a conforming to God's will that should have taken place already in this life. The summit of perfection is the soul's union of love with God, undefiled by self.

U.B. da Genova, *S. Caterina Fieschi Adorra*, 2 vols., (1961–2). With critical text of *opus Caterinianum*.

S. Hughes (tr.), B. Groeschel (intro.), *Catherine of Genoa; Purgation and Purgatory, the Spiritual Dialogue*, (London, 1979).

See also *D. Spir.*

Catherine of Siena, St (*circa 1347–80*)
Born an uncertain number of years before 1347, in Siena; she died in Rome. She was ill-served by her biographers, as a certain unreality hangs over her childhood, for example, she is supposed to have taken a vow of virginity at the age of 4.

Her political entanglements are not our concern, except to note that it is rare even for a mystic to see straight in those crooked alleys. Her real fame, apart from helping to bring the Pope back to Rome, rests on her intimate union with God, and her marvellous capacity of expressing in words (*Dialogues*, 1377–8) her revelations from God, and also her remarkable sanity of judgement. The essence of her teaching, unlike that of the contemporary Rhineland and Dominican mystics – which was union with God in an inexpressible way – was simply love for God and the crucified Christ, a love which overflowed especially with apostolic zeal into love for the Church. In her eyes God was Christ. There was no Dionysian darkness, nor do we find speculations in the manner of the Rhineland mystics, nor psychological analyses in the 17th century manner, but supreme simplicity and humanity. In spite of her close association with the highly intellectual Dominican Order – she was a member of its Third Order – her manner of expression is unsophisticated, yet completely orthodox. Her letters are even more direct than the *Dialogues*. She shows herself a woman of great sympathy and of strong will. It must be remembered that she remained always a lay woman and never married.

The *Dialogues* are answers from God – who for her is Christ – to four questions, of which the first is: 'Discretion, what is it?'; and the reply: 'It is none other than true knowledge of self and of Me' (chs. 2–16); 'Know, my daughter, that I am He who is and that you are she who is not.' The second, third and fourth questions are concerned with reform in the Church and the world.

See *D. Spir.*, Vol. 2.

Caussade, Jean-Pierre de, SJ
(*1675–1751*)
A French Jesuit. In his lifetime he published one book, *Instructions spirituelles en forme de dialogues* (1741).

In 1861 another Jesuit, P. Ramière, edited some of his letters and treatises under the title *L'Abandon à la Providence divine*. De Caussade had for many years been director of the Visitation nuns at Nancy. His doctrine is that of ⟋Francis of Sales and Jeanne de Chantal, tempered by the critical judgement of ⟋Bossuet. The latter in attacking ⟋Fénelon had also criticized Francis. De Caussade by judicious handling of a controversial matter produced a sound statement of the great theme of spiritual abandonment to divine Providence in all circumstances. It is clear that such an abandonment makes all life a prayer of conformity to God's will. To make doubly sure, ⟋John of the Cross would refuse any consolation; de Caussade accepts the pleasant with the unpleasant in all simplicity. The modern interpreter of this spirituality is Soeur ⟋Thérèse of Lisieux.

K. Muggeridge, *The Sacrament of the Present Moment*, (London, 1981). Translated from the original text.

A. Thorold (tr.), *Self Abandonment to Divine Providence*, (London, 1962).

Chapman, John (*1865–1933*)
A monk, first in England at Erdington in Birmingham then in Wales at Caldey. He was made prior there before moving to Downside, of which he was elected Abbot in 1929. He was a considerable authority on New Testament studies and on the very early Church. But for our purposes his importance lies in a considerable number of letters on the spiritual life, on prayer in particular and religious studies, especially to monks and nuns. These were gathered and edited after his death by Dom Roger Hudleston. They blew a breath of fresh air, reasonableness and common sense

into a somewhat esoteric subject, that of the more advanced stages of prayer, which he maintained many religious and lay folk were capable of and even approached but, for lack of proper guidance, failed to achieve. Especially he was interested in the 'ligature' or the point in time when, at prayer, it becomes in practice impossible to think any more, and when therefore one should start praying wordlessly.

J. Chapman, *St Benedict and the Sixth Century*, (London, 1929).

R. Hudleston, OSB, (ed.), *The Spiritual Letters of Dom John Chapman*, (London, 1935).

Charismatic Movement
A more appropriate title than the Pentecostal Movement, because it is concerned with the Gifts (Greek *charismata*) of the Holy Spirit and not precisely with Pentecost, which was a special occasion, and not – at least in the same manner – to be repeated, except for Cornelius and the Samaritans for a special reason. We receive the Spirit at baptism (*cf.* St Paul's baptism in Acts 9:17–19). Nevertheless the Spirit does manifest himself in the Church throughout its history in innumerable and unexpected ways, for no merit of the individual concerned and often enough not through the ministration of the structures of the Church, though it remains to the latter to test the spirit, to see whether it is of God or of the devil (Discerning of Spirits). The movement is one of openness to the Spirit and more fittingly should be called the movement of the Holy Spirit.

The charismatic gifts (1 Cor 12–14) are: speaking with wisdom, with knowledge (the gift is for the Church not for the individual); the gift of faith, of healing, of performing miracles, of prophesying, of discernment of prophets, the gift of tongues, the interpretation of tongues. St Paul has little use for uninterpreted tongues (14). The highest of all the gifts, he says, is prophecy; but above prophecy itself is love or charity. These accounts (in 1 Cor) are of considerable interest today when the same gifts are appearing in profusion through the spread of the Charismatic Movement, not only among the less structured Churches but even among Episcopalians and Catholics.

Besides the gifts mentioned above, Paul also mentions (Rom 12:6–8), those of being prophets, teachers, workers of mercy, the gift of administration.

Today there are examples of speaking with tongues, of healing, of prophesying; also of the higher gifts, especially love. Any, today, who claim to be led by the Spirit, but are destructive of unity, are suspect.

cf. ↗Pentecostal Movement.

Charismatic Prayer Meetings
Groups have sprung up all over the United States and in England and elsewhere. It is impossible to generalize as to their essence. These meetings are spontaneous. An example of one meeting may give some idea. There is a hall capable of holding 200–300 people, with seats arranged in a semicircle. At 8.30 p.m. little groups begin to gather, a young couple perhaps with a small child; an older man, perhaps a clergyman, a few young people, teenagers; a married couple in middle age; a youngish man alone; a priest and some sisters. The general character of the group as it builds up is on the young side, cheerful and earnest. A guitar picks out a song;

and · all join in the refrain. Then silence perhaps for three to five minutes. A passage of Scripture is read; the leader comments very shortly upon it. A pause – someone begins to pray spontaneously aloud, usually in praise of God, and in thanksgiving for all his great goodness to men. Someone else will pick up the theme and begin reciting a well-known prayer, and all join in. Another silence; then a hymn is started 'from the floor', people pick it up. At the same time a sporadic speaking with tongues here and there, in low tones; now and then a prophetic utterance or a reading from Scripture. All this rolls on easily, unaided, or almost, for about one and a half to two hours.

This particular group here described began very simply as a group of four or five people with a priest. Gradually, without pressure or advertising, it grew to 200 or more.

Some meetings have a pause at the two-hour point or a little earlier and then break up into groups for laying on of hands for the ↗'Baptism' of the Spirit; or for healing. Others gather towards a corner or room where someone has the power of discerning of spirits, of guidance. The whole evening . will last from two and a half to three hours.

It has to be realized that an element may enter into the group destructive of unity and critical of institutional religion and attempting to use the meeting for propaganda purposes. There is only one way of dealing with this, and that is to ask those who so behave to leave. Of course if the meeting is called under un-denominational or 'leftish' auspices the situation is more delicate. You yourself might have to retire from the meetings. Signs of hatred are not of the Spirit, only love.

Charisms

(From the Greek *charisma*, a favour.) These extraordinary gifts of the Spirit, until recently thought to have been confined to the apostolic age and therefore to be of somewhat academic concern today, have become a matter of intense interest with the influx of the ↗Pentecostal or ↗Charismatic Movement into the bosom of the Catholic and Episcopalian Churches. St Paul examines these gifts (1 Cor 12–14), because of the disorder and discontent in the Corinthian church, especially on account of the strange or unintelligible utterances of those 'speaking with tongues'. He said that this rowdy gift was the least among them all; the most important was love, and the second, prophecy. He held that gifts are given not for the recipient but for the Church (1 Cor 14:12).

But in another place, using a different word, *fruit*, he enumerates many gifts that are not spectacular but rather might be called 'ordinary' gifts for market-place and home: 'Love, joy, peace, patience, kindness, generosity, forbearance, gentleness, faith, courtesy, temperateness, purity' (Gal 5:22). From this and other references in St Paul (for example Rom 12:6, where among other gifts he mentions administration, teaching, preaching; and Eph 4:11 ff) it seems that the Spirit may enter into any Christian activity and support with a special gift any virtuous act. Hence it is well to examine every way of life to see what are the specific virtues for that life and which would be the appropriate gifts. For example in monastic communities there might be the gifts of obedience, humility and chastity, also of a sense of community which would appear as joy and peace and considerateness; in family life especially the gift of love and forbearance, of teaching, of administration, and so on; in the professions, prudence and constancy.

The Charismatic Movement has concentrated, perhaps to its own detriment, on tongues, prophecy, and healing – extraordinary gifts, although (as they are gifts and not to be called up at the will of man), if they come they are to be accepted. Nevertheless from the point of view of the ordinary Christian it would be well to broaden the base of the movement, to recognize those 'little' gifts which are so close to sanctity: peace and joy and considerateness. The virtue is our part, with the grace of God; the gifts associated with every virtue are our response to the discreet promptings of the Spirit, if we would let Him act within us with His Life.

The most profound and universal Gift of the Spirit is Love (Rom 5:5), and its wide-reaching effects (1 Cor 13).

See also ↗Pentecostal Movement.

Chastity

The due restraint of the sex instinct is according to traditional Christian teaching incumbent on all Christians. Even within marriage unbridled sex indulgence is wrong. But chastity is a word usually associated with 'the vow' of chastity by which is meant the vow not to marry or indulge in sexual relationships. This strand of the ideal of chastity, which was both practised and praised by Christ (Mt 19:10 ff) and by St Paul (1 Cor 7) is part of the Christian heritage. Unlike some Gnostic sects and the Manichees, who acclaimed celibacy as the only right procedure and declared marriage as bad though unavoidable,

the Church on the one hand proclaimed marriage a sacrament and on the other celibacy as a holy state. Christians believe that all creation, being from God, is good, including the human body and its appetites, and procreation in particular. They also believe that created things may be left behind, put on one side, for something greater. Celibacy or chastity is a leaving behind of a very good thing in order to cling more closely to the greatest, God himself. As Christ said, let him take it, who can (Mt 19:12). This form of chastity is only for those who are called to it by a special vocation, for the sake of the kingdom (Lk 18:29), namely in order to be free to help the promotion of God's work in the world. It is a means not an end in itself. The end is the love of God and our neighbour. The vow of chastity has also an eschatological value. It stands as a sign, as do the other vows and the religious life generally, for a recognition in the Church that above and beyond this present life is the one of heaven which is eternal.

Childlikeness

Unless a man receives the Kingdom of God as a little child does, he shall not enter it, so runs the saying of Christ (Mt 18:2 and Lk 18:17).

At first sight this is confusing, since Paul (1 Cor 13:11) seems to say the opposite, that once we are grown up, we should put away childish behaviour, attitudes of mind, ways. There is a difference between childishness and childlikeness. The former is partly a mannerism, partly lack of self-control, emotionalism, irrational behaviour; whereas childlikeness is meant to signify the child's attitude of trustful love. Just as a child reposes complete confidence in his parents, so spiritual persons are never anxious, putting all their trust in God. As ↗Julian of Norwich wrote, 'All will be well, all manner of things will be well'. The child's trust may be misplaced, not so the Christian's, for God has such care of us (*cf.* I Pet 5:7).

The *Autobiography* of Soeur Thérèse is the *locus classicus* for this spirituality.

The basis for this unshakeable trust is the certainty of faith in God who has infinite love for each one and the power to do as He wills. It is not our love for God which is the root of this trust, but God's infinite love for us. In ↗John's Gospel it is recorded that God so loved the world as to send His only Son to save us (Jn 3:16). He died for us, even to the death of a cross (Phil 2:8) and in spite of the evil in us. Jesus who said, no greater love had any man than to lay down his life for his friends, is here dying for those who live as though he meant nothing to them (Rom 5: 8–9).

Clare, St (*1193/4–1253*)

Contemplative and foundress of the Second Order of St Francis, commonly called 'Poor Clares'. She came of a rich and noble family. At 18 on the night of Palm Sunday 1212, she fled from the city of Assisi by the Gate of the Dead to join Francis and his band of brothers. They met her with lighted torches. He cut off her hair, clothed her in the rough sackcloth of the Franciscan habit and that night settled her in a Benedictine convent, then a few days later in another one, where her sister Agnes joined her. Finally the house next door to the chapel he had rebuilt – San Damiano – was chosen and there she stayed and wanted to stay for the rest of her life.

A year before she had been fired with an intense love of God, listening to Francis preaching the Lenten sermons. During that year they had met to discuss her future. The flight was the first step of that future.

In 1215, by which time she had a community round her, Francis made her their abbess. While Francis was to roam the world telling of God's love, she was to remain there at San Damiano taking a special vow not to leave the enclosure. But an even greater desire was absolute poverty, not merely personal poverty but community poverty, possessing nothing, neither land nor rents nor buildings, subsisting on God's loving care of them and if need be by begging. Not even a cardinal or a Pope could shake her determination in this. Her austerity matched her poverty: under the sackcloth dress a hair shirt, no meat ever, bread and water for Lent, sleeping on the floor. Francis saw to it that she slept on a mattress and that she changed from eating every other day to every day. It was too late however to save her from 28 years of illness which followed. The experience explains her letter to a Poor Clare in Prague, Blessed Agnes of Bohemia: 'Since our bodies are not made of brass and our strength not the strength of stone but rather we are weak and subject to corporal infirmities, I implore you strongly in the Lord to refrain from excessive rigour of abstinence ... so that you may offer him a reasonable service and sacrifice seasoned with the salt of prudence.' She treated the great with firmness but little people, especially her own sisters, with most delicate attention, washing and kissing their feet as they returned from begging. Last to bed, first astir, during the night she would tuck in a stray covering over a sleeping sister. More than once she was found in ecstasy. Her greatest devotion was to the Blessed Sacrament.

Francis was her guide, but she at times guided him, persuading him, for example, that preaching was his vocation. At her death three followers of Francis were with her: Juniper, Leo and Angelo, and as for Francis so for her, they read to her the Passion. Among her last words were – speaking to herself: 'Go forth in peace, for you have followed the good road. Go forth without fear, for He that created you has sanctified you ... and loves you as a mother. Blessed be thou, O God, for having created me.'

P. Robinson, OFM, *Contemporary Life by Thomas of Celano*. Together with her *Rule*. (London, 1910).

There are also five letters of St Clare, her *Testament* and the documents of her canonization during the pontificate of Alexander IV (1255); for which see *Acta Sanctorum*, for 11 August, pp. 754–67.

See also 'Claire' in both *D.H.G.E.* and *D. Spir.*

Cloud of Unknowing, The
A short medieval English treatise on prayer by an unknown hand, a priest (ch. 75) from the East Midlands – to judge from the dialect – written in the second half of the 14th century. His chief sources, apart from the Bible, are ↗Richard of St Victor and the Pseudo-↗Denis. We may expect to find his teaching on prayer cataphatic, i.e. along the negative way, *via negativa*. He stresses the unknowableness of God. God is known in a cloud, as he 'showed' himself to Moses in a cloud on Mount Sinai. But the author of *The Cloud* is far from esoteric in his style, down to earth as he is both in language and thought. 'Lift up your heart to God with a meek stirring of love' (ch. 3). 'Though it be good to

think upon the kindness of God, and to love him and praise him for it; yet it is far better to think upon the naked being of him, and to love him and praise him for himself' (ch. 5). The last expresses the general tone of *The Cloud*.

This little work is not for those who find their support in meditation, but for those who cannot meditate and would yet love. *The Cloud* suggests an uncomplicated kind of prayer that it calls *stirrings*, almost without words, movements of the heart in love towards God. It suggests the use of words rich in meaning and short in extent – preferably of one syllable – such as 'God' or 'sin'; let them be repeated at intervals, to give substance to the prayer.

The Cloud is part of a 14th and 15th century movement away from communal prayer towards private individual prayer, also away from the *via positiva* to the Dark Night that St ↗John of the Cross was later to describe so thoroughly.

P. Hodgson, *The Cloud of Unknowing*, (Oxford, 1958).

D. Knowles, *The English Mystical Tradition*, (London and New York, 1961).

J. McCann (ed.), *The Cloud of Unknowing and other Treatises*, (London, 1924).

C. Wolters (ed.), *The Cloud of Unknowing*, (Harmondsworth, 1961).

Confession
The Sacrament of – sometimes called the Sacrament of Penance. Neither word is satisfactory, as the fundamental meaning of the rite is *metanoia*, or change of heart, and forgiveness of sins by God through the ministry of the priest, who says

the words of absolution in accordance with the promise of Christ, 'whose sins you shall forgive, they are forgiven' (Jn 20:23; *cf*. Mt. 16:19). More recently the name Sacrament of Reconciliation has been suggested, or the Sacrament of Peace – peace between the soul and God and between the individual and the Church.

The reception of Communion has the power to annul minor sins, since the very act of receiving is on our part a *metanoia* and on Christ's it is redemptive. Only weighty sins (mortal so called because they have destroyed the divine life in us) need absolutely the Sacrament of Penance. Should then lesser sins be mentioned in Confession? There is no absolute obligation, but doing so is both an act of humility and of contrition, as well as bringing us up against our faults, vanities, meanness, lustfulness. A further question; is it useful, if one has no consciousness of serious sin, to go nevertheless to Confession? The answer is much the same as above. We are stirred to repentance and receive the grace of the Sacrament. While it is doubtful what immediate effect the routine Confessions of children have upon them, at least going regularly makes them accustomed to the idea.

Now that many have abandoned frequent Confession, it would perhaps be an opportunity to establish new rites for partially communal Confession, e.g. a communal reading of suitable Scripture lessons, a homily, acts of contrition, a probing of conscience.

Once again the Charismatic Movement has cast a bright light upon this ancient practice of Reconciliation or Penance by its emphasis on ↗ *Healing*. Christ himself more than once linked a miracle of physical healing with spiritual healing. He said to the paralytic: your sins are forgiven you (Mk 2:5). Indeed the miracles of healing are in a sense a prelude and parable of the healing of the soul. The Sacrament *is* Christ in that, through his body the Church, he is healing his members of their spiritual sickness.

Confessor

Used here not in the sense of a saint who was not martyred – e.g. Edward the Confessor – but to designate the priest who hears confessions and often acts as director to penitents. The rise in importance of the confessor-director coincides with the Counter-Reformation and the renewal of the spirituality of the laity, especially the newly educated laity of the Western world. The leaders in the new look were the Jesuits who transferred their own spirituality of obedience to superiors to their penitents through the instrumentality of the director. Penitents were expected to be guided by the director in all spiritual matters and receive permission for practices of piety and for any major activity in their lives. This resulted in the most zealous lay folk, and these were of remarkable and courageous assistance in those troubled and dangerous times.

There is no doubt that in spiritual matters all Christians need guidance, as we very easily deceive ourselves in the obscurity of faith; and the laity need the asceticism of obedience just as much as religious. It needs the skill of spiritual discernment on the part of the confessor and of the director to know when to take the lead and when to withdraw, to allow the soul to expand under the guiding hand of God.

Today we think more in terms of counsellor, of one who is prepared to listen and, by careful and wise probing, to lead the person concerned to find his or her own decision. To be fully human, people must make their own decisions.

The confessor, being aware over a long period of time of the spiritual longings, the sins and propensities of his penitents, is in a good position to give advice and to lead souls towards God.

Conscience

The final judge for deciding that an action is either right or wrong. The way to come to this conclusion is immensely complex. We may even not be aware of how we have come to it; a whole lifetime of decisions may be at the back of a clear decision of conscience that this or that is wrong, or right.

In general it may be said that the Christian conscience is formed by the innate search for the good, by the exterior admonitions of Sacred Scripture and of the Church, whether in the form of parental training, the local Christian group, the local teacher or minister, the bishop or bishops, or the Pope himself. At the centre is the guidance by the Spirit within. It is however not always easy to distinguish the leadings of the Spirit from the desires of the carnal man. It is for this that exterior help is important, more especially as we Christians know that our nature is somewhat warped by a basic flaw in our being as well as by our past propensities to sin, and our actual failures.

For a person entering upon a serious intent to live a good Christian life, conscience in the early stages plays some tricks. For instance, one may become over-scrupulous through being so conscious of the need to purify one's motives. If the scrupulous person cannot be rid of the gnawing fear of guilt, the answer

is to consult a wise counsellor, and *do what he says*; or, if such a one is not easily available, to put complete confidence in God and do whatever at the moment seems good, after having prayed over it; and not to go back over the problem. Another twist is to become exceedingly critical of others' behaviour. The answer here is to realize that we do not know the inner motives of people, and what seems to us irresponsible or even evil, may prove, should we ever learn the hidden motives, to have been subjectively at least a good act. A third quirk is to become extremely unconcerned about right and wrong, leaving it all to God. This was the pitfall of the ↗Quietists. It is not something that only occurred in the 17th century, but is a permanent hazard for those who abandon themselves to the will of God. 'Whatever happens' is not necessarily his will, but whatever happens that is according to his known will, in Scripture and tradition.

In the modern world the call of conscience for Christians is often agonizing, because the world is not guided by Christian principles and yet Christians are involved in the intricate workings of the world around them; and in a manner that has a degree of intimacy it never had before. We know what is going on, not only in our own village but throughout the world and almost instantaneously. We know of social injustice in our own country and also abroad. So in a sense we are all involved in the sin of world-wide social injustice unless we, following our conscience, in so far as we can, do something to overcome it. Whether we will it or not we are engulfed in innumerable unjust transactions, from workmen's pay in East Africa – those for instance who pick the tea which we drink – or the miners' pay in Zambia – those who provide the copper for the pipes along which our fresh water runs. We use what they provide, but for a wage that is hideously low. Meanwhile the capitalist gets an unfair share of the profit.

The solutions are not easy, and wild demonstrations and wilder theories will probably not help. But we have a duty to help form a conscientious public opinion; this requires serious study of these problems and co-operation with those who show concern.

In another area conscience plays an important role, that of marriage, with special reference to abortion and birth control. The Church – most recently in *Humanae vitae* – has attempted to legislate, and with considerable success, in the area of birth control, but to find a complete answer in writing for every single case has not proved altogether satisfying either to theologians, the medical profession or to the couples concerned and there is a tendency, wisely, to fall back, after all teaching from on high has been treated with all the respect it deserves and has been carefully weighed, upon individual conscience. This would appear to be the teaching of St Thomas who recognized so clearly that circumstances made a profound difference in moral matters.

Contemplation

A word that has had a shift of meaning. The early Jesuit tradition (see the *Spiritual Exercises* of ⌐Ignatius) would use the word contemplation for prayer done with the help of the imagination, memory, mind and will. Today 'meditation' is the recognized term for this, practical and useful for active people, who are distracted by many things, and therefore find it difficult to keep in God's presence. But meditation is not suitable for all. Among the Fathers of the Church, notably ⌐Augustine, ⌐Gregory and ⌐Bernard and for medieval writers, contemplation meant a form of prayer which does not require discursive reasoning (ratiocination), but in which the soul is aware that God is close and so stays with him in an attitude of humble praise, thanks, sorrow, adoration and longing. This meaning is now once again the standard one. There are however several stages in the prayer of contemplation. The early stage of this is a form of prayer that should not be considered reserved for the very few, but rather open to all who take appropriate means.

The phrase '*acquired contemplation*' is used, especially in the Carmelite tradition of ⌐John of the Cross to signify a form of prayer which dispenses with the imagination and memory and is akin to peaceful abiding in the presence of God with a minimum of thinking and a maximum of ⌐loving attention. This could be achieved by practice by all devout and diligent Christians and is therefore suitably called 'acquired'. Undoubtedly on the technical side, of quieting all the exterior activities, it has affinities with the ⌐Buddhist contemplation and approach to enlightenment. All mystics assert – without proof – the existence of a kind of 'knowing' which is deeper than concepts, than reasoning; and also more real and satisfying. Many serious Christians, religious and lay, fight shy of allowing themselves to accept contemplation which is open to them, because of a humble fear that contemplation is only for the few. Acquired contemplation is open to all. There is further, '*passive contemplation*', a phrase used by ⌐John of the Cross to describe the condition of someone praying who has already reached the acquired contemplation or peaceful, tranquil remaining in the presence of God without concepts but who now, moved by the Spirit to prayer, is granted a form of union with God which is above the capacity of human effort with grace to achieve. It is seen to be wholly God's work and quite beyond the capacity of words to describe. It is a pure gift. In this condition it is unwise to attempt to be active in the old sense of exercising the imagination or mental processes. On the other hand love is greatly increased. Love can be wordless, and it is so in this case.

Catholic writers prefer 'contemplation' to 'mysticism'. It has acquired more precise meanings.

C. Butler, *Western Mysticism*, (London, 1928).

E. Allison Peers (ed. and tr.), 'John of the Cross', *Ascent of Mount Carmel*, Bk. 3, ch. 13, ss. 3–5, in *The Complete Works of St John of the Cross*, 3 vols in 1, (London and New York, 1964).

Contrition
Derived from *cum*: completely, and *tritum*, from *terere* (Latin) to rub or crush or bruise; therefore, completely bruised or crushed by a sense of guilt from offending God (sin). Traditional theology specified that contrition was sorrow for sin because one's action or inaction was an offence against God's love. A modern reaction to this is to find it difficult to see God as hurt by anything we can do or not do. Sin would appear to be an offence against oneself. In a real sense this is true. But God made us and therefore sin is against his plan. Another reaction is to deny sin altogether: we make mistakes, but are not wilful. Facts bely this. People kill for money or

love, lie for reputation's sake, even at the expense of another's reputation. Perhaps too we do not want to admit that we do wrong; this is compounding the evil deed with pride. If men would admit to guilt, and so acknowledge their weakness, then in true contrition they could appeal to God for help, 'Lord have mercy' – and the Spirit would be active in their lives again.

See 'Contrition' in *D. Spir.*

Conversion
Translates New Testament *metanoia*, a turning back to God, a change of heart. The cry of the Baptist was, 'be converted, for the kingdom of heaven is at hand' (Mt 3:2); see also Christ's call (Mt 4:17).

It is a pre-requisite of redemption as Peter points out preaching in Acts: 'You must be converted (repent)' (2:38). It has two aspects: turning away from idols (1 Thess 1:9) and a turning towards God, as manifested in the Lord Jesus (2 Cor 3:16). The New Testament frequently refers back to (Is 6:10) man's blindness and consequent inability to be converted.

Conversion is an important idea in monastic literature. ⟋Benedict asks of the novice whether he 'truly seeks God', which means a turning towards God. ⟋Ignatius set the stage in the *Exercises* for an 'election' which is a profound conversion of manners. ⟋Paul's experience on the road to Damascus is peculiar in that it was transparently supernatural, and also an 'experience', as much as an intellectual decision. Protestant conversion (*cf.* also ⟋Pascal's conversion as described in the 'memorial') also includes experience. It was John ⟋Wesley's worry that, at first, though converted, he was not convinced he had received an 'experience'. Revivalism and the

↗Pentecostal Movement all seem to require this element, and they have some corroboration from Paul's description of the happenings in Corinth (1 Cor 11 ff). But conversion, whether with or without an 'experience' is only the first step; there must follow the life in the Spirit.

Conversion, second

The phrase second conversion is used to express a deepening of the life of the spirit that may occur as late as middle age, even old age. ↗Pascal's famous experience is perhaps a typical example, as already he was a sincere Christian. It usually includes a sense of deeper commitment, of greater loyalty to the inspirations of God. It resembles somewhat the experience described by Pentecostalists – confusingly – as the ↗Baptism of the Spirit. The Jesuit Tertianship itself resembles this, being an effort to recover the first fervour. Any retreat might result in a 'second conversion', and as such would be of profound importance in the spiritual life of an individual, and an opportunity not to be ignored. In thise sense the spiritual life is never standing still, but always either going forward or falling back, a continual conversion, or repeated falling away.

See 'Conversion' and 'Repentance' in *D.B.T.*

Crashaw, Richard (*circa 1613–49*)

'Poet and Saint', as his friend the poet Abraham Cowley wrote in his poem *On the Death of Mr Crashaw*. The poet we know, with all his magic with symbol, rhyme and rhythm; the saint needs more facts than are now available.

Crashaw had an earnest Pres-byterian father, a preacher at the Inner Temple. His schooling was at Charterhouse, where the memory of the Carthusian martyrs must still have lingered. At Cambridge he was at Pembroke College and in 1637 gained a fellowship at what is now called Peterhouse. Both these were High Church in the Laudian tradition. At Cambridge he lived in a circle of poets including Beaumont, Cowley, and met Nicholas Ferrar, whom he visited at Little Gidding, that village of high seriousness where he would meet George Herbert. Among his friends at Cambridge he was already known as 'chaplaine of the Virgin myld'. In the Civil War he refused to align himself with the Puritans and resigned his fellowship for conscience-sake, fleeing first to Holland, then to Oxford to join Charles I. There, at the nadir of any Catholic hopes, he became a Catholic and fled to Paris. Cowley found him there in abject poverty. Queen Henrietta Maria sent him on his way to Rome. In the household of Cardinal Palotta he dared expose its unchristian living, whereupon the cardinal got him safely out of Rome to Loretto. He served the shrine in some lowly ecclesiastic post and shortly died, as Cowley wrote: 'The most divine and richest off'ring of Loretto's shrine.'

It was the life and writings of St Teresa of Avila that had first set Crashaw's heart aflame. He wrote that through her 'I learnt to know that love is eloquence'. All his poetry was a pouring out of 'divine song': songs to Mary – the translation of the *Stabat Mater*, a poem on the Glorious Assumption of Our Blessed Lady; songs in honour of the Blessed Sacrament: translations of the *Lauda Sion*, the *Adoro te devote*, and the well-known poem on Mary Magdalene, *The Weeper*. But his lodestar was St Teresa (canonized in

1622); he acclaimed her in three poems. *The Hymn to Saint Teresa* was written while he was still an Anglican, then *An Apologie*. Her language, he explains, is 'not Spanish but heaven'. The third was *The Flaming Heart*, which has the magnificent ending: 'O thou undaunted daughter of desires / By all thy dowr of Lights and Fires . . . / Let me so read thy life, that I / Unto all life of mine may dy.'

Crashaw's writings were published as *Steps to the Temple, Delights of the Muses and Other Poems*, edited by A.R. Waller, (Cambridge, 1904). Also *The Poems, English Latin and Greek of Richard Crashaw*, edited by L.C. Martin, (Oxford, revised edition 1957).

Creeds

The most solemn professions of the faith of the Universal Church, hammered out at the great early Councils, especially at Nicaea and Chalcedon. Thus they provide strong material for prayer, especially in times of doubt and darkness. Each section or 'article' of the Creed may be taken separately and repeated, as one would the ↗Jesus Prayer.

The Creeds are expansions of the Christian Baptismal belief. We are baptized in the name of (by the power of) the Father, Son and Holy Spirit. Prayer is Communion, talking with God, Three-in-One. The Creeds expand, unfold the meaning of each of them. The Father creates, the Son becomes man, dies for us and rises from the dead. The Spirit spoke through the Prophets, he lives on in the Church. All this is rich material for prayer.

But it is worth remembering that the Creeds are 'occasional' documents, produced to respond to a particular threat: to Arius, to

Nestorius. There are therefore, other facets of God's nature which might be used for meditation: God the Mother, God who ties his own hands by his gift to us of liberty, all-wise, all-provident, unknowable, the beyond all concepts, beyond all reality.

Then Jesus Christ, the suffering Servant, the healer of ills, the compassionate friend, lover, sharer of our life, our sorrows, etc. The Holy Spirit, the God-life, love, power to the infinite and all the titles of the mystics of other religions – the 100 names in Islam. The Creeds then are a start and a safeguard, an assurance and re-assurance, no more, no less.

J.N.D. Kelly, *Early Christian Creeds*, (London, 1949).

See also ↗Catherine of Siena, ↗Pseudo-Denis and ↗Ruysbroeck.

Cyprian, St (?–258)

Bishop and martyr, one of the glories of the early North African Church. Though beyond the scope of this book, mention at least must be made of his famous treatise *De Catholica Ecclesiae Unitate* (251). A late convert, and a distinguished rhetorician, within two years of his conversion he was elected Bishop of Carthage, the most important see of North Africa (248). In the plain, below the modern city, the unkempt, ruinous remains of his basilica and the site of his martyrdom nearby can be visited.

The account of that martyrdom still survives, one of the earliest to give us, possibly *verbatim*, the very text of the trial. Among his short treatises on spiritual matters are: *In praise of virginity*, another on *Alms giving* and among the earliest of commentaries on the *Lord's Prayer*.

D

Dante Alighieri (*1265–1321*)
Politician, philosopher, theologian,
mystic and poet first and last. He was
born in Florence; he loved it. But half
his grown life he was exiled (1301–
21) for political reasons (he was a
prior), thus living as a fugitive, a
refugee, in poverty and humiliation,
and dying in Ravenna. Dante would
have us believe that at the age of 9 he
met a girl, Beatrice (just younger
than himself), in a street of Florence
and that immediately and per-
manently he fell in love with that
lovely image. They never spoke,
though he met her nine years later
and she saluted him. In 1290 she
died, causing him, so he says, to
despair, to live wildly and lose his
faith. But he tells us also that she
appeared to him in a vision and his
pure youthful love returned. That
love grew until it embraced the
whole world, and found its
consummation in God. Then it was
he resolved to compose in her
honour a poem incomparably
beautiful. The *Divina Commedia* is
the result. For this end he studied
philosophy, history, theology, all
the knowledge of his time and left
his *Convivio*, unfinished, which
together with the *Vita Nuova* (1292)
provide us with the account of this
love.

The *Divina Commedia* was perhaps
begun in 1305, and he worked at it
for most of his remaining years. At
its simplest, it is the account of a
pilgrimage Dante makes, he
imagines, through hell, purgatory
and into paradise, towards the very
vision of God; but in the process he
gathers up into one mighty whole
the total world of Italy and beyond,
the cosmos itself into a great
movement of love. In hell he
describes the fate of those who had
sinned grievously, but more, he sees

in their sin his own weakness, if not
his fall. Virgil guides him there. On
reaching the highest point of
purgatory, Virgil hands him over to
Beatrice who leads him into
paradise, when St Bernard appears
and takes him towards the Blessed
Virgin, whose praises Bernard had
sung, and she places Dante before the
ineffable vision of God.

Since the poem contains
innumerable meetings with the dead,
Dante grasps the opportunity to
make use of his vast knowledge of
past and contemporary history
ecclesiastic and lay, of law and of the
sciences, of language and art, to
create a work which in the language
of poetry gathers all that constituted
the complex panorama of medieval
life and thought into an intelligible
whole. He was perhaps the last of
that Christian age, so full of the good
and the bad, to have the chance and
capability to do so, before the
ultimate disintegration set in.

K. Foster, op, *The Two Dantes, and
other Studies*, (London, 1977).

E. Gilson, 'Dante et Beatrice' in
Etudes dantesques, (Paris, 1974).

J. Sinclair (tr.), Italian text, *The
Divine Comedy*, (Oxford, 1971).

F. Vandenbroucke, osb, *H.C.S.*,
Vol. 2, pp. 364 ff.

Death
The dissolution of that complex
entity we call the human being. For
those who consider man no more
than a complex material organism,
this will be his final extinction. Even
some, who believe in a spiritual
principle underlying the visible, see
death as the end of that particular
being, who is absorbed, sucked back
into the Absolute Reality. Others
consider that men, unless they have

achieved perfect detachment from desire, will exist separately yet again until perfect detachment is achieved. This is common Hindu teaching. Some Hindus and Buddhists hold that the I is extinguished with death. Christians see death as the entrance for each individual into a new and everlasting life in union with God. At death the union between body and spirit for a time dissolves, as can be seen; but according to the revelation and example of Christ, that union will be restored, but in a spiritual manner. Just as Christ died but rose from the dead, and proved it by living with his disciples after the Resurrection, so we shall rise again. But, for the Christian, death also is a time of reckoning: heaven or hell.

For Christians death signifies much more than disintegration, since it is seen as a sharing in the death of Christ, a death that is a victory because, once accepted as God's will, as it was by Christ in his case, it becomes the entrance to eternal life. Recently much study has been made of the process of dying, and it has been seen to have four phases, not necessarily in every case in identical sequence. They are: fear, anger, disbelief, acceptance. *Fear* of the unknown, of pain, of a judgement. That fear is natural enough. A strong Christian faith overcomes all that. *Anger* is a reaction of one's sense of justice: why me? And again, faith in God who knows and loves each one, reduces anger to acceptance. *Disbelief* that this could be happening to me is our instinctive reaction of pushing unpleasant possibilities 'under the mat'. *Acceptance* is an honest facing of the facts. This comes as the moment of death approaches. For a Christian death is a passage to the fulness of life, and by the mercy of God to seeing him as he is, infinite beauty, face to face.

L. Boros, *The Moment of Truth*, (London and New York, 1965).

P.S. Chaney, *Dealing with Death and Dying*, (Beckenham, 1976).

M. Oraison, *Death . . . and then What?*, (London, 1969).

Deification

Master ↗Eckhart and ↗John of the Cross were not afraid to use the word, which is common among the Great Fathers of the Eastern Church. Its justification is the daring sentence in 2 Pet 1:4, 'You are to share the divine nature.' The 'eternal life' of John's gospel, 4:14, the 'new creation' of Paul's epistles are different words for the same thing. How could this come about? By union with the humanity of Christ, through the Eucharist (Jn 6). Christ is the vine, we the branches; Christ the Head, we the body. The purpose: that being made God-like, we may share in his life of knowing and loving. This is Christian prayer in all its richness. In the next life 'we shall see him (God) as he is' (1 Jn 3:2).

Deification or Absolutization (for those who prefer to think of the ultimate reality in impersonal terms) presents a complex problem to students of mystical experience in world religions. Not only do the means towards the end seem to have close similarities, but perhaps the end itself may be the same, expressed in different ways. Some would see the end as identification, others as absorption, others as a sinking into the absolute, others as union amounting to unity in God, others as annihilation of self, others as a realization that only the Great Self is, and that 'I am that'. These same experiences have been put into poetical terms, such as marriage, or as a drop is absorbed in the vast ocean. The question remains: are these experiences identical? Are they different experiences approaching the same ultimate reality? Are they experiences that cannot be expressed adequately in logical terms? And are they not always in their expression influenced by the preconceived philosophy of the one who experiences them?

From a Christian point of view here are a few very tentative suggestions:

(i) Christians believe that God – the ultimate reality – made all men so that they could share by his gift (grace) in his absolute happiness; but whether the Christian achieved this union depended for each on his acceptance. God has led men by many ways, many covenants, many revelations. They claim that the ultimate is Jesus Christ through whom all, by sharing in his Eucharist, may be brought to union with God. This is the meaning of the Christian prayer that survives from the very early Roman Mass: 'By the mystery (sign) of this water and wine may we come to share in his divinity who humbled himself to share in our humanity.'

(ii) Christians go on to assert that all men may have a part in this great and perfect gift through Christ, even unknowingly, so long as they in humility seek God and implore his aid. This they achieve in good faith through their own religion in so far as it has been a true revelation of God's love.

(iii) This 'deification' is not merely a presence of God in the ground of our being. This is of course true, but true also for animals and everything in the universe. Nor is it simply an awareness of this fact. Christians believe that God takes over our lives. As Paul wrote, 'now not I live but Christ lives within me' (Gal 2:20). Note, however, that though he wrote that we no longer live our lives, he did write that the new life is within *me*. In some way therefore he too knows that he still lives on. It is a new self, no longer completely separate from God, now almost identical with him, a soul absorbed in God, identified in life, with an identity still distinct, an infinitesimal dot on an infinitely wide screen.

(iv) Here in this life the mystic swings from one extreme to the other, from a sense of complete absorption in the super-essential reality of God back to the realization of his own wretched creaturely existence. In heaven there will be no need to return; the Infinite will be all in all, even though the 'dot' exists.

(v) When any true mystic, who has abandoned self, looks within, he will see the divine reflection in the mirror of his own being. This is a sublime and shattering experience, enough to account for the ecstasies of a ↗Teresa or the wild sayings of ↗Al-Hallaj. But neither the ecstasy nor the wild sayings are the experience; these are but the reactions on the human level in the human psyche. The experience is the 'dim silence' of a ↗Ruysbroeck, perhaps even the One of Plotinus, the ↗Atman or the ↗Nirvana of the East.

(vi) The great mystics are those who attempt to describe this deification, this God-likeness, this sonship, this intimate sharing in God's own life. But the wonder-fact is that all Christians, all true and faithful seekers of the *God who saves*, are also in the depth of their being deified, united with the very God; and it is only the crust of selfishness that prevents us being aware of it in any fulness. The deep awareness is a gift of God.

Denis the Areopagite

An Athenian converted by the

preaching of Paul (Acts 17:34). In the very early 5th century there appeared works attributed to him. Only one person seriously challenged this attribution of the works until the 16th century. The influence of these writings was immense, as they seemed to have almost apostolic authority. The identity of the 'Pseudo Denis' or 'Dionysius' has remained a mystery even to this day. All we can say with some assurance is that he lived in Asia Minor and that he was closely linked with ↗Gregory of Nyssa (*circa* 330–*circa* 395). ↗Thomas Aquinas quotes him liberally; the works of ↗John of the Cross are clearly related to his theories. The English mystic, author of ↗ *The Cloud of Unknowing*, is not only indebted to him for the title of his work but also for much of the underlying teaching. Denis taught that God is unknowable in his essence, except by the *via negativa*; in this he seems to echo the Hindu teaching; God is neither this nor that: '*neti, neti*'. God is utterly transcendent, the superessence. No matter what name we may give God – super essential or super divine – they are all inadequate. Nevertheless the *via negativa* must depend on a *via positiva*, otherwise God would be equivalent to nothing, and neither Denis nor his contemporaries meant that. Behind the 'cloud' was the great light. Or the light is so dazzling that men are blinded by it. Both for Denis and for Gregory of Nyssa the image of Moses seeing God in the cloud on Mount Sinai was crucial.

It has been said that Denis is more Hindu than Christian. Not only does he have this negative approach to God but he seems to be more intellectual than volitional. It is claimed that loving is not part of his thinking; that in his work the Christian dogmas are lacking. This criticism is important but beside the mark if we keep in mind that behind the famous treatise on the *Divine Names* are thoroughly Christian ones: the *Ecclesiastical Hierarchy*, the *Celestial Hierarchy*, *Mystical Theology*. Further, even in the treatise on the *Divine Names* there are such passages as:

'Thus everything tends towards the Beautiful-and-Good; he is the object of all loving desire and of all charitable love. It is through the Beautiful-and-Good, because of the Beautiful-and-Good, that beings love one another, that the lower turn to the higher, that those of the same rank unite with their like . . . Doer of good in everything, this loving desire, which pre-exists in a superabundant way in the very heart of 'the Good, would not have permitted him to remain sterile and turn in on himself, but rather sets him astir so that he acts in accord with the superabundant power of universal giving-birth.' (ch. 4. Section 10).

In our time, which has witnessed the discovery of immeasurable space and galaxies of stars 'stacked' beyond one another, together with the mysteries of quasars and the infinitely small, the God of the Bible has seemed mightier yet, more mysterious than ever with the consequence that writers such as Denis come into their own, and the need for an Incarnation, or breakthrough by God into this world more than ever needed, to give humanity something by which to glimpse those attributes of God other than size, or else Pascal's famous *pensée* '*Le silence éternel des espaces infinis m'effraie*', would appear to be more terrifyingly true than ever.

Not everyone is called to pray according to the nameless dark night. Rather we should remain in customary prayer, at least with some words or images, until such time as these are found to be no longer relevant to our state. Then would be the time, as the cloud closes in, to accept it, though not seek it, in faith and courage.

The *Opera omnia* are in process of being published by the monks of Solesmes, France.

Desert Fathers

Led by the example of Antony the Hermit (251–356) thousands, possibly tens of thousands of men and women fled the world in the 4th and 5th centuries to hide themselves in the remote desert solitudes, not only of Egypt (Nitria and Scete), but also of Palestine and Syria, indeed throughout the Christian world, from Trier in the north-west to Arabia in the south-east. In the track of Edward Gibbon, writers have for long written disparagingly of them, emphasizing their eccentricities – and these existed. But in recent years the humanity as well as the austerity of the ancient ascetics has been appreciated. Helen Waddell's book *The Desert Fathers*, a masterpiece of presentation, translation and selection, has had a notable impact, reviving sympathetic interest. Some lived alone as anchorites or hermits; others lived in groups called monasteries (*Cenobia*); others again in a group of hermits called a *laura*. The founder of the monastery style was St Pachomius. For us their austerities are frightening and unhelpful. Yet they taught succeeding generations: that God is best sought in solitude; that no Christian achievement is possible without denial of self; that there are degrees of praying. Nor is it true that they had no thought for their fellow men and women. Shiploads of grain that they had grown would be sent down the Nile from their remote colonies, and directed to the poor, for instance, of Alexandria.

The Desert Fathers sought to be free of the world in order to be free for God. They sought *custodia cordis* a guarded heart. Their spirituality has been gathered in their Sayings and in the works of ↗ Cassian. ↗ Benedict in the 6th century distilled from all this the essential elements, interiorizing their austerities and ordering the daily round.

Athanasius of Alexandria, R.T. Meyer (tr.), *Life of St Antony*, (*A.C.W.*, 1950), x.

E. Walter Budge (tr. and ed.), *The Paradise Garden of the Holy Fathers*, (London, 1907).

Palladius, R.T. Meyer (tr. and ed.), *Lausiac History*, (*A.C.W.*, 1965), xxxiv.

H. Waddell, *The Desert Fathers*, (London, 1937).

B. Ward, *The Sayings of the Desert Fathers*, (London, 1975).

See also ↗ Cassian and ↗ Evagrius.

Desire

Plays a central role in Christian and Buddhist spirituality. All spiritual guides encourage, even require a purgative period in the learner stage, for the beginners, the novices. They need to strip themselves of all unnecessary 'baggage' for the ascent. Part of this baggage is desire. In classical Buddhism it is all desire that has to be eliminated, even the desire for ↗ Nirvana, the desire to live. The logic of it runs thus: all life is painful, therefore desire not life. When all desire is quenched, then the stage of Nirvana is reached. Nirvana as a word means the blowing out of all desire.

The Christian tradition hesitated. The ↗Desert Fathers approached very nearly to this absolute stamping out of desire. But with the advent of ↗Augustine a more balanced view prevailed. He expounds his considered view in the *City of God* (Bks. 9:5 and 14:5). He said that neither Jesus Christ nor St Paul aimed at extinguishing all desire or emotion (*City of God*, Bk. 14:9). The question therefore is 'not whether the devout soul is angry, but why; not whether it is sad, but why, what causes its sadness; not whether it is afraid but what is the object of its fear'. (Bk. 9:5). 'Cicero', he writes, 'did not hesitate to call compassion a virtue, while the stoics did not scruple to class it a vice'. (Bk. 9:5). Later: 'If these emotions and feelings, that spring from love of the good and from holy charity, are to be called faults, then let us allow that real faults should be called virtues.' (Bk. 14:9). He concludes: 'It comes to this then: we must lead a right life to reach the God of a life of felicity; and this right kind of life exhibits all these emotions in the right way.' (Bk. 14:9).

H. Bettenson (tr.), *The City of God*, (Harmondsworth, 1972).

Detachment
There is only one from whom we should not be detached, that is God: But even there, we need to be detached from our ideas of God – which are not God. Always there are deeper depths to fathom. So too 'touches' of God, visions, locutions, sensible devotion, are not God, and we must be ready to cast them aside.

Normally the word detachment, in the context of prayer, means detachment from people and things. There may be here a difference between Christian and Buddhist

thought, though the fulness of compassion that the Buddha himself showed for all living creatures leads one to believe that his and the Christian ideal in this matter are closer than once thought. No creature has the absolute value that God has, and to be attached or to be unwilling to let go seems to point to an egocentric attitude to the other, or at least an over-emphasis on the other (*cf. Confessions* of ↗Augustine, Bk. 9:12). Christian thought, relying on Christ's command to love one another, proclaims the good of human love in marriage and in friendship and in love for enemies. Here we have an unselfish love, the authentic mark of the Christian message, exemplified in the life and death of Christ himself. Christians are also told to be ready to give up all for God's sake. That is rather non-attachment than detachment: the readiness to forego a good thing for a better, yet never denying its goodness.

Devil
A familiar figure in Christian literature and life, and in Judaism, from the Garden of Eden, through the temptations of Christ in the desert on to the lives of the saints, particularly the Fathers of the Desert and medieval saints, right up to the 'happenings' at Ars in the time of the holy Curé, whose bed was burned (still on view) during his three or four hours' sleep. We in our age are somewhat sceptical about him and his tribe, seeing that much human temptation attributed to the devil could just as readily come from one's own depraved nature, while many so-called possessions are hallucinations of deranged minds. On the other hand the devil and his legions would like nothing better

than that humans would think he did not exist.

G. Bazin and others, C. Moeller (tr.), *Satan.* (*Etudes Carmelitaines*), (London, 1951).

Devotio Moderna

Devotion was the favourite word used by Gerhard ↗Groote to describe the attitude of mind with regard to religion of himself and his followers. Modern it was at the time (15th century) as it was a reaction against the scholastic ratiocination and stylized religious life such as it had become in the generation or two before the Reformation. While *devotio moderna* was 'anti' in the sense that it was disinterested in religious orders and particularly vows, it was eager for community, for frugality, for hard work which earned one's daily bread; against prayer in common (choir) but eager for private meditation. It was an inward-looking movement, inward to Jesus at the centre of the soul. It was for women as well as men.

Its geographical centre was Deventer, Groote's native town, in the Low Countries, and neighbouring little towns like Zwolle and Windesheim. The ecclesiastical 'Establishment' was so nervous about lay movements at this time – compare anxiety over the *Opus Dei* in Spain in the late-20th century and see ↗Lay Movements – that finally Groote allowed his follower Florentus Radewyns to give some of the groups of disciples the Rule of ↗Augustine as being most free of regulation, and the Congregation of Windesheim developed in consequence. They themselves fought shy of having a 'name' like Benedictine or Franciscan. They did not even call themselves the Brethren of the Common Life, but simply 'the Brethren living together at Zwolle' or wherever it was. Their work was at first manual and craft but the Guilds resented their intrusion in their own preserves, and this led the brothers to concentrate on copying MSS books, and later printing and writing books of devotion, the fine flower of which was the ↗*Imitation of Christ* by ↗Thomas a Kempis. They also conducted schools. Many leaders in the next generation in Europe had been influenced one way or another by their spirit, ↗Catherine of Genoa, ↗Nicholas of Cusa, Gerson brought it to Paris, the College de Montaigu was under its influence. ↗Luther met it at Magdeburg, Pope Adrian VI, ↗Erasmus, ↗Ignatius, Calvin breathed its air. Like the Franciscans the movement began mostly as lay, but the priestly caste soon got control. Its anti-intellectual temper made it difficult for it to withstand the intellectual storms of the 16th century.

Fliche et Martin, *Histoire de L'Église*, Vol. 14b, p. 938 ff.

R.W. Southern, *Western Society and the Church in the Middle Ages*, (Harmondsworth, 1970), p. 331 ff. Very useful.

Director, Spiritual

One who is chosen by a person wishing to progress in the life of the spirit, not only for advice but often as one to be obeyed, in view of the fallible judgement we ourselves have.

Jesus in the episode of Paul's vision, did not himself tell Paul what to do, rather he told him to go to Damascus and Ananias would tell him (Acts 9:6). The Fathers saw in this an example to follow. God directs through human instrumentality. But it is the Fathers of the Desert, beginning in the late 4th century, who represent the earliest known variant of the genus 'director'. The hermits, new to the Desert, would seek out a wise and holy ancient, a father, to ask him for a 'word', or piece of advice, which he would give, often, in some pithy even enigmatic saying. The response would provide material for meditation over the coming months; then, the saying being exhausted, the neophyte would come seeking another. This custom lies at the back of those collections of Sayings of the Fathers, ↗*Apophthegmata Patrum*.

Jerome in Rome and ↗Augustine at Hippo were directing men and women along the Way; so too was Pelagius but with dire results. The tradition was carried on through the Benedictine centuries, ending with Peter the Venerable (who cared for Héloïse) and St Anselm. Then ↗Bernard and ↗Aelred were the guides of their century. During the Counter-Reformation ↗Teresa was lamenting the lack of good directors and the absolute need for them. She put prudence first on her list of qualities for a good director, then experience in spiritual matters, then learning. As she warmed to the subject it seemed as though, at least for those who had progressed some way in the life of the spirit, for her, learning came first on the list. (See the *Autobiography*, c. xiii, 16 ff B.A.C.)

John of the Cross wrote his commentaries because there was so little help from uninformed directors. The great directors of souls in that Golden Age were ↗Ignatius with his insistence on the gift of discernment of spirits, ↗Francis of Sales, so gentle in manner but firm in substance. His method can be followed in the collections of his admirable letters. That was a period of great confusion, a new world coming to birth. The need for clear strong guidance was evident. Direction took on a strongly obediential character. The penitent put himself or herself under the direction of the spiritual director and his word had in a sense the authority of God. In supernatural prayer a guide is an assurance.

The Venerable Fr ↗Baker (d. 1641) was much in favour of direction but suggested that, as the one directed progressed in the life of grace, the Holy Spirit should be allowed to play its part more immediately (*cf.* Jer 31:34). It was the method he used with his nuns at Cambrai and particularly with Dame Gertrude ↗More (*Holy Wisdom*, Treatise I. 2, ch. 2).

Today the temper of the times is to proclaim that as Christians we have come of age, we are mature and that therefore so tight a rein is no longer desirable. Education has changed everything. But is not our world in even greater turmoil than before? We are all very bad judges in our own case. Moral problems seem more acutely difficult to solve than previously. The method that is emerging is perhaps more flexible and more suited to our temper than the very authoritarian methods of bygone times. Direction is seen as, first consultation with an exposition of the problem, then a mutual discussion as to the way to proceed, then preferably that the directed one come to see the rightness of a particular course of action, and finally this course is blessed and approved by the one consulted. But the old method has its strong adherents: let the director decide after discussion. This echoes the way of ↗Benedict and his monks. When they had a problem, the whole community would discuss and propose ways of proceeding, but in the end it was for the Father (the abbot) to make the decision.

Among the most distinguished directors of modern times are the Abbé ↗Huvelin and Abbot ↗Marmion, Fr Bede Jarrett, OP, Fr C.C. Martindale, SJ, Fr M. D'arcy, SJ.

Abbot Chapman, OSB, R. Hudleston (ed.), *Spiritual Letters of Dom John Chapman*, OSB, (London, 1935).

St Francis of Sales, E. Stopp (tr.), *Selected Letters*, (London, 1960).

See 'Direction Spirituelle' in *D. Spir.*, Vol. 3.

Discernment of Spirits

An old-fashioned term for sorting out motives in one's spiritual life. Clearly this can be done more surely with the help of another (↗Director sometimes called), and he or she, clerical or lay should have intelligence, instruction, experience and judgement. (↗Teresa of Avila preferred an intelligent man to a holy one.) At no point on the road of the spiritual life is one free of self-deception. 'The last temptation is the greatest treason / to do the right deed for the wrong reason' (T.S. Eliot, *Murder in the Cathedral*). If the object aimed at is good and according to one's way of life, then the motivation is likely to be good too. If the effects are joy and peace, likewise; but if the effects are pride or slackness or despondency, the motive is likely to be bad. In deeper levels of prayer a person may easily be deceived. The safe way is that of humility and obedience even in little things as well as great, and to trust God with loving care.

Discipline

The word is used by the ancient monastic writers for the monastic way of life, (*cf. Rule* of ↗Benedict, chs. 2:62 and 56:6, etc.). Connected as it is with 'disciple' or learner, its root is *discere* (Latin) to learn. A monk is a learner, first from his monk guide, and then from God himself through Scripture, tradition, inspiration. But discipline has come to mean a physical restraint, even harsh treatment of the body. A discipline may even signify a scourge that ascetics use upon themselves to tame the flesh. Modern guides are chary of advising such methods, being now conscious of the strange paradoxical effects of physical pain whether inflicted by oneself or by others. Some form of self-discipline however is very necessary for progress in the life of the spirit, to free us from all our selfishnesses, of mind, affections, tastes, sexuality. Since ↗Francis of Sales, spiritual writers have wisely concentrated on control of the will. In this they are harking back to Benedict, whose asceticism is obedience, poverty and chastity, hard work, the regular life. No one without discipline of mind and body can be open to a spiritual depth which God might want to impart. It would be like expecting fine playing on a slack violin, or clear sight through dirty lenses. Self-control is the first requirement and the ancients called it the ↗Purgative Way, a liberation from the thrall of body, sense, vanity, greed, hatred. The same path has to be trod today. We are still slothful, vain, greedy, irritable, lustful.

Distractions

In prayer, these are almost to be expected, even though they may disclose to ourselves our nakedness, our shortcomings; to be expected because the object of prayer, God, is not tangible, visible, audible, and all our senses are at a loose end, wanting to cling to something. That is the distraction. Our minds, unaccustomed to pondering on God, who is beyond the grasp of the mind, wanders off on thoughts, memories and imaginings that are more immediately attractive. The will, accustomed to being linked with natural desires, emotions, the senses, feels naked, cold. This is part of the slow weaning from this world of sense.

Distraction may come from a habit of sin or imperfection, too strong an attachment, a failure to forgive, from frivolous reading. The remedy is clear if difficult. But distraction may come from a faulty method of prayer. The solution is to change the method in time, perhaps a change from meditation to a prayer mostly of listening. It may be the time of day, the place, posture, or one's health. Each of these has its solution.

The old way to combat distractions was to thrust them firmly but gently aside. This was suitable in a contemplative setting; in the modern bustling world of action less so. ↗Ignatius of Loyola saw this clearly and made popular the methods of ↗meditation that are common today, using the imagination upon scenes in the New Testament. With the passage of time this prayerful meditation has almost ousted the more contemplative forms of prayer, to the detriment and impoverishment of Christian spirituality.

Another approach to distractions is to ignore them, as we ignore the wind while contemplating a landscape from a great height, or as we let a dancing stream hurry by our ankles as we stand mid-stream enthralled by the beauty of the glinting water. The mind is fixed elsewhere. Thus when we use a phrase, the ↗Jesus prayer for example, the imagination,

the memory, all our senses may be 'registering' something – those chores, the shopping list, a journey to the dentist; that meeting in the city, those tax-returns – but the heart is fixed on God and we let all the rest pass us by.

Divine Office
A form of Christian prayer that comes from the earliest stratum of Christian piety. The Christians are not merely a group of individuals but in the words of Paul, 'The body of Christ', and the New People of God, from which it follows that they will want to express this wonderful truth outwardly and indeed publicly. From this follows, by a theological necessity, communal prayer: first the Eucharist, and then as here the Divine Office. Its ingredients are: Psalms and Canticles from the Old Testament and the canticles from the New; pious readings from them; hymns composed by ↗Ambrose and others; readings from the Fathers of the Church; short lives of the saints as their feasts come round in the yearly cycle; finally, concluding prayers. Traditionally there were seven times in the day that the brethren gathered to pray together in church: Matins or Vigils, Lauds, Prime, Terce, Sext, None and Vespers. Compline was added about the time of ↗Benedict. Prime was also a late comer, put in by a wily abbot who suspected his monks went back to bed at that time. The Jews in the time of the early Church in Jerusalem had three times of prayer that the Christians kept up among themselves when they were cast out of the synagogues; Terce, Sext and None. But the basic communal prayer was Lauds in the early morning and Vespers at nightfall. In the Egyptian desert there were according to ↗Cassian only two periods of communal

prayer – morning and night. The monastic prayer was mostly private and not communal. It was the laity who built up these group prayers, they and the clergy in the great cathedral cities, especially the basilican clergy of Rome. The monks gradually adopted pieces from both.

This prayer of the Church is a telling sign of its unity in love, and prepares the way for the supreme celebration of the Eucharist, both the sign and the reality of that love, through the Church and Godwards through Christ. But an external sign is useless unless it comes from within the heart of each individual worshipper. Indeed it is this internal worship alone that has any value before God who is not interested in those who only pray with their lips, no matter how splendidly.

A group, a Church, grounded in spirituality on liturgical prayer, receives inestimable gifts. In the first place it is non-self-centred, but an outgoing form of prayer of praise and adoration. The expression, secondly, is sober and not over-romantic or emotional. The latter wears thin very soon. Thirdly it is a prayer open to the needs of the world. Fourthly it keeps to the front the great truths of revelation: the Holy Trinity, God's love, the Incarnation, Redemption, the Kingdom.

J. Crichton, *Christian Celebration: The Prayer of the Church*, (London, 1976).

C. Cary Elwes, *The Way*, suppl. 40, (Exeter, 1981), pp. 25–7.

C. Jones, E. Yarnold and G. Wainwright (eds.), *The Study of the Liturgy*, (London, 1978).

Dominic, St (*1170–1221*)
Founder of the Order of Preachers.

His birthplace in Spain was Calaruega near S. Domingo de Silos in Old Castille. Priest and then canon in the diocese of Osma, he accompanied his bishop to Languedoc in southern France, in connection with converting the Albigensians. There they met three Cistercian abbots with their splendid retinue. He realized that only reasonableness, learning and the evangelical life of poverty could convert the heretics. He was both very austere and yet a very attractive man, a leader and also an organizer. Many joined him and the Dominican Order came into being. He willed that the Dominicans should maintain the ideal of community life of the old Orders and also the Divine Office in common. But whereas the Benedictines have each house or monastery autonomous, the Dominicans are a true Order with a Master General. The heart of their apostolate is the dissemination of truth, thus they have been closely linked with the rise of universities in Europe and as far afield as Peru and the Philippines.

Unlike the Cistercians and the Jesuits, Dominic was happy to have a female branch to his Order. When dying he confessed that though he had kept his virginity intact, he had preferred conversing with young women rather than with old ones.

He designed the government of his Order in a spirit of freedom, yet with strong leadership, a Master General, Provincials and Priors, but with many checks and balances, so that the wishes of all the friars could be heard, and voted upon. He and his Order were battling by persuasion against the deadly heresy of the revived Manichees who had contempt for the body. Dominic had respect for all that God had made and saw was good. His thought is reflected in the writings of the greatest of his sons, ↗Thomas Aquinas.

Bede Jarret, OP, *Life of Saint Dominic*, (London, 1924).

M. H. Vicaire, *Life and Times of Saint Dominic*, (London, 1964).

Donne, John (*1571/2–1631*)
Poet, controversialist, preacher, Dean of St Paul's. His father died when he was 4; he went to Oxford in 1584, transferred to Cambridge in 1587 and was admitted to Lincoln's Inn in 1602. The following year his younger brother died, in prison for his Catholic faith; the family was strongly recusant, with two of his uncles Jesuits in exile, and closely connected with the family of St Thomas ↗More (m. 1535). John's great-great-grandmother was More's sister Elizabeth and all the generations in between lived in banishment for the 'old faith'. John lapsed more through conduct than from conviction. His *Songs and Sonnets* were the outcome of that early period of love, now sensuous now spiritual. In 1601 he eloped with Ann More and found himself in prison for it and penniless, except for the bounty of rich friends. He was persuaded to write against the Catholic faith, first the *Pseudo Martyr* (1610), at a hint from King James, then a brilliant, scurrilous and regrettable diatribe against the Jesuits, *Ignatius His Conclave* (1611), which at times he must have felt was a double betrayal of his faith and his family. King James had blocked a preferment in the State service; now personally he offered Donne one in the State religion. Donne hesitated three years, but finally accepted and rose to be Dean of St Paul's and a noted preacher. During this time he wrote his *Divine Poems*, among them

the *Holy Sonnets*, also *Devotions* (or meditations) and a number of *Sermons*. In 1617 his beloved wife had died in childbirth of the twelfth child. Donne's thoughts are full of doom, of death, of pre-destination, the wrath of God, though occasionally the cloud lifts. He was torn in two by his own nature, by the times in which he lived. His is the perfect expression of that agonizing loss of direction, similar to the predicament of our own age.

Sir H.J.C. Grierson (ed.), *The Poems of John Donne*, (London, 1939).

E. Hardy, *Donne, A Spirit in Conflict*, (London, 1942).

J. Haywood (ed.), *Complete Poetry and Selected Prose of John Donne*, (London, 1936).

Drugs
A number are being used in order to heighten perception – marijuana (pot, grass) accentuates the sense perception, sensual awareness, sex; the 'sacred mushroom' of Mexico, psilocybin, and mescaline, a synthetic form of peyote, acts likewise. LSD or lysergic acid diethylamide is the most potent of all, producing all the desired effects and at once. Marijuana, Mescalin, LSD and the others have the effect of liberating various levels of consciousness from 'controls' which in ordinary life prevent the various levels of consciousness from being more active. We seem to have a screening process which limits our powers of perception in order to think clearly. The concentration on the senses and not on their making sense, i.e. no rationalization, causes an immense concentration on the object as such, a kind of randomness, a sense of floating, a serenity: no meaning beyond the experience it-

self. When reasoning is subdued, each sense becomes master. There are states also beyond sense, a kind of illumination about the past. Most of these drugs are found to have a permanent damaging effect on the brain.

It is claimed that these states are equivalents of mystical experiences of East and West, which is patently false of the Christian mystics. It is possible that certain physical reactions from a mystical experience might resemble physical reactions produced by drugs. But any reader of, for instance, ↗John of the Cross, will know that the physical reaction is not the experience of God. Nevertheless these experiments have cast some light on the stranger experiences of holy people.

L. Goodman and A. Gilman, *The Pharmacological Basis of Therapeutics*, 4th ed., (New York, 1970).

R. C. Zaehner, *Drugs, Mysticism and Make-Believe*, (London, 1972).

Dryness

A form of spiritual boredom, almost revulsion, resulting from too frequent a repetition; and this is not unnatural since God is unseen. At first, emotions and imagination may spur us along, give fervour to our prayer. But, as Chesterton wrote, five miles of even Michelangelo's statues might pall; so too these 'images' or substitutes for God himself will pall, and we reach a stage of dryness. What should be done? At first perhaps we simply change our method of prayer, from, say, ↗meditation with composition of place to ↗affective prayer, or by using prayers known by heart. If none of these expedients revive the fervour, we should stay quiet in an atmosphere of attentive love, perhaps even wordlessly, except for an occasional phrase, as it were, to keep the prow of the little skiff pointing towards the true harbour of desire.

The period of dryness, which envelops a beginner in a sense of unrest and a strong urge to quit, is crucial for the advancement in prayer or closeness to God. It must be recognized as a weaning process when the tyro learns that those helps that come at the start are only props – emotional experiences of warmth and peace – that must not become substitutes for God, who can only be reached by faith.

cf. 'Nights', in *The Cloud of Unknowing*.

Duns Scotus, John *(circa 1265– 1308)*

The greatest Franciscan philosopher and theologian of the Middle Ages. He was born in Scotland, became a Franciscan *(circa* 1280), probably went to Cambridge University, studied under William of Ware at Oxford and went on from there to Paris. He was ordained in 1291. Between 1297 and 1302–3 he lectured successively at Cambridge, Oxford and Paris, where he became regent in 1305. In 1307 he was moved to Cologne and died the following year. Several of his ideas have profoundly affected Christian spirituality. St Thomas Aquinas held that the primary activity of the human being in heaven is the vision of God, Duns Scotus maintained that it was love for God, since the essence of God is love (1 Jn, 4:16). The Franciscan approach to the spiritual life has been affective rather than intellectual. The centre of Scotus's thought is love. Again St Thomas was cautious about the doctrine of the Immaculate Conception, but Duns Scotus was its champion, on the grounds that God, 'foreseeing' the redemption through Christ's death, made Our Lady free of sin even at her conception. Again he disagreed with St Thomas on whether the Incarnation would have happened even if there had been no original sin. Thomas thought not. Scotus had an immensely subtle mind – why he was dubbed *Doctor Subtilis* – but his works are not easily available, and those that are make difficult reading. The best known is the *Tractatus de Primo Principio*; the other is his *Commentaries on the Book of Sentences* (of Peter Lombard).

D.T.C. IV (1911), 865–1947, by P. Raymond, OFM; *N.C.E.* IV (1967), by C. Balic, OFM. An excellent exposition of his theological thought.

An English translation of *De Primo Principio* and text, E. Roche, OFM, (tr.), (New York and Louvain, 1949).

E. Gilson, *Jean Duns Scotus, Introduction à ses Positions fondamentales* (Études de Philosophie médiévale, XLII, 1952).

See *O.D.C.C.* for further bibliography.

E

Eckhart, Meister, OP (*circa 1260–1327*)
One of the most profound and controversial mystics of all time. He was born at Hochheim in Thuringia and became a Dominican friar, lectured at Paris university, became Provincial of his Order in Saxony and later Vicar General of the whole Order. He returned to Paris 1311–4 where he again lectured; after that

the Archbishop of Cologne set up an enquiry into his orthodoxy (1326). Eckhart went to Avignon where he defended himself before the Pope. The accusations and his responses have recently been discovered. But in 1329, two years after his death, Pope John XXII condemned 28 propositions taken from his Latin works. The point at which his teaching seemed heretical was his apparent conviction that the soul and God are absolutely one with no distinction. If this were his real teaching, his mystical theory would approach very nearly to that of the great Hindu philosopher and mystic Sankara who claimed that the atman and Brahman were one. Pope John and his theologians are perfectly correct in condemning this teaching as unchristian. It does however remain a question whether Eckhart ever really intended to say this. He was a man who delighted in paradox and in antitheses. If one took only one half of what he said it would be easy to find fault with his orthodoxy. Besides, Eckhart had almost a private vocabulary. This is important with regard to his orthodoxy. When he uses the word Godhead, he means God in himself in his unknowable beyondness. On the other hand he uses the word God for God as understood by us. He sees us already in the Godhead before creation, by which he means the 'idea' of us: and in this sense he can speak of us being God, eternal, uncreated. On the other hand, we, meaning us as we are, created, are created in time. He also has a way of writing about our return to God as though it were complete absorption. But once again this is not meant absolutely, as other passages show: 'God has left her (the soul) one little point from which to get back to herself and find herself and know herself as creature.' (*Tractate* 11.)

Only eleven of Eckhart's German sermons have survived, and they are only shorthand accounts taken down as he spoke. Three Latin Tractates have recently been found by the Dominican scholar P. Denifle. As to the corpus of Eckhart's work, the style and the meaning are so abstract as to be unsure on vital matters, except perhaps for the most erudite.

J. Ancelet-Hustache, *Master Eckhart.* Translated into English. (London, 1957).

E. Colledge (tr.), B. McGinn (intro.), *Meister Eckhart: The Essential Sermons, Commentaries, Treatises and Defense,* 2 vols., (London, 1981).

Ecstasy
From the Greek, 'outside oneself'. In a trance the bodily side of a person operates as in a dream. In an ecstasy it does not act at all, the *mind* is very active. Consciousness is absorbed away from what is all around into the vision. There are degrees of this. Rapture is the word used for the most complete form and it usually overcomes a person suddenly. ↗Teresa of Avila underwent many ecstasies, which she records with great fidelity in her works (*Interior Castle, Mansion 5 and 6* and *Life* ch. 20). ↗John of the Cross writes little of them because he says that Teresa has already done so admirably. He suggests that ecstasy is a passing phase resulting from the weakness of the human frame, not able to bear the tremendous wonder of God's revelations. (*cf. Spiritual Canticle* 12, 5–6 and ↗Francis of Sales, *Love of God,* Bk. 7 chs. 4, 5, 7.)

Edith Stein
See ↗Carmelite Spirituality.

Elizabeth of the Holy Trinity, St
See ↗Carmelite Spirituality.

Elizabeth of Hungary, St (*1207– 31*)
Born in the old capital of Slovakia, Bratislava (Pressburg) and died at Marburg in Germany. At 14 she was made to marry, for political reasons, the Landgrave of Thuringia, Ludwig IV. It proved a love match but short-lived, as he died at Oranto in 1227. On hearing the news she went screaming through the castle in an agony of grief. Recovered, she gave herself up to an extremely ascetical life under the brutal and imprudent guidance of Master Conrad of Marburg. He allowed her to dispose of the care of her children, imposed excessive mortifications, administered the discipline, but did not restrain her in her charitable works. She, however, though frightened of him, sprang up, as she said, strong and unharmed like grass (sedge) after rain. When Ludwig's brother Henry wished to expel her from his domain, she abandoned all her wealth and gave herself over entirely to serving the poor, making clothes for them, even fishing to provide them with food. She was only 24 when she died, wife and widow, a lay woman in love with the poor to the extent of giving her life to them.

H. Thurston and D. Attwater, *Butler's Lives of the Saints,* (London, 1956), Vol. 4, pp. 386.

Emotions
Part of the human make-up. Some, the Stoics and certain Buddhists, would deny man his emotions, for peace sake. 'The strong silent British Sahib' of Imperial days was their distant heir. The Christians, recognizing that the emotions are

disorderly, as is all man's make-up, lacking integrity, would 'order' them. ↗Augustine in the *City of God* wrestled with the Stoics on this, and pointed out that both Christ and ↗Paul manifested much emotion: Jesus wept over Jerusalem, and for Lazarus; he was angry with the sellers in the Temple, had compassion for the crowds, affection for children (*cf. City of God* Bk. 9.4.5. and Bk. 14.9). Both Stoics and Buddhists admit compassion. It is the motive of the emotions that make them good or bad. Well-ordered, they are an enrichment to the personality.

People vary in degrees of emotion: some are very emotional, some scarcely at all. The latter find it hard to be compassionate; the former hard to reason coolly. Maturity is partly control – not elimination – of emotions. A strange phenomenon is that we enjoy emotions, even sadness; so that we do not want to be drawn out of such a condition, e.g. anger and pleasure, exaggerated laughter. These are unreasonable and unworthy of man. Emotions cannot always be 'turned off', like a tap – or turned on – but distraction is the practical way to break, for instance a melancholy mood.

Those who have a neurosis may have to 'live' with their problem. The heightened experiences, sense of frustration, if overcome, can be a source of help to others. Abandonment to the Divine Will should be in normal circumstances the best medicine for all emotional disturbances; though even that will not always enable one to shake off one's moods. But these are not necessarily faults. More frequently they are a sickness, like any other.

Emotional tensions are often an expression of a mental disturbance, which lies below the surface of consciousness. This is not necessarily a sickness; yet it can be most unfortunate for the sufferer. Here the priest and the doctor need to co-operate. What seems a moral failure is in fact nothing of the sort, but rather the subconscious forcing a reaction that cannot be resisted, or scarcely, at the conscious level. For some, shock treatment alleviates; for others, pills; for yet others, depth psychology. All psychoanalysis however needs heroic co-operation from the patient. The analyst can bring him to self-revelation, but cannot necessarily bring the cure, or acceptance. So, in some cases there remains the patient acceptance of a cross not of one's making and certainly not a moral failing; a cross that is, though unknowingly, a great grace, sharing in Christ's dereliction.

Enlightenment

The quest of all Buddhists, since the Buddha – the Enlightened One – gave to the world his message, after his experience under the Bhote tree, as to how this should be done (see ↗Buddhist Terms: The Fourfold Noble Truths, the Eightfold Noble Path; and ↗Nirvana). Early European travellers thought that Nirvana or enlightenment was pure negation; and this was the European view up to this century, when it was recognized that this interpretation of Buddhist texts was a misunderstanding and that the negation was only of the superficial self, and of the world of *maya*. Yet, what the positive content of this enlightenment was, remained a mystery, because the Buddha refused to say.

In general, enlightenment in Buddhist teaching is considered to be something one may acquire by one's own powers. This would appear to put Buddhist enlightenment in a different order of experience from that of the Christian mystics. The way of negation in both cases may be similar but the objectives do not appear to be the same.

In this supra-rational experience the possibility of confusion is manifold. East and West may be describing exactly the same experience but, because of their philosophical predispositions, describing it, one as union of two, the other as complete unity. Or East and West may be describing different experiences and both sides trying ecumenically to see them as the same. The possible relationships with God are infinite from his side and the likelihood that two experiences are the same is extremely remote. From a Christian point of view, it is certain that there is and remains a real distinction between the creature and the Creator, even though the union is immeasurably great, so great that 'enlightenment' may seem to be fusion.

See ↗Eckhart.

Erasmus, Desiderius (Didier)
(1469[?]–1536)

Born at Rotterdam in the Low Countries; his father was probably a priest, and all his life Erasmus felt the stigma. His life spanned the passing of the Middle Ages and the dawn of the Reformation. His upbringing was immersed in the spirit of ↗Groote and his disciples of the ↗Devotio Moderna, with their return to the pure Gospel, their revulsion from the meaningless intricacies of the later Scholastics, their austere life. He attended a school run by the Brothers of the Common Life at Bois-le-Duc, (1484–7) after which he joined the Canons of St Augustine at Steyn, a group closely linked with the community of Windesheim, itself, too, linked with Groote. But

there at Steyn, he and two other brothers became bewitched by the New Learning, reading all the Latin classics they could lay their hands on and works of the Fathers of the Church. What leanings Erasmus may have had for the religious life soon evaporated. Once ordained to the priesthood (1492) he got permission to visit Rome, Mecca of humanists, among whom he was later to be the acknowledged leader. Back in Paris (1495) he went to the College of Montaigu, once again an establishment dominated by the spirit of Groote. But its austere life was too much for Erasmus. He accepted an invitation to visit England (1499) where he met Thomas ↗More and Dean Colet, both distinguished humanists, but also earnest Christians. Colet determined the direction of Erasmus' future towards editing a Greek New Testament and some of the great Fathers of the Church. These two aims were now central to Erasmus' life. But he also had one other task to fulfil, to ridicule all those elements of medieval spirituality which he considered wrong or superstitious. A number of devastating attacks followed, not by any means all negative in character; but which helped to change the whole spiritual climate of opinion of Western Europe. This was 'the egg' that he laid and that – as he wrote – Luther hatched out in misshapen form. The first broadside was the book *The Enchiridion or Handbook of the Christian Warrior* (1504), with a popular edition in the following year. There followed *In Praise of Folly* (1509), which contained a biting attack on monasticism, and the *Colloquies* (1518). The editions of the Fathers included his favourite, St Jerome (9 vols), Ambrose, Augustine and Origen, whom he was editing at the time of his death at Basle. Thus he stands at the source of modern biblical scholarship and also at the source of modern patristic interest, with the French Benedictine scholars of the 18th century and with Newman of the Oxford Movement. But it is his new approach to Christian living that helped powerfully to change the climate of Christian devotion. Away with superstitions, miraculous statues, with interminable pilgrimages, with concentration on outward performance of religious duties; instead, a return to internal devotion and the simple life of the early Christians. He favours throwing off all those human rules and regulations that had hidden the practice of the pure Gospel. Away with all the hairsplittings of the theologians, all that latter-day Scholastic verbiage which entangled the heart in mere words. It was heady stuff; and, when Luther followed, even Erasmus himself regretted some of his too free criticisms. He now defended virginity, frequent oral Confession, devotion to Mary and the Mass. Pope Paul III had offered him a Cardinal's hat. Popes Paul IV and Sixtus V wanted all his works condemned. He died a Catholic at Basle with these words on his lips: 'O Jesus, mercy! Lord, have mercy on me! O Mother of God, remember me! *Lieve* God!'

R.H. Bainton, *Erasmus of Christendom*, (London, 1970).

L. Bouyer, F.X. Murphy (tr.), *Erasmus and the Humanist Experiment*, (London, 1957).

J.D. Dolan, *The Essential Erasmus*, (London, 1964).

J.D. Dolan (tr. and ed.), *Erasmus, Handbook of the Militant Christian*, (Notre Dame, Ind., 1962).

See also, 'Erasme' in D. *Spir*.

Eschatology

From the Greek *eschata*, the Last Things, and *logos*, the study of them. In the New Testament there is much about the Kingdom of God, of Christ, the Coming of the Son of Man, the Parousia, the fulfilment, the Last Judgement, the great signs of the End, of the Day of the Lord. But the peculiarity of this element in the teaching of Christ is the question: *when* is all this to happen? This question has exercised the exegetes much for a century, though today some measure of consensus has been achieved, and from the spiritual point of view new insights. This entry will be confined to the latter.

Some of the references in the Gospels undoubtedly refer to something that is imminent, in fact already present. John the Baptist said: 'the Kingdom of God is at hand' (Mt 1:2), and Jesus, when asked when all this was to happen, replied: 'the Kingdom of God is among you' (Lk 17:21), that is, it has already happened, and almost certainly he seems to be implying that the Kingdom was himself. Other texts lead to the same conclusion: that he himself was the Kingdom (the reign of God). And yet often, also, the texts are saying that the Kingdom or reign, the Day of the Lord, is at the end of time, when all will have passed away. Not that Jesus ever said whether this would happen soon or late. More than once he said that not even the Son of Man himself knew when it was to come about.

We have then two apparently irreconcilable pronouncements: the Kingdom is *now*, and the Kingdom is at some indeterminate time in the *future*. But Jesus himself has pointed towards how to reconcile them. Perhaps the simplest way of showing this is to take the parable of the mustard seed – told as a description of the Kingdom. The mustard seed (the Kingdom) is the smallest of seeds when planted; but as it *grows* and reaches fulfilment (*parousia*) it is greater than all the trees and the birds of the air can make their home in it. So the Kingdom is *now* among us as a seed, almost unseen, growing. It is the People of God, but in the process of growing. It will have reached its fulfilment at the end of time.

This process of growth is known to us at at many levels of being. It is present in the life of Jesus himself from the Incarnation to the Resurrection, all of which is the beginning of the Last Things, the end of the ancient world of paganism. It is also in process of coming in each human being: accepting or refusing the gift of God's coming and his death, and so moving inexorably towards the Day of Judgement. It is visible in the Church as such, the Body of Christ, which must share in his death in order to share in his Resurrection and the final Glory of his second Coming. It is visible too in a mysterious way in the whole cosmos, as St Paul describes in the first chapter of both the epistles to the Ephesians and to the Colossians. When, therefore, we say, as Jesus told us, in the Our Father, 'thy Kingdom come', we mean *now* in our own hearts, *now* in the Church and in the whole universe, but also progressively through history to the Day of the Lord, when all shall be judged and receive either doom or divine destiny in heaven, and all things be made new.

A word on the imagery of a world cataclysm, falling stars and final Judgement of the Last Things. This can mostly be found in Daniel (7). This is not scientific truth but truth of divine things beyond the capacity of our pigmy words to describe, and only expressible at all in poetic – metaphorical – language. The magnitude of the transformation from the old creation to the new *in* Christ Jesus is so vast and deep that it has to be expressed in symbols. Likewise the Judgement dramatizations express vividly the tremendous awesome confrontation of God's infinite justice and mercy with each human being and every single thing that we have done or failed to do, whether good or ill.

A vast number of books and articles have appeared. A very clear summary has been made by J. McKenzie in his *Dictionary of the Bible*, (London 1965). See also the footnotes to the key words as they are noted in the Index to the *Jerusalem Bible*.

Espousals
The first stage of the state of union with God that is called by some – ↗Ruysbroeck and ↗John of the Cross – a mystical marriage. At this first stage of Espousals or Betrothal, the soul has truly given itself *all* to God; indeed God has already stripped it of all delight in created things which could interfere with the total giving, and the total union which is to come. Now all is done for love, whether sweet or bitter. Every part of the person, sensual or intellectual, is handed over to God. Such a one is lost for God, doing all for him and nothing for self.

But such a condition is a pure gift from God, and is only given after a profound and painful purgation, a purgatory on earth, for it leads to that complete union in which God shows himself.

cf. E. Allison Peers (revised edition), John of the Cross, *The Spiritual Canticle*, Vol. 2, Stanzas 18 and 19, pp. 103–12.

Eucharist
Greek *eukaristia* meaning praise and

thanksgiving. Hebrew, Aramaic and Syriac had no word for thanksgiving, using for it words such as bless or love. This word is the oldest word for the Christian rite, derived from that of the Last Supper. It has always been central to the Church's understanding of Christ's mission and to Christian spirituality. Contained within it are the basic truths of the Incarnation and Redemption, the redeeming act of Christ and the Messianic promise. It is the heart of the Christian prayer-pattern of union with Christ, of praying with him and through him to the Father. It has been the source of marvellous artistic inspiration in architecture (the cathedrals of all times), in music (Palestrina and Vitoria, Byrd, the *Lauda Sion* and *Ave Verum*), and the other arts.

The emphasis placed by Christians on the Eucharist has varied through the centuries. At first, communion was very frequent, then for centuries very rare. Today it is almost daily for many. Now the sacrificial element has been stressed, at other times the meal element, or the Real Presence. The last gave rise to elaborate tabernacles and reredoses, to great eucharistic processions, to the devotion of the forty hours (*quarantore*). The less the Reformers seemed to recognize the Real Presence, the more the Catholics accentuated it, until the more basic nature of the Eucharist became obscured.

In both East and West the Eucharist is a celebration of the memorial (Greek *anamnesis*) of Christ's Passion, Death and Resurrection, by the Church under the leadership – presidency – of the local bishop. It derives from Christ's action at the Last Supper at which he inaugurated a rite when he said 'do this in memory of me' (Lk 22:19; 1 Cor 11:24). The primitive Church obeyed his command (*cf.* Acts 2:42,46) in the 'breaking of the bread'. ↗Paul gives us the earliest account of an early Christian Eucharist (1 Cor 11:23 ff). The Epistle to the Hebrews considers Christ the High Priest and Calvary the unique sacrifice. The Eucharist can only be sacrifice in sign, as Christ does not shed his blood again. But truly there is Christ offered by the Church. In Revelation Christ is seen as the eternal victim – note the repeated use of the title 'Lamb' for Christ in heaven. ↗Ignatius of Antioch centres his pastoral apostolate on the communal Eucharist. The earliest account outside the New Testament is in St Justin's first *Apology*. The most comprehensive early account is in Hippolytus' *Apostolic Tradition*, where the basic structure as we still know it is already present.

The Eucharist must not be separated from the Last Supper if one hopes to penetrate its meaning. The Paschal Supper was the Mosaic rite of thanksgiving for all the wonders (*Mirabilia*) of God's mercy to his Chosen People: the delivery from the slavery of Egypt, the giving of the Covenant on Mount Sinai, the leading to the Promised Land. Christ transformed this ancient rite into a prayer of praise, a sacrifice of thanksgiving for liberation from sin through his death, the giving of the new law of love written on the heart, and the promise of the heavenly kingdom – the Messianic meal (*cf.* Jer 31:31). That the Last Supper was the Passover meal is shown by many indications (especially Lk 22:15: 'I have longed to share this Paschal meal with you.') The shedding of Christ's blood on the Cross is foreshadowed, prefigured by the separate consecrations of bread as body and wine as blood, and by the words used.

Beyond this symbolism is the further reality, expressed in the statement, 'Take and eat . . . take and drink', which points to the intimate union between Christ and his followers, and also to the means for effecting it. 'Now not I live but Christ lives in me' is ⟋Paul's way of putting it. Thus the doctrine of union with Christ is already there in the synoptic accounts of the Last Supper, though not spelt out.

The Eucharist or Mass has a clearly defined shape. It begins with a greeting and a hymn; both are designed to draw the congregation together, because the Mass is a community event, together with Christ himself. Suitably there follows a penitential rite acknowledging one's unworthiness to be present and asking forgiveness. Then follows the Liturgy of the Word, as it culminates in the readings from Scripture. This is completed by a homily that should apply the Scriptures read to the lives of the congregation, and by the prayer of the faithful that should link what they have learnt about their Christianity to *action*. The offertory section is preparatory to the Eucharist proper, the sacrificial meal. The latter essentially, is a long prayer of praise and thanksgiving to God culminating in the account of the Supper followed by the offering of Christ and his Church to the Father, which reaches its climax in the great Doxology 'through Christ, with him, and in him . . .'. After that comes the Communion, the return gift of the Father, namely his own Son, to us his children, followed by a concluding prayer.

COMMUNION In the communion the faithful receive the body and blood of Christ. When Christ used the words 'body' and 'blood' at the Last Supper they had a richer meaning in the Jewish language than

they have in English, as the Jewish idea of the *body* was the *whole man*. So it would be fair to believe that he meant his humanity, his human nature. Likewise blood has a richer meaning, namely the very life of a person since 'blood' stood for, and was seen as *the source* of life. Therefore on receiving Christ, the Christians share his humanity and his life, and through his humanity they share in his God-life. This is filled out in the letter to the Colossians: 'In his body lives the fulness of divinity, and in him you too find your own fulfilment.' (2:9). But communion also exists between all the members of the Church both living and dead. It is a time for heightened awareness of union with Christ and, in his life, of union also with the suffering Church and with those in heaven.

EUCHARIST AND SACRIFICE The Orthodox and Catholic theologies recognize a sacrificial element in the Eucharist. But the Christian idea of sacrifice should not be enclosed within the confines of Old Testament concepts. Calvary was no ritual, it was starkly real. ⟋Augustine points out (*City of God*, Bk. 10:5–6) that in the idea of sacrifice, of the two elements, *external expression* and *internal intent*, the latter is the more important, quoting the Psalm: 'My sacrifice is a humble and contrite heart' (Ps 51:17). The Epistle to the Hebrews quotes another Psalm: 'I came to do your will, O Lord' (Heb 10:7). This submission of will to the Father was Christ's inward sacrifice, expressed throughout his life in his actions and culminating in the acceptance of death (*cf.* Jn 10:11 ff). This is how the faithful can share in his sacrifice, in that they, part of the Body of Christ, conform their minds and hearts, their wills to his in offering him and themselves to the Father. In so far as the Mass shares in all the sacrificial elements of Calvary, it also shares in its expiatory and intercessory power.

N. Lash, *His Presence in the Word. A study of Eucharistic worship and theology*, (London, 1968).

J. Martimort (ed.), *The Church at Prayer*, Vol. 1 (London, 1968); Vol. 2 (Shannon, 1973).

E. Masure, *The Christian Sacrifice*, (London, 1943).

J.M. Powers, sj, *Eucharistic Theology*, (London and New York, 1968).

S.J. de la Taille, sj, *The Mystery of the Faith*, Bk. I (London, 1941); Bk. II (London, 1951).

Evagrius of Pontus (*346–99*)
No doubt he was born in Pontus and died in the Nitrian desert of Egypt. This is an abstruse subject but for those interested in the history of Christian prayer of considerable importance. For centuries he was little more than a name and his works had mostly vanished. Though he began life in the north central province of Asia Minor (Pontus) he moved to Constantinople to join his friend ↗Gregory Nazianzus. From there he moved to Palestine, ending his days in the desert of Scete among the ascetics of whom he became the intellectual leader. It is told in the *Lausiac History* that he went to India. In ancient times 'India' could designate any place from Ethiopia to India proper. But in his case, in view of the close affinity of his thought with Buddhist ideas, it is quite possible that he really did visit it. For it was thought that his theories approached far more closely to the passionless state of Buddhism than they do to the loving mysticism of Christianity. His influence, it has been maintained, was among those that nearly diverted Christian asceticism and mysticism into oriental modes of thought. For him, it was thought, prayer is a mental or intellectual exercise of concentration and denudation, reaching a point of total abnegation after which one can expect that enlightenment will follow. So runs the traditional opinion on Evagrius, but on insufficient documentation.

He was also a follower of ↗Origen and was engulfed in the condemnation of the latter which resulted from the onslaught against Origen by ↗Jerome. Origenism was condemned in 553 (The fifth Council of Constantinople). Almost none of his writings has been translated into English. Passages may be found in the ↗*Philocalia*, translated into French and English. These come from his *Centuries*, a collection of groups of a hundred sentences. The vision of God 'is in a mirror; the mirror of a pure heart. It is an experimental knowledge of the Holy Trinity, but it requires a perfect nudity of the intellect, a state above forms' (*Centuries* 7:2). 'When the *nous* (intellect) has been stripped of the old man and put on the man of grace, then he will see his own proper state at the time of prayer like sapphire and the colour of the sky' (7:25; cf. also *Prakticos* 1:70). Evagrius identifies 'the seeing of his own state' and seeing 'the place of God', for he says it is 'in oneself that one sees the place of God' (*Prakticos* 1:71). 'The place of God. It is thus that is called he who is in prayer, clothed in the light without form' (*Centuries* 7:21). 'Hasten', he writes, 'to transform your image into the likeness of the archtype' (*Gnosticos* 151).

Until the work of I. Hausherr, sj and others, some felt that the condemnations of his doctrine were harsh, others that his mysticism was pure negation and lacked love. Since the discovery of his *Kephalaia Gnostica* (Syriac version found 1952) and the correct attribution to him, and not to St Nilus of Sinai, of *Chapters on Prayer* the former shows that his cosmology was rightly condemned (e.g. pre-existence of souls and that Christ was like angels, men and demons an 'intellect' but sinless); but that on the other hand the latter work shows him as the teacher of ↗Cassian and his *custodia cordis*. Evagrius says '↗Agape is the progeny of ↗apatheia. Love is the child of unattachment. Apatheia is the very flower of ascesis', i.e. love is the flower of peace of heart, and peace of heart is the flower of self control (*cf*. ch. 81). ↗Augustine rightly condemned the apathy of Stoicism (*cf. City of God* Bk. 9:4,5 and Bk. 14:9). Had Evagrius used the phrase 'control of the passions' instead of 'impossibility' it would have been orthodox.

Evagrius's works include: *Praktikos, Gnostikos, Kephalaia Gnostica, Chapters on Prayer, Sentences for Monks, Antirrheticos, Exhortations to a Virgin, Hypotyposis, Treatise to the Monk Eulogius, On Evil Thoughts, Letters, Biblical Commentaries:* for his life see Palladius' *Lausiac History*.

J.E. Bamberger (Intro. and notes and tr.), *Evagrius Ponticus, the Praktikos. Chapters on Prayer*, (Spencer, Mass., 1970). A useful bibliography and with comment on Evagrius's doctrines.

I. Hausherr, SJ, *Les Leçons d'un Contemplatif. Le Traité de l'Oraison d'Evagre le Pontique*, (Paris, 1960). Excellent.

See also 'Eckhart', by A. and C. Guillaumont, in *D. Spir*.

Examination of Conscience

The Confessions of ↗Augustine are in one sense a prolonged examination of conscience. This aspect of ascetical practice has never been absent from Christian living. But it was ↗Ignatius of Loyola who first organized it in his famous *Spiritual Exercises*. He begins with it, and demands of the retreatant an examination of conscience for a quarter of an hour twice a day. If this were mere introspection it would be harmful. Rather it is a facing-up to the reality of our behaviour in the presence of God and his Law. The Buddha in his Eightfold Path is aiming at approximately the same immediate end: true self-knowledge for the sake of amendment, which will lead to enlightenment. The Greeks taught the same: man know thyself. In the Christian context, at least, self-knowledge leads to a recognition of one's inadequacy, of failure, as well as of successes. The failures are attributed to self and ultimately the success to God. Man needs God's help to raise him from his weaknesses. Man may – as Buddhists rightly stress – pull himself up by his own shoe strings. Some have the will. Others have not. But in the Christian context we are not only speaking of the natural order but of the order of Grace. If we lose God's Grace, only he can restore it. Thus examination of conscience for a Christian includes also contrition and prayer for the restoration of God's love and grace.

Superficiality is the curse of the examination of conscience. We note irritation, melancholy, sexual indulgence, cruelty. These may be only symptoms of a deeper ailment, of vanity, lack of faith, selfishness, jealousy. The question to be asked is: Why do we behave like that?

Self-examination of a negative kind is inadequate. It would be better also to ask: Have we loved those we are with? This is matter for the second commandment. Also we could ask ourselves, have we loved God, as Christ showed, by obeying his will? These two questions sum up our whole obligation, since these two commands cover the whole Law and the Prophets.

F

Faculties of the Soul

In prayer it is impossible to separate or exclude any part of the immensely complex structural make-up of the human psyche. Even the body plays its part by its sluggishness or alertness. Posture – a bodily function, as the East reminds us – can help concentration. Excessive asceticism or laxity likewise could either cause weariness or distaste. The mind must be master and the body disciplined. The five senses play their part. The liturgy is a stylized recognition of the value of the senses: sacred ↗music, colour, statues, ↗icons, the liturgy of the word. The sensual and sexual parts of man too enter into prayer, even in the highest, sometimes as an unwelcome guest. The imagination, crossroads of the human consciousness, has to be tamed, or it will conquer. All thought is echoed in the imagination. The emotions are there to support the will, but are unpredictable and cannot be turned on at will. Love, sorrow, humility, repentance, etc., are not emotions but movements of the will. We in the West tend to consider only reasoning as valuable; in prayer it may be at times the only kind of thought that is nearly valueless. It is the will adhering to God that counts in Christian prayer. The rest is ancillary, not useless but not primary, at best means not ends.

Faith

A gift of God by which we are able to accept the revealed truth of the Christian religion. It is therefore concerned with knowing; but, as what is known by faith in God and his message is beyond proving up to the hilt, it is also an act of the will. We say: we will believe. The centre of our belief, our faith, is God himself, who will not let us down. He is all Truth, all Love. We have faith and trust in him. What irrigation is to parched soil, or petrol to an engine, faith is to religion. It provides the motive force, the life. As religion is concerned with the unseen, even though there are tangible indications of its truths, its certainty is not self-evident. Faith, in the first instance, is trust in God, such as is found in the case of Abraham (Gen 12 ff). His act was a mixture of belief and hope, of recognition that God is and that he is trustworthy. Such is the usual meaning of faith in Scripture. The apostles trusted Jesus and gave their lives to him, as the Saviour and the Word of God. Faith can also be said to be a way of knowing. All knowledge depends on some sure grounds, either immediate perception or a process of reasoning, whether logical (syllogistic) or instinctive. Faith is not immediate perception, but an acceptance of truths dependent on the veracity of God, of truths that unaided we could not have reached.

All historical certainties, to a scientific mind, sound somewhat faulty; but they are as sure, in their own way, as scientific truth, and of a far deeper quality. We cannot deny that America was discovered in the 15th century, but the evidence is complex and intangible. The evidence for God speaking through Christ is of that kind. Our desires, our stances, our past behaviour, all could cloud our power of perception and our willingness to accept a truth that might be unpalatable to our present way of life.

All succeeding generations receive this message of God through Christ by means of the Church. Some have a personal awareness which reassures them of the truth of the faith. All, if faithful, are conscious that Christ is alive among his people. But often faith is like night-flying, it is obscure and even difficult. Times come in the life of every Christian when the strong flame may be reduced to a faint flicker. This may be from wilful sinning, pride, sensuality or sloth. Only one remedy for that – a renewal of the spiritual life. A Christian may find his faith almost meaningless, especially if he is deeply engaged in worldly – even if innocent – activities. Traditional teaching is: let that Christian not abandon his Christian practice, but be specially loyal to prayer and the sacraments; read about the faith, and be reassured. The Cloud or the Night, it is said, is bound to descend on every zealous Christian at some time or another.

Reason works upon the object of faith to evolve further truths; but in so far as these conclusions are conclusions of reason alone they are not '*de fide*', of faith; in fact they suffer from the same malady as all human reasonings, they may be faulty. It is immensely important not to be deceived into imagining oneself to be bound by faith to all these reasoned conclusions. Being human they are fallible. Christ, however, did guarantee certainty to his Church, and so certain pronouncements of the teaching Church are a sure interpretation of Revelation, comparable to the certainty that God spoke through the Prophets; yet the Church claims only to interpret accurately something already revealed.

Fasting

In the Old Testament this exercise is not part of asceticism, self-discipline, rather it is a physical expression of sorrow for sin, a prayer in act: the outward expression of a desire to escape from God's just punishment, and so a freeing of the soul from the association with the sin which was calling out for that punishment. It seems to be a human attempt to show what we deserve, as, in our misery, we face the all-holiness of God.

A simple expression of all this occurs in the story of Jonah and the wicked city of Nineveh. When Jonah finally got round to giving it God's message, 'the people of Nineveh believed in God; they proclaimed a fast and put on sackcloth' (Jon 3:5). The Prophets said that fasting which had become a routine with no inward significance had no spiritual value, (*cf.* Zech 7:5–6). What God wants is kindness and compassion – that is true fasting.

Jesus is not particularly concerned with fasting. His disciples cannot be expected to fast when they have Him, the Bridegroom, with them, the very one who saves them from their sins. Only when he has gone will they mourn. Note that he moves to the inward meaning: the longing for forgiveness (Mk 2:18–22).

The Fathers of the Desert, led by St Antony, went to extremes in fasting, possibly egged on by Manichean monks in the vicinity – and the motives were mixed: sign of repentance, ascetical practice, competitive spiritual athleticism. Perhaps some of the strange disturbances from demons could be explained by an empty stomach. We are too far off to judge.

The modern Church is nearer the Biblical understanding of fasting, as an outward expression of mourning for sin, and in believing that the latter is the more important. But we lose something by ignoring physical fasting altogether.

See 'Fasting' in John L. McKenzie, *Dictionary of the Bible*, (London, 1965).

Fear
An emotional and physical reaction to danger or the unknown which seems dangerous. It is almost the natural condition of man in view of his littleness and weakness and the immensity of all around, with its indifference if not its hostility to him. We are all afraid of being proved inadequate, failures. In the depth of our being we know we are so – we are afraid and we are right. At the very centre of our being is an in-adequacy, a dependence, a limited-ness, which in isolation is not able to live up to the demands made upon us. Then, too, we are out of complete harmony with our selves, like so many cracked bells ringing an uncertain note. Fear is the natural result. But an answer exists. If we recognize our dependence on God, the creator and the redeemer, fear is overcome. Those without faith often suffer from a mad-making fear; they lack the humility; which is truth about ourselves. Those with faith are at peace. Fear is the distortion of humility. The latter brings peace. The knowledge that God loves us casts out fear (*cf.* 1 Jn 4:18).

Christians have fear of not 'living up to' the demands of Christ. But this is precisely what he was trying to free them from, since no longer were they to be saved by 'keeping the law' but by the utter mercy of God their loving Father. Indeed this 'despair' of Christians could be put to good account, if it forces them to appeal like the monks in the Desert: 'God come to my aid, O Lord make haste to help me', in the words of the Psalmist (Ps 39 40:13).

C.G. Jung, *Psychology and Religion: West and East* (London, 1977). Has many useful insights.

Feast
The meaning of a feast is almost lost in modern Western society. The cocktail party has taken its place. The feast in many cultures has a deep symbolic significance and is usually linked with religion, since food is the means of life and its sign; and as food is recognized as a gift from God it stands for life itself. Most sacrifices therefore will be found to be connected with sharing a meal with God himself. Probably the most primitive sacrifice in the world, that of the Pygmies of the Congo (as described by Fr Trilles) is sharing a honeycomb with God and with the cuckoo who found it in the dense forest of their homeland.

A feast is a celebration of union, not only with God, but with men. Jethro, the future father-in-law of Moses, invites the stranger to share a meal with the family (Ex 2:20). A feast is a memorial. Even today it celebrates the memorial of births and marriages. But in ancient times, especially among the Jews, the Passover meal, for example, celebrated the whole chain of events of the liberation of the Jewish people from the thralldom of Egypt and the receiving of the covenant and gift of the Promised Land.

In the Christian dispensation this very Paschal meal is taken over to commemorate a deeper liberation –

from sin – and a New Covenant, that of love, written in men's hearts, and the promise of the kingdom, begun already on earth, and consummated after death in heaven.

The word feast is also used of anniversary celebrations of saints' days, especially their 'nativity', the day they died and were 'born' into heaven. Thus the feast day of ↗Ignatius of Loyola is the day he died, 1 August, and of Soeur Thérèse, 2 October. There are also feast days of the events in Christ's life: his Nativity (Christmas), his Resurrection (Easter). Thirdly there are feasts connected with doctrine: e.g. Corpus Christi, connected with the doctrine of the Holy Eucharist; Trinity Sunday (every Sunday is a feast commemorating Christ's Resurrection).

In so far as every event in the life of Christ was a divine event as well as a human one, it has an eternal dimension and is outside time, has an ever-presentness. So, when we celebrate an event in Christ's life we are in a way made present to it and can share in it. That is a traditional way of understanding the celebration of the feasts connected with the life of Christ.

Fénelon

François de Salignac de la Mothe was born at Fénelon in 1651 and died as Bishop of Cambrai in 1715, the year of Louis XIV's death. Ordained priest in 1675, he was appointed tutor to Louis XIV's grandson the Duc de Bourgogne. For him he wrote the political novel *Télémaque*. The following year (1688) he became acquainted with ↗Mme Guyon, an exceedingly pious widow who undoubtedly had great insight into prayer. But she had had no theological training. She was accused of being ↗Quietist. Fénelon de-

fended her. But in 1696 he signed the Thirty-four articles of Issy which condemned Quietism. However a year later he published a book, *L'Explication des maximes des saints sur la vie intérieure*. These considerations roused the ire of ↗Bossuet. A fierce controversy ensued in which it seemed that the very teaching of ↗Francis of Sales himself was being attacked under the disguise of an attack on Fénelon. In the end the Holy See very reluctantly condemned 23 propositions from the book and Fénelon submitted. He never had any doubt of the authority of the Holy See. Fénelon's standing as a great spiritual writer continues to rise.

Acton, *Lectures on Modern History*, (London, 1906), pp. 5–6.

M. de la Bédoyère, *The Archbishop and The Lady*, (London, 1956).

See 'Fénelon' and 'Madame Guyon' in *D. Spir.*

Ferrar, Nicholas (*1592–1637*)

Scholar and devout Christian. He was born in London, his father a prosperous London merchant and his mother a very fervent Anglican. As a child he read the Bible and Foxe's *Book of Martyrs*. At 14 we find him at Clare Hall, Cambridge; in 1610 he gained his B.A. and was elected a Fellow of his college. His interest was medicine, perhaps fortunately as he himself was dogged by ill-health, so seriously that in 1612 he was advised to travel. He visited Holland, Germany, stayed in Venice and Rome, walked through Spain between 1616 and 1618 when he returned to England, but not to Cambridge. His father had died and he found himself responsible for the latter's commercial interests, in particular those connected with the

Virginia Company. Its patent was withdrawn (1623). Elected to Parliament in 1624, he withdrew foreseeing the inevitable Civil War. He had been offered a Readership; proposals were made that he should marry an eligible heiress. He decided to remain single and retire to the country. In 1624 his mother bought Little Gidding in Huntingdonshire: one shepherd's hut, a ruinous manor house and a church being used as a barn. Here he, his mother, his brother, wife and family and children, his brother-in-law John Collet with his wife and fourteen or more children plus servants, in all thirty souls came to live there, all of one mind: to cultivate a devout life, putting prayer first. This was a unique experiment, not a monastery, but an 'extended' family living in common, a serious Christian life in retirement. The daily timetable was as follows: they rose at 4 a.m. and Matins were said in church at 6 a.m. Evensong was also said in church, the remainder of the canonical hours were said in the house. At night watch was kept by two in the first half, two in the second. They would recite the whole psalter on their knees. The little community was linked with the neighbourhood: a school for the children, a dispensary, an infirmary were organized. The rest of the waking hours were divided between study, book-binding and pious discussion. Both Charles I and Archbishop Laud approved of the experiment. In 1637 Nicholas died and then the Civil War overtook the community. A violent book against the enterprise was published: *The Arminian Nunnery* (1646). In the same year the settlement was sacked, everything stolen or destroyed or burnt. The little group dispersed. Together with the poems of George Herbert, Nicholas's friend, and the noble death of Archbishop Laud, Little Gidding stood and stands for a high Anglican religious ideal, dignified, austere, intelligent, peaceful.

A.L. Maycock, *Nicholas Ferrar of Little Gidding*, (London, 1938).

J.R.H. Moorman, *A History of the Church in England*, (London, 1953).

See 'Nicholas Ferrar' in *D.N.B.*

Flight from the World

Fuga mundi was supposed to be the motive for a monk withdrawing into the desert or to his monastery. This may have been the case for some, but the prime motive was not flight from but flight to someone, God. Nor is this selfish as is sometimes in-sinuated, since the monk believes that all should seek first God and then all other things will be added. By his action he is beckoning the men in the world to follow him, each in his own manner, to put God first.

In any case the word 'world' is ambiguous. In Christian literature it has acquired several meanings, even in the Old Testament and the New Testament: (i) It can mean the whole universe, the cosmos, the universe. We can scarcely escape from that. Besides, God in creating it said it was *good*. (Gen 1). The only true evil is in men's hearts. Nor can we flee our own hearts, as the Desert Fathers were the first to realize; (ii) In ↗John's Gospel, often, the 'world' stands for those who oppose Christ, and are wicked. Since Vatican II the emphasis has been rather to go into that world, to convert it, and not to flee it entirely. Such an approach needs courage and caution, courage to grapple with the evil, and caution so as not to be contaminated. Those who withdraw are witnesses of the ultimate aim of all mankind and they are also those who pray for the success of the apostolic effort of others.

Foucauld, Charles de (1858–1916)

French aristocrat, rake, explorer in Morocco, hermit. He was born in Strasbourg and was orphaned at the age of 6, inheriting considerable wealth. He entered St Cyr, joined the cavalry, lived an openly dissolute life and in the process lost his faith. Sent to Morocco to calm down, he made a remarkable exploratory journey through that country disguised as a Jewish itinerant trader. The result was *Reconnaissance au Maroc*; and on its publication, he became famous overnight (1888). Meanwhile he was slowly recovering his childhood faith. The Abbé ↗Huvelin became his Confessor. First Charles became a Trappist in France, then was sent to Akbés in Syria, a daughter house; then, withdrawing from the Trappists, he moved to Nazareth where he lived as a hermit and odd-job man for the Franciscan Sisters. He lived for a time in Jerusalem, where he was persuaded to accept the priesthood. But his heart was set on Africa. After ordination in France (1901) he settled at Beni Abbès deep in the Sahara, but moved further south to Tamanrasset in the Touareg country in 1905. It was there he was murdered by an anti-French native group in 1916.

That, however, was the new beginning, as both his life and his writings (more than 2,000 letters extant and a number of meditations) have been the source of a great movement within the Church, comparable in spirit with the Franciscan one in the 13th century. His life, once converted, was an ever-deeper penetration into the poverty and meekness of Jesus: the little hut at Nazareth, the hermitage at Tamanrasset, the utter poverty; his

example of silence and contemplation for many hours a day; that burning desire to be *one* with the poorest of the poor wherever they might be found, have all been the inspiration of his followers – the Little Brothers of Jesus, and the Little Sisters – from Alaska to Onitcha to Nairobi to Sydney. His own personal austerity was too great for any to follow, but René Voillaume, his disciple, has given his ideals a setting practical enough to draw very many in the footstep of Jesus the poor man.

Charles de Foucauld, Oeuvres Spirituelles, Anthologie, (Paris, 1958).

R. Bazin, *Charles de Foucauld, Hermit and Explorer*, (London, 1923).

M. Trouncer, *Charles de Foucauld*, (London, 1974).

R. Voillaume, *Seeds of the Desert, The Legacy of Charles de Foucauld*, (London, 1955).

Francis of Assisi, St (1181/2–1226)

Born in Assisi and died at the Portiuncula. He was the son of a successful cloth merchant, but, led by dreams and visions, saw the danger to society and the Church of idolizing riches. It is instructive that he did not at first grasp the meaning of the 'messages'. When told to rebuild God's church, Francis took this literally to mean the crumbling church of San Damiano. Gradually he realized he was destined to restore the Church of God by dedicating himself to his Lady Poverty, that is the Church, especially the Church of the poor.

His life was prayer: he praised God in all his creation (see the *Canticle to the Sun*), sun, moon, stars, wind, fire, water and even sister Death. Having given all, he received all back: a multitude of disciples, Sister

Clare and 'Brother' Jacobo too; all the birds and fishes, even Brother Wolf. Never was there a mere man who reflected so perfectly the human-divine character of his Master, even to bearing his five wounds. His form of prayer was simple. On Mount Verna Brother Leo recalls that he spent the night saying 'My God and my All'. He was subject to ecstasy. During one such experience he received the stigmata – the first man in the history of the Church to do so, unless ↗Paul's sting of the flesh (2 Cor 4:10 ff) was so also.

He was torn – as his Order has been ever since – between the desire to preach Jesus to the world (he even went to Egypt to preach to Saladin) and to flee the world to find his Lord in the solitude of a cave on Mount Verna. In fact he did both, thus fulfilling the judgement of ↗Thomas Aquinas that the perfect life was to give to others what one had received in contemplation.

His prayer was centred on Christ, as revealed in the Gospels: his humanity, from the crib to the Cross. In this Francis is the successor of ↗Bernard. He thus impressed his style of devotion on the Western Church, which became increasingly Christ-centred as the centuries accumulated: the crib, the Rosary, the House of Loretto, the Sacred Heart, the relics of the Passion, the sacred wounds.

G.K. Chesterton, *Saint Francis of Assisi*, (London, 1923).

Fr Cuthbert, OSFC, *Saint Francis of Assisi*, (London, 1912).

Francis of Osuna (*circa 1492–1540/1*) Spanish Franciscan writer and mystic. A student of Alcalá University, he was ordained priest 1519–20. As a Friar Minor he was sent to a retreat house at Osuna near Seville in 1523. There he wrote six 'Alphabets' on the spiritual life. The *Third Alphabet* (1527) was to influence St Teresa profoundly by describing the prayer of *recogimiento* (recollection). She writes in her *Autobiography* that after nine months of practice she entered the prayer of quiet and even once of union (*La Vida*, ch. 4, 6). But his writings have their own intrinsic value also.

Francis of Osuna, M.E. Giles (Intro. and tr.), *The Third Alphabet*, Classics of Western Spirituality, (London and New York, 1981).

Francis of Sales, St (*1567–1622*) Bishop of Geneva and doctor of the Church. He was born at Annecy in Haute Savoie and died in Lyons. He never lived in his cathedral city though he visited it several times to persuade Beza the Calvinist leader to return to the Catholic Church. He had great apostolic zeal, was a writer of spiritual books which have had wide influence even beyond the Catholic Church, the most famous of which, *An Introduction to the Devout Life*, was translated from the French almost immediately into most European languages. It is a work of genius, expressing for the educated laity of his time the Christian ideal which others had described for religious. Holiness, according to Francis, is for every man and woman. They are lay people, and therefore their ways of following Christ would not be like a Carthusian's or a Benedictine's way, but as a soldier or wife or merchant. He was aware of the dangers to Christian morals in the frivolous, flirtatious life led by young people of his time, but he was not censorious. A girl should, he thought, try to look attractive but beware of sentimental attachments. He analysed the movements of the heart like a Jane Austen with a Christian edge. Friendship he approved of among religious, but not one whose *centre* was the emotions. The second masterpiece, *On the Love of God*, was specifically written for his friend ↗Jeanne de Chantal, describing for her the stages of the higher reaches of contemplative prayer, in a style both florid and limpidly clear. At first one finds the icing on the cake here and in his letters too sweet, but the substance is strong. His treatment of the prayer of Quiet led ↗Fénelon into statements that might be confused with ↗Quietism, though Francis himself was never accused of this; he is a doctor of the Church. His teaching on prayer keeps to the middle of the road; that on mortification is partially new, as he is against extraordinary physical mortifications, and considers that the slings and arrows of ordinary misfortunes provide ample occasion for asceticism. But for those who wish more, he teaches the *acceptance of everything* from the hand of God, an ↗abandonment to the Divine Will. From this germ, good in itself, there grew by exaggeration: total indifference, leading to Quietism. But the true descendant of Francis is Soeur ↗Thérèse of the Infant Jesus with her little way which echoes his.

The two main sources for Francis's teaching on prayer are *An Introduction to a Devout Life* and *On the Love of God*. In the *Introduction* he follows ↗Ignatius, but simplifying the methods. He even goes so far as to say that for some the best method is to have none. In *On the Love of God* he reaches deeper into the more profound stages of prayer. His guide is love. In this treatise he follows closely the degrees as laid down by ↗Teresa of Avila, even to the names. But once again he simplifies,

seeing conformity to the Divine Will and holy indifference to all else as the summit of all.

Francis was one of the pioneers in encouraging frequent Communion and Confession; he followed Ignatius in encouraging people to have a spiritual ↗director. The attractiveness of Francis's personality comes through in the extensive collection of his *letters* and also in the memoir by his friend Bishop Camus, a manageable abridgement of which was published in New York in 1952, entitled *The Spirit of St Francis of Sales*.

Oeuvres Complètes, 26 vols., (Annecy 1892–1932).

M. de la Bédoyère, *Francis of Sales*, (London, 1960).

Mgr Trochu, *S. François de Sales* (2 vols., Paris, 1946).

Bremond, Vols. 2, 7.

Freedom

Freedom, or liberty, of spirit is a fundamentally Christian attitude. ↗Paul, in Romans, hopes that human nature will 'share in the glorious liberty of the sons of God' (Rom 8:21). He writes (2 Cor 3:18): 'Where the spirit of the Lord is, there is liberty.' In Galatians he sees the very call to be a Christian as a signal for liberation: 'Freedom claimed you when you were called' (5:1). Christ himself put his finger on the cause: 'The truth will make you free' (Jn 8:32). The Christian message, then, is essentially linked with the gift of freedom, both a freedom from the slavery of sin or of the Old Law, and also freedom to live the life of a son of God. Christ began his ministry in Nazareth by reading the prophetic passage concerning the messianic time being one of freedom (Is 61:1–2).

The Christian is free because he realizes he is no longer bound by an impossible aim beyond his capacity, and now knows he is saved by the infinite mercy of God. It is apparently one of the most difficult teachings of Christ to accept. We are always inclined to think and act as though it is we who save ourselves. The heresy of Pelagius (4th–5th centuries) is an expression of that. An excess in the opposite direction would be despair, knowing self-help to be not enough and not expecting God to supply all that is needed. Another error is to suppose that as God's mercy saves, therefore we need do nothing. It all depends on God but not without our co-operation, which itself depends on God's enabling grace.

B. Häring, *Free and Faithful to Christ*, Vols. I and II, (Slough, 1978, 1979).

Friendship

A mutual relationship of love between two of either sex, the sexual element playing a minimum part if at all. Friendship can be either selfish, even obsessive or selfless and free. The former is not made to last. True friendship is a mutual delight and love for the other for his or her sake, and for the sake of a common purpose or interest. It is a mutual sharing of each other's riches and each other's pains. Jesus showed the origin of friendship in his mutual relationship of knowing with his Father. We can be friends with God because he has raised us up to his Life by his grace. Spiritual writers have in the past warned heavily against human friendship as an obstacle to God (*cf. The Imitation of ↗Christ*, 2:7). ↗Teresa of Avila wrote against particular friendships, as did ↗Claude de la Colombière and others. Yet the greatest among the saints have had great friendships: Teresa herself with ↗John of the Cross, ↗Francis of Sales with ↗Jeanne de Chantal. Francis however puts at the summit of human friendship – and his own for her – a regard for God alone in the other. Yet ↗Aelred (12th century) in his treatise on *Friendship* – and he was a Cistercian – says that if God is love then by implication, he must be friendship too. As all true love goes out to the other, so we should also go out in love or friendship to others. True deep friendship, he says, is likely to be with few. ↗Bernard in his commentary on the ↗*Songs of Songs* laments the death of his brother monk in an almost excessive display of love. Should we then perhaps say that God made man for friendship with himself, and that human friendship is an image, an encouragement to this supreme friendship? It is not an absolute, it passes; but that very passing is its purification.

It is the emotional and sensual element in friendship against which spiritual writers are really warning us. Yet here again human nature includes those elements and in themselves they are not bad but good. It is when they take the centre of the stage, and the friend is only a friend in order that one may experience these emotions, that such a friendship is entirely selfish and unworthy of man or woman.

We have to learn how we can control all the various levels of our psyche: its genital, sexual, sensual, emotional and affectionate elements, so that they serve the true love we have. True love is derived from God, who is Love. True love in its exercise, in a Christian setting, is activated by God himself, and it also tends towards God as its ultimate aim, since no human love can fully satisfy the human heart.

For a summary traditional teaching, and references, *cf.* Tanqueray, *The Spiritual Life*, (Westminster, Md., 1948), pp. 595–606.

St Aelred, H. Talbot (tr.), *Christian Friendship*, (London, 1942).

G

Garrigou-Lagrange, Reginald,
OP (*1877–1964*)

He early became a Dominican, taught at the Saulchoir near Paris, then from 1909 till 1960 taught theology according to ↗Thomas at the Angelicum, the Dominican university in Rome, and for many years was consultor to the Holy Office. Most of his writings were commentaries on various parts of the *Summa Theologica* of Thomas Aquinas but he was also a director of souls and wrote important books on the spiritual life, *L'amour de Dieu et la Croix de Jésus* (Juvisy, 1929), *L'éternelle vie et la profondeur de l'âme* (Paris, 1950), *Christian Perfection and Contemplation*, (London, 1937), *The Three Ages of the Interior Life*, 2 vols., (London, 1947, 1948).

He was at the centre of an important discussion: whether holiness is for all? He held that it was. His view prevailed and is expressed in the *Constitution on the Church* (of Vatican II, ch. 5). This controversy included the question of whether contemplative prayer was open to all. Again he took the side of those who affirmed that it was, since all baptized Christians have the supernatural life with the gifts of the Holy Spirit, and it is these that become active in prayer when a Christian tries seriously to live according to the Sermon on the Mount. It remains to be examined how in our time these deeper forms of prayer are expressed and experienced by lay people in their busy but holy lives.

C. Butler, OSB, *Western Mysticism*, (London, 1927).

A. Poulain, SJ, *Graces of Interior Prayer*, (London, 1930). For the discussion on the nature of Contemplative Prayer.

A. Sandreau, *The Life of Union with God*, (London, 1927).

See also, for the life and works of Garrigou-Lagrange, D. Spir.

Gerson, John (*1363–1429*)

Priest, Chancellor of the University of Paris, theologian, pastor of souls (*doctor christianissimus*). He came from a very poor home and the little ones of this earth remained his special care. Five of his sisters vowed themselves to God, but in the world. Many of his writings, 'spiritual exercises', were for such. He was in touch with the Brothers of the Common life and the Beguines, having spent some time in Bruges (1397–1401) as Dean of St Donatian. Though in his youth a brilliant student, he never allowed his learning to smother him in the sterile disputes of the schools. Though friendly to the mystic Ruysbroeck, he was on his guard against the possible danger of pantheism. Later, when Ruysbroeck explained, Gerson modified his opinion. During the final stages of the Great Schism – with its three Popes – he was deeply involved, but always as a peacemaker. Most loyal to the Papacy, yet he saw the importance of the General Council (in this instance of Constance) and of the theologians. He has been seen as a Gallican before his time – with considerable truth.

Today, perhaps, we also are more aware of the rich complexity of the service of authority within the Church. He went further afield with his ecumenical approach, this time to the Eastern Church, trying to separate out the essential from the non-essential in the dispute: for example, did it matter what kind of bread should be used in the Eucharist?

His last ten years were spent at Lyons in peaceful obscurity. St Francis of Sales in his time felt a spiritual kinship with John Gerson – praise enough.

The Mountain of Contemplation, (1397). No English translation.

J.L. Connolly, *John Gerson, Reformer and Mystic*, (Louvain, 1928).

See 'Gerson' and bibliography in *D. Spir.*

See also *O.D.C.C.*

Gertrude the Great, St (*1256–circa 1302*)
Born at Helfta in Saxony and died there. She was a German Benedictine (or Cistercian) nun, a mystic, not in the speculative tradition, but Christ-centred, love-motivated, intimately structured on the liturgy. Her mystical and communal prayer were completely integrated. Through devotion to the humanity of Christ she was raised to union with the Holy Trinity; also she saw the Sacred Heart of Jesus – centuries before ↗Margaret Mary Alacoque – as the centre of his love for men. But the 'heart' for her was the heart in the biblical sense. The liturgy with its Scriptural readings, its poetry and theology provided her with a solid base for her private prayer.

Her writings (which are in Latin, edited by the monks of Solesmes, 1875) have been translated into French and published by Editions du Cerf (Paris) in their series *Sources Chrétiennes*, nos. 127, 139 and 143, namely *Les Exercices*, (1 vol.) and *Le Héraut*, (2 vols.).

See 'St Gertrude' and bibliographies in *N.C.E.* and *D. Spir.*

Gifts of the Spirit, Old Testament
In Isaiah occurs a list – famous in theology – of those Gifts of the Spirit which were to be granted to the future Messiah (Is 11:1f). In the theology of the 13th century much thought was given to these; ↗Thomas Aquinas devoted a special section of the *Summa* to them and he relates them to the various virtues (see *S.Th.*, Ia, IIae, qq. 68–70). St ↗Bonaventure also has much to say on the subject, scattered through his works. Modern theological scholarship considers that perhaps too much importance has been given to this seven-fold *division* of the Gifts, though theologians would not of course deny that in themselves these gifts are among the most fundamental; yet they point to the considerable list of other Gifts of the Spirit mentioned especially in the New Testament (see Charisms). Aquinas, however, as always, has penetrating things to say, including the description of gifts as: that in our soul which makes us responsive to the prompting of the Holy Spirit. The virtues lead us to act according to our rational and supernatural nature, the gifts lead us to act rather with docility in accordance with the purpose and *prompting* of God himself. That is why the gifts seem to give a spontaneity to our actions, while the slower moving virtues require forethought. The gifts mentioned in Isaiah are: wisdom, understanding, counsel, fortitude, knowledge and godliness (the last

one, godliness or piety does not occur in the Hebrew Bible, only in the Septuagint and the Vulgate). Tradition has associated the various intellectual Gifts with various ways of knowing and according to what the object of our knowing is – God in himself, God in his ways with men and so on. These Gifts have been incorporated into two famous hymns: the Eucharistic Sequence for Pentecost, *Veni Sancte Spiritus*, and the Vesper hymn *Veni Creator*.

Thomas Aquinas, *Summa Theologica*, Vol. 24 (Ia, IIae, 68–70).

A. Gardeil, OP, *Les Dons*, in *D.T.C.*

A. Gardeil, OP, *The Holy Spirit in the Christian Life*, (London, 1953).

D. Hughes, OP, (tr. and ed.), *John of St Thomas, The Gifts of the Holy Spirit*, (London, 1951).

R. Hudleston, OSB, (ed.), *The Spiritual Letters of John Chapman*, OSB, (London, 1935).

E. O'Connor, OSC, (ed.), *The Gifts of the Spirit*, (London, 1974).

Gita
The Bhagavad-Gita, a unique work (*circa* 200 BC–200 AD) that forms only an infinitesimal part of an immense epic of much greater age, has been for centuries the spiritual guide for millions of Hindus. For Ghandi it was his most precious possession. A Westerner may find it difficult to assess, but even if by Western standards it seems to hold contradictions, it remains a little masterpiece. The story runs as follows: a civil war is in progress, and a battle imminent. A young prince, Arjuna, speaks to his charioteer – who turns out to be the 'incarnation' of the God Krishna – to question whether to fight is justified, especially as he may kill his own and dearest friends. Krishna replies that death is of no moment, as this world is in any case unreal. Each must do his duty according to his nature and condition. The discussion moves to whether activity has any spiritual value. The answer comes that some are led one way, some another. He, Arjuna, is led by the way of devotion (↗ *bhakti*) or love. Here is perhaps the bridge point between Christianity and the Eastern religions, namely love. Krishna tells Arjuna that beyond Brahman is someone who loves, and he must love that someone in return. But this stage can only be reached by entire detachment, disinterestedness, desirelessness, self-mastery, total freedom; then, united to Brahman, he will reach beyond, to love. Krishna at the poem's end says, 'Give your whole heart, love and adore me'. This is the secret of secrets.

cf. C. Isherwood, Swami Prabhavananda (tr.), *Bhagavad-Gita*, (New York, 1944).

R.C. Zaehner, *Concordant Discord*, (London, 1970).

R.C. Zaehner (tr. and notes), *Bhagavad-Gita*, (London, 1976).

Gnosticism
A conglomeration of sects claiming secret knowledge (Greek *gnosis*) of God, of creation and man's destiny. It seems to have been in existence about the time of Christ (protognosticism) and become linked with Jewish thought soon after, then in the 2nd century it began to penetrate Christianity in Asia Minor, Egypt and elsewhere. Perhaps St Paul is tilting at Gnostics in his epistles (Ph 2:9; Eph 1:10) on the subject of genealogies and 'powers'. St John may be reacting against them in his emphasis on Christ's real humanity

and equality with the Father. But we are on sure ground with St Irenaeus (*circa* 130–*circa* 200, Bishop of Lyons but originating from Smyrna in Asia Minor) who wrote a great book on them, *Against Heresies*. His information has been startlingly confirmed by a recent find in Egypt at Nag-Hammadi (1945–6). These sects had a way of using the genuine Gospels dressing them up in Gnostic theology, *The Gospel of Thomas* for example. But here we are only concerned with the impact of all this on the spirituality of the early Church. This can be put under a number of headings:

(i) They claimed that God did not create but a Demiurge of his did. Sometimes this is said to be Jesus. Thus here is a denial of the true divinity of Christ.

(ii) They generally claimed that the universe is made of good (spirits) and bad material (beings).

(iii) God could not have made the bad, therefore either the Demiurge who made them was a kind of rival to God, or else he was a fallen angel. This is simply a form of the Dualism of the ancient East. So the Old Testament, rightly seen, would be not about the Christian God but about a Demiurge and his activities. The Church reacted strongly and reasserted the divine origin of creation and of the accounts in the Old Testament.

(iv) Since the material universe including man is evil of its nature, so they claimed, Christ could not really have become incarnate nor could he conceivably have died on the Cross. At most he could only have 'seemed' to do so. The church reacted strongly to assert that man's saving is not merely 'knowing' (*gnosis*) but by the action of Jesus who is Saviour.

(v) As for all this secret information supposedly derived from Jesus, the Church reacted by saying that Jesus set up his Church upon the twelve apostles, and, if there had been secret information, it would have been told them by Jesus and to their successors (tradition). Therefore, to know the truth, we must appeal to the apostolic churches, especially to Rome.

For Irenaeus the Eucharist was a proof that Christ truly became man, for, as he writes, the Eucharist really being the body and blood of Christ, the faithful by receiving them have the promise of the resurrection, sharing through them in the life-giving humanity of Christ.

Among the Gnostic sects or churches were the Valentinians, the Mandeans, the Montanists, the Marcionites, the Manicheans.

M.R. Grant, *Gnosticism, An Anthology*, (London, 1961).

E. Pagels, *The Gnostic Gospels*, (London, 1979).

St Irenaeus, *Adversus Haereses*, several translations.

See 'Gnostics', in *N.C.E.* and *O.D.C.C.*

God

As the object of prayer, God is someone who knows and loves us; and prayer as normally understood is the raising of the mind and heart to him. One does not raise up one's heart to an abstraction. In this sense ↗Pascal's insight is true: not the God of the philosophers but the God of Abraham, Isaac and Jacob, Jesus Christ (*Pensées*, no. 737). Yet the God discerned by reason and the God revealed in the Old and New Testaments are not contradictory but complementary; the one is rational and no more, the other is revealed to us at a deeper level. ↗Thomas Aquinas still used, in his *Summa*

Theologica, reason almost alone to establish the fundamental nature of God in so far as that is possible to a creaturely mind: that he is Being, One, Infinite.

Aquinas himself admits that God is the unknowable, and while the Pseudo-↗Denis has given us the most telling expression of that, Nicolas of Cusa sees God as Truth, which is the reconciler of opposites. But, as Pascal sensed, all this is cold and – for most – not conducive to devotion. In the Bible on the other hand are innumerable insights or profound sayings on God, often expressed simply as titles of the Divine: Lord of Peace, Justice, Love, Compassion. He is the *Deus absconditus*, the hidden God. He is infinite, the Creator, Judge, Saviour; Shepherd, our Rock, our Fortress, Shield and King. Finally he is our Father.

God himself, as the object of our prayer, is none of these descriptions. He is behind and beyond them, inscrutable. In prayer we do not concentrate on words, propositions, definitions, even though they direct our hearts to God; we penetrate by faith and love, in darkness, into the mystery – *mysterium tremendum* – of God. Yet it is a relationship of me to you, an I-Thou relationship, as Buber insisted.

For Jewish, Christian and Muslim worshippers God is a person, Some One; not a person in our limited sense, but one who knows and loves, in a way that is beyond knowing and loving. As Scripture tries to express it: God is Knowledge: 'In the beginning was Wisdom (*logos*)' (Jn 1:1); God is love: '*Deus caritas est*' (1 Jn 4:16). He is someone with whom we can communicate; not an object, a dead stone, nor merely a faceless absolute.

The mysticism of the eastern religions has, generally speaking, two characteristics which distinguish it from Christian mysticism: (i) It often asserts that there is no real distinction between the subject of the meditation and its object. In fact its aim is to make one become aware by meditation that 'I am that', that Atman and Brahman are one; (ii) This leaves little room for the other element of Christian prayer, namely love, except the compassion for all creatures so well demonstrated by the Buddha.

As pointed out earlier (↗Gita), this de-emphasis on love or devotion (*bhakti*) is not universal in Eastern mysticism. Likewise, in Christian mysticism there can be found a tradition that emphasizes the 'awareness' element and the closeness of the creature to the Creator, to such an extent as almost to blur the distinction (*cf.* ↗Eckhart).

See also ↗God the Father, ↗God the Son, ↗God the Spirit.

God the Father

Not the most common title of God in the Old Testament though the idea of the Fatherhood of God does occur half a dozen times, signifying God the provider, the compassionate and the loving God: e.g., Ps 68:5, 'Father of the fatherless'; Ps 103:13, 'as a father pities his children'; Prov 3:12, 'God corrects as a father'. In Isaiah the One who is to come, is to be called 'everlasting Father' (Is 9:6). In Jeremiah (31:9) God is Father to Israel. In Malachy (2:10) 'Have we all not one Father?' In the Old Testament it is never used as a title of prayer.

But this idea of the Fatherhood of God receives its full flowering in the New Testament and on the lips of Jesus. Prof Joachim Jeremias in *The Prayers of Jesus* explains how this address, 'Abba', was peculiar to Jesus as an address *to* God in prayer. It had been the child-name for 'father' as 'papa' might be with modern children. But it had become a grown-up term by Jesus's time too. Thus its English equivalent might be 'dear father'. Jesus told his disciples to pray to God as their father. No one else should be so called. Clearly he meant that there was an intimate relationship, which makes it one of the most precious revelations that Jesus made about God.

It is clear from the teaching of ↗John's Gospel and the writings of ↗Paul that this title is not a mere metaphor, rather it is an analogy. By baptism we die and rise with Christ, sharing his new life. Now Christ lives in us, now not we live but he lives in us. We are therefore sons of God by adoption and by 'grafting'. Christ is the vine stock, we the branches. We are co-heirs with Christ. He is God's son, we share his life, through the Eucharist. Unless we eat his flesh and drink his blood we shall not have life – his life in us. By 'flesh and blood' is meant Christ's humanity, his life. By 'eat' is meant, 'become one with', *cf.* Rom 6:3,4; Gal 2:20; 1 Jn 3:1–2; Jn 15:5; Rom 8:17; Jn 6:54 ff. For 'Our Father' *cf.* Mt 6:9 ff and Lk 11:1 ff.

J. Jeremias, *The Prayers of Jesus*, (London and New York, 1977).

God the Son, Jesus Christ

According to Christian teaching, God manifests himself (his glory, power, beauty) on earth not only through nature, through pre-Jewish prophetic figures, through the Law, the Prophets and in the very history of the Jewish people. He also manifested himself, and in a supreme manner, in his Son, Jesus Christ (Heb 1:1–3; *cf.* Jn 14:9: 'He who sees

me sees the Father'). During the first five centuries of the Christian era, especially at the Council of Chalcedon (451), the Church hammered out as clear a description of this mystery as it could; delimiting positions beyond which it was not orthodox to stray. Jesus, they said, is wholly man, but also wholly God; like us in all things except sin (Heb 4:15); the Son of the Father, co-equal with the Father, of one substance with Him (*cf.* Jn 1:1 ff). In the beginning was the *logos* (creative Word, Wisdom) and the Word was with God, and the Word was God (*cf.* Col 1:15–20). The climax comes with, 'and the Word was made flesh' (i.e. human) (Jn 1:14). This is all central matter for prayer for Christians: the wonder of God's own Tri-une life, his condescension: 'God so loved the world as to send his only Son' (Jn 3:16).

The saving act of Christ has been variously expressed in East and West. Eastern Orthodoxy likes to express it as God, in Christ, sharing our nature, so as to raise our nature in Christ into the God-nature, the God-life, which is the Spirit. For the Western Church the act of Redemption, through Christ's crucifixion and Resurrection, is seen as the sign of God's saving love for us, and as the effective means of our saving on the one hand and as the supreme sign of the New Adam's (Christ's) love for his Father in heaven on the other, thus restoring peace between God and man. This most loving self-giving of Jesus coaxes us to love in return. The two approaches, of East and West, are not contrary but complementary to one another. Irenaeus, in the West, but an Easterner, could represent both traditions.

The Western insight has at times deteriorated into a somewhat legalistic approach, in which Christ *satisfies* for our sins by his suffering, by accepting the punishment due to sin. ↗Thomas Aquinas, however, points out that Christ satisfied (did enough) by *doing enough loving*, to make up for all our lack of love, and so provoking us to love in return (*cf.* S. *Th.*, III, q.46, a. 2).

Devotion to Jesus has taken many forms through the centuries. The early Christians prayed to him as the Good Shepherd (*cf.* mosaics), as the victorious King (*cf.* St Polycarp) who conquered death, as the Beloved Child of the Father (*cf.* early poems, and ↗Origen). In medieval times, under the influence of ↗Bernard and ↗Francis of Assisi, greater emphasis was put upon Christ's human nature, as described in the Gospels – the historical Jesus; a useful counterweight to the great previous emphasis on Christ's divinity, necessary of course to counter the Arian heresy. The Middle Ages stress Christ's human love, his sufferings on the Cross in devotions such as the Way of the Cross, the agonized crucifix, the manger, crib, house of Loreto. By the 17th century this form of Christian piety had concentrated on Jesus's love for men, symbolized by his Sacred Heart (St Margaret Mary, M. Olier). Today in the wake of a deepening of Christology and also of the insights of ↗Teilhard de Chardin and Durwell, we are very aware of the Risen Christ, making all (even the whole cosmos), one in himself. All of these insights are rich sources of prayer and meditation.

God the Spirit

Pneuma (Greek) and *ruah* (Hebrew) both mean: wind, breath, breath of life, life, God's life. In the Old Testament the spirit of God, which hovered over the water at creation (Gen 1:2) is not seen, even at the most profound (Wis 7:1 ff), as in any way a person distinct from God. But in the light of the New Testament the Old Testament Spirit is seen as God, active in creation, inspirer of judges, kings, and prophets (*cf.* Num 11:17,26; 1 Sam 10:10; Ez 3:14).

In the New Testament the Spirit comes into his own: he is at the New Creation, when the Archangel tells Mary she is to conceive Jesus – 'The Holy Spirit will come upon you . . .' that is how the New Creation is explained (Lk 1:35). Christ himself, the perfect Man, is led into the desert by the Spirit, who has descended upon him at his Baptism (Mk 1:10,12). At the Baptism all three persons interact – the Father who speaks, the Spirit who appears, the Son being baptized.

Throughout his life Jesus follows the same pattern. At its end he promises to send his Spirit upon the Church, to make it strong (to *comfort* it) to guide it into all truth (*cf.* Jn 14 and 16). The greatest of the Gifts is the Spirit himself: he *dwells* in *us* (Rom 8:9). In Acts the promise is fulfilled at Pentecost, and at several other spectacular givings of the Spirit himself. Acts could well be called, the Acts of the Spirit, and the modern Christian would do well for his own spiritual life to see how the early Christians were led by the Spirit (Acts *passim*). ↗Paul in various epistles enlarges on the place of the Spirit in our lives: (Rom 8:26), the Spirit and our prayer; (Rom 12:6), gifts for the good of the Church; (1 Cor 12:14), different kinds of gifts, and their chief – Charity (*cf.* also Eph 4:4; Gal 5:22 ff).

In some of the earliest documents of the Church, for example in the *Didache* and the *Shepherd of Hermas*, the working of the gifts of the Spirit, especially prophecy, can be seen. But, by the time of Tertullian (*circa* 160–*circa* 225), the Montanists had used prophecy to distort doctrine and to refuse obedience. The Eastern Church developed, especially among the ascetics and monks, a whole spirituality of the Spirit. In the West ⁊Irenaeus, ⁊Augustine, ⁊Hilary kept the richness of the doctrine of the Spirit alive. But in the Middle Ages Joachim of Flora caused alarm with his teaching of the three ages, the third – his time – being that of the Spirit. Again at the Reformation the Anabaptists and others emphasized the Spirit, in reaction perhaps at the over-legalized condition of the Roman Church. Likewise mystics in Spain were suspected of indulging in private revelations – *illuminati* (see ⁊Illuminism). Almost alone Augustine ⁊Baker openly encourages his penitents as they grow in discernment, to follow the guidance of the Spirit.

The 18th century, the Age of Reason, also saw the resurgence of Spirit-guided Christians, the most notable being John ⁊Wesley and his friends. Today, once again, devotion to the Spirit has revived, and this time in the bosom of the Episcopalian and Catholic Churches; as proved by the ⁊Pentecostal, or ⁊Charismatic Movement, better called the Movement of the Spirit.

The second Vatican Council also emphasized the place of the Spirit in the life of the Church (see specially *Constitution on the Church*, ch. 12). A renewal of devotion to ⁊Baptism and ⁊Confirmation also brings out the place of the Spirit. The liturgical revival has disclosed to us the importance of the Spirit in the ⁊Eucharist, by highlighting the two aspects of the epiclesis, namely the prayer asking the Spirit to effect the change of the bread and wine into the Body and Blood of Christ, and also the prayer to effect the unity of Christians in Christ. The anointing of the sick is seen to be the coming of the Spirit to strengthen them on their journey.

It is impossible to describe in short the richness of the relationship between the Church and the Spirit and Christians and the Spirit. The supreme gift is love (1 Cor. 12:31 ff) and God being love, this seems to identify the Spirit with love. In tradition especially as exemplified by Augustine and ⁊Thomas Aquinas, the way to express the mystery of the Holy Trinity, and the place of the Spirit in it, is to show that in some way the Spirit is the love of God for himself, the love of the Father for the Son and of the Son for the Father. This spreads into the love of God for his Church, the Bride of Christ. But the Church is made up of individual Christians, and these too are filled with the Spirit, indeed they become, according to the words of the New Testament, conjoined in spirit with the Spirit (*cf.* Rom 8:16). While we retain our own persons we are in a mysterious way made one in the very life of God (*cf.* Gal 5:25), living by the Spirit to such an extent that ⁊Paul can say that it is the Spirit who prays in us, who 'cries out in our hearts' (Gal 4:6).

This love that comes from the Spirit unites all the members of the Church together, and makes each member of the Church conjoined with all the others. It is a union of love which transcends our understanding (*cf.* 1 Cor 13).

Good Works

The New Testament leaves no doubt of their necessity, especially the Gospel of St Matthew (25:31 ff), where the Son of Man will separate us as a shepherd separates sheep from goats. Not only is helping the helpless doing so to Christ, but failure in this merits eternal damnation. Dives, the rich man, refused to help Lazarus, the beggar. He too finds himself in hell (Lk 16:19 ff). Only the Samaritan is commended by Jesus in the story of the man caught by robbers on the way from Jerusalem to Jericho (Lk 10:30 ff). Jesus said that the second commandment was like the first: love your neighbour as yourself.

Motives for Good Works are not all of them worthy, some are from self-interest, unconnected with true love: self-aggrandisement, vanity, political promotion, occupational therapy. Christ requires us to do them out of love. Nor are cool, dispassionate, ineffectual *feelings* of compassion enough.

From the earliest time, Christians have visited slaves and prisoners, conscripts and the sick. These great works of mercy go on to our own day, starting with the world-wide Society of St Vincent de Paul and culminating in recent years with the work of Mother Teresa and her disciples. The laity very often are taking the lead in all this fulfilment of Christ's command, especially in the 'basic christian communities'.

The spiritual works of mercy still hold: prayer, penance, preaching the gospel, consoling, admonishing and the like. Yet it was often enough through the corporal works of mercy that the greatest of the saints found their vocation – ↗Francis of Assisi embracing the leper, ↗Ignatius of Loyola and his companions working in the hospitals of Venice, ↗Catherine of Genoa and her husband managing a hospital in their native town.

Grace

This word stands at the centre of great theological battles reaching back to those of ↗Augustine's time, through the Reformation and later

still to those connected with Jansenism. It is wise for those attempting to live a spiritual life to keep clear of all that polemic, yet they must have a steady appreciation of the place of the Divine and human action in Christian living. The following attempts to keep clear of controversy and presents a simple outline, inevitably almost *simpliste* and possibly one-sided. The word Grace translates the Greek word *charis*. It has a wide range of related meanings; three are fundamental.

(i) Grace can mean God's good pleasure, his merciful intent to save fallen man. This is sometimes called *Uncreated grace*. In the spiritual life this is the most important, as it expresses God's infinite love for us. 'God so loved the world ...' (Jn 3:16). In Ephesians we read, 'Before the world was made, he (God) chose us, chose us in Christ ... to make us praise the glory of his grace (*charis*), his free gift to us in the Beloved. Such is the richness of the grace (*charis*) which he has showered on us ...' (Eph 1:4, 6, 7). The word *charis* here is best understood as meaning God's benevolent love (*cf.* also Eph 2:7). There are many passages where *charis* could mean either this freely given love of God for us or a gift that transforms us, also freely given.

(ii) *Sanctifying grace.* Here the word *charis* seems to mean not so much God's attitude to us as the result of that attitude, namely a free gift. This is clear in Rom 6:22, 23: 'You get a reward leading to your sanctification and ending in eternal life. For the wage paid by sin is death; the present (*charis*) given by God is eternal life in Christ Jesus our Lord.' Here *charis* (grace) is used to represent the deep transformation in the human soul for which the New Testament uses a great many different words and images, since it cannot be adequately described by any one image alone: life (Jn 11:21), as here, Divine life, the life of the vine in the branches (Jn 15:1 ff), life of the spirit (Rev 11:11), the living water (Jn 4:11), being members of the Body of Christ (Col 1:18), sharing in the divine nature (2 Pet 1:4). Here grace stands for the transformation of the soul, a gift from God, by which we are made to share in the life of the New Man (Eph 2:15), The New Creation (2 Cor 5:17), so that one day we may see God as he is and know him as we are known by him (1 Cor 13:12).

(iii) Grace can also signify *Actual Grace*. Again intensely heated discussions have flared up over the relationship in time of human endeavour and God's help. Today all would agree that no matter what the human element in the good act may be, it is always preceded by a Divine aid. Today we are more concerned to realize how much of one's ordinary life is in fact 'actual grace'. The very presence of certain people can be an inestimably gracious help. The very gifts of our character – no one is completely bad – are all God's gifts. The assistance that has come our way through life, either by favourable circumstance or a kindly word, is also part of a Divine plan, a gift. In other words every aid along the way to heaven, from a sermon to a kindly chuckle when we feel depressed, every support in difficulties, may be called actual graces.

Another group of charismata or gifts or graces from God form part of the Christian landscape. These are technically called the ↗Gifts of the Holy Spirit, or the ↗Charisms.

Gregory the Great, St (*circa 540–604*)
Born of patrician family, he became chief administrator of Rome (prefect), but seeing the futility of mere human remedies withdrew to become a monk in his own palace on the Coelian Hill. He also established six other monasteries on his estates in Sicily. The greatness of Gregory lies both in what he did and wrote and even more in the conditions under which he succeeded in doing these things. In the first place it was at a time of extreme economic, political and moral collapse in the West; the Western Roman Empire in his day consisting of little more than Rome itself and that in ruins. At the same time he was himself physically very sick, unable often to rise from bed. He is the patron saint of those who carry on when all seems utterly lost. In 590 he was elected Pope. Despite chronic illness he took immediate action in the anxious years of his pontificate; he sent Augustine and forty monk-companions to England, saved Rome from famine, from the ravages of barbarians, from pestilence. At the same time he wrote books which provided the groundwork of medieval spirituality, e.g. the *22 homilies on Ezechiel* (593) dealing with the active and contemplative lives, prayer, the theological virtues, the priesthood; *the Moralia*, or extended commentary on the book of Job, in fact a discursive treatment of morals and also again on prayer; the *Pastoral Care*, a *vade mecum* for bishops and priests. *The Dialogues*, whose second book describes the life of ↗Benedict, were written in an easy, unlearned way. Gregory, a monk himself, presented the monastic way as the highest form of Christian life, both in his life and his writings, especially his letters and the life of Benedict. Yet his monastic ideal was not inactive, it was monks he sent to evangelize Britain. This became the pattern in the early Middle Ages, with Willibrord, Wilfrid and Boniface, each going out in their turn

to evangelize the barbarians in Northern Europe.

What part Gregory played in the renewal of the liturgy is not certain; it is known that he introduced the *Kyrie* into the Roman Mass and placed the *Pater* after the canon.

C. Butler, *Western Mysticism*, 2nd ed., (London, 1927).

F.H. Dudden, *Gregory the Great*, 2 vols., (London, 1905).

Fliche et Martin, *Histoire de l'église*, Vol. 5, (Louvain, 1978).

Gregory Nazianzus, St (*329–89*)
One of the three great Cappadocian Fathers of the Church, together with ↗Basil the Great and ↗Gregory of Nyssa. His father, Gregory the Elder, gave him an excellent Christian and pagan education, the first at Caesarea and Alexandria and the second at Athens where he again met Basil and where they became fast friends. After returning home he joined Basil at his hermitage in Pontus (358–9) where they made an anthology of Origen's works, called the ↗*Philocalia*. Home once again, Gregory's father – now a bishop – practically forced his son to be ordained priest. He fled back to Basil, but (362) only to be persuaded to return to Nazianzus. This was the occasion of his writing the famous *Apologeticus de fuga*, which in fact was a splendid statement of what the priesthood is. Now comes an extraordinary misadventure: Basil persuading him against his desire to be made bishop. In the event he never even visited his diocese, but assisted his father at Nazianzus. Once again, on his father's death he withdrew to solitude (374), yet again he was persuaded to emerge, this time to support the poor small remnant of Catholics left in the great capital, Constantinople, after the death of the Arian Emperor Valens. Gregory turned his home there into a chapel, in which he pronounced his famous five *Orations* or discourses on the Holy Trinity, which proved to be the turning point in winning back the Christians of the city and beyond to the Catholic faith. Elected archbishop of the city, he soon found the political intrigues and disloyalties more than his sensitive soul could stand, and for the last time he escaped from the world, back to his family estates where he cultivated his garden in peace, wrote his remarkable autobiography in verse and many letters. In his will he gave his property to the poor of Nazianzus.

We know him through his 45 discourses, his letters, his poetry. Like Augustine his theological thinking was intimately linked with his personal spiritual life. For him the doctrine of the Incarnation meant that he personally and Christ were one, he being divinized by Christ. His affectionate nature made his relationship with Jesus such that he could call him 'my Jesus'. At the same time his mind was so penetrating that his statement of the mystery of the Incarnation and of the Trinity in the letters and elsewhere became stepping stones towards an orthodox statement of these fundamental Christian doctrines. His panegyrics are also famous: especially that on his friend Basil, all misunderstandings of the past being forgotten.

See *D. Spir.*, both for his spiritual significance and for bibliography; J. Quastens, *Patrology*, Vol. III, for outline of his theology and bibliography.

See also *O.D.C.C.* for bibliography.

Gregory of Nyssa, St (*circa 330– circa 395*)

Born at Caesarea in Cappadocia, he died in Constantinople. His father, brothers and sisters were saints, including his brother ↗Basil the Great. In early life he married, but some time later became a monk, and Basil persuaded him to be consecrated bishop. The latter had only himself to blame if Gregory was not a success as a bishop. Strangely enough after his elder brother's death, Gregory developed into an intellectual leader in the Church. He is its earliest systematic mystical theologian and together with ↗Evagrius of Pontus, his friend, he set a pattern which influences us to this day. His thought has logical consistency, and his explanations of the mystical experience are based on the scriptural and doctrinal truth that man is made to the image and likeness of God, and in a sense returns to knowledge of God through sharing in Christ's likeness to God the Father. He insists however on the complete transcendence of God. In his *Life of Moses* can already be found the symbolism of ↗ *The Cloud of Unknowing*, soon to be associated with the writings of the Pseudo-↗Denis, and which later will provide the title for a famous English medieval book on prayer.

Gregory's writings even may have a Buddhist flavour. But the relationship between East and West at this period is still very obscure.

J. Daniélou (ed.), *From Glory to Glory, Texts from St Gregory of Nyssa's mystical writings*, (New York, 1961).

Gregory Palamas, St (*circa 1296– 1359*)

Became a monk at Mount ↗Athos in 1318, was ordained priest in 1326 and consecrated Archbishop of Thessalonica in 1347. It was only in 1337 that he found himself involved in a tiresome controversy which was to make him one of the great doctors of the Orthodox Church, almost of the standing of ↗Basil and John Chrysostom. He became the defender of the ↗Hesychast tradition, practised especially by the monks of Mount Athos. The dispute began with the arrival in the East at Constantinople of Barlaam, a Greek monk from Calabria in southern Italy, full of the new learning, that is the rediscovery of neo–Platonic thought; and full of the Pseudo-↗Denis, and with a nominalist philosophy. To the Orthodox he seemed to reduce all theology to reason and to despise the body as a prison. Thus on encountering the ↗Hesychast tradition among the monks of the East he was startled at their claim to know God in himself and through the bodily powers, while their prayer techniques and their rhythmic breathing were distasteful to him. God he said was unknowable, completely other, thus exaggerating the teaching of Denis. Gregory Palamas answered Barlaam's attack with his *Triads in Defence of the Holy Hesychasts*. The monks of Mount Athos came to the support of their champion with the *Hagioritic Tome*.

The two protagonists became embroiled in the question of the Divine Light that the Hesychasts claimed to see with mortal eyes, just as the apostles saw the light at the Transfiguration. Gregory agreed with Barlaam that without baptism that would be impossible, that is in the natural order, but given baptism and the whole man, body and soul, being transformed into the life of Christ, the ascetic would share in the Divine Light (*cf.* the phrase in the

88 Groote, Gerhard

Prologue of ⟋Benedict's Rule, *deificum lumen*). Perhaps Barlaam might have been silenced but Gregory claimed that this light was God himself. Barlaam declared that no one in this life can see the essence of God. Gregory replied that this was true; but the Light was the *energia* of God, God in his creatures and still God himself that they see.

The Council of Bishops in Constantinople supported Gregory in 1341. By some twist of political fortunes another condemned him in 1344 as a heretic. In 1347 and 1351 the Great Synod reversed that decision decisively and showed their approval of Gregory by having him elected as bishop. The triumph of the Hesychasts explains the great emphasis on the feast of the Transfiguration in the Eastern Church. The matter, as Gregory saw it, had a wide significance. It involved the purpose of the Incarnation, which was to renew and deify the whole man body and soul.

J. Meyendorff, *A Study of Gregory Palamas*, (Leighton Buzzard, 1966).

J. Meyendorff, *St Gregory Palamas and Orthodox Spirituality*, (New York, 1974).

Timothy Ware, *The Orthodox Church*, (Harmondsworth, 1964), pp. 72–80.

Groote, Gerhard (*1340–84*)

Born at Deventer in the Netherlands. He withdrew from a prominent ecclesiastical career to live for two years in retirement with the Carthusians of Monnikhuizen. This is an early example of the unobtrusive but profound influence the Carthusians were to have on the movement for reform in the Church over the next 300 years. Groote then preached throughout the Low Countries – though he was not a priest – against abuses and in favour of reform. He founded the Sisters of the Common Life, and after his death the Brothers of the Common Life sprang up according to his spirit. He wanted religious life without vows, that is lay people living according to the Gospel and working for their living. His prayer was not mystical in the Rhineland style; he reacted strongly against the intellectualism of the late scholastics, against seeking preferments or honorific academic titles. He was a drop-out from the 14th century academic, religious world, but not against the Church as such. His spirit is parallel to that of many today, who might learn from his courage and honesty of mind, but also from his humility and obedience to due authority. At the end, owing to pressure from the Orders, he did adopt in his foundation at Windesheim, near Deventer, the so-called Rule of ⟋Augustine, as the least structured statement of the religious life. Most of Groote's disciples remained free even of that Rule, and called themselves simply 'the brethren living together at Zwolle' or wherever it was. They came to be known as the Brethren of the Common Life and were the source of the ⟋*Devotio moderna*, which had so wide an influence before the Reformation. The ⟋*Imitation* was the choice flower of this spirituality inaugurated by Gerhard Groote.

T.P. van Flijl, *G. Groote, Ascetic and Reformer (1340–1384)*, (Catholic University of America Studies in Medieval History, New Series, 18, 1963).

R.W. Southern, *Western Society and the Church in the Middle Ages* (Harmondsworth, 1970), pp. 331–58.

Guyon, Madame (*1648–1717*)
Her married name. *Née* Jeanne Marie Bouvier de la Motte, her childhood was spent in convents where she read much piety, including the works of ↗ *Francis of Sales* at about the age of 12, also the life of ↗ *Jeanne de Chantal*. These had a lasting influence upon her. In 1664 she was married; in 1668 she had her first mystical experiences. She read ↗ *Catherine of Genoa*, ↗ *Benet of Canfield* and ↗ *Molinos*. In 1676 her husband died, and with the feelings of a prophetess she set about spreading her doctrine of prayer. Her first book was published in 1685: *Moyen court et facile pour l'oraison*. The descriptions of passive states of prayer therein were not always felicitous. In 1686 she was in Paris and helping Mme de Maintenon at St Cyr. Two years later she met the Abbé *Fénelon*, who at first cautious, became a devoted follower. After the first enthusiasm, he took her and her writings in hand.

Mme de Maintenon was jealous of her influence; ↗ Bossuet, brought in to examine her doctrine, gave an unfavourable report in 1694. A more solemn examination took place at Issy, and, in 1695, 34 propositions of hers were condemned, though her morals were not found wanting. The basic objections were, first to her account of passive contemplation which did not allow for any activity to the soul, and secondly to pure love, or disinterested love, which seemed akin to the heresy of ↗ *Molinos* condemned only a few years before (1687) i.e. a form of ↗ *Quietism*. Meanwhile Mme Guyon was put now in the prison of Vincennes, now in the Bastille, now under surveyance in this or that convent and died in 1717.

She was not the first prophetess who directed her directors, nor the last. Nor is she alone in having deep mystical experiences but with insufficient theological education to be able accurately to express them. Fénelon, of great learning, sensitivity, holiness and discernment, believed in her, while recognizing the element of exaltation. The story is an object lesson in the problems of the guidance of such personalities.

Various articles on these subjects by L. Cognet in *Catholicisme Hier, Aujourd' hui, Demain*; see 'Pourrat' and 'Quiétisme' in *D.T.C.*, which takes a hostile stance with regard to both Mme Guyon and Fénelon. See also 'Fénelon' and 'Bossuet' in *D. Spir.*

H

Hail Mary, The
Made up of two parts. The first is from the New Testament. 'Hail (Mary) full of grace, the Lord is with thee', the greeting of the angel Gabriel to Mary at the Annunciation; and 'Blessed art thou among women, and blessed is the fruit of thy womb (Jesus)', the greeting of Elizabeth to her at the Visitation, both from Luke (1). The second half: 'Holy Mary Mother of God, pray for us sinners, now and at the hour of our death', seems not to have been added before the end of the 15th century. Savonarola's little work on the Hail Mary (1495) has it almost word for word. It is first quoted exactly in the Mercedarian, Cam-aldolese and Franciscan breviaries in 1514, 1515 and 1525 respectively. On the other hand the first part occurs in 6th-century liturgies, those of ↗ James and ↗ Mark, and the Ethiopic. The intrusion of the name Jesus probably was made by Pope Urban VI (1261–4). The first part is not a petition but a salutation. The

Catechism of the Council of Trent approved of the addition as making a suitable prayer of petition to Mary.

In the Middle Ages the short form of the Hail Mary was repeated fifty or a hundred times and usually with a genuflection or even prostration each time. In the West it seems to have been treated much as the ↗Jesus prayer was used in the East.

H. Thurston, *Familiar Prayers*, (London, 1950).

See also 'Rosary' and 'Hail Mary' in *N.C.E.*

Harphius, Henry
Variously spelt Erp, Herp, Arp, Herpff, Harpius, Herpius. Born at Herp at the beginning of the 15th century. Just as ↗Origen and ↗Evagrius are the basic but shrouded figures of Patristic spiritual theology, so Harphius stands at the source of the great mystical revival in Spain and France of the Counter-Reformation period. In both cases their ideas were amply used and unacknowledged; in both cases modern scholarship has recognized the borrowings (*cf.* references to Harphius in *H.C.S.*, Vol. II, pp. 469 ff, also Louis Cognet, *Post-Reformation Spirituality, passim*).

As a youth he became a Brother of the Common Life (*cf.* ↗Groote) and became Rector of their house at Delft. In 1450, in Rome, he became a Franciscan Observant of the Ara Coeli. He became Guardian at Malines, provincial of Lower Germany (Cologne), dying in Malines in 1477.

His own thought is influenced by the Pseudo-↗Denis, by ↗Bernard (devotion to the humanity of Christ and affective approach to prayer) also in the same sense following ↗Bonaventure. He is profoundly influenced by ↗Eckhart and

through ↗Tauler, also by ↗Ruysbroeck. It is chiefly through Harphius that the Rhino-Flemish mystical tradition spread to Spain and France. Certainly indirectly he influenced ↗Teresa, and very probably directly ↗John of the Cross, though cautiously and selectively used by him; he is the master of another Observant, ↗Benet of Canfield, himself the Master of the French School.

He wrote many sermons and letters, but also mystical works, the most mature being *Speculum perfectionis* or *Directorum contemplativorum* (English translation, *The Mirror of Perfection*). He distinguishes three Mansions in the soul: (i) That of the heart and sensibility; (ii) The place of the intellect and will; (iii) The essence of the soul, the *apex mentis*, the point of the spirit.

Linked with these are three stages of prayer: (i) Meditation; (ii) Prayer of the gifts of the Holy Spirit; (iii) The super-essential life, where in rapture the soul experiences the vision of the essence of God. It was this last of which Rome disapproved; and ↗John of the Cross does not follow him here. Another point of dispute was his admitting the 'by-passing' of the divine humanity of Christ in higher degrees of prayer. It has to be admitted however that his devotion to Jesus was great and he recognized that all Christian life including prayer derives its power from Christ. One element of Eckhart and Ruysbroeck he leaves on one side, namely the Platonic theory of the ideal self being pre-existent in God, and that this is the centre of our being. His mystical works were published by the Carthusians of Cologne from 1509, and in 1538 they were published there in Latin, so that his doctrine spread throughout the West. One of those who acknowledged Harphius was Augustine ↗Baker the English Benedictine mystic. He also propagated the method of 'aspirations' advocated by Harphius. The Jesuits and ↗Francis of Sales approached him with caution. The Franciscan Order keep his feast, 13th July.

Healing
Jesus began his public life with healings of the body. He meant these miracles as 'signs' of a deeper, spiritual healing. 'Go, sin no more.' He used the healing of the paralytic let down from the roof to show that he had the power to forgive sins. He expected his disciples to do miracles of healing, 'When you enter a city . . . heal those who are sick there' (Lk 10:9; *cf*. also the end of Mk 16:18). The Acts are full of such miracles.

Today, by the instrumentality of the Pentecostal movement, this charism of healing has become prominent in the Church once again. The Episcopal Church has led the way in instituting services in church of laying on of hands over the sick following the example of the freelance Pentecostalists. And cures are undoubtedly effected. It has been found that there are three grades of healing, that of the body, that of the mind, and deeper, that of the spirit, putting at rest some deep wound. There is also claimed a healing from possession. It is God who heals and man is his instrument.

The two sacraments, Confession (or Reconciliation, perhaps even better the Sacrament of Healing or of Peace) and the Sacrament of the Anointing of the Sick, have been, throughout the history of the Church, the regular instruments of healing; but the former was in danger of becoming routine, the second a sign that the sick person was about to die. The Charismatic Movement has changed all that and these

Sacraments are seen for what they are, truly instruments of healing. The Sacraments not only heal the wounds caused by sin but absolve from the sin itself. God uses the lay person to help heal those wounds.

T. Kelsey, *Healing and Christianity*, (San Francisco, Calif., 1973).

F. MacNutt, OP, *Healing*, (Notre Dame, Ind., 1976).

A. Sanford, *The Healing Gifts of the Spirit*, (New York, 1966).

Herbert, George (*1593–1633*)
One of the formative figures in Anglican spirituality, he was born at Montgomery Castle in Wales into an ancient and distinguished family. His elder brother Edward, created Lord Herbert of Cherbury by Charles I, was a noted courtier and diplomat as well as a philosopher and poet, and George himself aspired to a career at court. But after he had become Fellow of Trinity College, Cambridge and Public Orator of the University, his most powerful patrons died, and he gave up the idea of a secular career. He became a deacon in 1625 and in 1630 he married and was ordained priest, spending the remainder of his life (only three years) as a country parson at Bemerton in Wiltshire.

Herbert shared with his close friend Nicholas ↗Ferrar of Little Gidding (who acted as his literary executor) a 'high' view of the priesthood and the Church and during his three years as a parish priest was noted for gentleness and sanctity of life, qualities which are reflected in his verse. At his induction as Rector of Bemerton he prostrated himself for a long time alone before the altar in prayer, setting himself rules for the conduct of his priesthood and vowing to keep them – rules afterwards set out in a little book called *The Country Parson*. But it is his verse which captured and conveys the quality of his spirituality and of his holiness. Written with disciplined elegance, compression and a frequent use of analogy, it nevertheless manages to express with passionate intensity the classic internal struggle of the Christian life between self-will and submission to the will of God. His greatest poems are in effect prayers, which reflect in various forms a direct dialogue with our Lord. In perhaps the most famous of his poems of struggle, 'The Collar', he formulates the cry of the emotions against the constraints of the Christian life: '. . . leave thy cold dispute / Of what is fit, and not. Forsake thy cage, / Thy rope of sands / Which pettie thoughts have made, and made to thee / Good cable to enforce and draw, / And be thy law . . .' and ends: 'But as I rav'd and grew more fierce and wilde / At every word / Me thoughts I heard one calling, *Child*; / And I reply'd, My Lord. The love and gentleness of Christ are constant themes, as in Bitter-Sweet: Ah my dear angrie Lord, / Since thou dost love, yet strike / Cast down, yet help afford; / Sure I will do the like . . .' And most intensely of all, in the concluding couplet of 'The Agonie' (in effect, a meditation on the Passion): 'Love is that liquor sweet and most divine / Which my God feels as bloud: but I, as wine.' But whether the tone of the dialogue is reproachful, submissive or joyful, at its best it is written, as Dame Helen Gardiner has said, 'in the tone of one opening his heart to a friend'. It is this immediacy which has given Herbert a place among the mystics and accounts for the timelessness of his appeal.

G. Herbert, Helen Gardiner (ed.), *Poems*, 2nd ed., (Oxford, 1961).

I. Walton, *Life of Mr George Herbert*, (1670).

Hermits
The eremitical life is as old as the Church and is found in religions other than the Christian. At the threshold stands John the Baptist, always the patron of hermits and contemplative life. ↗Benedict dedicated a chapel at Monte Cassino to him; the Cistercians have a chapel to him in all their churches. He is the solitary par excellence, the ascetic, the penitential figure, pleading for *metanoia* (conversion of heart). Note, he was not above preaching – he preached Christ; he had to become less, that Christ might be all in all. In Church history the earliest hermit is ↗Jerome's figure: Paul the Hermit; better authenticated is ↗Antony of the Desert, the life of whom by ↗Athanasius, Patriarch of Alexandria, made Antony the symbol of the great eremitical and monastic experiments. Hermits and monasteries sprang up all over Europe, as far as Trier in the north west, in the hills of Subiaco where ↗Benedict was to find his cave; in Asia Minor and far eastward. After the Barbarian invasions the eremitical life again flourished: Romuald (d. 1027) founded his 'laura' or cluster of hermitages at Camaldoli in Italy; ↗*Bruno* (d. 1101) followed with the Grande Chartreuse. The 12th century was especially the hermits' century – the Carmelites emerged from Mount Carmel. The tradition continued through the Middle Ages, with ↗Richard Rolle in England among many, St Nicolas ↗von Flue in Switzerland, St Colette at Corbie in France and right up to the Reformation, with St John ↗Fisher installing two hermits in his diocese of Rochester. In France and Spain they survived as a way of life up to the

Napoleonic wars. In England they had in the 18th century become a romantic dream (*cf. English Eccentrics* by Edith Sitwell), but once again in the 20th century a revival has taken place, not only among the contemplative orders, as the Cistercians, but also among those following the mixed life and even the active life. The ideal still is to find God by shutting out all that is not God. But note how hermits of all ages have found beauty of nature to be a way to God, if it be only the bare and desolate beauty of the desert. Hermits practise penance as well as prayer, and, following the doctrine of the unity of all men in Christ, believe that what they do influences others for good. Besides, their life of prayer, though this is not the reason for it, does bear witness to the necessity and primacy of direct communication with God. Sooner or later men and women come to seek their advice: Benedict at Subiaco, Simeon the Stylite and Nicolas of Flue are notable examples.

See 'Hermites' in *D.Spir.* And also Charles ↗de Foucauld, ↗Ancren Rule, ↗Julian of Norwich, ↗Nicolas of Flue.

See also the writings of Thomas Merton, *passim.*

Hesychia

Tranquillity, solitude; and *hesychast* the solitary. Later it acquired the specific meaning of one who sought to see the Light of God. ↗Benedict of Nursia says 'Let us open our eyes to the deific (God-making) light' (Prologue of *Rule*). The means to acquire this, in the Orthodox monasticism, is the ↗Jesus Prayer.

HESYCHASM A method of prayer, the first mention of which seems to be in the life of John the Hesychast, monk of Jerusalem (5th century). ↗John Climacus (d. 649) describes it in his *Ladder of Paradise* (ch. 27) as a prayer method of the monastery on Mount Sinai. It consisted in a continuous repetition of the Jesus Prayer, 'Lord Jesus, Son of the Father, have mercy on me', or a close equivalent. This was to be combined with careful ↗breath control, correct ↗posture of the body; from which would follow perfect calm and enlightenment. With Symeon the Theologian (949–1022) the nature of the enlightenment became the object of controversy. Was it light that emanated from God or Christ, or were such visions of the devil? ↗Gregory Palamas claimed that God in himself was transcendent, in his being, but his energy could be experienced in the form of light. In 1344 Palamas's theory was condemned, but in 1347 and 1351 two synods at Constantinople reversed this decision and Gregory Palamas's teaching became the official teaching on the subject in the Orthodox Church.

See *H.C.S.*, Vol. 2, pp. 576–89.

See also *D.T.C.*, Vol. XI, pt. 2, cols. 1777–818 (Jugie).

Hilton, Walter

A Canon regular of Augustine, an English mystic, author of the *Scale of Perfection* which was one of the first books to be printed in England (Wynkyn de Worde, 1494). The *Scale* is a work of great power. The author avoids the extremes of the Pseudo-Dionysians by his strong Christo-centric approach to prayer. According to Abbot Cuthbert Butler he follows in the great Western mystical tradition of ↗Augustine,

↗Gregory and ↗Bernard, though he was aware of the Pseudo-↗Denis and of the ↗Victorines.

Hilton also makes it plain that the perfect following of Christ need not necessarily be in the cloister (*cf.* ↗Groote and ↗Devotio Moderna). In the *Scale* is the ancient imagery of the pilgrim, and the sentence quoted together with the Pilgrim passage: 'I am nought, I have nought, I desire only one thing, and that is Our Lord Jesus Christ, and to be with him in peace at Jerusalem' (Sect 1. ch. 6).

A number of other treatises are attributed to Hilton: (i) *A Mixed Life*; (ii) *Eight Chapters on Perfection*; (iii) *Qui Habitat*; (iv) *Bonum Est*; (v) *Benedictus*.

He died on the vigil of the Assumption at the monastery of St Peter, Thurgarton, Notts, 1395.

D. Jones (ed.), *The Minor Works of Walter Hilton*, (London, 1929).

M.D. Knowles, *The English Mystical Tradition*, (London, 1961).

G. Sitwell (ed. and tr.), *The Scale of Perfection*, (London, 1953).

Holiness

A characteristic of all Christians in view of their faith, their Baptism and their consequent union with Christ as sons of God. It is gift of the Holy Spirit, as John the Baptist said, 'He (Christ) will baptize you with the Holy Spirit and with fire' (Lk 3:16 f). 'Holy' as a word often has the meaning of apart, transcendent, sacred (as opposed to profane), the absolutely other (*cf.* Rudolph Otto, *The Idea of the Holy*, 1923), something mysterious, compelling but frightening. But, in the Old Testament, God the Holy One *reveals* himself as just and mighty, merciful and faithful. By being associated with him the Israelites are

also holy, set apart from other peoples. In the New Testament, the new People of God are also holy on account of an even closer association, namely by being remade in Christ, and being the Temples of the Holy Spirit.

That is the first stage of a Christian's holiness, something *given*, but then he must co-operate with the Holy Spirit, live by him, by his life. This will be manifest in the theological virtues and in the ↗Gifts, as well as in the virtues appropriate to each one's state of life, aided by the Sacraments.

God made all for perfection: 'Be you perfect as your heavenly Father is perfect' (Mt 5:48), an echo of Lev 19:2, where the word used is 'holy', and it applies to *all*. Vatican II has this as one of its main themes: 'The followers of Christ are called by God, not according to their accomplishments, but according to His own purpose and grace. They are justified in the Lord Jesus, and through baptism, sought in faith, they truly become the sons of God and sharers in the divine nature. In this way they are really made holy. Then, too, by God's gifts they must hold on to and complete in their lives this holiness which they have received.' (*Constitution on the Church*, n. 40). And later: 'Thus it is evident to everyone that all the faithful of Christ of whatever rank or status are called to the fulness of the Christian life and to the perfection of charity.' (*ibid.*, para. 3).

The more this is realized and the laity are led the way of holiness by the Holy Spirit, the more will the infinite variety of holiness become apparent. A widow's holiness will not be like that of a busy general practitioner, or a factory worker's resemble that of a journalist, a politician's that of a postmaster, a university student's that of a sailor.

Hope

The Christian theological virtue which looks to God to fulfil his promise that we will share in his glory, and to provide the means to achieve this, if we keep in his love. It is primarily self-regarding, a hope in the reward: the vision of God, hope in the means for reaching there, which in short is God's merciful grace. Is it wrong to be self-regarding, should one have only 'pure love', that is, altruistic love? ↗Francis of Sales, and the author of the famous sonnet on the Crucifix (attributed wrongly to Francis Xavier), and others have imagined themselves as prepared to forgo heaven if this were the loving will of God. ↗Paul himself approaches the same state of mind (Rom 9:3). God made us for himself, to share in his life for ever. Therefore it would follow that we are fulfilling his will by seeking the end for which he made us. Hope then is the *love of desire, amor concupiscentiae* supported by a certainty that God, the Loved One, will give us all that is needed to reach him. Yet it must be distinguished from presumption which expects God to do all on his side, and we to do nothing in our turn, but rather follow our own wayward will regardless of God's commands. Despair is the opposite vice: a failure of hope, on the grounds that God cannot be concerned with one so wicked and useless as oneself. But we have the examples in the Gospels of two who hoped against hope, Mary Magdalen and the 'good' thief. He was good because he hoped. Indeed Jesus preferred those who recognized their sinfulness and therefore needed and knew they needed his help – they were exercising the virtue of hope.

Is there any relationship between natural hope and Christian hope, i.e. hope in earthly well-being, earthly goods, friendships and the like, and the hope of heaven? In other words, to work and pray for such, is that exercising the virtue of hope? Ask and you shall receive? Is that only to be applied to supernatural objects? Some would refuse to ask for earthly things. Soeur Thérèse asked for snow on her profession day and saw nothing incongruous in that. Perhaps the answer is that we may pray for such with an understood clause – if this is in conformity to the final will of God. Besides, to do so may be more in conformity with our nature as dependent beings, since such prayers are an exercise in dependence, humility, creatureliness.

The ground for hope is that 'God wills that all men should be saved' (1 Tim 2:4). If that is his will, then he wills the means, namely saving grace. But he leaves us free (the mystery of predestination). We can say that God acts according to our nature.

The above approach, in line with scholastic understanding, has been enriched in our time by a return to biblical insights. In the Old Testament the hope of Israel is what God promised, grounded on his fidelity, truthfulness, power. These promises were made to the People of God, as such, and their fulfilments in history were the *magnalia Dei*, which the Israelites commemorated in their great feasts, especially the Passover (Deut 6:20–5). Hope was trust in God's promises and his trustworthiness (*cf.* Ps. 26). These fulfilments were pledges of further wonders. Israel's hope, enlarged and deepened, is the prototype of our growth in hope. Their earthly hopes proved fragile: the Jews were exiled, their kingdom destroyed, the line of kings deposed. The prophets, Isaiah particularly, transformed that hope spiritually (*cf.* the Songs of the Suffering Servant). Yet, all the time, the future life was still nebulous and uninviting. Job, hoping against hope, could not grasp why the wicked should prosper and the just be ill-used. Yet Israel's hope slowly became the hope for all men, though veiled in mystery. Then, in the New Testament, Hope dawned, Jesus Christ. The Christian's hope is inseparable from his person. He is his hope (1 Tim 1:1). He already gives us a foretaste of fulfilment in his own Resurrection (1 Pet 3:21). Christ had risen, wrote ↗Paul, and if that were not so, then our faith (hope) was vain (1 Cor 15:14); and not merely did this rising again prove his divinity, but proved that death was not the end; and not only that, but that already we share the new life (Rom 8:10–11). Christ is still living among/in us (Mt 12:28). This the early Christians 'realized' in the Eucharist. But there was still a second coming: the Thessalonians (1 Th 5:1 ff) thought it was 'now'). This is the tension throughout Christian history. The early monks withdrew from the 'world' to establish the fulfilment as best they could; the emigrants to America founded their Concordias and Harmonies for the same reason. Today we recognize that Christians must also live *in* the world to transform it through the power of Christ (which is his Spirit), by out-going love and justice. But, aware that men remain weak, Christians know that here and now the fulfilment can only be partial and unstable, for it can only be made perfect in heaven.

Hope, then, is not a passive state, waiting for the second coming, but an active state co-operating with Christ in establishing a world in which that second coming (for each of us) is already a partial reality, and in which the Christian can suitably prepare for the full vision of God's glory.

The Christian then, through the virtue of hope, is one who looks not merely backwards to the *magnalia Dei* in the past, but also to the future, which, even in this world, he can, with the power of Christ, transform for the better. Here lines cross with the Marxists' future-look. For them the future in this world can be a utopia. We would be forced to reply: (i) That that does not help those who have gone before; and (ii) That human nature is not so completely to be restored to perfection as to make this possible; besides with each generation one has to begin again; (iii) Finally, the pleasures of this life are unsubstantial for the spirit of man that seeks the absolute and it is a universal experience that they pall, and we die. Nevertheless, both we and the Communists are seeking to ameliorate the lot of men in this life, and this comes from the element of *hope.* The one sees that amelioration as an end, the other (the Christian) as a means, so that 'the least' of this world, and yet God's precious ones, may have 'room' to seek God's will here and now.

Hopkins, Gerald Manley (*1844–89*) English poet and Jesuit. He was nurtured in the High Anglican tradition, was schooled at Highgate Grammar School, won an award to Balliol College, Oxford, where he graduated with first class honours in classics in 1867. In the previous year he had been received into the Catholic Church by ↗Newman. In 1868 he joined the Society of Jesus and passed through the usual Jesuit establishments: Roehampton, Stony-hurst, St Beuno's in North Wales. But after his ordination to the priesthood (1877) it seems that his superiors were at a loss to find a suitable niche for him. Various parishes were tried: London, Oxford and Liverpool, likewise school posts at Mount St Mary's and Stonyhurst. Apparently he failed at them all. Meanwhile he had destroyed all his poems, thinking them contrary to the spirit of the Order – fortunately not so his friends. But in 1875 his superior at St Beuno's suggested he write a poem on a recent tragic shipwreck. Thus ended the great silence. He wrote 'I long had haunting my ears the echo of a new rhythm'. The great work entitled 'The Wreck of the Deutschland' was the outcome. It attempts to express lyrically Hopkins's profound con- viction that, under the mastery of God, there is a unity in all creation with God 'throned behind Death', God who uses even natural disasters as a means of reconciling sinful man to himself. This is the tension that grips all Hopkins's finer poems. Nature, for Hopkins, was each *individual* creature: the skylark, the falcon, man, the bluebell (in each of which he could see Christ). Duns Scotus's belief that the very distinctiveness of each individual thing (the *haecceitas*, the 'thisness') was what we know, fitted admirably into Hopkins's instinctive vision, the 'inscape'. His whole purpose was to grasp – in words – that inscape. 'The world is charged with the grandeur of God.' But all decays. A child's tears for dead leaves falling set Hopkins explaining to her, that what was inexplicable then was in fact our common lot. 'It was the blight man was born for, / It is Margaret you mourn for.' ('Spring and Fall'.) But death is not the end, that is the burden of the 'Leaden Echo and the Golden Echo'. How to keep beauty from vanishing away? We can do nothing but 'be beginning to despair'. Yet God has kept it 'with fonder a care', so that 'not a hair is,

not an eyelash, not the least lash lost'. The reason is that we will rise again with Christ.

At the end, in Dublin, cut off from England, he despaired, almost, and wrote in rapid succession the 'terrible' or rather the deeply Christian sonnets, 'Carrion Comfort' and the others. He, a failure; his work meaningless; God silent. Yet he stood firm:

'Not, I'll not, carrion comfort, Despair, not feast on thee; / Not untwist – slack they may be – these last strands of man / In me or, most weary, cry *I can no more.* I can.'

Suddenly his spirits rise again and he can write in 'That Nature is a Heraclitean Fire and of the Comfort of the Resurrection', the final lines: 'In a flash, at a trumpet crash, / I am all at once what Christ is, since he is what I am, and / This Jack, joke, poor potsherd, patch, matchwood, immortal diamond, / Is immortal diamond.' He died in Dublin of typhoid fever. The best commentary on Hopkins's mind and poetry is found in his Journal, Sermons and correspondence.

C. Devlin, SJ, (ed.), *The Sermons and Devotional Writings of Gerald Manley Hopkins*, (London, 1959).

W.H. Gardner and N.H. MacKenzie (eds.), *The Poems of Gerald Manley Hopkins*. 4th edition, revised and enlarged. (London, 1978).

H. House and G. Storey (eds.), *Journals and Papers of Gerald Manley Hopkins*, (London, 1959).

There are various editions of Hopkins's letters; to Robert Bridges, and between Hopkins and Richard Watson Dixon and others.

Hugh of St Victor (*1095–1142*)
The greatest of the Victorines. He

entered (*circa* 1115–8) the abbey of St Victor on the outskirts of Paris to become a canon; a considerable theologian for his time, well-versed in Scripture and ↗Augustine; he corresponded with ↗Bernard, especially over Abelard. His writings are voluminous, on the Church, Sacraments, the heavenly Hierarchy of the Pseudo-↗Denis, and especially on religious formation, in which he treats of prayer, from spiritual reading to meditation, which for him is a *search*, on to contemplation which he says is *possession*. But in between these two last comes '*speculation*' or fascination and admiration of Truth, a condition that is possible because at this stage one is freed from the passions. Upon that follows the profound peace of contemplation, as a natural consequence of the love of the truth which is seen. It may be that occasionally God, the Spouse of the soul, will give signs of his love; these are pure gifts, and the soul remains passive. His teaching was much used by the medieval writers on prayer that succeeded him, not least by the English, among them ↗Hilton.

Though St Victor is called an abbey, a monastery, in the time of Hugh it had become a house of Canons Regular of Augustine, having been established by William of Champeaux (d. 1121), the unfortunate opponent of Abelard.

See 'Hugh of St Victor' in *D.T.C.*

Humanity of Christ

Whether Christ was truly man, how the humanity is united with Christ's divinity, these questions we here take as settled in the sense the Church has made decisions about them. This is not a dictionary of dogmatic or positive theology, but one of the life of the Spirit. Christ is truly man in all

save sin, (Heb 4:15). He is truly God and the union is in the Person of the Logos, the Son of the Father. Our question is: how has the humanity of Christ affected the spirituality, the life and prayer of Christians through the ages? The New Testament has in germ all the ways that later Christians appreciated the humanity of Christ. The writers cherish all the humanity of Christ, his humble circumstances, poverty, his compassion, his sufferings, his firmness, his courage, the Passion. Christ's own teaching reveals a twofold approach: he is the way, i.e. we follow in his footsteps; he is also the bread of life. We must eat his flesh and drink his blood sacramentally, so as to have life in us. Here his humanity is the instrument of our union with him and through him with the Holy Trinity. ↗Paul too sees Christ the man as someone to imitate: imitate me as I imitate Christ (1 Cor 4:16) and in Philippians (2:5–8) he outlines the way a Christian should follow Christ in humility and obedience even to death. But in Hebrews (1:1 ff) Christ's humanity is seen as the image of the unseen God, it is the final manifestation of God's glory. Christ himself had said: 'He who sees me sees the Father' (Jn 14:9). The contemplation of the human life of Jesus gives us deep insights into the nature of God, for that life of Christ is God-behaving-as-a-man. Through his humanity, the apostles came to be aware of Christ's divinity.

The early Church had all these interests in Christ's humanity: the martyrs from Ignatius to Polycarp, to those of Lyons and beyond are thought of, in their passions, as paralleling the Passion of Christ (*cf.* particularly Polycarp's). ↗*Irenaeus* (d. *circa* 202) penetrates the mystery of our recapitulation into God's life through the humanity of Christ, especially in the act of Communion. ↗*Augustine* frequently refers to the union between men and God through the Body of Christ. But the Fathers are not so much interested in the *details* of Christ's life (as things to imitate), as in the *main outline*, the spirit in which he lived it, in humility and obedience and love, and how he offered his life on the cross. When martyrdom was no more, it was the monks who in a 'living crucifixion' imitated Christ's Passion. ↗*Benedict*, at the end of this period, through the doctrine of the mystical body, sees Christ in all: the abbot, the sick, guests, the poor.

Not many prayers to Christ are found in the early Church, unless we except the hymns to Christ the Child and occasional prayers such as those of ↗Origen; usually Christ is thought of as by our side, within us, in whose life we share; we go with him to the Father, which accounts for the endings of the ancient liturgical prayers, *per Christum Dominum nostrum*. We rarely find crucifixes, as the sight of criminals dying on a cross was still too present a spectacle – until Constantine forbade the penalty of crucifixion – for Christians to want to portray their God-made-man dying nailed to a cross. He was most often portrayed in frescos and mosaics as the risen, triumphal Christ who had conquered death. However, the Eastern monks were already by the 6th century portraying the almost naked Christ on a cross (cf. 'Crucifix' in *N.C.E.*). In what follows only tendencies can be noted.

A change occurred in the West, culminating in the 12th century, with innumerable groups seeking to live an evangelical life, the *vita evangelica*, among them the poor of Christ, the poor of Lyons; these wanted to imitate Christ even in the details of his life, especially in his

poverty. ↗Bernard of Clairvaux (d. 1153) is the mouthpiece and fulfilment of this movement. From his pen and those of his friends, for example, ↗Aelred of Rievaulx, come meditations on the babyhood, the childhood of Jesus; every little detail of that life becomes precious. ↗Francis of Assisi and his disciples in the next century turned a monkish devotion into a people's devotion – the crib, the stations of the cross, the five wounds, the relics of the Passion. The ↗Rosary – a late medieval devotion – is not only a devotion to Mary, but also to Christ since the purpose of it is to meditate on the mysteries of Christ's life and death and resurrection in the company of his mother, rather than to concentrate on the actual Hail Marys.

By the 15th century and the '*Imitation*', devotion had concentrated on the Passion of Christ. The full flowering comes in the Exercises of ↗Ignatius where Jesus is all in all. With ↗Margaret Mary, we find further concentration, now upon the Sacred Heart of Jesus, sign of Jesus' love for men. This devotion was saved from sentimentality by the great French School led by Cardinal ↗Bérulle who, following Paul, taught that we should live by the interior dispositions of Jesus Christ, since we share his life.

Today we seem to be heirs of all these streams: Charles de ↗Foucauld would imitate Jesus in his hidden life, his poverty, even in his food; the theology of the Mystical Body has enriched our appreciation of Christ living in us, and made us aware of our obligation in love to all the poor of the world; we are more aware again that the Christ who lives in us is the Risen, victorious Christ, and through him we are one with God. But we are also aware that for us the way to sharing in Christ's Risen life is to share first in his Crucifixion. Besides, the contemplation of his dying for us is the massive incentive to make us love him in return.

BY-PASSING THE HUMANITY OF CHRIST A number of mystics have been accused of saying that in the higher regions of prayer, just as one has to put aside all earthly things, so too one should 'by-pass' the humanity of Christ. Among these so it is said are: the Pseudo-↗Denis, ↗Eckhart, ↗Benet of Canfield and even ↗John of the Cross. In a summary fashion the following distinctions are appropriate. Three points of view have to be considered, the ontological, the causal and the psychological. None, not even the Pseudo-Denis would maintain that ontologically the humanity of Christ can be put aside. All Catholic mystics hold that we can only be saved through Christ and by incorporation into his Body. ↗Denis writes about the sacraments as do all others; we know that Eckhart and Benet of Canfield and the other 'suspects' were devout to the Eucharist, celebrated Mass and received the Sacraments.

Likewise 'causally' no Catholic mystic – including those mentioned – would deny that we are saved through the power of Christ, through his Passion, Death and Resurrection, that we are united to the life of the Trinity *in* the Body of Christ. But when it comes to the psychological aspect of the matter, it seems very probable that many a mystic would have to admit that in certain states of prayer he is *not conscious* of the humanity of Christ. We cannot normally think of more than one thing at a time, and if a person praying is contemplating the mystery of the Holy Trinity, it is quite likely that the aspect of it which includes the Incarnation and the humanity of Christ does not enter his consciousness.

On the other hand, one should not consciously exclude the humanity of Christ. He himself said that he was the Way, and also that he who sees him sees the Father. ↗Teresa of Avila strongly emphasized the utility of the practice of going into prayer with and through Jesus Christ. But in passive prayer, the initiative does not come from the human side, it comes from the Spirit himself; and where he leads there the soul follows. Nevertheless, no Christian can be certain or even expect that at any time he will be led in prayer along the passive way. It is wiser and more humble to be ready to begin, as Teresa advises, with the humanity of Jesus Christ.

Humility

Latin root *humus*, earth, so, earthbound, littleness. In the Old Testament the humble or poor (*anawim*, Hebr) were thought to be idle (Pr 10:4), but in the Prophets seen as the oppressed and needy (Am 2:6 ff; Is 10:2). With Zephaniah they are the chosen ones of God, those to receive the promise (Zp 2:3; 3:11–13). This prepares the way for the splendour of Mary's *Magnificat* (Lk 1:46–55). For her, humility includes truthfulness. She is not afraid to say that God had done great things for her. She expresses the great spiritual truth that it is those who recognize that they are and have nothing who can be enriched by God. A noticeable quality of her hymn to humility is her joy; it begins with praise and thanksgiving. Christ's own way of life was that of the *anawim*, the poor folk. From his birth in a stable to his death on the cross, he claimed no exceptional treatment. No one was afraid to speak with him, neither prostitute nor robber, nor child. Yet he was not subservient; the Pharisees and Herod, the High Priest received a clear statement of the truth from him. He taught that prayer should be humble, notably in the parable of the publican and the Pharisee (Lk 18:10 ff). He would have us imitate himself who was meek and humble of heart (Mt 11:28). ↗Paul, in Phil 2, describes Christ's humility as an emptying of his 'equality with God' so as to become as a slave. This seems to mean, not that he ceased to be God but that *in his humanity* he refused to allow his divinity to burst through, take over, but wished to remain mere man, 'Son of man'.

The doctor of humility might reasonably be said to be ↗Benedict. He bases his spirituality upon that virtue, giving twelve degrees, beginning with the interior dispositions which then instinctively express themselves outwardly. His understanding of humility is all-embracing, leading to obedience or a loving acceptance of the Divine Will, and includes patience and joy. It is the expression of our share in the Passion, when we are asked to do 'the impossible'. But all saints are grounded upon humility. St Leo (the Great) said that the deeper the foundations of humility the higher the holiness. The mystics proclaim the importance of the same, especially ↗John of the Cross with his *nada*, or nothingness before God. (Yet for the young, who lack assurance, it is important to begin not with nothingness but with the qualities that God has given, and then proceed to recognition that all comes from God. Besides, we are in the Christian dispensation, far from nothing: we are children of God.) It is noteworthy that ↗Ignatius in the *Exercises* equates humility with obedience in his first degree: to prefer the will of God to anything in the world, even our life. The second is 'indifference' to all, provided God's purposes are forwarded. The third prefers the sole love of Jesus to all, even to our salvation, if that would be to God's glory. (*cf.* second week of *Exercises*).

↗Francis of Sales in the *Devout Life* (Bk. 3, ch. 4) exposes the vanity of his time. Vanity differs from pride in that it either takes pleasure in praise for qualities that are ours but are unworthy of notice; or delights in praise for qualities that in fact one does not possess. Among his examples are: our distinguished ancestry, the splendid horse we ride, fine clothes; our well-groomed hair, skill at dancing; our smattering of learning. Today we might have a list such as the following: we wish to be praised for the clubs we frequent, the people we claim to know, the expensive car we drive, our handicap at golf, the letters after our names; our coiffure, figure, wardrobe, the people we are seen with.

Soeur Thérèse in her *History of a Soul* defined humility as truth. This is only partially true. We may know the truth about ourselves and not like the look of it. ↗Thomas Aquinas more penetratingly put humility under the general heading of temperance. He saw that in man there are immensely strong drives, and among them the drive towards excellence, or as he puts it 'to excel'. These drives are part of the process of each man's becoming, since he starts not with ready-made qualities or virtues, but with the potentiality to become this or that. So, God placed in man, not only the sexual drive – which we hear so much about – but equally important this drive towards the development of one's potentialities. However, as in all man's activities, there is a flaw; we need balance, restraint, and that we do not naturally have. It too has to be acquired. This restraint of the urge to excel is understood by ↗Thomas to be humility (*S. Th.*, II, qq. 131, 132).

Humility for modern Western man is difficult to assimilate. He lives in a world of competition for position; in business, in politics, in the forces, in the professions. He is trained from childhood in self-assertion, in struggle for survival, for excellence. Ambition is a prime 'virtue', humility derided or mis-understood. Even some Christians think it means self-effacement, self-denigration, an acrobatic feat of pretending not to have gifts that in fact we do. How then can a Christian compete in the modern world and still be 'meek and humble of heart' (*cf.* Mt 11:29).

At a deep psychological and theological level Thomas grapples with this problem (he, the most intelligent man of his age, must have needed to clarify it for himself!); the references are: ambition (*S. Th.*, IIa, IIae, q. 132), humility (*ibid*, q. 161) and pride (*ibid,* q. 162). To summarize, with an eye on today, let the following suffice: he recognizes that man must be strenuous and aim high; to achieve excellence requires magnanimity. But to aim beyond one's capacities is pride, to restrain one's ambitions within one's powers humility. God has given us qualities, they should be used for the good of mankind; but we should not attribute them to ourselves, but to God. All we have that is completely our own is our failures. This provides food for a just estimate of ourselves. Yet it is part of our nature to want to excel, but this must not be done for vainglory, to hear people praise us. Yet, though their praise is of no intrinsic worth, it has a value, in that it makes us more able to do good, and we can turn it to God's glory. Thus a doctor, whose reputation is growing, can rightly be

happy since he can do more good, and he can say, '*non nobis Domine, non nobis, sed nomini tuo da gloriam*' (Ps 115:1). A politician who is arduously climbing the ladder, is well advised to hope that his fellows think well of him, not because their opinion is of intrinsic worth, but because he hopes to do more good. A priest may hope to be a bishop, not for the glory of the mitre (if that attracts him) but so that the area where he can do good is wider.

Ambition is not the desire for fame but the desire of it for the wrong reason or for a matter that deserves it not at all.

St Augustine, *The Confessions, passim.*

C. Butler, *Benedictine Monachism*, (London, 1924).

Thomas à Kempis, *The Imitation of Christ*, Bk. 1.

Lord Longford, *Humility*, (London, 1969).

A. Tanqueray, *The Spiritual Life*, (Westminster, Md., 1948).

W.B. Ullathorne, *The Groundwork of the Christian Virtues*, (London, 1882). In fact the book is entirely about Humility.

Huvelin, Abbé (*1838–1910*)

A justly renowned spiritual guide in Paris. In his youth he studied the Greek classics at the École Normale, but decided to become a priest rather than a professor. For seven years he was priest at St Eugène in Paris, then, from 1875 to his death in 1910, unpaid curate of the well-known church of St Augustin, also in Paris, where he would spend at certain seasons between twelve to fourteen hours in the confessional and towards the second half of his life receive visitors of all classes in his room between 2 and 5 p.m. Among his visitors and penitents were ↗Baron von Hugel, ↗Charles de Foucauld and Paul Claudel. He wrote little; as he said 'it is better to write on souls than on paper'. That was the Abbé Huvelin's own way. People were attracted to him not by his learning but by his holiness. He loved them all, sought which way God was leading them and shared their search. For many years he was immobilized by rheumatism and suffered intense pain.

Abbé Huvelin, *Some Spiritual Guides of the Seventeenth Century*, (London, 1927). Translation of notes taken during the conferences or talks he gave in the crypt of St Augustin. J. Leonard, CM, (tr.).

I

Icons and Images

An icon is a two-dimensional image of Christ, his blessed mother and his saints, usually a painting on wood, often covered except for head and hands with a silver surface. In the West images include statues, murals, etc. They serve in East and West much the same purpose, to excite devotion to those represented: Christ, Mary, the angels and saints. But in the East, as a result of the violent struggle during the Iconoclastic controversies (*circa* 727–843), a complex theology of the icon emerged. An image is part the same and part different from what it represents. If it were totally different, it would not represent at all; if entirely the same, it would be identical. As the icon is partly the same, it has something of the original in it; thus an icon of Christ has something of Christ in it and should therefore in itself be given special worship (not that of God, but of a holy thing). Consequently in the East we find prostrations, kissings, incensing and lights before them. The attack against them was stemmed temporarily at the Council of Nicaea (II) in 787, which was attended by Pope Hadrian I. It established the doctrine: 'By these images we understand those of Jesus Christ, of his immaculate Mother, of the holy angels and of all the holy persons. The more one looks at these images, the more will the spectator be reminded of the one who is represented, will try to imitate him, will feel himself drawn to show him respect and veneration, without however giving him divine honours that belong to God alone. But he will offer to the images, in sign of his veneration, incense and lights, as is done for images of the holy cross and for the holy Gospels' (Mansi xiii, 377–80).

The Orthodox Church has integrated the icon in a beautiful way into the liturgy and architecture of the Churches and into family life. While not having the power of, say, the Eucharist, icons are seen as channels of grace, since they lead to the very source of grace, namely God. The Council of Trent omits the words 'holy angels'. Images 'are to be retained especially in the churches and due honour and reverence given to them; not, however, that any divinity or virtue is believed to be in them by reason of which they are to be venerated, or that something is to be asked of them, or that trust is to be placed in images . . . but because the honour which is shown them is referred to the prototypes which they represent, so that by means of the images which we kiss and before which we uncover our heads and prostrate ourselves, we adore and venerate the saints whose likeness they bear.' (25th session, 1563; *cf.* K.

Rahner, *The Teaching of the Catholic Church*.) The Eastern Church has maintained a very lofty view of the place of the artist who paints the icon. He must put his prayer into his work; he must follow the tradition of the great icons which were painted in a manner symbolic of austerity, holiness and splendour, sharing in some way the austerity, holiness and splendour of the God-Man Christ and of his blessed Mother, the angels and saints. Mere naturalism or sensual beauty was eschewed as unworthy and inadequate for the making of icons. In the West dissolute men have even portrayed their paramours as the Blessed Virgin. A welcome return to a more symbolic representation should restore western icons to their holy origins.

K. Rahner (ed.), *The Teaching of the Catholic Church*, (Staten Island, N.Y., 1967).

D.T. Rice, *Russian Icons*, (Harmondsworth, 1947).

See also 'St John of the Cross', *Ascent* 3. chs. 35–7.

Ignatius of Loyola, St (*circa 1492– 1556*)

The chief source of the spirituality of the Counter-Reformation, one in which those born before Vatican II were immersed, requires special treatment. He was essentially a layman, a courtier, an active soldier, converted to Christ; and, as a Spaniard (Basque) of the *Reconquista*, filled with triumphant and chivalresque imagery. Converted, recovering from a broken leg at the siege of Pamplona, he read the *Lives of the Saints* by Voragino and the *Life of Christ* by Louis the Carthusian of Cologne, through which he was linked with the ↗*Devotio Moderna*. Then at Montserrat he encountered the *Ejercitario* of García de Cisneros, the faint model for his own *Exercises*. At Manresa he experienced high mystical prayer and wrote the first sketch of the *Spiritual Exercises*. Like ↗Francis he wanted above all to go convert the Moslems in the Holy Land. There only nineteen days, he returned to seek education with children, then he moved to the universities of Alcalá, Salamanca and Paris. He was now ready; and companions joined him, including ↗Francis Xavier. In Venice they encountered the Theatines tending the sick in hospital. In Rome they put themselves under the special protection of and as auxiliaries to the Holy See. Ignatius and his followers turned two ways, first to the turmoil in Europe where they combated heresy, and second to the new world of the West and old world of the Far East. The Church became once again mission-minded – other orders joined in, notably the Augustinian, Franciscans and Dominicans. But in Europe Ignatius's followers and others, with the Jesuits in the lead, fashioned a spirituality suited to the new times, and which still persists to this day, but visibly being transformed in its turn.

St Ignatius' special contribution was to establish a spiritual attitude of mind, exceedingly active: that of a soldier of Christ, an apostle, going forth to convert the whole world, to refute heretics, to bring all men to the standard of Christ; a spirituality ideally suited to an age and a Europe at the gateway of great discoveries and immense activity in every direction. At the same time, for these active souls, he established a way of prayer that would prevent activity dissipating the initial spiritual motive. The *Exercises* are the vital instrument in the Jesuit spirituality: meditation, particular examen, contemplation of the life of Jesus

Christ, the need for a spiritual director; the centrality of obedience; election-choice of Christ.

In passing: St Ignatius uses 'contemplation' in a sense peculiar to himself, i.e. to mean the imaginative representation of scenes of Christ's life. He had been put in prison by the Inquisition as a suspected *Alumbrado* (*cf.* ↗Illuminism), and consequently never described his own mystical experiences, and kept his teaching on prayer in the foothills of contemplation, and mostly on the plain of meditation. The emphasis on examining one's conscience and ↗obedience almost created the need for spiritual direction, to avoid scruples and help make life-decisions. The absolute obedience to the ↗ director was perhaps part of the absolutism of the times. Today there is some break away from so close a dependence. But as the ↗Charismatic renewal gathers force, it may become apparent that the spiritual director, or discerner of spirits, will be even more necessary, to prevent self-deception. The relationship between private inspiration and external authority will always be delicate, yet the authority of the Church should always have the last say together with conscience. But not all Church decisions are infallible; and the prophet has his place to speak in the Church – and also to be silent if so bidden.

The concentration on the historical life of Christ, which Ignatius inherited from the late Middle Ages, is being modified today by a greater attention to the Risen Christ.

The devotion to the papacy, so necessary at that time of disintegration, became almost an obsession in the Tridentine Church. We recognize better today the place of the bishops and the limits of papal authority and infallibility. This eases

consciences, as one may be committed to obey though not *always* to agree, except in cases of most solemn pronouncements.

Devotion to the Blessed Sacrament, which developed special features in the same period and was much encouraged by the Society of Jesus, with devotions such as Forty Hours, great Processions, Expositions etc., was not peculiar to them. Nevertheless, with the present Liturgical revival, much of that is seen as less central than full participation in the Mass.

J. Brodrick, SJ, *The Origin of the Jesuits*, (London, 1940).

L. Cognet, *Counter-Reformation Spirituality*, (London, 1959).

Obras completas de San Ignacio de Loyola, in *B.A.C.*, (Madrid, 1963).

Illuminism

Alumbrados formed groups of laity and religious living retired lives and claiming personal illumination from the Holy Spirit. It was a Spanish preoccupation of 16th and 17th centuries. Even a work of St Francis Borgia was put on the Index. It is possible that the origins of the movement were Muslim or Jewish, but the evidence is not adequate. As early as 1525 two trends show themselves; the '*recojidos*' (the recollected ones), and the '*dejados*' (self-abandoned); the former concentrated on a form of prayer, passive to all created things, even including the Incarnation, and concentration on God alone, in order to let God act on the soul. This could lead to Quietism, but it is doubtful whether it was itself heretical, though the Spanish Inquisition found occasion to condemn a number of notable saints, including Francis Borgia and John of Avila.

↗Teresa received immense help from both of these, and from the *Third Spiritual Alphabet*, by a holy Franciscan, Francisco de Osuna (d. 1527). He would have the soul ignore the senses, imagination, intellect and will, and turn lovingly to God alone. ↗Teresa of Avila does not follow him in by-passing the humanity of Christ.

The *recojidos* were mostly found among the religious; the *dejados* among the laity. The word '*alumbrados*' (illumined ones) applied to them all, as they emphasized illumination from God to the individual, provided the self-abandonment was complete enough. It was a time when the Church authorities felt there were altogether too many prophets; consequently the Inquisition suppressed these groups. The overall result was a shrinking of writings concerning the deeper regions of prayer. It is noteworthy that neither Luis of Granada nor ↗Luis of Leon ventured in their writing on this area, and this is a loss to the Church. Today, once again, the Spirit is speaking to people in their hearts. The Church authorities have two approaches, the one of condemnations, the other of guidance; but those who receive these Gifts of the Spirit must also co-operate. One of the signs of the genuineness of the Spirit is the humility and obedience of the recipient.

L. Cognet, *Post-Reformation Spirituality*, (London, 1959).

Illuminative Way
A spiritual condition occurring after a period of darkness, occurring in all periods. It is the second of three states, the first being the Purgative Way, the third the Unitive Way. The entrance into the illuminative way is

through the purification of the senses and the spirit (↗'John of the Cross' Active Dark Night; *The Ascent of Mount Carmel*, Bk. 1, chs. 1–13). The gateway beyond the illuminative way is the Passive Dark Night of the senses and of the spirit (*cf. The Ascent*, Bks. 2 and 3; and *The Dark Night*, Bk. 2). The word 'illuminative' signifies rather the experience than the dying to self that it entails. At this stage of prayer, the Spirit begins to illumine the soul through the ↗Gifts of intelligence and knowledge, not in any logical or verbal manner: insight is the best word. Likewise the prayer itself will be less wordy, rationalized, and become simpler – as ch. 8 of Romans says, the Spirit himself intercedes for us knowing better than we what to say (*cf.* vv. 26 & 27). The experience is of shafts of love, 'stirrings' as ↗ *The Cloud of Unknowing* describes them. Thus two sides emerge in this 'Way' – the negative or ascetical and the positive, or divine action. Has all this any relevance to the life of Christians in the world, whether priest or lay? Holiness is for all. Therefore – and especially today when the laity are being encouraged to commit themselves to Christ more and more – it is certain that God will respond to their generosity with like generosity, especially in prayer. The illuminative way will surely be experienced, only in a different way from that of the enclosed religious. Many laymen experience the aridity of faith, especially with their immersion in the materialistic world where they have to live. The truths of faith seem completely unreal even though they practise their religion with devotion. They hold on with a naked faith without any joy of the senses or of the spirit. At the same time their prayer becomes simplified, wordless; it is more an attitude of heart and mind, an acceptance of the divine will, however obscure that may be; and now and then, perhaps more frequently, the cloud disperses and the things of God make sense, or the things of earth do, in the light of faith. Then the cloud returns, but they have been strengthened. This surely is the illuminative way, only in a different setting. Should lay people become slack, praying little, becoming entangled in worldly objectives, careless about marriage loyalty, then the aridity is not a prelude to the Illuminative Way, but a form of ↗accidie and perilous.

The devout laity, not realizing that this is a trial and not a sin, imagine that these obscurities in faith, in some way, must be a fault, or the result of some fault in them. This could be so, if they were not living up to their ideals. But granted that they are dedicated and have compunction, this 'black-out' in faith is a blessing in disguise: light is on the way.

Imitating of Christ, the
Jesus himself encouraged us in the words: 'Learn of me who am meek and humble of heart' (Mt 11:29). When Philip asked Jesus: Show us the Father, Jesus answered: 'He who sees me sees the Father' (Jn 14:9). ↗Paul had no doubt: 'Imitate me as I imitate Christ' (1 Thess 1:6); and in Phil 2 he tells the Philippians to imitate the humility of Christ. Some saints have been eager to imitate him in minute detail: ↗Francis of Assisi in his poverty, ↗Charles de Foucauld in his manner of living, when he went to Bethlehem. Another word 'follow' shifts the meaning of imitate, that is, answering a call: 'Come follow me'. And: 'Take up your cross daily and follow me'. Francis and Charles perhaps were answering a very

special personal call – neither succeeded in having their followers live just as they lived. It had to be, rather, the spirit of their example that could be followed. So with Christ. Christians follow Christ, imitate him in his virtues: his humility, meekness, obedience, patience, compassion, prayerfulness, his faith as man, his hope, love, in his skill as teacher and healer of souls, his courage, chastity, prudence (note not all of these are Aristotelian categories).

This is a task of a life-time both as meditation and action. There is a deeper level at which imitation and following become subsumed into sharing his very life. We no longer are said to imitate but rather to share, for example, in his love for others, his patience, because *he lives in us.* 'Now not I live, as ↗Paul cried, but Christ lives in me' (Gal 2:20). This is the action of ↗Grace. Thus the Christian life is not so much a search as a following of a call from God, a ready acceptance of co-operation in the work and the very life of Christ himself.

See 'Imitation of Christ' in *D. Spir.*, Vol. 7, pt. 2, cols. 1536–62.

Imitation of Christ, the
This book appeared in manuscript in 1418. Endless controversy and immense scholarship have developed over it, very contrary to its own spirit, yet useful for those who read it. It is generally agreed that Thomas à Kempis compiled it out of four small books which again he had put together from his readings and own meditations; all this being much in character with the spirit of the Brethren of the Common Life to which he belonged and in the manner of the ↗*Devotio Moderna* of his time and of Gerhard ↗Groote. It is a

forest of quotations: over a thousand from Scripture, some from ↗Bernard, ↗William of St Thierry, ↗Gregory the Great and ↗Gerhard Groote. Book I is that which gave to the whole its name: *The Imitation of Christ*, being a lesson in the stripping of self and the acquiring of the humble virtues. Book II continues the thought of the first but directs the soul to approach God closely in prayers. Book III is full of the consolation that comes from listening to God, while Book IV is a colloquy between the soul and Christ in Holy Communion.

The spirit of the whole is uncompromising, not about religious activities, but about interior dispositions. It has in recent times seemed anti-intellectual and lacking in humanity. The intellectualism of à Kempis' day, against which he reacted, was the 'dead' end of scholasticism. Thomas à Kempis would reply to the accusation of inhumanity by saying that unless the Cross is accepted, no spiritual advance can be made. The test of the book's value is the number of saints that have used it including ↗Soeur Thérèse.

R.A. Knox and M. Oakley (trs.), *The Imitation of Christ*, (London, 1959).

See 'Imitation of Christ' in both *N.C.E.* and *D. Spir.*

Immanence

A key word and key idea in a spirituality that emphasized the presence of God *within* us. The word was first adopted by Thomas Cajetan, OP, (d. 1534) and by John of St Thomas (*circa* 1644), but as an idea it goes back to ancient cultures such as the Hindu and Greek, and was poetically described in 1 Kings 19:9 ff where Elijah is presented with all the old epiphanies of God – mighty wind, earthquake, fire, thunderbolt – but God is in none of these, only in the sound of a gentle breeze, symbol for something hidden and inward. Christ himself emphasizes the hiddenness of God's presence, 'the kingdom of God (i.e. God) is among/in you' (Lk 17:21). The idea of God being 'within' us is accentuated by the practice and contemplation of the Eucharist, by the image of the spring of water, welling up from within (Jn 4:14); and this is confirmed by ↗Paul's teaching: we are the temple of God, the body of Christ. Inversely, 'In him we live and move and have our being' (Acts 17:28).

↗Thomas Aquinas says that God is within us by his creative power, by his preserving us in being, by his knowledge and by his grace. (*S. Th.*, I, q. 8, art 3); we might add, God is present in us by his love (*cf.* also *loc. cit.* q. 43, art 3).

Far Eastern thought also concentrates on this immanence of God or the Absolute, particularly from the time of the writing of the Upanishads (*circa* 8th to 6th century BC), in which there is oscillation between an absolute unity between the atman (inward self) and Brahman (the absolute Transcendent) and a profound *union* yet a *distinction*, as in the Katha Upanishad: 'Of the measure of a thumb is (this) Person The Immortal Self, in the heart of creatures abiding ever. Stand firm! and from the body wrench him out,/Like pith extricated from a reed./Pure and immortal He. So, know Him!/So, know Him: pure and immortal He.'

The same ambiguity appears in the European thinking on the idea of the immanence of God. With Spinoza it evolves into pantheism, and with Hegel into an ideal monism. But with Blondel, the Catholic lay philosopher (1861–1949) and his *Action* (1893) and the *Letter* also by Blondel, though used in a much controverted sense for apologetics, the idea returns, making it familiar to Christians. ↗Teilhard de Chardin carried it a stage further with his theory of the immanence of Christ in the whole cosmos: every rock is in some way leading up to the fulfilment of the universe in Christ (*cf. The Phenomenon of Man, passim*). Among Protestant theologians, such as Tillich, 'the Ground of Being' recurs as a description of God, more suited to our demythologized minds. But it lacks the element of Person.

See ↗Indwelling.

Imperfections
A lapse from the perfect following of Christ but less than a sin. According to Proverbs, even the just man 'sins seven times a day' (Pr 24:16). Therefore the sooner one adapts to the situation the better. We could pretend we are not imperfect; that way madness lies; or recognize our imperfections but throw in the sponge; or live with them, almost cherish them, as ↗Francis of Sales used to write: 'mes chères imperfections'. Why? because they kept him and his penitents humble.

A sin is a fully voluntary act, turning towards a 'good' which is against our best interests, and therefore against God's will: excessive drink, lusting after another man's wife, excessive desire for money or honour. The less serious the deviation, the less serious is the sin; the greater the provocation from outside, again the less serious it is. An imperfection is not a turning towards a lesser good in place of God, but a not-full giving of ourselves to God in a particular situation, being half-hearted, or at least not full-hearted: making

sluggish movements of the will in prayer, yet prayer; an unenthusiastic welcome to a guest, yet a welcome; a not total dedication to work, yet work; a grudging forgiveness, yet forgiveness – these are not a turning away but a tepid response. They come from the root evil in us, both that aboriginal lack of integrity and our own past habits of sin. Spiritual writers have usually envisaged imperfections from the latter angle. It is better to judge them from the point of view of love and less love.

In this way it becomes clear, first that imperfections can be a major obstacle to the growth in holiness, since holiness is love and any act of love below the perfect drags the soul to that level, whereas perfect love reaches ever higher, and God, as it were, can respond accordingly. Secondly, this explains why it is good to confess one's minor sins and imperfections, partly for humility and truth's sake, partly for the grace to resist the lukewarmness of our hearts, and partly to keep ourselves aware that it is precisely these which set up barriers to the grace of God, and therefore growth in holiness.

Incarnation
The key text for the orthodox understanding or expression of the mystery, from the Council of Chalcedon (451) reads: 'We confess one and the same Christ, the Son, the Lord, the Only-Begotten, in two natures unconfused, unchangeable, undivided and inseparable. The difference of natures will never be abolished by their being united, but rather the properties of each remain unimpaired, both coming together in one person ...' (*cf.* K. Rahner [ed.], *The Teaching of the Catholic Church*, p. 154).

The early Church, e.g. ↗Ignatius of Antioch, emphasized the

humanity of Christ against Gnostics; the great Patristic age emphasized his divinity against Arians and others. The Middle Ages came back to a devotion to Christ's *humanity*. Today two trends are visible:

(i) An appreciation of the part played by the Incarnation in the whole salvation process especially the Risen Christ. We are not simply saved by God but through Christ. He is the new creation, the New Man. ↗Teilhard de Chardin has given us a heightened sense of the unity of all creation *in* Christ. The Scripture references are: the New Man, Eph 2:15; everything reunited in Christ, Eph 1:10, i.e. the whole universe; *cf.* Eph 4:10, by everything is meant the whole cosmos; *cf.* Col 1:19f, also Rom 8:19–22.

(ii) With the advent of biblical theology, many have become more aware of the limitations which Christ seems to have imposed upon his knowledge in his life on earth. The Scholastics evolved a theory that Jesus had the vision of God from the first moment of his conception. The extreme opposite view today would say: Christ, in order to be 'like us in all things but sin' would deny himself this knowledge. Others point out (Karl Rahner among them) that it is impossible for one person not to be aware of his own identity even in his human nature. But the extent to which he might allow this to play a part in his human conscious life remains mysterious. However we are given some indications in the New Testament. He grew in maturity (Lk 2:40) as a child. He professed ignorance several times: as to the time of the Second Coming: 'But as for that day and hour, nobody knows it, neither the angels of heaven, nor the Son' (Mt 24:36). He did not know who had touched the hem of his garment (Mk 5:30). So while existentially he was conscious

of his oneness in the Godhead, though not necessarily formulated in words, at the conscious, in-tellectualized human level many things could remain obscure, not 'known'. He could in a sense refuse to think about things that in the depths of his being even as a man, in the 'vision of God' he possessed but did not conceptualize. This explains the mysterious text in Phil 2 in which Christ is said to have emptied himself of his Godhead (v. 7) this cannot mean that he ceased to be God, rather than he voluntarily refused the glory of the Godhead, including the knowledge that naturally would be his as man united in the one Person of the Son of the Father. If this is true then our reading of the Gospels takes on a more 'real' aspect. Certain incidents become alive, which seemed unreal before, such as the temptations in the desert. Jesus allowed himself to 'discover' the right way of being the Messiah. The short cuts would have been overpowering miracles, to force belief; or by power, coming as a great king. The Jews expected both. But Christ took, in the desert, the way of the suffering Servant, which had been hinted at by the Father at his baptism, 'You are my beloved Son/Servant' (Mk 1:11). The fear of death, and the horrors that would accompany his, were not alleviated by the light of beatitude inundating his consciousness. He had to 'set his face' towards Jerusalem, that last time (Lk 9:51). The agony in the Garden was real, he was not bathed in celestial light but in a sweat that was like blood (Lk 22:44). There was a real struggle between the upper and the lower man, between the physical horror of the coming Passion and the determination to do his Father's will (Lk 22:41–4). The cry, 'My God, my God why have you forsaken me?' (Mk 15:34) was surely not a mere quotation from the Psalm (22:1), but the derelection of dying, and apparently being totally abandoned, thus sharing with the saints that supreme Dark Night in which only dark Faith survives, and the flickering flame of love which is conformity of will, but with no answer back. Is this compatible with an existential realization of his divine Self? It is difficult for us to understand how; but if he shut that off from the levels of intellectual realization, at those levels he could be desolate and alone.

Teilhard de Chardin, *The Divine Milieu*, (London and New York, 1960).

K. Rahner, *Theological Investigations*, Vol. 5, (London and New York, 1956), pp. 193–215.

K. Rahner and H. Vorgrimler (eds.), article 'Knowledge of Christ' in *A Concise Theological Dictionary*, (London and New York, 1965).

Indwelling
Derives from John (14:23): 'If any man loves me, he will keep my word, and my Father will love him, and we shall come and dwell with him.' This is 'immanence' but with a difference, due to revealed truth. Christians are certain that God is personal and that within the Godhead are Three Persons. Thus our relationship with God, as Christians, is assured as an interpersonal one.

God is not a Trinity only for Christians, but for all men, though they may not be aware of this. It is the awareness which is significant in the 'indwelling', but of such a kind and degree that we could not have conceived it possible, namely a Sonship (Jn 1:12), and truly so, for we read in 1 John (3:1): 'Think of the

love that the Father has lavished on us, by letting us be called God's children, *and that is what we are.*' ↗Peter puts it differently: 'We share in the divine nature' (2 Pet 1:4). This sharing makes our awareness of the transcendent God real; and it is promoted by the Holy Spirit (Jn 15:15) who will teach us all things; is our support, especially in prayer (Rom 8:26), but also in trials (Rom 8:13).

The imagery is changed from a 'home' to 'temple' (1 Cor 6:19), God lives in us as in a Temple; at other times it is we who live in God, e.g. John 14:2: 'There are many mansions in my Father's house.' ↗Teresa uses this imagery for *The Interior Castle*.

Prayer, in the light of this revelation, will be a humble adoration of the Holy Trinity whose life the Christian shares so intimately; a sharing of the love within the Trinity; a burning desire to be made worthy of this fellowship, of being co-heirs with Christ, members of God's household, sons and daughters. We are to be holy as God is holy, not in the same way – that would be impossible – but because he is holy, we should be so in our degree, and through the power of the Spirit. We also see in others the presence of the Holy Trinity.

Infused Contemplation
Used in contradistinction to 'acquired' contemplation – a modern pair of terms, not found in the classical writers. ↗John of the Cross uses 'active' and 'passive'. All Christian prayer is assisted by grace; all is a gift. But in acquired or active contemplation the human effort takes the forefront. In infused or passive contemplation, the Spirit acts upon the soul as a harpist on the harp, or as wind over water. But the word

'passive' does not mean dead, rather 'acted upon', so that it itself becomes active, yet in a new way. This is often called: attention, savouring, absorption.

Many different conditions and stages are included under this head – the sweetness described by ↗Bernard and the aridity of the passive Dark Nights by ↗John of the Cross; their common characteristic being that these experiences are not self-induced but are from the Spirit who overwhelms the soul. While ↗Teresa of Avila writes of joys, ↗John of the Cross, her contemporary, writes of the Nights, though not always; he knows a beyond.

These experiences do not occur in the discursive reasoning, nor in the surface level of the will, but as is frequently said, in the point of the spirit, the centre of the soul. The Spirit may stir the depths of the mind to know in an indescribable way, or the heart to love likewise. The senses remain outside this activity, sometimes straying, at others dormant. These activities at the centre of one's being may be transitory or more or less permanent.

Thomas Aquinas, *S. Th.*, IIa, IIae, q. 180 particularly art. 3 c.

John of the Cross, *Ascent* 1.1.2; *Dark Night*, 1.8; *The Flame*, Stanza 3.

Teresa of Avila, *Way of Perfection* ch. 31 and *passim*.

See also ↗Ways or Degrees of Prayer.

J

Jacopone da Todi (*circa 1230–circa 1306*)

Franciscan mystic and poet. Supposedly a successful lawyer, he married a noble lady, Vanna, but she was crushed to death by the collapse of a building, and he, rushing to her, found that under her lovely dress she wore a hair shirt. All this so disturbed his mind, reminding him of his great sinfulness, that he went 'mad for love of God' his Saviour, wandering the dusty roads of Umbria, distraught, singing his *Laude*, or religious songs that he composed himself. For ten years (1268–78) this continued until Franciscan Friars took him in. They were 'Spirituals', that is of the group determined to preserve the primitive ideal of Francis. When Pope Boniface VIII came to the see of Peter, Jacopone wrote against him. Promptly the poet was imprisoned, and though he wrote two poems to the Pope (which have survived) asking forgiveness, it was not until the following pontificate of Benedict XI that he was set free, *circa* 1303. In 1306 he died in a Poor Clare convent, having written his last poem to Mary, *Donna del Paradiso* (XCIII). In the Franciscan Order he has always been venerated as a Blessed and his name is in their martyrology.

His poetry is warm, almost fiery with its extreme pleas for austerity. Among the most famous of his poems are *La Santa Poverta* (LX), and the dialogue between the soul and the body (III). His espousing the teaching of Denis the Pseudo-Areopagite made him suspect in the 16th and 17th centuries. It is probably impossible to come to a sure judgement on his poetry because of the uncertainty as to which poems are authentically his.

Giovanni Ferri (ed.), *Le Laure*, Jacopone da Todi, (Bari, 1930). This second edition reproduces the first printed edition of Florence, 1490.

See 'Jacopone da Todi' in *O.D.C.C.*, *N.C.E.* and *D. Spir.*

Jansenism

At its birth, with the posthumous publication of *Augustinus* (1640), by Jansenius, Bishop of Cambrai, it was doubtless a well-intentioned movement of reform by Cornelius Jansenius (1585–1638) and Jean Duvergier de Hauranne, Abbé of St Cyran (1581–1643). They had been conspiring together at Bayonne for several years with the intent of a great reform of the Church, in the moral order and on the subject of grace. They judged that casuistry – in simple terms the effort by moralists to judge each case (*casus*) as leniently as possible within the framework of the canons – had gone so far in leniency as to be gravely lax. Likewise, these two reformers decided that the Church had strayed from St Augustine's teaching on grace, by allowing too much freedom to the human will. They were entering perilous seas, since the Society of Jesus, the most powerful Order of the day, was thus indirectly attacked. With the publication (1656–7) of the *Provincial Letters* of ↗Pascal, the attack was direct and very unfair – but this is beyond the scope of this Dictionary. Meanwhile Pope Innocent X had condemned five propositions (1653) which were said to be the teaching of the *Augustinus*. The Jansenists admitted that the five propositions were heretical but denied they expressed the mind of Jansenius or of his book. Jansenius was not there to defend himself, but the Party, led by Antoine, le Grand Arnauld (1612–94) and his sister the Abbess, Mère Angélique (1591–1661) of Port Royal, stood their ground. Port Royal was disbanded in 1709 and finally pulled down in 1710–3. But the sect lived on, a tragic object-lesson of the evil of division, of the *odium theologicum* and of the danger of zeal for renewal without obedience, which leads to schism; and of obedience without zeal, which leads to death. The quarrel embittered the religious life of France, until all was swept away by the French Revolution. The work of Pope Pius X (1835–1914) helped to restore the warmth and practice of normal Christian life, especially his Decree on Frequent Communion (1905).

Bremond, Vol. 4.

L. Cognet, 'Jansenism' in *N.C.E.*

R.A. Knox, *Enthusiasm*, (Oxford, 1950).

Jesus and Prayer

Jesus both prayed and taught how to pray. He prayed as a man to God his Father, both in a liturgical context and privately; going up to the great feasts of his people. He used the symbolism of the Jewish liturgy in his teaching: water, light, the Passover itself, transformed into the prayer of the Eucharist. In personal prayer he always spoke of God as Father (using an affectionate form, ↗Abba). He respected the holiness of the Temple. At crucial moments he prayed specially: before the beginning of his preaching, forty days; all night before choosing his apostles; through the night in the Garden before the Passion. To be free from the crowds he would slip away early into the silent hills to pray (Mk 6:46). The words he used: the Our ↗Father, the thanksgiving prayer (Mt 11:25 ff; Lk 10:21–2) are typical of Jewish blessings in form, i.e. the Divine name followed by an epithet, 'Lord of heaven and earth', and then mention of the reason for thanksgiving, that God has revealed himself to little ones. How close this prayer is to the Magnificat! It is a prayer of gratitude and abandonment to the Divine Will, as was also the prayer in the Garden. Here Jesus is a consolation to all his followers because he allows the natural struggle between his desire to live and his Father's providential arrangement that he should accept death to appear: 'Not my will, but thine be done' (Lk 22:42). The only resolution of man's problems is acceptance of the Divine Will, even if he cannot see the way ahead. On the cross Jesus prayed for his executioners, and at the end he gave that cry, 'My God, my God, why have you forsaken me?' (Mk 15:34). True, this comes from a psalm (22:1) but clearly too it is a cry of a man in agony, in the darkest night, a not-knowing in his human consciousness; thus he shared our Dark Nights, of faith, hope, no gleam of intelligibility, no glow of dawn. At the end there was peace. The long prayer at the Last Supper is of a different order, full of compassion for his chosen ones, and that longing for unity among them, such as exists always between him and his Father.

Jesus's teaching, which includes the Our Father, is first, that prayer should be praise and only then petition. We should pray always (Lk 18:1), but long prayers are useless (Mk 12:40), gabbling likewise. It should not be done for show but secretly in one's room (Mt 6:5–6). Prayer should be confident, 'Ask and you will receive' (Mt 7:7 ff). The importunate friend, the widow and the judge are examples of persistence in prayer (Lk 11:5–8; 18:1–8). We must pray as children to a loving Father (Mt 7:11).

Jesus and the Spiritual Life

Recognized as the teacher (Rabbi), so too the Buddha or Confucius; as the Example for men to follow, so too Socrates; Jesus is both, but more. For Christians his life, death and resurrection have not only an exemplary relationship with us, they are the *cause* of our salvation, the means by which we can live a spiritual life – the life of the Spirit. He does not merely show the way, and then leave the stage; he *is* the Way. He not merely tells us what is true; his very life and death and resurrection are the truth, and our being one with him also. He does not merely tell us about the true life; he is that Life. This was clear to the early Christians (*cf.* ↗Humanity of Christ). Later generations tended to concentrate now on this now on that aspect of Jesus. An extreme Protestantism today would declare that we cannot know the historical Jesus. Catholic theology that is close to the Bible has returned to an ancient biblical insight, of recognizing that it is the Christ who is alive today who is our life, that faith is faith in him as Lord and Saviour. We therefore go with him and through him as Man to the Father, and worship him also as God. 'With Christ I hang upon the cross, and yet I am alive, or rather, not I, but Christ who lives within me' (Gal 2:19–20).

That being said, nevertheless Jesus is the Exemplar for his followers, because he is perfect and perfectly man. If it be accepted that Phil 2 refers to Jesus' determination not to let his Godhead, as it were, interfere with the full natural activity of his human nature (*cf.* ↗Humanity of Christ), then we can even say that he had, in some sense as man, the theological virtues not only of charity but also of faith and hope, also all the other virtues. Certainly he appears to be exercising to the ultimate the virtues of faith and hope in the darkness that came over him on the cross. He prayed with hope at the Last Supper that his Church would always remain one. Outstanding is his hope in all mankind, i.e. that God would have mercy on us all. Of course his love is never in doubt; he came out of love, he died from love, to provoke us to love in return. Then we have telling examples of other virtues in his life. Once he told us to imitate him: 'Learn of me; for I am meek and humble of heart' (Mt 11:29). With people he was generally gentle and compassionate; but with the insincere he was straight and unflinching. His courage was supreme. In all these ways and many others, we should follow him. But once again there is more to it than that, we actually share his *life* and share his very virtues, '*I am* the Way'.

Jesus is also the teacher; as to the nature of God, not only in word but in act, since he is God working through a human nature: 'He who sees me, sees the Father' (Jn 14:9). Therefore to contemplate Jesus is to contemplate God through his actions. By word and action he taught us the central mystery of man's salvation. His life, death and resurrection are our salvation; this truth is inextricably interwoven in his life. In that sense he is that truth. Three times before the Passion he told how he had to suffer. It was ↗Paul who expounded the mystery (specially in the Letter to the Ephesians). Man must live spiritually by this mystery, realizing that salvation is a new start with Christ. We are the New Man, and made one with him, by baptism and the Eucharist. It is through these that we receive the Spirit (*pneuma*), the Life of Christ, which is the Life of God.

To share in the life of Jesus is central to Christian living. ↗Paul remembered how the voice had said: 'Why do you persecute *me*, that is Christ *in* his members.' Christians remember the account of the Last

Judgement: 'If you gave it to the least of my little ones, you gave it to me' (Mt 25:31 ff). The Church is seen as the Body of Christ; and it is a praying community, with Christ, in him and to him (as God). Thus we must say with him that he '*is* the·Life'.

↗John's Gospel only confirms this. Like Nicodemus, the Christian must be born again (Jn 3:3); with the Samaritan woman (Jn 4:13), they must drink the living water (life); unless we eat his flesh and drink his blood, we will not have life in us (Jn 6:53): that is the God-life; Christ is the vine, his followers receive his life by being the branches (Jn 15:1 ff). The Christian life is sharing Jesus' life. This life was a child-life, a private life, a prayerful life; a public life, doing his Father's will; also a death accepted in obedience. He neither spared himself the humility of a human birth nor the humiliation of a human and inhuman death.

At the same time, though completely man, he was and is God. Thus he is the bridge between creation and the Creator. Man's aim is to return to the Father, and it is done through Christ. We must make that initial act of faith, going out of self into the world of Hope, which says: 'Jesus is Lord and Saviour' (2 Pet 1:11).

Jesus Prayer
The usual forms are 'Lord Jesus, Son of the Father, have mercy on me', or 'Lord Jesus have mercy on me', or simply the name 'Jesus'. Its origins are lost in antiquity; today it is much used, not only by the monks of Mount ↗Athos, but all over the Christian world. Though it may have originated on Mount Sinai, the first certain reference is in *The Ladder* of ↗John Climacus (d. *circa* 649) 'Let the memory of Jesus be joined to your breathing and then you will

know the usefulness of repose in God (↗hesychia)' (*P.G.* t. 88 col. 1112 c, quoted in *H.C.S.*, Vol. 2, ch. 'Byzantine Spirituality', *passim*).

Here for the first time are brought together the name Jesus, breath and hesychia. In the *Centuries* or sayings attributed to Hesychius of Jerusalem (but from Mount Sinai), is the continuous saying of the prayer all day, fulfilling the divine command and the interior illumination, which guarantees the living presence of Christ within. Nicephorus, monk of Mount Athos (mid-14th century), is the chief systematizer of the Jesus Prayer, through whom it spread throughout the Orthodox Churches. The outline of the method is:

Retire to your cell, become recollected, sit down, let your head fall forward over the chest, look at (your navel) the middle of your stomach, expel breath, make a strong effort to 'find the place of the heart', to imagine its shape, at the same time repeating the 'epiclesis of Jesus' (*cf. H.C.S.*, *loc. cit.*). At first there is only discomfort, obscurity, but some kind of light appears. It is supposed that the Jesus prayer gradually takes the place of psalmody, and in time a condition of 'theoria' is achieved. This we can do of ourselves – so the teaching says – then Christ will come and God will aid us.

Some have thought that the *method* – *technique* – has affinities with Indian Chakras technique, which may have influenced some Greek Fathers – i.e. the combination of breath control and the repetition of a series of words; for example, ↗Evagrius of Pontus, ↗Gregory of Nyssa and Macarius of Egypt, also Theodoret of Cyr (*cf. N.R.E.* 7:971). There is nothing to prevent Christians from learning physical techniques for praying from other religions.

The effect of this prayer, the light, has been the source of much controversy (*cf.* ↗Hesychia and ↗Gregory Palamas). Today the theological tensions have relaxed. The prayer has degrees: first the word – Jesus – then its meaning, and after a long period the meaning becomes a living reality in the soul.

Anon., *The Way of the Pilgrim*, (London, 1973).

G.E.H. Palmer (ed.), *Philokalia*, (London, 1962).

John Climacus, St (*circa 570–649*)
Monk and later abbot of the monastery on Mount Sinai. He wrote *The Ladder* (Gk *klimax*) hence the name. It describes thirty steps on the ladder to holiness for a monk, corresponding to the thirty years of Christ's life before his public career. Each step represents a virtue or vice. Step thirty is faith, hope and charity. The work influenced ascetical writers both in East and West. The ↗Jesus Prayer is clearly described for the first time.

John Climacus, L. Moore (tr.), M. Heppell (intro.), *Ladder of Divine Ascent*, (London, 1959).

John of the Cross, St (*1542–91*)
Born at Fontiveros (Castile), and died at Ubeda in the deep south. He was a Castilian and one of the glories of the Golden Age of Spanish literature, an exact contemporary of ↗Teresa, ↗Luis of Leon, Luis of Granada, Cervantes and the rest. Poet of genius, acute theologian in the scholastic mould, saint and mystic of the highest order, he had a rare combination of qualities. In his close friendship with ↗Teresa she tempered his extreme asceticism and

he her ecstatic transport. Between them they renewed the Carmelite Order, restoring its austerity, its silence, its spirit of prayer and return to the eremitical ideal. For his reforming ideals he was imprisoned in a disused toilet for eight months by his unreformed brethren. During this period, with astonishing serenity, he composed most of the poem *The Spiritual Canticle*, probably *The Dark Night* and several other poems. He did not disdain to use the beautiful Renaissance rhythms of Garcilaso and Boscán, or to take a love poem and *vuelto a lo divino* (turned to divine purposes) transpose its meaning (*Un Pastorcico*). Later, for Carmelite nuns, he wrote commentaries on the poem *En una noche escura, On a Dark Night*, on the *Spiritual Canticle*, on *The Living Flame of Love*. The book *The Ascent of Mount Carmel* refers to the transition from the stage of 'beginner' to that of 'proficient'. The book *The Dark Night* refers chiefly to that second main stage in the life of prayer as it leads from 'proficient' or early stages of passive prayer to the summit, or unitive way. These two books form a whole. But even here he did not complete his commentary on the poem. The commentary on *The Spiritual Canticle* is concerned with the ↗unitive way. The story of the manuscripts is confusing, and the scholars are not yet agreed as to their relationship, as there are two somewhat different versions of the poem. The manuscript of Jaen is generally being accepted as the final revision by ↗John of the Cross himself (*cf. Vida y Obras* in *B.A.C.* p. 696).

It may surprise some readers to find that the two major prose works, *The Ascent* and *The Dark Night* are mostly concerned with the ↗purgations, first the active purgation of the senses and the spirit, then the passive purgation of the same. But ↗John's

doctrine is that of ↗*nada* or nothing in order that we may gain *all*, namely God. Nothing should take the place of God, whether it be sentiment, or the highest vision; God is beyond everything. However it must always be borne in mind that he was writing for Carmelite nuns of the reform. If all Christians in different walks of life were to follow to the letter his practical advice on abnegation, it could lead to exhaustion and tedium; therefore he must be read with discrimination.

↗Francis of Sales reaches the same heights but by a more humane method, though it too is surprisingly austere if fully carried out. As L. Cognet points out, ↗John gives no references whatever apart from the Bible. It is certain however that he knew a work entitled ↗*Opera Tauleri*, therefore indirectly ↗Eckhart; he had read ↗Catherine of Genoa; was well acquainted with the Pseudo-↗Denis, ↗Thomas ↗Bonaventure, etc. There seem to be echoes of the English medieval mystics but nothing can be proved (*cf.* Cognet's reference to J. Orcibal, *Jean de la Croix et les mystiques rheno-flamande*, Paris, 1966).

↗John, despite his doctrine of the *nada*, delighted in nature, as can be seen from his poems, and from his life; he would seek solitude in the mountains; the stars sent him off into a whole night's ecstasy at Segovia. He loved ↗Teresa, and wrote to a Prioress, 'where love is not, put love and you will draw love out'.

A Benedictine of Stanbrook Abbey, *The Medieval Mystical Tradition and St John of the Cross*, (1954).

P. Crisólogo, ODC, 'Vida y Obras de San Juan de la Cruz' in *B.A.C.*, 7th (revised) edition published in Madrid (1973). Excellent.

Bruno de Jesus Marie, *St John of the*

Cross, (London, 1932). A good English-language life.

E.A. Peers, *Studies of the Spanish Mystics,* Vol. 1, (London, 1951).

E.A. Peers (tr.), *The Complete Works of St John of the Cross.* 3 vols. in one. The revised edition (London, 1953) is the most accurate in English.

See ↗Night, ↗Illuminative Way, ↗Unitive Way, ↗Nada.

See also, for further bibliographical material, *O.D.C.C.*

John the Evangelist, St

His Gospel and First Epistle shows over and over again, with great simplicity and great profundity, that Jesus and his message are inseparable, indeed that Jesus is the message. The synoptics do not deny the centrality of Jesus in the spiritual life; it is they who record the institution of the Eucharist, which is the means to union with God through the body and blood of Christ. But they concentrate on his words and deeds, while John concentrates on Jesus as the Light and our Life: (*cf.* 1:12) those who welcome Christ will become children of God, by a special birth. This is repeated (ch. 3) where Nicodemus is told he has to be born again, of water and the Spirit. The Samaritan woman (ch. 4) is told that Christ gives living water – this is a symbol of the Life of the Spirit. Then (ch. 6) the great mystery is revealed; that this new life *is* his own life and it is received through the Eucharist. In John's Gospel, Jesus, we find, *is* also the Way and the Truth and the Life. It is absolutely clear that the message is inseparable from the Messenger. It follows that belief in him is the first step forward. He is the Light of the world, that is the Truth revealed by God; and men must follow that Light

(12:44 ff). But this new life does not excuse the follower from action: 'If you love me, keep my commandments' (14:15). Yet another image is given (ch. 15): that of the vine and the branches, all sharing the same life. Finally Jesus gives the promise at the Last Supper that he will send the Spirit of the Father, his Life, to remain with them for all time (*cf.* especially 16:7–16). The first Epistle confirms the Gospel. God is love, and the Christian must live by that love, in this way God's life which is love will be in him, and he in God (4:16). But now the emphasis is on loving one another. As God has shown such love for us, we must show love for one another; an idea already expressed in the Gospel: his command is that we should love one another (15:12).

W. Grossouw, *Revelation and Redemption, an Introduction to the Theology of St John,* (London, 1966).

John of St Thomas (*1589–1644*)

A profound theologian, probably Portuguese. He became a Dominican, professor at Alcalá; at one time he was confessor to Philip IV of Spain. His notable work is *The Gifts of the Holy Spirit.* His importance lies in his theological analysis of the truth that the soul in grace is in the presence of God, and the mystical experiences that occur must be understood as following from this fact. The work, *La structure de l' âme et l'expérience mystique,* by a modern Dominican theologian, P. Gardeil, OP, is based on the writings of John of St Thomas.

John of St Thomas, D. Hughes, OP, (ed. and tr. and notes), *The Gifts of the Holy Ghost,* (London, 1951).

Julian of Norwich

Born (*circa* 1342–4) though still alive in 1413, she was dead by 1423. She was possibly a Benedictine nun of Carrow Priory who became a recluse by the church of Julian of Norwich, which belonged to that Priory, or she may have been a lay woman to whom the Priory gave the place. There at the age of 30 she had her fifteen 'shewings' all on one day and the sixteenth on the following. For twenty years she pondered on these divine revelations and then wrote her still famous book *Sixteen Revelations of Divine Love* in homely, lively, practical, imaginative language, full of wisdom and insight, profoundly centred on Jesus whom she calls Mother. The main theme is an understanding of sin and sorrow in the world, in the light of God's infinite love. The answer is in the phrase: 'All will be well, all manner of things will be well.' She is one of the few mystics to write of the Motherhood of God (ch. 58). She wished to be as submissive to the Church as a child to her parents. God is in every creature yet distinct. We find God in all creatures. Fifteen years after her revelations, her 'shewings', she asked God to explain all. The reply was: 'Would you learn your Lord's meaning in this thing? Learn it well. Love was his meaning who shewed it to you. What did he shew you? Love. Wherefore did he shew it? For Love. Hold firm therein and then you will learn and know more in the same. But you will never know or learn therein any other thing without end' (ch. 86, slightly modernized). We may pray to the saints, but, 'We may ask of our lover (God) all that we will' (ch. 6).

A.M. Allchin and others, *Julian of Norwich: Four Studies*, (Oxford, 1973).

Julian of Norwich, J. Leclercq, DOM,

(tr.), *Shewings*. From the critical text with an introduction by E. Colledge, OSA, and J. Walsh, SJ. (New York, 1978).

P. Molinare, *The Teaching of a Fourteenth Century English Mystic*, (1958).

J. Walsh, SJ, (tr.), *The Revelations of Divine Love*, (London and New York, 1961).

K

Karma

In general, for Hindus and Buddhists, it is the weight or effect of one's own past deeds, good or bad, 'inherited' from one's past existences, especially the accumulated effect of wrong action. 'Whatever deeds a man may do, be they delightful, be they bad, they make a heritage for him; deeds do not vanish without trace', (from the Sanskrit *Dharmapada*, ch. on Karma, in E. Conze, *Buddhist Scriptures*, Harmondsworth, 1959, p. 83). Man can free himself from this burden by good actions; no one else can do it for him, so they teach.

Kempe, Margery (*circa 1373–circa 1433*)

Wife and mystic. Her father was Mayor of Lynn (Norfolk), her husband a burgess. She had fourteen children. For a time she went out of her mind; after visions she had a conversion with an intense sense of the love that Christ had shown in dying for our sins. This sent her into paroxysms of weeping and crying out, which happened often, naturally enough, when a priest was preaching on the Passion from the pulpit. Thus she became a public nuisance and was almost forced to leave Lynn. Then began her pilgrimages, first to Canterbury where she rebuked the bishop, as well as the Bishop of Lincoln, then to the Holy Land, Compostela, Scandinavia and Rome. Everywhere her crying and weeping disturbed the peace of the congregations. Finally she was persuaded to recount her life, which she did simply, admitting her early vanities: wanting to look the fine lady, being extravagant in dresses, but also telling of her communing with Jesus as though with a husband – she gives surprisingly down-to-earth comparisons in her Bridal spirituality. Yet she was well acquainted with the spiritual writers of her time including the works of Hilton. She once visited Julian of Norwich for counsel.

She is scarcely imitable except in her trust in her Lord, Jesus, her genuine experience of God's love. This possibly was too much for her self-control in view of her bout of madness, and resulted in un-controlled 'boisterous' weeping and crying.

Until 1936 the *Book of Margery Kempe* was not known to have survived. It was then for the first time published by its owner, W. Butler-Bowden, (London, 1936).

M.D. Knowles, osb, *The English Mystical Tradition*, (London, 1961).

H. Thurston, sj, *Surprising Mystics*, (London, 1955), pp. 27–37.

J. Walsh, sj, *Pre-Reformation English Spirituality*, (London, 1960).

Kiss of God

Symbolism, found for instance in the writing of ↗Teresa of Avila, to describe a form of close union between the soul and God himself, likened to that of two lovers, who express union with a kiss. The symbol goes back at least to the *Song of Songs* (1:1): 'Let him kiss me with the kisses of his mouth.' The sign of the kiss is ambivalent: pointing towards sexual intercourse, or representing spiritual love between parent and child, or between friends. As ↗Teresa wrote 'Who would dare, my king, to use these words, if it were not by your permission' (*Meditations on the Song of Songs*, (1:11), and: 'The kiss is the sign of peace and great friendship between two people' (*ibid*).)

William of St Thierry, M. Columba Hart, osb, (tr.), *Exposition of the Song of Songs*, (Shannon, 1970).

Koan

In ↗Zen schools of Buddhism, the name for those enigmatic, apparently pointless, irrational sayings made by the master to his disciple, whose very irrationality shocks the latter into a deeper mode of knowing, and so leads to ↗*satori* – or enlightenment. At first the koan seems senseless, but with puzzling over – not reasoning – the disciple acquires a new, wider, deeper dimension. A purpose of a koan is to stop the intellect reasoning. But a koan also has a hidden sense which only becomes clear with satori. A famous koan is: 'Who is the Buddha?' – answer, 'Three chin of flax'. According to some Christian writers the New Testament has a number of Christian koans, e.g. the crucified God; one God, three Persons; to save one's life, one must lose it. A Christian would endorse the Zen principle that a human being must be ready to go beyond reason to reach the Ultimate Reality, and would add that the reaching it would be the act of God, as in for example the 'unknowing' of ↗*The Cloud of Unknowing*.

L

Laity

The New Testament was mostly written for these, the People of God. It is hard to see how the Ancient World was converted to Christ except by the action of the laity, who by their example fired others to accept Christ and often the cross of martyrdom.

As time went on the clergy 'took over' and the laity tended to be more passive than active, though of course by no means always. We forget perhaps that the vast monastic movements of the 4th to the 12th century were lay rather than clerical. St ↗Benedict was cautious about priests. St ↗Francis of Assisi remained a layman. The Cistercians brought the lay brothers to the fore again. It was the Reformation which truly broke through the clericalized mesh – no doubt to excess, but it was ↗Luther and Calvin specially who reminded us all that the People of God share in the triple office of Christ, as Priest, Prophet and King. ↗Newman gently reintroduced it into the Catholic blood-stream and in Vatican II it has come to stay.

Since the documents of Vatican II, the place of the laity in the life of the Church and the dimensions of their own spirituality have been enormously extended. (The relevant documents are the Dogmatic Constitution on the Church, the Constitution on the Sacred Liturgy, the Decree on the Apostolate of the Laity, and the Pastoral Constitution on the Church in the Modern World.) While these documents take for granted the need for self-improvement in the Christian sense, they see the baptized laity as sharing in the missionary thrust of the Church, as of their very nature. From the fact of their baptism they share in the priesthood, the

prophetic character and the kingship of Christ. The laity are called to holiness, they are not second-class citizens of the kingdom of God. Their holiness is: to take part in the work of Christ, in bringing the mystery of Christ to the world, *in* which they live out their lives. One of the characteristics of the laity is that their life as Christians is enveloped in the world, the non-Christian world around them. It is not the intention of the Church today to protect them by encouraging a ghetto mentality, but to make them seize the opportunity to transform the world, by the power of the Holy Spirit, all in their own areas of work: as worker, business man or woman, lawyer, doctor, politician, journalist, artist; and not least in family life. The same themes occur in the New Canon Law.

Thus, by sharing the prophetic character of Christ, they bear witness to his teaching, not only in word but by their lives and possibly by dying for it. There is a right order in the life of the world, an order of justice and charity, which is so often broken. The laity, who form part of that order or disorder, are there precisely to help restore the right order. In this work they share also in the kingship of Christ, whose right order it is. If men would keep his commandments, then peace would be restored in the world, in industrial disputes, in political ones. The laity also offer their spiritual sacrifices to the Father, and they offer themselves at Mass with the priest, and offer Christ as the Victim. Not that they claim to share in the hierarchical priesthood, rather they share in the priesthood of all the faithful; and this is Christ's own. They cannot bring Christ on the altar; nor be the ritual priest but they are the Church and as such they too offer Christ and themselves united to him, as a perfect sacrifice. (*cf.* ↗Lay Spirituality).

Law

The authoritative statement of the rights and duties of those within a sovereign State. Canon law is the Church's statement concerning the People of God in their lives as Christians. Law therefore plays a wide and intimate part in the lives of ordinary people. Laws, if made at the whim of the ruler, are tyranny. Laws must be grounded on justice. Justice rests on what it is reasonable to do. What is reasonable, for a Christian, is what is in accord with human nature and the designs of God as known by Revelation. Therefore law is closely associated with religion. In the Old Testament 'The Law' became so important that to keep it was to be saved. It was the very expression of God's wisdom. Christ in the New Testament kept the law but rejected the burdensome additions of the Rabbis. Further he rejected the idea that men could save themselves by keeping the law. Salvation was a gift of God through his Messiah. ↗Paul expanded this, especially in the Epistle to the Romans (*cf.* chs. 6 and 9). The details of the law were for the Jews a sign of sin; the Christian Church was to be free of them. What then is the place of law in Christian spirituality? ↗Thomas Aquinas distinguished between the 'Eternal Law' which approximates to God's Providence, and Christians lovingly finding it in their life, even in its sorrows; and 'Divine Law' which is the mind of God as expressed in Revelation and applicable to human living, e.g. the Ten Commandments, and Christ's own two: to love God and our neighbours as ourselves. Then there is the 'Natural Law', so much attacked by the early Protestants, and which was for ↗Thomas Aquinas the basic principles by which men live: to seek good and to avoid evil, from which all the rest derive. We must accept the way God has made us, and to diverge from that plan in any notable area is a breaking of the Natural Law, which itself derives from the Eternal Law. However, we are not saved by the minute keeping of the law, much as we must keep it; but by the mercy of God who makes it possible for us to keep that Law of Love, which Jesus taught us. Love and law are not contrary. We can want others to have their rights, from love of them. It is probable that without love, law would both be administered selfishly and even the law itself not be laid down for the benefit of the humble. Further, love can go beyond law, and give to the weak even more than they can claim. The law Christ gave was to love one another (*cf.* 1 John, *passim*).

B. Häring, *Free and Faithful to Christ*, Vols I, II. (New York and Slough, 1978, 1979.)

Thomas Aquinas, *S. Th.*, I, qq. 90–108.

See also ↗Legalism, ↗Obedience, ↗Providence, ↗Abandonment.

Lawrence of the Resurrection, Bro (*circa 1605–91*)

He was born in Lorraine and died in Paris, a Discalced Carmelite lay-brother, who had served eighteen years in the army, then thirty years as cook to the friars, and who finally went blind. He published nothing, though he wrote some notes and a few letters. These were gathered together in two books after his death by Joseph de Beaufort, Vicar General of the diocese of Paris, which were published in 1692 and 1694. These are best known, in English, as the single volume *The Practice of the Presence of God*. Its spirituality is the quintessence of that 17th century spirituality of the presence of God and abandonment to the Divine Will, but in simple language; a spirituality familiar to us in ↗*Francis of Sales* and others; the work has little or nothing on liturgy or the Sacraments.

D. Attwater (tr.), *The Practice of the Presence of God*, (Springfield, Ill., and London, 1977).

Lay Movements, Modern
The oldest is the monastic movement to the Egyptian desert, but that finally became an Order and even clericalized. The oldest modern lay movement is perhaps the *Society of St Vincent de Paul*, not founded by him but inspired by him; Frédéric Ozanam (d. 1853) was its originator. It still retains its vitality, with its limited aim of helping the poor not primarily with money but with compassion and advice. Among the oldest of this century are the Legion of Mary – spread from Ireland as far as China – itself an offspring of the S.V.P., with its regular structured religious meetings, its concern for the poor and those in spiritual trouble.

From Belgium came the *Young Christian Workers* (*YCW*) and parallel groups for students, farmers, etc., founded by Canon (later Cardinal) Cardijn. Its aim was to save the young from the corrupting influence of a pagan milieu, but also to turn the young themselves into apostles of their fellows. Like must help like. He saw work as part of the holiness of the worker. The *Opus Dei* founded in Spain by Jose María Escrivá brought this principle to a fine point, following in the wake of the theology of St Francis of Sales. Your work is your spirituality, it is your prayer. Not that 'straight' prayer is unnecessary – far from it – but work is prayer too, because it is fulfilling with our whole being, mind, heart and body, the will of God. Thus the apostolate of work follows naturally to seek excellence in one's trade or profession, in order to bring Christ into the very structure of human society.

These are all thoroughly immersed in the world, but also in varying degrees share in the spirituality of religious life, by vows or promises and hierarchic organization, even having their own priests (in the case of the *Opus Dei*). But their aim is to remain *lay*.

Another, more difficult to categorize, is the *Society of the Little Brothers and Sisters of Jesus*, founded in the spirit of Charles de ↗Foucauld, (d. 1916). They live with the very poor, share their work, become one of them, and yet they have the equivalent of vows and in fact live a contemplative life right in the world. They never preach; it is their lives that speak. On the other hand, also a very recent arrival, the Focolari, begun by three young girls from Trent (Italy) is completely lay and its message is: 'where two or three are gathered together in my name, there am I in their midst', and 'Love one another as I have loved you'. They really mean it.

Appearing over the horizon are those '*basic communities*' that have sprung up in many parts of the world, more especially in the Third World of South America and Africa, made up of small groups of lay people in this village or that, who for lack of a priest between them do all that they can to build up the kingdom in their small surroundings: one is leader, others visit the sick, administer communion, care for the lonely, catechize the young and those to be baptized, prepare couples for marriage. Here indeed is a flowering of Vatican II.

Lay Spirituality

The way the laity apply the teachings of Christ to their own life-settings. All this was deeply studied and preached by the Rhineland Dominicans, ↗Eckhart, ↗Tauler and Suso, and at about the same time by the group known as the school of ↗*Devotio Moderna*. These were followed by the Spaniards, particularly Juan Luis Vives, ↗Luis de León and ↗Luis de Granada, and contemporaneously by Thomas ↗More and ↗Erasmus. Then came ↗Ignatius of Loyola and his disciples, then pre-eminently and with great discernment, ↗Francis of Sales; and now the second Vatican Council.

The principles of the spiritual life are changeless but the circumstances in which they are applied vary, as does the emphasis given to this or that aspect of the whole. Not *whether* the laity should pray is in question, but *how*? Not whether they should perform good works or not, but which and when? The temptations against faith and hope and love are as strong in the world as in the cloister but of a different kind. The dark nights will come from the overwhelming proximity of the world and its clamours and vanities, from the apparent lack of divine providence in such a setting. There is no holiness without sorrow, self-denial, abnegation. In the world, they are ready-made; there is no need to invent them, they are all the harder to bear and understand; the nagging wife, the ruthless, selfish husband, the rebellious child, the loss of wealth or standing in men's eyes, all are as good 'crosses' as hair shirts, fasts and disciplines; to say

nothing of the great struggle to bring Christian principles to bear upon life in the world, as Vatican II says is the laity's task.

Time for prayer will be circumscribed by the complexities and unpredictability of life; it will be snatched in buses, trains, queues; but also in the very stuff of life – the daily chores, the disappointments as well as the loves, fears, pains – all part of the loving guidance and care of God. Words are often unnecessary; it suffices to *see* the meaning and accept, grasp and love the divine will discovered in every nook and cranny of life.

The basic means of grace remain the same for all: baptism and the Eucharist, the sacraments of Confirmation, Reconciliation, Marriage and Anointing. They create and build up and restore the life of Christ in the soul; they open the heart to the action of the Holy Spirit; then the holy Scriptures, messages from God, the story of the saving of us all.

See ↗Abandonment, ↗Prayer, ↗Marriage, ↗Lay Movements, ↗Laity.

Lectio Divina

'Divine Reading' is the ancient and medieval term in most monastic circles for meditative pondering, 'chewing' or masticating, assimilating the text of Sacred Scripture, the opposite of speed reading. Normally the reading would be aloud with the object of learning by heart, so as to continue the assimilation during the day. Other religious books also might be read in the same way – St Augustine's commentary on the Psalms or St Bernard's on the *Song of Songs*, which themselves resemble *lectio divina*. Modern reading has as object information or recreation; *lectio divina*'s purpose is to provide fuel for the mind and heart to raise the soul to God in contemplation. To make sure that the reading of Scripture does not lose its meditative aim, it is a practice to devote part of the day specifically to meditation, from half an hour to two hours in the day.

J. Leclercq, OSB, *The Love of Learning and the Desire for God*, (London, 1974).

D. Rees *et al. Consider Your Call, A Theology of Monastic Life Today*, (London, 1978).

Legalism
In the spiritual context, an exaggerated adherence to the letter of the law, human or ecclesiastical, which attempts to express the mind of God in particular circumstances. The principles do not change but the circumstances do. The legalistic mind finds it impossible to accept this, clinging to the letter of the law, failing to grasp the reason for the law and for the change. Christ said that the Sabbath was made for man, not man for the Sabbath (Mk 2:27).

Legalism creeps in also when what is done is done not for love but simply because it is the law. Note also the Pharisaic type of legalism, in which it is supposed that keeping the law saves (Lk 18:9–14), when we are saved by the mercy of God.

Soeur Thérèse promoted the practice of 'the little way', namely doing all, even the most insignificant actions, for the love of God and therefore all of them with complete dedication. Her followers could be in danger of concentrating on the minutiae and forgetting the motive.

Laws are necessary to preserve the rights and liberties of all. It is one thing to safeguard the law for the sake of the liberty of the sons of God, and another simply for its own sake.

Formalism is a particular kind of legalism, in which the exterior performance of a rite or law is considered, either subconsciously or consciously, adequate. Christ, and the Prophets before him, were scathing on this (Amos 5:25; Lk 11:41–2; Jn 4:21–4).

Lent
Emerged in the early 4th century as forty days of preparation for the Paschal feast. After some variations it reached the present arrangement, starting on Ash Wednesday, and leaving out the Sundays (since these are days commemorating always the triumph of the Resurrection). Lent has from ancient times been used for reconciliation of sinners and also as preparation of the catechumens for baptism on the Vigil of Easter. The emphasis during the first two weeks' readings in the liturgy is on repentance, conversion, *metanoia*, a change of heart, a turning away from sin and towards God. Associated with this came fasting, but only in the 6th century. The Sunday readings include Christ's own forty days in the desert – all this a liturgical expression of the Purgative Way. Soon the theme of God's mercy intrudes, and hope or trust in God, exemplified by Abraham. In the second week the readings are more positive: concern to do good; also premonitions of the Passion – the virtuous life, (*cf.* the Illuminative Way). In the third week, water becomes central as symbol of baptism; also miracles of healing and the universality of salvation. In the fourth week, water and life and the Passion are dominant. In the fifth, the Cross and death of Christ. In the last week, Holy Week, each day follows the Gospel story as we know it.

Lent is for us modern Christians a time for taking stock, attempting at least during that short time to live as we should the year through. But it is wise to concentrate on one or two aspects of the Christian life: one's prayer, charity towards others, self-control in food and drink (not however simply for slimming purposes), restraint in sensuality, good reading, our work. Not all these but a selection, and then we will find the others benefit too.

J.A. Jungmann, SJ, *The Early Liturgy*, (London, 1959).

Rule of S. Benedict, ch. 49.

Life, Supernatural
This is the sharing in the life of God that is granted to Christians as a result of dying with Christ in ↗baptism and being reborn in him (Rom 6:1–4). It is obviously one of the most important elements in the Christian revelation. Jesus himself expounded it, as recorded in John's gospel, when Nicodemus came to him by night (ch. 3). This Master in Israel was taught that he had to be born again of water (Baptism) and the Holy Spirit (Confirmation). The Samaritan woman was told that she could have living water for the asking (ch. 4). Jesus explained the relationship by a parallel: he was the root of the vine and we the branches, thus sharing the life of the root, unless the branch was snapped off by sin (ch. 15). Jesus gave his followers the sign of that life in the ↗Eucharist, the sign and the means (ch. 6).
↗Paul was very conscious of the reality in his life of the marvellous transformation. He cried, that now not he lived, but Christ lived in him. He was simply experiencing what our Lord himself had proclaimed:

that he himself was the Life (Jn 14:6). Paul had another way of seeing it, for him Christ was the head and the Church his body, each member having his part to play (1 Cor 12:12). Finally Paul links up with the teaching of the Synoptics when he enlarges on Jesus' teaching there, claiming that he is the Son of God, and his followers share his sonship. The Our Father of Matthew (6) and Luke (11) are a profound revelation which Paul recognizes as another way of expressing this union between us poor human creatures and God himself: we are co-heirs with Christ, being able now to cry 'Abba, Father' (Rom 8:15). Christ is the new Temple of God (Rev 21:22), the shrine within which the Godhead resides, we are the very Temple (1 Cor 3:16). These are all efforts to describe the ineffable mystery of God's marvellous condescension and love in making us one with him that Christ came to reveal. As Peter wrote, we share the divine nature (2 Pet 1:4). It is not possible to go further into the mystery than that in describing the life of ↗Grace.

Abbot Marmion, *Christ the Life of the Soul*, (London, 1922).

Liturgical Cycles
The series of feasts sharing a topic throughout the year. Although each liturgical event, whether the Eucharist or any other sacrament, recalls and represents the whole paschal mystery, yet the Church has through different feasts emphasized certain aspects of this great mystery. Every Sunday the people of God celebrates the death and resurrection of Christ, and has been doing so since the beginning of the Church. Gradually two major series or cycles of feasts built up: the Easter cycle, which now begins with Lent and

ends with Pentecost; the Christmas cycle which begins with Advent and ends with the Octave of the Epiphany. Each has subsidiary feasts: the instituting of the Eucharist, Maundy Thursday, the Crucifixion, Good Friday, Ascension Day, for the first cycle; and the feast of the Holy Innocents, the Motherhood of Mary, the Baptism of Jesus for the second. It will be seen that the Easter cycle is more profoundly expressive of salvation history. Minor cycles also exist, that of Mary – from her Immaculate Conception to her Assumption – that of St John the Baptist. The Saints' days are normally the day of their 'nativity', i.e. of their death, when they were 'born' into heaven. Most of such in Lent have been transferred. Other feasts commemorate certain aspects of Christ's work: Corpus Christi, the Precious Blood, his Kingship. The last fittingly concludes the cycle of the saints before Advent.

See following 'Liturgy' for bibliography.

Liturgy
From Greek *leitourgia*, a public service; divine service (New Testament). It comes into Church use as: the public prayer of the people of God, officially sanctioned by the authorities in the Church, primarily the bishop in his own diocese (*cf.* nn. 22, 39, 40 *Constitution on the Sacred Liturgy*. In the Roman Rite, it must also be sanctioned by the Holy See; the Eastern Rites have a greater autonomy. Some public prayers are on the fringes of the liturgy, e.g. Benediction and public Rosary. Other denominations either have their own governing body to decide on the manner of the liturgy or must have it approved by Parliament, as for the established Church of England.

Prayer for a Christian is *never a private affair*, since always he is united with the whole and Christ the Priest, as a member of his Body; only so can his prayer be valuable. The supreme prayer is the Eucharist, where the whole Church with and in and through Christ the Priest, gives glory to the Father by a sacrifice of praise. The form of the prayers expresses our solidarity with one another and with Christ; it is objective and free of individualistic idiosyncrasies; being ancient it is rich in content with the accumulated thought of centuries; grounded in Scripture, the liturgy relates to the whole man both exteriorly – all his senses – and interiorly – and so welcomes all the arts.

Liturgical prayer is not true prayer if it is only external. If on the other hand it is also interior, then, being a Christ-prayer and the offering of the whole man, it is the supreme expression of prayer that men can make. Nevertheless private contemplation also has its place in Christian spirituality, since it derives its power from the liturgy, especially from the holy Eucharist, and also by its fervour enriches the very liturgy itself.

The liturgy is a community act, but the community is not distinct from those who make it up; therefore each individual taking part must be involved not merely with voice and eye but with mind and heart. This requires readings and singing and actions, but also periods of recollection, so that all that is being done and said may be assimilated, shared and accepted. In the Eucharist there are specific times for silence: in the Penitential rite, at the 'Let us pray', after the readings from Scripture, after Communion. The 'Amen' is typical of the liturgy, expressing as it does an affirmation of and agreement with the great action that is going on, and this 'Amen' is the affirmation and agreement of the laity, each individually and as a whole group, namely the Body of Christ, his Church. (*See* ↗Eucharist.)

A. Baumstark, *Comparative Liturgy*, (London, 1958).

J.D. Crichton, *Christian Celebration, the Mass*, (London, 1971).

G. Dix, *The Shape of the Liturgy*, (Westminster, Md., 1952).

J.A. Jungmann, sj, *The Mass of the Roman Rite; its Origins and Development*, 2 vols, (New York and London, 1951, 1955).

J.A. Jungmann, sj, *The Eucharistic Prayer – a Study of the Canon of the Mass*, (London, 1966).

A.G. Martimort (ed.), *The Church at Prayer*, Vols 1 and 2, (Dublin, 1965 and 1973; to be continued).

Llull (or Lull), Bl Ramon (*circa 1233–circa 1315*)
Franciscan Tertiary, born in Majorca and died as result of ill-treatment by Muslims in North Africa, 1316. After a profligate youth and early marriage, at 30 he was converted and left his family to dedicate his life to the conversion of Jews and Muslims. He travelled through North Africa and as far as the borders of India to study the problem; learned Arabic so thoroughly that several of his works are in that language. At a time when the Christian world thought the best way to convert was by force of arms and Crusades, Llull favoured reason and persuasion. Perhaps he exaggerated the power of reason, thinking to establish the reasonableness of the doctrine of the Trinity by reason alone; he did this after a vision of the

Trinity on Mount Randa in Majorca *circa* 1272. He is a pioneer in the wider ecumenism spoken of today, as he travelled from Rome to the other courts of Europe to persuade princes to found colleges for the study of Arabic (Islamic) literature with a view to evangelization. His only success here was the College of Miramar in his native Majorca. His literary output was stupendous. Two mystical works stand out, the *Llibro de Contemplacio* and a little work, the *Llibro d'Amic e d'Arnat*, both written in Catalan, his native tongue.

E.A. Peers (tr. and ed.), *The Book of the Lover and the Beloved*, (London, 1923).

E.A. Peers, *Ramon Lull, A Biography*, (London, 1929).

E. Longpré, ofm, in *D.T.C.*, Vol 9, pt i, cols 1072–1141.

Locutions
An old word for perennial experiences: words heard with the ear, or in the mind or heart and thought to come in some way from God. Today we are conditioned to be cautious, and suggest schizophrenia whereas in the past people welcomed such experiences though they feared the devil. ↗John of the Cross was alive to these pitfalls (*cf. Ascent*, Bk. 2, chapters 11 and 28–31). All exterior 'locutions' or words heard with the ear, he says, must be rejected, being far from God; and one is easily deceived. The second kind of locution occurs when in meditation we carry on a veritable conversation as though with another person, and the subject matter is profoundly examined. It is of course ourselves with whom we are conversing, though the Holy Spirit may well be helping; and the danger

remains that we may imagine we are really conversing with the Holy Spirit! Sometimes, thirdly, a word or phrase comes to us 'out of the blue'. He calls them formal locutions – they may be for our instruction. If they make for humility, possibly they are from God, otherwise from the devil; and advice should always be sought before acting on them. A fourth kind of locution ('substantial'), he says, is a species of the last, but with this difference, that God's word does what it says, e.g. 'Love thou me', and the soul finds an immense increase in love. He says the soul should do nothing about such, neither desire nor shun them. If of God, they do their work; if not, then no harm comes. He is more interested in the 'touches' of God, either in the will or in the substance of the soul. These touches overflow into the understanding; and the person himself, not God, tries to express them in words; which words are always inadequate, often inaccurate and are taken to be of God, and are not, and thus could ruin the profound effect that the unverbalized 'touches' of God have of themselves.

Today we still weigh up spiritual matters in our minds – the Spirit will surely be guiding. We still have those moments of clarity, and a thought is verbalized with extreme precision; we still have those moments when God is near and without words our soul is consoled or illumined; at others we are flooded with a realization of his love and are moved also to love more. In all these ways the guidelines of John of the Cross are still useful.

Love of God for us

Since the Bible shows us the Source of all being as personal, it is possible to see God as someone who loves. In the Old Testament this is brought out frequently. He loves his people as a husband his bride, even when she abandons him (*cf.* Hosea 1–3, Jer 31; Ezek 16:59–63). The Covenant can be seen as a marriage agreement between God and his People (Ezek 16:6–14). In the *Song of Songs* this love becomes a mutual dialogue, the interplay of lovers. In Isaiah comes the comparison 'Does a woman forget her baby at the breast, or fail to cherish the son of her womb? Yet even if these forget, I will never forget you' (49:15). The very fact of creating was a sign of surpassing love, and God's promise of future forgiveness yet another. The fulfilment in the New Testament exceeded any hope that the Jews may have had, since God so loved the world as to send his only Son; and that son died for the world's salvation (*cf.* Jn 3:16). Finally it is revealed in 1 John 4:16 that God himself *is love*; it follows that all true love on our part flows from that absolute love. It must always be remembered that 'God loved us first' (1 Jn 4:10).

Love, Human

Man's love of people is primarily self-regarding, a desire to possess (Greek *eros*) and enjoy. It also flows into the desire that the other be perfect in his degree and be perfected (Greek *agape*). These two are neither exclusive of one another nor contradictory. But man being thirsty for boundless good, can never be satisfied with less than the infinite; and so is in danger of divinizing the limited love that he loves, not realizing its limitations. The other human being, though lovable, should be recognized as a sign of something greater, beyond all limitation. Once human beings step out of themselves in love, they step into the infinite dimension, their thirst being fulfilled with nothing less, whether they know it or not. They are in fact seeking God.

CHRISTIAN LOVE Both for God and for men, is a sharing in the divine love within the Trinity itself, since by the gift of justification and of grace – the grace that makes holy, by bringing man into the orbit of life of God who is holy – the Christian shares the divine life, is caught up in the spiral of God's mutual love. Here the Christian need not fear satiety, such as he experiences in human love; nor need he limit his own surrender, since God has loved us first.

LOVE OF ONE'S NEIGHBOUR A specifically Christian thing, in that it is universal in its application, not confined to friends or relations, one's tribe or country, or to intelligent or friendly or 'good people', but to all, particularly the needy; it is also to the limit of the humanly possible, in imitation of Christ who accepted even death on a cross and for his enemies. It is therefore a love which is totally other-directed, unselfish, and if achieved is the perfection of human love. This is the meaning of Jesus saying that he is giving us a new commandment, to love one another in the way, to the extent he has loved us (Jn 13:34).

SEXUAL LOVE Of its nature can be a beautiful and profound expression of the complete giving of two to each other in love; it can easily slip from that height to merely a mutual sharing of sexual pleasure, and lower still to a demand of one for the use of the other's body for the former's self gratification, regardless of the inclination of the latter, showing a total disregard of the other as a person, and so destroying true love – treating the other as a thing. (See ↗Marriage.)

LOVE OF ↗FRIENDSHIP A mutual appreciation of the other's worth and a sharing in common interests, a mutual exploration of the other's ways of thought and appreciation. While it will include sentiment, it eschews sexuality in the gross sense of the term. It may be asked whether this is a Christian thing, compatible with the Gospel. Christ himself showed special affection for John the beloved disciple, for Lazarus and Martha and Mary, for children he took in his arms. Christians are not Stoics who avoid love for fear of disturbing their ↗apatheia, but people who keep a custody over their heart, that is a restraint and moderation, since none except God can receive our unlimited love; all must be subordinated to that. So long as friendship and other human loves are motivated primarily by mutual desire for the good of the other, and by love for God, then they will profit the soul, and as ↗Francis of Sales points out, the signs or demonstrations of it must be moderated 'so that what began in heaven does not end in hell' (*cf. Introduction to Devout Life*, pt. III, chs. 17–22).

LOVE AND EMOTIONS Man is all of a piece, and what happens in one part of him tends to affect the rest, whence human love, which may begin by being spiritual, easily spreads across into the emotions – adolescent friendship is most often this – and it can also spread into sensuality and sexuality. That it has this tendency is human not sinful, unless indulged in; restraint is Christian.

C.S. Lewis, *Four Loves*, (London, 1960). Especially chapter 4.

C. Spicq, *Agape* I, II, III, (London, 1963–5).

C. Spicq, *Charité et Liberté*, (Paris, 1964).

St Aelred, *Spiritual Friendship*, tr. C.F.S. (Kalamazoo, 1977).

Loving Attention, prayer of

St John of the Cross' name for a state of prayer which among the writers on the subject has acquired a number of different names. Teresa of Avila calls it Interior Recollection; Francis of Sales, Prayer of Simple Commitment; Jeanne de Chantal, Calm Attention to God; Bossuet, Prayer of the Faith, or Prayer of Simplicity – this has been favoured by other writers; Augustine Baker, Prayer of Interior Silence. Each attribute of these titles helps us to grasp its meaning more clearly.

Those who seek God in earnest usually begin with meditation, called 'discursive' because the mind and imagination are given full play on the subject to be meditated on, whether a passage from the New Testament or some doctrine, such as the Eucharist or the Trinity. But meditation, in the prayer context, includes as its objective and conclusion 'affective prayer', the stirring of the heart, the will, using thinking on the subject and the emotions in order to elicit affective prayer. But a time comes when this kind of praying no longer helps, the meditating itself becomes barren and unproductive of affective prayer as the affections themselves are not aroused. It all becomes distasteful, counter-productive, and the one meditating is strongly tempted to give up praying altogether.

Of course this distaste could come from causes other than God weaning one from this method. They are enumerated by John of the Cross in *The Ascent*, XIII. His advice and that of most authorities today is: once meditation becomes barren, then leave reasoning aside, leave any effort to rouse 'affections', leave the imagination, everything, and simply be attentive in a loving way to the God who is present in the soul. For as Christians we know by faith that God is present as a Father, a friend, as Christ, the head and we the members of his body, so that we share in the very divinity of God, and this sharing comes by sharing in his Life, the very life of God, which is one of Truth and of Love. Now Truth, now Love will predominate. This, however, is not for us to decide but for God to give. We must wait upon him, in faith, in love, silently, attentively, still.

This loving attention comes with the purifying of the 'sensible' part of the soul; it is happy in this condition. Later God may even also deprive the soul of this delight in the spiritual part (*cf. Dark Night*, Bk. 2, chs. 11 ff).

Luis de Granada (*1504–88*)

A Spanish Dominican. He refused professorships and the archbishopric of Braga, preferring to pray, preach and write. His most famous works are (1554) *Libro de la oración y meditación* (*Book of Prayer and Meditation*), and (1556–7) *Guía de Pecadores* (*Guide for Sinners*). His purpose was to bring Christian perfection within the reach of all, laity as well as priests and religious. He was harried by the Inquisition, but twice exonerated. His writings influenced especially Charles Borromeo, ↗Francis of Sales and ↗Teresa of Avila. He laid down simple methods of prayer – being more concerned over interior prayer than with prayers – particularly meditating on the life of Christ. He encouraged all Christians to become Christ-like. Undoubtedly he could have given deep instruction on contemplative prayer, but the conditions in Spain were unfavourable owing to the witch-hunt for *alumbrados*.

cf. E.A. Peers, *Studies in the Spanish Mystics*, 2 vols, (London, 1930).

Luis de León (*1527–91*)

He was an exact contemporary of ↗John of the Cross; a Spanish Augustinian, probably of partly Jewish descent, which may have given him his profound feeling for the Old Testament and which resulted in his magnificent commentaries on the *Song of Songs, Job* and the masterpiece, *The Names of Christ*, which was put in the form of a Platonic dialogue on some of Christ's Names in the Old Testament. Professor at Salamanca University, he was imprisoned by the Inquisition for his commentary on the *Song of Songs*, but later released. His poetry is unequalled, though without the mystical depths of ↗John of the Cross. If he had any desire to expound mystical experience, he was dissuaded by the adverse winds caused by the Inquisition. But it was he who was chosen by the Carmelites to be the first editor of the work of his friend and disciple ↗Teresa of Avila. His book *The Perfect Wife* is an early attempt to bring the spiritual life to the laity, and lay women particularly.

A.F. Bell, *Luis de León*, (Oxford, 1925).

M. Duran, W. Kluback (ed.), *The Names of Christ*, (London, 1984).

F. Gracia (ed.), *Obras Completas castellanas de Fray Luis de León*, (Madrid, 1944).

Luther, Martin (*1483–1546*)

The life is known, the spiritual significance is overlaid with polemics, politics and war. Primarily Luther was a spiritual reformer. He changed the way that millions have followed Christ. This derives from the experience of his own conversion. There are parallels between his and the conversions of St Paul and St Augustine. They derived their teaching partly from that intimate experience. Luther's experience was one of despair at his sinfulness and his inability to make himself just before the Lord. Over a number of years – not in a blinding flash – he grew in a mighty realization that he was saved by the mercy of God and nothing else; all he had to do was to believe that: *sola fides*, faith alone. How had he got into that predicament? Partly from an exceedingly scrupulous temperament, partly, perhaps chiefly, from the current atmosphere of late medieval Catholic piety, which seemed to make salvation depend on pilgrimages, miraculous statues, multiplication of Masses, indulgences, indeed on *works*. Luther was right to see the great danger of this approach. We all have to throw ourselves into the merciful arms of God. The confrontation came over indulgences. Luther was excommunicated for his opinions and he burnt the bull of excommunication, thus concluding the breach. He found himself, unwillingly, with a Church on his hands. He had to start afresh. How should the people of God practise their religion, if so much of the immediate past was thrown overboard? In place of pilgrimages and Pardons, etc. what? To a considerable extent Luther took over the spirit of the ↗*Devotio Moderna* and the love of Jesus crucified. Luther opened the Bible to his followers, first by translating it himself while the printers did the rest, then by assuring his followers that they themselves had the Spirit of God, they shared the priesthood of Christ, and they themselves could interpret Scripture. Private judgement and conscience were supreme. He wrote hymns and set them to music, for singing, first by the hearth, but also in church. His was primarily a lay Church, while the old Church seemed to be a clerical one. The Mass – which he was devoted to particularly as a real Presence of Jesus – again, he wanted to be for the People, translating it into the vernacular. In place of shrines and rosaries, he made the preaching of the Word central to worship and the singing of Psalms in the home, in the family circle. It is attractive to find him writing a very long letter to his barber, Master Peter, telling him how to pray: meditate, he says, on the Our Father, the Commandments and the Creed. And he gives an example of his own prayer on these (see *Devotional Writings*, Vol. 2, Philadelphia, Pa., 1969). The old fire is still there. In a meditation on the Passion he writes: 'They contemplate the Passion aright who view it with terror-stricken heart and a despairing conscience' (*ibid*). Always he comes back to the fearfulness of sin and the only remedy – casting oneself on the mercy of God.

Martin Luther, *The Shorter Catechism*, 1529; *The Ten Commandments*; *The Sacraments*; *The Appendix I, How the Master of the House should teach his household to commend themselves to God both night and day*. cf. H. Bettenson, *Documents of the Christian Church*.

G. Casalis, *Luther et L'Eglise confessante*, (Paris, 1962).

O. Chadwick, *The Reformation*, (Harmondsworth, 1964).

G. Rupp, *The Righteousness of God*, (Birbeck Lectures, 1947, 1953).

M

Macarius
There are four, easily confused with one another:

(i) St Macarius of Alexandria, a hermit who lived in the desert near ↗Antony, 4th century. Little can be said of him with certainty.

(ii) St Macarius, bishop of Jerusalem (d. *circa* 334), who built the church of the Holy Sepulchre at the instigation of the Emperor Constantine.

(iii) St Macarius of Egypt, called also St Macarius the Great (*circa* 300–90). He founded a monastery in the desert of Skete, was associated with ↗Antony and ↗Athanasius (*cf*. Palladius's *Lausiac History*). According to Meyerdorff he was the master of ↗Evagrius who spent the last years of his life at Skete.

The little ↗*Philocalia* quotes him as saying: 'They asked of Macarius: how should one pray? The old man (*geron*; in Russian, *starets*) answered: "There is no need to waste time with words. It is enough to hold out your hands and say: 'Lord, according to your desire and to your wisdom, have mercy'. If you are hard pressed in the struggle, say: 'Lord, save me!' He knows what is best for you, and he will have mercy on you."' As Prof Meyendorff says: 'In its primitive form the ↗Jesus Prayer seems in fact to be the *Kyrie eleison* ("Lord, have mercy") whose constant repetition in the Eastern liturgies goes back to the Fathers of the desert.' (*cf. St Gregory* ↗ *Palamas and Orthodox Spirituality*, [New York, 1974], p. 24).

(iv) 'Macarius Magnes' or the Homilist (but the homilies referred to were not by him) or perhaps 'the apologist'. The homilies attributed to this Macarius are by an author unknown and were written in the late-4th century. This author ('Macarius') together with St Maximus stemmed the movement within the spiritual life of the Church towards a neoplatonic concept of prayer. It is the whole man, body as well as soul that prays, 'heart and soul'; the Christian being incorporated by the sacraments into Christ and so united to God.

Manichaeism

Religion of Manes, or Mani, born at Seleucia 216 and killed perhaps by the influence of the Magi *circa* 276–7. As a result of a vision which he had in 240 he inaugurated a new religion, to be the final religion of mankind, including within it all the best of the others, especially those of Zoroaster, the Buddha and Jesus. The tenets of Manichaeism can be summarized as follows. It claimed to be the ultimate religion; held a dualistic view of the world and man, subject to two principles, one Good, the other Evil; all matter was evil, spirit was good; hence marriage, which perpetuated the imprisoning of spirit in matter, was an abomination; hence too God could not be incarnate and die; yet Jesus and the Paraclete were part of Mani's salvation doctrine, at least in the Christian part of the Manichaeian diaspora; only the elect or perfect needed to concern themselves with the destruction of their materiality. Others could hope for a better life in a rebirth (Indian borrowing). Manichaeism spread from Iraq to China and India to North Africa where ↗ Augustine fell under its spell; and in the Middle Ages its descendants the Cathars (Albigensians) still disturbed the Church. The influence of Manichaeism on the Church was considerable, either by leading it to emulate it or to react strongly against it: thus the Fathers of the Desert and their sometimes excessive asceticism; the medieval concentration on devotion to all connected with the human life of Jesus.

Our information on Mani has been confirmed and enlarged by the discoveries of Manichaean manuscripts made in Turfan, Central Asia in 1904 and at Medinet Madi in Upper Egypt in 1930, especially the latter.

H-Ch. Puech, *Le Manichéisme*, (Paris, 1949).

A. Voobus, *History of Asceticism in the Syrian Orient*, 2 vols. (Louvain). His opinions are not completely accepted by other scholars.

Marmion, Columba (*1858–1923*)

Was born in Ireland and, by a series of providential accidents, in 1886 became a monk of Maredsous in Belgium, a foundation from Beuron in Germany. In this exile-existence he was following the tradition of his namesake and of the old Irish saints. He became abbot in 1909. His significance in Christian spirituality is that he wrote or rather spoke in the ancient manner, not in arid syllogisms. His conferences were meditative ponderings on Scripture in the spirit of the old monastic *lectio divina* (Divine Reading). His conferences were taken down and published after his death. They are a combination of personal commentary on Scripture and the thought of ↗Thomas Aquinas. The part of Scripture that he was most attracted to were the writings of ↗Paul. Thus the teaching on the Body of Christ – which became so central to the thinking of the Church between the wars and after – stems partly from his writings and also from the immediate appeal to Scripture. For him grace was not a 'counter' but the life of Christ in the soul. Lastly his spirituality was liturgical; the Divine Office and the Mass and the sacraments stand out as central in his thought. His mind was spacious, doctrinal not legalistic. His thought reminds one of the Fathers of the Church with whom he was well acquainted. He died in 1923. There is a movement to have him canonized by the Holy See. It is progressing slowly.

R. Thibaut, *Life*, English translation, (1932).

English translation of the *Works: Christ the Life of the Soul*, (London, 1922); *Christ in his Mysteries*, (London, 1924); *Christ the Ideal of the Monk*, (London, 1926).

Marriage
Christ graced the marriage at Cana by his presence (Jn 2:1 ff), thus showing that this most fundamental of human institutions is ratified in heaven. The fact that he himself remained celibate, therefore, did not imply any disparagement of marriage. In gracing the marriage at Cana he may be said to have graced all marriages. At Cana he even performed a miracle in order to help the embarrassed family out of an awkward situation. Water he turned into wine as he will turn human love, which is weak and vacillating, into strong, sure Christian love. ↗Paul

went so far as to compare the union of Christ with his Church to the union of man and wife (Eph 5:24 ff). As one is indissoluble, so must the other be.

Traditionally three intrinsic purposes are seen in marriage: the bringing to be and the nurturing of children, mutual love between husband and wife, and the satisfying of concupiscence or sexual desire. All three are achieved, in principle, in the very act of intercourse itself, but also in much else in married life. Procreation and mutual love strengthen the marriage bond, but especially mutual love, since this of its nature tends to permanence and, in conjunction with intercourse, creates a deep union of body and soul – the merging of two human beings into one – as was written long ago 'They become one body' (Gen 2:24).

In line with a number of modern Catholic theologians it is worth mentioning another and more biblical way of stating the underlying tradition of the previous paragraph. Marriage is not only a contract concerning intercourse, it is a covenant between two human beings to share their life, to have a common destiny, which means a commitment to one another not only in the comparatively narrow area of rights over each other's bodies for procreation but in a shared personhood, in a common life, arising from the deepest mutual love. Sharing in the desire to 'create' other human beings, a family, is of course a prominent aspect of such a covenant, yet not the only one and not necessarily the chief.

The sexual urge, concupiscence, is no longer seen as something somehow guilt-laden. Sexuality is part of our God-given nature, and so very good, and its fulfilment comes in the rich relationship of marriage. The sexuality of either sex is fulfilled in that of the other, for man and woman are incomplete without the other. By unselfish giving of one self to the other, both find their peace (*cf. The Bond of Marriage, An Ecumenical and Interdisciplinary Study*, William W. Bassett (ed.), London, 1968).

Marriage for a Christian is expressed in the form of a ↗ *sacrament*. The outward sign is the mutual vow of loving fidelity expressed to one another by the engaged couple, before a witness representing the Church; and he – usually a priest – blesses them. The peculiarity of this sacrament is that the two recipients themselves give the sacrament to each other. At the deepest level, it is Christ who unites them, through their vow, since he is present within them, because they have .been baptized already in his death and risen with him and share his life. Thus the power of the Christian marriage comes from the power of the risen Christ himself.

Marriage is a permanent condition, not just a flash in the pan – a wedding with its ceremonial, its bridesmaids, wedding cake, reception, the presents, the speeches, the champagne. It persists, *the grace of it persists*, 'until death do us part'. This is the beauty and wonder of marriage and can be its agony. But when a marriage reaches out to its perfection, then, of all human relationships, it is the most full of wonder and mystery, unfathomable in the richness of its love.

Every humdrum item, through the alchemy of human love and the enrichment of divine grace, becomes transmuted; the swift departure for work, the awaited return, the very turn of the latch; the call, the kiss, the recounting of the day's events, little confidences, news of the child, are all bathed in joy. Even what might seem to an outsider distasteful, the changing of those nappies, is a source of deep contentment, the being able to make the baby clean again; the delighted smile is rich reward. Those little disagreements are quickly healed by a gentle action, a smile, a tap, a word.

The love of husband and wife could be like the plucking of a perfectly tuned harp (the occasional discord an embellishment), liquid chords and trills coming at every human contact. The final union is but the culmination of all the above, gently, patiently, unselfishly, humorously, earnestly shared. The consummation itself becomes only a beginning: a child is heralded; that shared creation, the baby to be, is itself a sacrament of the love of the two and of the divine Source. The children are born, grow, leave the home, all this has intense joys. They are all recorded here simply to remind us that God, the origin of it all, is present throughout, and to be praised. These joys are never without great self-sacrifice, but, with love, easily borne.

TESTING TIMES So long as the covenanted love is there and the remembrance of the divine assistance, guidance is mostly from the heart itself. When that love is under strain, help may be needed. The following are instances of crises, all very common and all superable; forewarned is forearmed.

LACK OF MONEY Causes anxiety, weariness, bickering, irritation. Recrimination is not the answer but mutual concern and common prayer.

WEAKNESS The discovery of weaknesses of character in the other. This must not be allowed to reach tension point but be dispersed by openness, with easy seriousness. Mature love expects limitations; we are not marrying a god or goddess. If we love, then these very limitations, foibles or failures are lovable.

SICKNESS Sickness or real defects of character may emerge – paralysis or alcoholism to take extreme examples – they may seem sometimes to smother love and yet this need not be true. It is a time for living our love, as it were, by faith in a kind of dark night. There may be no sense of pleasure; all has gone grey, even distasteful, wretched, dreary; even prayer has become meaningless. This is the time to trust with great, deep strength in the loving care of God and come close to Christ on Calvary. A more profound sense of love and compassion will emerge and a yet deeper sense of the presence of God will be experienced through the pain.

INFIDELITY This shatters one's self esteem. Can I not hold my man, my woman? The realization that so much has been a sham, so much has been deceit, can be crushing. Here we learn to forgive, to understand, to be immensely patient. The passage in Paul's first letter to the Corinthians (13:4) acquires its full meaning: 'Love is always patient . . .'.

This can be a deeper Night yet. It requires full truthfulness about one's own part in the tragedy, an acceptance of the agony, a complete casting of oneself on the infinite understanding, power and mercy of God.

In all these cases and many others – each marriage has its own pilgrimage – guidance from outside should be sought. We might in every situation recall the phrase of Paul: 'My grace is sufficient for you' (2 Cor 12:9). How marvellous it can be, when all has been restored, as by some miracle, and the love once again grows stronger, more mature, and more

humble. As time goes on, each will need more room to grow, especially intellectually, neither letting himself or herself dominate. It is this growth that can become the new centre of mutual interest in middle age and beyond. Love has to be for ever cultivated or it withers, since its variety of expression is infinite.

Mary

These sections on the Virgin Mary are an attempt to express in simple language why Catholic and Orthodox and other Christian bodies have such veneration for Christ's Mother. Mary in the New Testament is portrayed as the perfect flowering of the Old Testament, the Daughter of Zion, 'full of grace' as the angel called her; fittingly it was she who received that first message of and that part in the coming of the Saviour, namely that she was to be Mother of Jesus. At the same time she is portrayed both by Matthew and Luke as the Virgin, whose motherhood would have a miraculous element. Her Son was to be born of God, the Spirit; in this way associating her with the Holy Trinity to a unique degree, though of course she still remaining a creature and herself redeemed, indeed the first of the redeemed. But this share in the work of God for men was to be accepted freely by her. She gave her humble *fiat*; 'may it be done to me according to thy word', was her reply. Again Luke records that not only was she to share in the birth of the Saviour but also in his Passion, as the prophecy foretells made to her by Simeon at the presenting of Jesus in the Temple: that a sword would pierce her soul, meaning she would share Christ's sorrows. John shows how this would be, by portraying her standing at the foot of the Cross, watching her Son die.

Mary, being so much one of us

and yet so close to Jesus, mirrors for us the perfect way of being a Christian. First, *she was faithful*, trusting the angel; believing even in darkness, e.g. when Jesus told her and Joseph that now at the age of 12 he must be about his Father's business; also when he turned away from the family circle at the beginning of his preaching; she never doubted he would answer her prayer for help at the marriage feast of Cana; she shared the darkness of his death. Secondly *she was humble*, the example of the *anawin* of the Old Testament (Zeph 2:3 – see J.B. note; also Is 61:1 where God promises that the Messiah will be sent to the 'poor', i.e. the humble). The *Magnificat* is the canticle of the *anawin*, the poor or humble of Israel, those who obey God's commands, and wait upon him for all, knowing that the rich will be sent empty away. Thirdly, *her love* is shown by her obedience, her *fiat*, her loyalty to the end at Calvary; her love for others in the story of the Visitation, that of the marriage feast of Cana – her concern for the married couple. When Christ gave his beloved disciple into her care at his crucifixion, he recognizes her love. Mary in that scene was given not only John but all Christ's disciples; as ↗Origen noted, John stands for the Church. She is Mother of the Church.

MARY IN THE HISTORY OF THE CHURCH She has played her humble part in leading Christians to her divine Son. St Irenaeus (d. *circa* 200) saw her as the second Eve, or the virgin soil from which sprang the second Adam, the New Creation. This leads naturally to seeing her as the type of the Church, and so much so that, in the works of ↗Augustine and other great Fathers of the Church it is not always easy to know whether they are writing of her or of the Church. Note already an ambiguity in Rev 12:1 ff: 'the woman clothed with the sun'. At the Council of Ephesus (431) it was the popular devotion to Mary as the Mother of God, the faith of the People of God, that helped the Fathers of the Council to see that Christ was not two persons but One. As part of the great wave of sensibility and affective devotion in the 12th century, led by ↗Bernard of Clairvaux, the human warmth of her relationship with Jesus was emphasized. But ↗Aelred, friend of Bernard, saw clearly her universal motherhood of the redeemed: though our own mothers are mothers of our body, he wrote, Mary is the Mother of our supernatural life. This strand of tradition developed strongly in the succeeding centuries, to end in such extreme and misleading titles as co-redemptrix. The second Vatican Council put a brake on this development. She had a unique relationship with her Son, but always herself as one of the redeemed by being preserved from ever being contaminated by original sin. Yet just as our own prayers have power because united with those of Christ, so do hers also and in a most perfect way. Her concern is not limited to this one soul or that, but embraces the whole Church. We must both see her as associated with *us* in the saving act of her Son, and see her also associated with *him* by her initial *fiat* and her whole life of union with Jesus. When Jesus on the cross said to John the apostle: 'Son, behold your Mother' (Jn 19:27), Christian writers from earliest times have seen him as representing the whole Church.

There are many devotions connected with Mary, but if examined closely they are seen to be devotions to Jesus her Son. The

Angelus is a reminder of that great mystery, the Incarnation; the *Regina caeli* of the Resurrection; the *Salve Regina*, said throughout the year, even in its lyrical outbursts, refer to her as Mother of Mercy, we are referred therefore to the merciful God as fount of all grace. The ↗Rosary is a continuing meditation on the great mysteries of · our Redemption from the Annunciation to the final consummation of Mary's assumption into heaven and the glory of the assembly of all the saints there too. Any devotion to her that fails to lead the soul to God is not acceptable to the Church (*cf.* Vatican II, *Constitution On The Church*, ss 55–69; also 'Mary' in *D.B.T.*).

MARY AND PRAYER It is not surprising that the Mother of Jesus should provide us with profound and simple forms of prayer, preserved in the Gospels. The first recorded is her acceptance of her role in the Incarnation and Redemption, 'may it be done to me according to your word' (Lk 1:38) – an openness to God's will, which in expression is perfect; a taking hold of the proposal, not mere resignation. The second occasion is her visit to her cousin Elizabeth. The latter says: 'How is it that the mother of my Lord should come to visit me? . . . Blessed are you for believing . . .'. As though to turn away the praise from herself, Mary exclaims, '*My* soul magnifies the Lord' (Lk 1:46, the *Magnificat*). This is a prayer, first of praise of God, then of joy at what he has done in her. She is not afraid to acknowledge that this is the fact. No mock humility here, but a recognition that *all* comes from God. This she then generalizes. It is the poor that God will make rich and the rich themselves will be sent away empty. It is spiritual poverty of which she is thinking. At Cana we have her

prayer of petition (Jn 2:11). She does not force her request, only: 'They have no wine', which is not even a request, but simply a statement. Nor does she give up when apparently rebuffed. 'Whatever he says to you', she says to the waiters, 'you do'. Her prayer on Calvary was silent compassion, a sharing in the acceptance of Christ. After the Resurrection we find her in the Acts sharing with the disciples the prayer of waiting on the Lord until he should send the Spirit (Acts 1:14).

Does she still pray for the world and the Church? Protestants are doubtful because they say that we have no scriptural evidence. That she does is a constant tradition of the Church – still preserved is the 2nd century prayer *Sub tuum praesidium*; and it was defined for the Catholic Church by the Council of Trent. But if we go back to the New Testament we have one clear piece of evidence that the saints pray for us in heaven from the Book of Revelation, where the 24 elders offer the prayers of the saints (5:8), which confirms what we would naturally expect: that if, as is sure, we pray for each other on earth – and ↗Paul repeats this over and over again – then we should, from love, do so in heaven. This is even more certain once we grasp the New Testament doctrine of the Body of Christ, the root and the branches. We and Mary especially share the one life with Christ and in him intercede for the world.

Mary of Nymeghen
See ↗Beguines.

Mary of Oignies, Bl
See ↗Beguines.

Maximus, St (*580–662*)
The last important link between the Eastern and Western Church, before

the final split (1054). Of high birth, he became a monk, then later abbot, but was called out of his monastery to become ecclesiastical secretary to the Emperor Heraclius, but when in 626 the Persians approached Skutari where he was a monk, he fled to Alexandria, Carthage and finally to Rome. There he supported Pope Martin I in his defence of the faith against the Emperor Constans II. Maximus was taken prisoner as reprisal, carried off to Constantinople, was imprisoned, flogged; his tongue was cut out and his right hand severed. He died near Batum (E. Black Sea). His *Four Centuries* – that is 400 short pithy sentences on the spiritual life – were a skilful synthesis, of what was best in the 'darkness' of the Pseudo-↗Denis and in the intellectual Light of ↗Evagrius.

English translation of *Liber Asceticus* and *Capita de Caritate* by Polycarp Sherwood, OSB, in *A.C.W.*, xxi, 1955.

See, for further biblio, *O.D.C.C.*

Mechtild of Magdeburg, St
See ↗Beguines.

Meditation
Through Latin from Greek *medomai*: think about. In the matter of prayer it can be described as a steady consideration, a careful reasoning on God or the things of God, more or less systematically, with introduction, consideration, conclusion. But this stylization was late in coming. The meditation of the earliest Fathers of the Desert was little more than the repetition of some short phrase from the Bible, or some pithy saying of one of the ancients. These were simple men, not trained to discursive reasoning. With ↗Augustine, for example, meditation is his normal way to God, forever searching to know God and his ways: the *de Trinitate*, and the *Confessions* are the meditations of a great mind and heart, since these thoughts lead to affective prayer: 'Late have I loved thee, Beauty so ancient and so new. Late have I loved thee!' (Bk. 10, ch. 27). This great tradition of meditation, in which man uses his highest faculty, the mind, to reach towards God, is continued, via monastic *lectio divina*, right up to the time of ↗Thomas Aquinas, who derives his doctrine from Augustine and the latter's disciples, ↗Hugh and ↗Richard of St Victor (12th century). The best examples of this strongly speculative – as well as affective – meditation are the three great saints Anselm, ↗Bernard and ↗Bonaventure. This is not to say that they had no experience of contemplation, which Thomas calls the intuition of divine truth; but it was in their tradition to use their minds to the full on the things of God.

However, Scholasticism, in its intellectual gymnastics of the later Middle Ages, became arid and lacking in that affective spirit which warmed these earlier works with divine love. Thus it was that spiritual writers, in Germany, England and the Low Countries particularly, began to turn away from speculative prayer or meditation, either towards that other tradition which stems from ↗Gregory of Nyssa, ↗Evagrius and the Pseudo-↗Denis, the tradition of darkness or ↗ *The Cloud of Unknowing* (notice, *un*knowing) or towards a simple imaginative approach to God. Thus in the 15th, 16th and 17th centuries meditation becomes the 'poor cousin' of contemplation and something that has to be passed through as soon as possible; whereas in ancient times it was considered as a noble occupation in itself, as well as being a necessary approach towards the mystery of God. The various complicated methods of the Counter-Reformation period were useful then, but they seem excessively stylized as well as poor in content today. Perhaps, with the renewal of scriptural studies and of theology, there will come a renewal of meditation, or the discursive search for meaning in God and his ways with men.

This is no attack on contemplation which is a gift of God and may crown one's life of meditation. But even the greatest exponents of the contemplative tradition from ↗Cassian to ↗Teresa recognize that these are moments only and, as she says, at the most a period of half an hour at a time. The normal way of men to God is through the mind, and the heart which is fed by it.

Meditation, methods of
The following notes are drawn from many sources including ↗Ignatius, ↗Teresa, ↗Francis of Sales, etc. The details of all these and others can be found in such compendia as Cardinal Lercaro's *Methods of Prayer*.

SUBJECTS The life of Jesus, applying it to oneself: the crucifixion, one's sins the cause; the saying of Jesus, particularly the parables; a passage from the Epistles, or the Old Testament; a theme such as one of the great mysteries of our faith: the Annunciation, Incarnation, Passion, Death, Resurrection of Christ; the Holy Trinity; the action of the Holy Spirit in our souls; or, the vices that ruin the life of Christ in the soul; the virtues that lead to God; the Four Last Things; the Names of Christ;

some well-known prayer; a chosen phrase, even a word.

PREPARATION Preferably overnight, but not too extensive or the freshness will evaporate. Have a book with the text applicable to the theme.

PLACE It should if possible be quiet, one's own room, a chapel, or a quiet path in the country or garden.

POSTURE Discomfort is not obligatory, rather the contrary, though lying down, which ↗Ignatius does not frown on, has its dangers. What is needed is a relaxed position, so that the breathing or the limbs do not begin to obtrude into consciousness.

THE BEGINNING Should always be with humility and faith; humility because we do not deserve to appear before God, and because all the good of the prayer will be a gift of God; faith, in order to put us into the presence of God, or more truly make us realize that we always are so. Then we should start on the theme chosen.

THE MIDDLE While we should not wantonly veer off the subject, yet, if the Holy Spirit, by simple inspiration, leads us along another fruitful path, we should not resist, so long as it helps us to pray.

THE END Many suggest we should gather up our prayer with good resolutions, or nosegays (Francis of Sales) that we carry around with us during the day. The essential is that our prayer be not wool-gathering, insubstantial, a concentration on nothing; and for this a final gathering up of the fruits is valuable. Yet it may be difficult to analyse what our prayer really was, except a loving care or a longing.

GENERAL REMARKS Our prayer will depend on our behaviour; if we are disloyal to God and his guidance, our prayer will be fruitless, unless we repent. If our lives are in concord with our prayer, then both will benefit. (*cf.* ↗Names of Jesus, ↗ *The Cloud of Unknowing,* ↗Distractions.)

No matter how hard we try, no method may work. We are in confusion, almost in revolt against systems. In this case pause and simply be lovingly attentive, almost wordlessly, to God, who is always there.

L. Cognet, *Meditation,* in *Cistercian Studies,* Vol. 8 (Kalamazoo, 1973), pp. 243–52.

J. Leclercq, *The Love of Learning and the Desire for God,* (London, 1974).

Luis of Granada, *Book on Prayer and Meditation* (Chester, tr. 1862).

J.H. Newman, *Works, passim.*

Richard of St Victor, *Benjamin major.*

St Anselm, *Cur Deus Homo?*

St Bernard, *de Consideratione.*

St Bonaventure, *Itinerarium mentis ad Deum.*

St Francis of Sales, *Introduction to a Devout Life.*

St Ignatius, *Spiritual Exercises.*

St Thomas, *S. Th.*, IIa, IIa, q. 180.

H. Urs von Balthasar, *Prayer,* (London, 1961).

Merton, Thomas (Fr Louis)
(1915–68)
Cistercian Trappist monk and spiritual writer. Born in France, his father and mother were both artists. His mother died when he was 6, his father died when Merton was 16; his life became rootless. Primary education he had in France, secondary at Oakham, England. His

university career at Cambridge was a disaster and the death of his illegitimate child and its mother during the London blitz of the Second World War, left in him an agony of guilt.

Columbia University, New York was a successful experience for him, and the impact of Gilson's *Spirit of Medieval Philosophy* set him off on his religious life-pilgrimage: baptism into the Catholic Church in 1938, entry into the Trappist monastery of Gethsemani in 1941, first vows 1944. He was ordained in 1949 and suffered a nervous breakdown. Merton himself would divide his life after becoming a monk into four periods: (i) The Noviciate up to 1944, with almost no writing; (ii) 1944–9, a preparation for the priesthood, and much writing; (iii) From 1949 to his appointment as Novice Master in 1955 during which the early and most popular works were published; (iv) The fourth period, 1955 up to 1961, when he was calling in question his over-romanticized Trappist monastic ideal. He wrote of these stages in his preface to *A Thomas Merton Reader* (1961).

The fifth period 1961 to his death in 1968 is one of ever-widening horizons. It is therefore important to know when the major works were written. *The Seven Storey Mountain* (called in England, *Elected Silence*) was mostly written in 1946 and published in 1948 (600,000 copies in hard-back sold). *Seeds of Contemplation,* written in 1947, was also published in 1948. In that year he wrote *The Waters of Siloe* (in England, *The Waters of Silence*) published in 1949. These were all Merton 'first phase'. *The Sign of Jonas* came out in 1953, but much of the material was of the early stage. It stands for the transition from the self-contained Merton, to the one now facing the world around. By

1955, when he became Novice Master, we have a probing Merton, entering into the world debates, about disarmament, the Third World, social justice, South America, with *Conjectures of a Guilty Bystander* in 1966; and next, stepping out of his own world into that of the Far East, he writes *Mystic and Zen Masters* together with the account of the fatal Asian journey which ended with his death in Bangkok, *The Asian Journal of Thomas Merton*, posthumously published in 1973 as was a group of very important chapters entitled, *Contemplation and a World in Action.*

Monica Furlong, *Thomas Merton, A Biography*, (London, 1980).

Mixed Life
It is a phrase so often used in spiritual writings, even from the time of ↗Augustine (*City of God*, Bk. 19, 2 and 19), that an explanation is called for. It is the third kind of life made up of a mixture of the contemplative and the active. We speak of the contemplative life, of contemplatives, of contemplation. Contemplative life occurs when the setting is such that the prayer of contemplation is assisted by it, by withdrawal from the world, by an avoidance of busyness, by regular periods of prayer in which the discursive kind gives way to that of simplicity. The active life, in modern parlance – already in ↗Augustine sometimes, and always with ↗Gregory – means a life in which good works predominate, though prayer of course is not absent. For the Fathers of the Desert, especially ↗Cassian (*passim*), the active life meant the one in which even in a contemplative setting one was chiefly concerned with eliminating evil habits. Now, by the mixed life traditionally was meant one

predominantly contemplative but in which some good works were admixed. Thus the Carthusians and Cistercians would be considered contemplatives, while most Benedictines, because they have some activity, would be living the mixed life. But just as there are some purely contemplative Benedictines (e.g. Solemnes) so there are active Cistercians (e.g. those of the University of Dallas). Likewise, some groups that were 'mixed' have become so full of good works that their contemplative setting has been disturbed, and they have in fact become active. A 'contemplative' only means one living in a contemplative setting, and he may not have reached any degree of contemplation in prayer. Many of those who lead the active or mixed life, though not called contemplatives, have in fact been granted by God, and not for any merits of their own, prayer which can only be described as contemplative, since the Spirit blows where it will.

↗Basil chose the mixed life; and, though the Eastern monks follow his 'Rule', they have taken the road of the purely contemplative life. The Rule of ↗Benedict has given rise to two interpretations: contemplative and mixed. But even in the former tradition, ↗Bernard remarks that in the life of a contemplative there are times for the active life alternating with the contemplative. For a full discussion of all these points see Cuthbert Butler's *Western Mysticism*, 2nd edition, (London, 1926).

At Vatican II, in the *Decree on the Appropriate Renewal of the Religious Life*, the Fathers of the Council did not make use of this terminology, but spoke rather of 'members of those communities which are totally dedicated to contemplation', (s. 7) thus avoiding the implication, had they used the words 'the contemplatives', that only such are ones who aim at contemplation. Nor do they use the phrase 'the apostolic life' or 'active life', as though such did not tend towards contemplation, but simply 'religious and lay institutions devoted to various aspects of the Apostolate' (s. 8).

In this way they avoided taking up a theoretical position concerning kinds of life, and merely stated what in fact existed in the Church. So, likewise the phrase 'mixed life' does not occur, since in one sense all Christian lives are mixed, having more or less activity, since no man or woman in this life can pray uninterruptedly – at least they have to sleep, and eat and do the usual chores. But of the third group the Fathers speak as follows: 'the venerable institution of monastic life' (s. 9); and here they make a distinction. Some of these are dedicated entirely to divine service, 'to divine worship'; 'or (take up) some apostolate or works of Christian charity' (*ibid.*), of course safeguarding their way of life. It will be seen that the third group, the monastic, and the first, the ones entirely dedicated to contemplation, partially overlap and this is as intended by the Fathers of Vatican II, since it is impossible to divide into watertight compartments anything so varied as ways of living the Christian life.

Some groups are primarily engaged in prayer – private and communal – and withdrawn more or less completely from the world; while other groups are primarily engaged in apostolic works and not withdraw from the world, but also pray; for these their work is part of their prayer. Those who have more or less withdrawn from the world nevertheless share as far as they are able in helping the Church and world by prayer and penance and a limited availability; while the apostolic group for their part cling to prayer.

Molinos, Miguel de (1640–97)

Born in Spain, the originator of ↗Quietism. In 1675 he published *A Spiritual Guide* which explained how to reach contemplative prayer, and claimed that the perfect Christian was distinguished from others by his practising of contemplation in contradistinction to ↗meditation, or any other more pedestrian prayer that was much promoted by the Jesuits. Molinos's contemplation however was so passive as to be without any effort at virtue or any positive avoidance of temptation. One resigned oneself to God's will, and if in this passivity one went through sensual acts of pleasure, even to sexual acts between the sexes, there would be no sin in this state, since they were not willed – the will was not willing anything, After twenty years of adulation as preacher and guide in Rome itself, in 1685 he was arrested by the Inquisition. At his accusation before an immense multitude in the Minerva, and with complete serenity, he admitted his guilt even to moral misconduct. He was kept in prison till his death in Rome on 28 December 1696.

cf. J. Paquier, 'Molinos' in *D.T.C.*

Monasticism

From Greek *monos*, alone, not married, celebate. It still flourishes in its many forms throughout the Christian world, in essence always the same though in manner surprisingly different. It has existed too in other cultures than the Christian, in China, India, Japan, Burma and among the Jews (Qumran). The essence is the seeking of God as the primary aim – not forgetting the love of neighbour – sometimes in complete solitude as hermits do (eremitical life);

sometimes in groups of like-minded people, but still in isolation – in the Eastern Church called lauras, in the West the Carthusians and Camaldolese are of this type; sometimes in communities under an abbot and sharing the common life. These are the cenobites of the Benedictine Rule, also the Cistercians; sometimes in friaries of contemplatives. The Carmelites, especially the women, are of this type.

Every reform has always been towards a restoration of the primary aim of seeking God first above all else. But with time it became apparent that with different temperaments, different situations and shifts of emphasis, different ways of achieving this have emerged. Thus some associated great austerities with the search for God, as for instance the Carthusians and Trappists; others followed the discretion of the Rule of ↗Benedict, allowing for the weakness of man and so reducing the physical austerities while emphasizing the ultimate one, that of giving up one's own will completely to God through the abbot and one's fellow monks. Others have concentrated on their need for no outside activity or even any share in the active apostolate, rather practising prayer and fasting. Again others have made allowance for some participation of the active apostolate. Thus ↗Basil and his way of life.

The essence remains the same. All the rest are means: silence, spiritual reading (*lectio divina*), the taking of vows, vigils, fastings, work, enclosure; all these support the essential of loving God and one's neighbour. Anyone interested in the monastic life first enters a monastery as a guest, then perhaps he takes part in some of the activities of the monks – this is the first tentative approach (postulant); next he asks to be allowed to share fully and becomes a novice under a wise monk (novice master). After a year or so he takes vows to live the life for a year, then perhaps for three years, until he is sure and then takes vows for life.

Monastic vows in the ancient tradition of Benedict are obedience, stability in that place under the abbot and his successors, and conversion of manners or determination to live no longer as a worldling but according to the Rule and with the desire to give himself in that way entirely to God. Poverty and chastity are included under this last vow of conversion of manners. The priesthood is not of the essence of the monastic life though it can be seen as its crown.

It has been claimed that the monastic life is higher than any other. This may be true in theory but not in practice. That vocation is higher for any individual which is most apt to lead him or her to God. Thus marriage – which after all is a Sacrament – is the better or higher for the vast majority. It depends on temperament, what Augustine calls *pondus* or tendency of the soul, the impulse of the Holy Spirit, the call from God and the acceptance by the monastic authorities. This can be decided after prayer and serious consultation and experience of one's own character.

C. Butler, *Benedictine Monachism*, (London, 1924).

T. Fry (ed.), *The Rule of St Benedict,* (Collegeville, Minn., 1981). Very comprehensive and scholarly.

M.D. Knowles, *Christian Monasticism*, (London, 1969).

P. Schmitz, *Histoire de l'Ordre de Saint-Benoît*, 7 vols., ↗(Maredsous).

See also ↗Antony, ↗Benedict, ↗Basil, ↗Bernard, etc.

More, Dame Gertrude (*1606–33*)
Great-great-grand-daughter of
↗Thomas More and one of the first
nine members of the English
Benedictine convent at Cambrai in
Flanders founded in 1623 (now at
Stanbrook) by the munificence of
her father, Cresacre More. She was
lively, gifted and affectionate. It
seems probable that at her simple
profession – when she first took
vows (1624) – she was not fully
aware of the implications, and
consequently for a time had scruples
over her position and was in great
misery. Meanwhile Fr Augustine
↗Baker had come to assist the
chaplain. His own teaching on
prayer was against the current tide of
meditation, composition of place
and the rest, pointing rather in the
direction of contemplative prayer,
that of aspirations, the prayer of
quiet. At first he had success but
Dame Gertrude held back and even
mocked his teaching. But at All-
hallows in 1625 she was persuaded to
take his counsel. Very soon her
attitude and whole life were
changed. The story of her agony, her
conversion and her progress in the
life of perfection and of prayer are
intimately known to us through her
own writings – particularly her
Idiot's Devotions – and through the
writings of Augustine Baker himself
who wrote her life. As she had a
'sensible affection' and a 'great
propensity' towards God (Baker's
phrase) and was of an 'affectionate
temper', he encouraged her in
sensible devotion in order that by the
use of her affections she should rise
to the pure love of God. Meanwhile
her scruples over her vows persisted
and to quiet her conscience she was
permitted to repeat them privately.
Baker's remedy for her scruples was
to teach her simply to cast all her
worries upon the mercy of God. She
died at the very early age of 33 having

reached a very high state of contemplative prayer. One peculiarity
of this was her ever increasing reliance on the internal guidance of
the Holy Spirit, as Fr Baker had expected. In this again his teaching was
unusual at that time, when direction
was at its height.

The Inner Life of Dame Gertrude More
Vols 1 and 2, revised and edited by
Dom Benedict Weld-Blundell
(London, 1910). This life is by
Augustine Baker.

The Writings of Dame Gertrude More,
revised and edited by Dom Benedict
Weld-Blundell (London, 1910). This
volume includes her *Idiot's Devotions*
called by Baker 'Confessiones
Amantis' (*Confessions of a Loving
Soul*). It also includes *The Apology of
Dame Gertrude More*.

The very confused and confusing
relationship between Baker's
writings and Dame Gertrude's can
be found sorted out in *The Lives of Fr
Augustine Baker 1575–1641* by Peter
Salvin and Serenus Cressy, edited by
Dom Justin McCann, osb, (London,
1932): see appendix III, pp. 202 ff.

More, Thomas (*1478–1535*)
Born in London and died for his
faith, being beheaded at the Tower.
It was a time when the nation States
were claiming complete sovereignty
over their subjects, even in matters
of religion. Render to Caesar the
things that are God's. He dared to
deny that; and the particular mode of
his denial was to maintain the age-
old supremacy of the Papacy in
religion against the royal claims,
even though he was fully aware of
the contemporary degradation of the
Papacy. He could not be a friend to
Erasmus and ignore it. The above
shows his great courage. But he was

a man for all seasons: boon companion – as his king appreciated – and loyal friend. No one could attack his friend Erasmus with impunity. A family man he was, though he spent some years undecided as to whether to become a monk or to marry, spending about four years living with the Carthusians even while practising law. His family life at Chelsea was the talk of Christendom: his daughters writing him letters in Latin; his monkey, his 'fool', the merriment, the music, the wit and at times high seriousness and devotion. He spent every Friday alone pondering the Passion of Christ. Every day he was at Mass in the parish church, not even a king could coax him from it. He had always been a scholar, since his teens at Oxford and then in London under Grocyn. While still a young man he lectured on the *City of God* of Augustine at Grocyn's church, St Lawrence Jewry. As scarcely more than a 'beardless boy' – so it was said – he dared as a very young member of Parliament to resist the extortions of Henry VII; while later, as Speaker of the House, he even withstood Henry VIII. But by profession he was a lawyer, always ready to help the litigants settle out of court to save their purses; as the old play had it: 'the best friend the poor e'er had'. Nor did he ever take a bribe or the semblance of one.

When his son-in-law, William Roper, embraced heretical views, he did not expel him from the house, but rather after failing in discussion to convince him of error, gave himself over to prayer and so won the young man back. But he did as a lawyer harass heretics to the ultimate penalty. In the King's Matter, he remained prudently silent in public, though his sovereign knew his mind. When however the time came to speak, he did not flinch but spoke with honesty and power.

Finally, on the scaffold, he uttered those words, a warning to all rulers and a guide to all citizens, saying he was 'The King's good servant, but God's first'. His writings match his life: the *Utopia* is a penetrating commentary on the politics and economics of his time. There are his intensely personal letters, particularly those to his daughter Meg; and finally those two long meditations composed when he was held prisoner in the Tower; the *Dialogue of Consolation* and the *History of the Passion*. His polemical works are not our concern, nor do they match the others in excellence. Thomas More for all his homely humour is a model of holiness for the family man, the lawyer, the statesman, politician, scholar, writer or friend. He was a Christian to the marrow of his bones.

The Complete Works of St Thomas More, (Yale, 1963 ff).

The Utopia (Yale).

R.W. Chambers, *Thomas More*, (London, 1935).

P.E. Hallett (ed.) and Mary Bassett (tr.), *The History of the Passion*, (London, 1941).

R. Marius, *Thomas More*, (London, 1985).

E.E. Reynolds, *St Thomas More*, (London and New York, 1953).

Elizabeth F. Rogers (ed.), *The Correspondence of Sir Thomas More*, (Princeton, 1947).

William Roper and Nicholas Harpsfield, *Lives of Thomas More*, (London, 1969).

Monica Stevens (ed.), *Dialogue of Comfort against Tribulation*, (London, 1973).

Music

The art nearest to contemplation, perhaps because it is wordless, therefore unreasoning and imageless in its message of beauty. One sense, hearing – pitch intensity, power, harmony and rhythm – holds all the senses and ratiocination in suspense, while intuition and contemplation hold sway. But like every art, which begins with the senses, it needs to pass beyond. Certain forms of music, fascinating in themselves, confine the listener in sense, or at most lead on only to emotion or sensuality. Why this is so may not be clear, but all are aware of it; thus some American negro music, dressed up for white consumption, though in its home-land of Africa it had an ecstatic quality, now at times becomes embedded in mere sensuality, when once it led to the divine. Plainsong (those melodies of the early Church) on the other hand, has a quality of peaceful tranquillity, of simple objectiveness and great beauty (of course there are uninspired passages). Plainsong is almost the symbol of Christian prayer-music. Any church music which is over-theatrical, self assertive, over-sophisticated, intellectual, even trivial or over-emphatic disturbs the mind; and the heart cannot speak. Yet some modern Church music is tender and strong, restrained and leading beyond itself to God.

Music has always been a part of Christian prayers. Paul mentions Christian singing (Col 3:16; Eph 5:19); Celsus, 3rd century, an anti-Christian writer, admits that church music was beautiful, too much so. Clement of Alexandria would admit music in Christian worship. ↗Basil introduced antiphonal singing; Ambrose composed hymns which were taken over by ↗Benedict for the Divine Office (*cf.* a short account

in Henry Chadwick's *The Early Church*, pp. 273–7).

A famous passage in ↗Augustine's *Confessions* deserves quoting: 'When those melodies that bear your life-giving words, catch my ear, and are sung sweetly with measured voice, I do, I have to admit, find in them some pleasure, yet not so great as to hold me too closely. I find it hard to judge their due place. At times I recognize that holy words set my mind aflame with piety and fervour, more when I hear them sung than when not ... I can remember shedding tears, moved by the sound of the Church's songs in the early days of my conversion ... I am moved not by the singing, but by the things sung – when they are sung with clarity and due modulation. I am inclined to approve the custom of singing in church so that by the pleasure of the ear weaker minds may be roused to feelings of devotion' (*Confessions*, Bk. 10:33).

In public divine service it is the words that count more than the music, since we are here not concerned with our private devotions but the prayer of Christ and his whole Church, the mystery of Redemption. The music should be subservient to the meaning, more especially as many have little appreciation of music.

Mysticism

The study or practice of union with God in prayer which goes beyond reasoning and appears to touch the divine in a unique way. It is still a 'dirty word' in some Christian quarters, e.g. see the Foreword to the English translation of the Russian *Philocalia* on the Prayer of the Heart which reads, 'Practice of the Jesus Prayer ... has nothing to do with mysticism which is the heritage of pagan ancestry' (p. 5). To a Greek-speaking Christian the word still carries about it a tang of mystery religions: orgies, secret rites, and midnight ceremonies of initiation. But in the West for long it has been associated with contemplative prayer. But the word mysticism is used indiscriminately for the immediate experience of God and for the theoretical basis of this experience, i.e. the practice itself and the underlying presuppositions.

Mysticism is a world-wide phenomenon (see ↗Mysticism, comparative). Here let it suffice to comment on *Biblical and Christian* mysticism. The Old Testament, while it preserves much law, is founded in mystical experiences, from that of Abraham and God's promise, through those of Moses at the burning bush and Mount Sinai, through all the Prophets, especially Elijah at the mouth of the cave on the mountainside, but also those ineffable experiences of Isaiah, Ezechiel, Jeremiah and Daniel; not forgetting those divine experiences of King David and his son Solomon. The whole book of the Psalms is an expression of a series of intimate experiences of Yahweh, and the Book of Job is one of the greatest expressions of the Dark Night ever penned. These are enough to dispel the absurd idea that the religion of the ancient Jewish race was simply legalistic; it is enshrined in the great library of books we call the Bible, in terms of love and often as a mystical marriage of the People of God with Yahweh.

As in the Old Testament so in the New, there is no theorizing, only expressions of the experience of God. Jesus himself is the summit of this union with God his Father – we are speaking of him as man – but because of the union of the two natures in one divine Person, the relationship is both unique and utterly mysterious. Yet there are moments when the veil is lifted, for example in the scene of his baptism, when the Father speaks to him; again in the desert where the devil tempts him; the ineffable divine light on Mount Tabor as later in the agony of the Garden of Olives and on Calvary. There the derelection is complete in order that the glory may also be complete. But the whole Gospel story gives the impression of a person who is at all times intimate with the Father. 'Only the Son knows the Father' (Mt 11:27). He does only what the Father wills. The Father and he are one.

In ↗Paul we have one of the supreme examples of Christian mysticism, though the expression, as with all mystics, remains obscure. Did he, as we also ask of Moses's vision, see the essence of God in his great experience described in 2 Cor 12 when he seemed 'out of the body'? It is in his intimate relationship with the living Christ within him and with the Spirit who guides him that we realize how close that experience of God was for him, yet always Christocentric. Now it was Christ living in him. So it began at his miraculous conversion, so it remained. He received locutions, lights, ecstasy, and always like his Master, with sufferings, the concomitant of deep experience of God. If Paul's experience of God has a strong intellectual element, that of ↗John, as expressed especially in his first Epistle, is most notably one of light and love: an intimate union of will: God is love and who remains in love, *remains in God and God in him* (1 Jn 4:16). The insights of the Gospel according to John could only be those of a mystic; his is truly a 'spiritual' Gospel, particularly the penetration into the mystery of the relationship between the Word and God in ch. 1.

CHRISTIAN MYSTICISM OR CON-
TEMPLATIVE PRAYER THROUGH
THE CENTURIES   Christian mysticism has remained all through
the centuries consistent with the
New Testament and with itself;
though two streams are discernible:
the one of darkness, the *via negativa*,
and the one of light and love, often
described in terms of a mystical
marriage. The former is the way
of the Pseudo-↗Denis and his
followers, the latter the way of
↗Origen, of ↗Augustine and
↗Bernard and many others. The
one takes the image of the ↗Cloud
in which God spoke to Moses; the
other the ↗ *Song of Songs*.

Certainly as far back as Origen (d.
254) were noted the three stages
through which a soul progressed
towards intimate union with God:
the purgative, illuminative and
unitive ways; though not always are
the same terms used to express this
scheme. For instance ↗Teresa of
Avila has a completely individual
terminology, though the structure
remains the same.

Six distinct periods may be
observed in the history of Christian
mysticism, especially in the West: (i)
The Patristic age; (ii) The monastic
centuries; (iii) The medieval
flowering, in two stages, pre-
scholastic and post-scholastic; (iv)
The Reformation period; (v) The
desert with oases; (vi) The modern
revival. (Detailed information is
given under individual writers and
saints to which the reader may refer.)

(i) In the early Church the East
had both mystics and theorists; the
former are represented by the
Fathers of the Desert; the latter – but
they too were mystics – particularly
by ↗Gregory of Nyssa, the Pseudo-
Denis and ↗Evagrius. In the West
three figures are outstanding:
Augustine and ↗Gregory the Great,
both great practitioners, the former

much influenced in terminology by
neo-Platonism, then also ↗Cassian
whose rôle was to pass to the West
both the practice and theory of the
East and with much prudence.

(ii) In both East and West the
contemplative life, its experience and
theory, was preserved during the
Dark Ages in the monasteries; in the
East with the ↗Hesychastic
tradition and the ↗Jesus Prayer, in
the West by ↗ *lectio divina* and the
preservation of the tradition especially of Cassian, Gregory and
Augustine. The writings of the
Pseudo-Denis were introduced there
in the 9th century but his influence
and that of the *via negativa* did not
become important till three centuries
later; while in the East his writings
immediately took on almost the
standing of Sacred Scripture (as they
did later in the West up to the
Renaissance). The outstanding and
typical figures of this period are
↗Anselm of Canterbury and the
German nun ↗Gertrude.

(iii) (a) With the emergence of
medieval culture in western Europe
came also a revival of mysticism,
particularly among the Cistercians
e.g. ↗Bernard, ↗Aelred and the
former's friend, ↗William of St
Thierry; these were still in the
tradition of Augustine, yet with a
new emphasis upon the humanity of
Jesus. This devotion reached its
climax in the next century with
↗Francis of Assisi and ↗Bona-
venture.

(b) Meanwhile, in the 12th
century come the beginnings of
scholasticism and its influence on
mystical theology; among the first
writers are ↗Hugh and ↗Richard of
St Victor near Paris. ↗Thomas
Aquinas in the next century laid
the foundation on Aristotelian lines
for the flowering, among the
Dominicans of the Rhineland, of a
school of prayer, led by Meister

↗Eckhart, ↗Tauler, and ↗Suso. Their tendency was towards the *via negativa* – one not alien to ↗Thomas, who maintained that all that we can know of God in himself is what he is not. A new height is reached with ↗Ruysbroeck of the Low Countries. He introduced what is called the Bridal mysticism of Origen and Bernard. England, a little apart, shows the same patterns: a glowing love for Jesus and a lightsomeness in Richard ↗Rolle and ↗Julian of Norwich; and in the tradition of Pseudo-↗Denis, the *via negativa* of ↗ *The Cloud of Unknowing* and the works of ↗Hilton. As the Reformation approaches, there appear the *Theologia germanica* (much cherished by Luther) and also the anonymous ↗ *Pearl*. A new note is heard with the ↗ *Imitation of Christ* – a return to more simple expressions of contemplative prayer, and in Italy a foretaste of the post-Reformation period in ↗Catherine of Genoa.

(iv) As the Church sank into the struggles of the Reformation, a tremendous upsurge of contemplative prayer took place, in Spain first. The richness of that renewal has been overshadowed by its two chief exponents, ↗Teresa of Avila, who was traditional except for her own peculiar terminology, and ↗John of the Cross who united in his person the two main streams: the *via negativa* and the bridal mysticism of ↗Ruysbroeck. The others include of course ↗Ignatius of Loyola and ↗Francis Borgia (both wrongly suspected of illuminism); the Dominican ↗Luis of Granada, the Augustinian ↗Luis of Leon, the Franciscans Laredo and ↗Peter of Alcantara.

(v) In France, when the civil wars were over, the Englishman and Franciscan ↗Benet of Canfield appeared in Paris, with ↗Francis of Sales – who outshines them all – and

not far behind, ↗Bérulle, Olier, ↗Fénelon and ↗Bossuet. But already a cloud had appeared which was almost completely to obscure the scene, which originated in Spain with the ↗ *Iluminados* and ↗ *Alumbrados*, appeared in Rome with the Spanish priest, ↗Molinos, and in France with Madame ↗Guyon. All this was ↗Quietism, against which the Church campaigned with anxious aggressiveness. A lone but important English figure at that time was Augustine ↗Baker.

(vi) At last, towards the end of last century, a revival occurred – in England with Evelyn Underhill, an Anglican, and in the Catholic Church with Cuthbert Butler, Bishop Hedley and Baron von ↗Hugel; in France and Belgium with Henri ↗Bergson and his *Deux Sources de la Morale*, the Jesuits, Poulain and Maréchal, the Benedictine Abbot Marmion, and the Dominican ↗Garrigou-Lagrange. As a result of their discussions mysticism, contemplative prayer, was once again recognized as a gift, not reserved for the very few, but for all those Christians who sincerely and persistently strove to keep close to Christ; a gift indeed, but legitimately hoped for and to be prayed for by Christians, in a state of grace and taking the necessary means on their part.

Mysticism, comparative

We live in an age when we attempt to compare all, not only of what is but of what was; not least in mysticism. There have been facile judgements as to the unity of all mystical experience. As more is known, scholars are more cautious. There are many distinctions to be made. With Prof Zaehner we may divide mystical experiences into three

152 *Mysticism, comparative*

categories: (i) When the mystic experiences oneness with the material universe – and Jean Jacques Rousseau in his *Rêveries d'un promeneur solitaire* may be taken as a typical example, possibly also Wordsworth; (ii) When he isolates himself from all around him to find his real Self, and here some Hindu and Buddhist mystics would be examples; (iii) When he in some way experiences God, and this would be typical of Jewish, Christian and Muslim mystics, though there are exceptions in all these religious traditions.

Of course both Hinduism and Buddhism are too vast and varied to be fitted neatly into such simple divisions. Thus even among the *Upanishads* (v. ↗Brahman) are found the unity-type and the I–Thou type, as these two can likewise be found in the later *Bhagavad ↗Gita* q.v. Further, while the West is accustomed to think of Hindu mysticism as an experience, not of union of two, but of unity realized – and this may be what the great Sankara meant in his writings – yet in the whole of the southern school in South India among the Shaivites (who are monotheists) the mysticism is love-laden (*bhakti*) and therefore dualist. Without going further than the excellent summary in Christmas Humphrey's *Buddhism*, it is clear that within its ample bosom Buddhism includes all varieties of mystical experiences. Perhaps the central theme, nevertheless, is a realization of indescribable bliss, Nirvana. The Buddha himself was wise enough not to attempt to describe it, he claimed however that it required no exterior help (grace).

It is possible to maintain that all these experiences objectively are the same, but that owing to the paucity of language and the uniqueness of the experience, those who experienced it have failed to describe it accurately, thus accounting for the differences and even apparent contradictions. If this be the case, then from a Christian point of view, all would be given God's grace, even though they did not know it (anonymous Christians); and naturally their expression of their experience would be coloured by their background and modes of thought.

Thus the relationship to the Absolute, the Ultimate Reality, is so close in this experience, and the self so insignificant, that almost inevitably some would express the experience in terms of absorption or complete unity. It is Prof Zaehner's contention that it is wiser to recognize that there is 'concordant discord', that here we may have a vast number of different experiences at different levels of consciousness, which are therefore up to a point discordant, but in reality referring all to the same ultimate reality, which Christians would say was God. Who is to say that the object of the experiences of Plato, of Plotinus is or is not the same as those of Catholic mystics?

In ultimate analysis the great tradition of Catholic and Orthodox prayer, at the deepest level, has three characteristics:

(i) It is Trinitarian, an entering into the life of the Holy Trinity.

(ii) The human soul, though enveloped in the being and life of the Trinity, and though made one with God, never loses its own identity.

(iii) The experiences of the Christian mystics are not self-induced, but *sheer gift* from God. We dispose ourselves; if he wills, he gives. Our part is to love. God is always beyond.

A.J. Arberry, *Sufism, An Account of the Mystics of Islam*, (London, 1950).

A.H. Armstrong (ed.), *The*

Cambridge History of Later Greek and Early Medieval Philosophy, (Cambridge, 1967).

E. Conze, *Buddhism, its Essence and Development.*

De Smet (ed.), *Religious Hinduism, A Presentation and Appraisal*, (Bombay, 2nd revised ed., 1964).

Sir C. Eliot, *Hinduism and Buddhism*, 2 vols.

L. Gardet, *Mohammedanism*, (London and New York, 1961).

The Bhagavad Gita, many translations by (*inter alia*) Arnold, Zaehner, Isherwood.

Hastings, *Encyclopaedia of Religion and Ethics*, art. 'Mysticism'.

M.D. Knowles, *What is Mysticism?*, (London and New York, 1967).

S. Mackenna (tr.), *The Enneads of Plotinus with Porphyry's Life*, 5 vols, (London, 1917–30).

K. Rahner, SJ, *Theological Investigations*, Vol 3 (London and New York, 1960), *Sacramentum Mundi*, 6 vols (London and New York, 1968–70), *A Concise Theological Dictionary* (London and New York, 1966).

D.T. Suzuki, *An Introduction to Zen Buddhism*, (London, 1970).

D.T. Suzuki, translations of Zen Buddhist texts.

E.J. Thomas, *The Life of the Buddha*, (London, 1927).

C.M. Vadakkekara, OSB, *Prayer and Contemplation, Studies in Christian and Hindu Spirituality* (Bangalore, 1979).

R.C. Zaehner, *The Upanishads, The Hindu Scriptures*, (London, 1966).

R.C. Zaehner, *Concordant Discord* (London, 1970).

R.C. Zaehner, *Concise Encyclopaedia of Living Faiths*, (London, 1977).

N

Nada
Spanish for 'nothing', a key word in ↗John of the Cross' writings; antithetical to '*todo*': all, or The All, i.e. God. 'In order to arrive at possessing all, desire to possess nothing (*Ascent*, Bk. 1, ch. 13. s. 11) or: 'In order to pass from all to the all, you must deny yourself totally in all' (*ibid*. s. 12). There is nothing new in this except its extreme statement, and the perennial starkness of actually attempting it. The same teaching is found in the Fathers of the Desert, and in the *Imitation*, Bk. 3, ch. 5.4: 'A man in love ... gives all for all'. They are all derived from Christ's own saying: 'He who loses his life will find it' (Lk 17:33). It is seen in the lives of St Paul of the Cross, of St John Vianney, indeed in that of all the saints. Even outside Christianity, *mutatis mutandis*, something similar is found: among the Muslim ↗Sufi, the ↗Zen Buddhist. The superficial self must be tamed (destroyed) in order to open the way for that other Self ...

The practice of the '*nada*' or of dying to self (mortification) is not an end in itself; and while all spiritual writers preach it, they vary over the extent, the forms and intensity of it, according to the types of persons involved. It would be imprudent for a married person to take too literally these lines of John of the Cross: 'In order to arrive at having pleasure in all (the *all*), desire to have pleasure in nothing' – suitable doubtless for a hermit, but not fair on the other party in a marriage. ↗Francis of_ Sales is a safer guide for those in the world. As mortification is but a means, we should choose the means to hand that are appropriate and proportionate to the goal aimed at; not destroy human nature but control it. Yet the principle remains the same: to reach God, we have to strip ourselves of selfishness. One dares to suggest that to possess in love another in marriage, selfishness also has to be stripped off.

Names of Jesus

In the Old Testament a name had deep significance: the name of God, 'I am' (Ex 3:14); the change of Abram's name to Abraham (Gen 17:5) and of Jacob to Israel (Gen 35:10), both signifying a development in God's relationship with the patriarchs. In the New Testament Peter's name was given him to point to his position. But most important of all is first the name given to the child of Mary: Jesus. It is in his name that all will receive salvation (1 Cor 6:11). The name of Jesus is central to the Christian message – it is above every other name (Phil 2:9–11). The reason is that the name for the Jews signified the very nature of the person and his work. Thus the ↗Jesus Prayer is precisely an attempt to penetrate to the meaning underlying the name.

But Christ had other names. Modern Christians of the West have received the Christian message through the media, the instrumentality of Greek thought and Scholasticism; that is, a rational statement, as far as this was possible, of the mystery of Christ, and in Greek philosophical language, from Nicaea, Ephesus, Chalcedon, the great constructions of ↗Thomas and Scotus. The Jews did not think in that way. To explain who someone was, the name sufficed. In Christ's case many names occur. A revival of interest in the Biblical approach to the mystery of Christ appears with such writings as the masterpiece of ↗Luis of León (probably of Jewish descent) entitled *The Names of Christ*; here the author is not concerned with

the pictorial, medieval attempt to return to the Christ of the Gospels, but with the biblical significance of the Names, particularly those used in the Old Testament, such as Lamb, Shepherd, Man of Sorrows, Son of Man. It will be seen that this is a subtle and poetic method, which allows of shades of meaning and discoveries, peculiarly suited to a prayerful study. In the New Testament there must be between thirty and forty names associated with Jesus, those pointing to his Godhead: Logos, Emmanuel, Lord, Son of God, Source of Life, the Beginning and End; those referring to his humanity, Son of Man – though this has divine undertones – Son of Mary; those referring to his work: Saviour, Christ, King, Priest, Prophet, the Way, the Truth, the Life, the Light, and Lamb. By comparison with the use of these in the Old Testament a richer understanding of the use in the New Testament emerges. Thus the Good Shepherd is connected with Ps 23 and Ez 34; the Rock with God, the Rock, and with the rock from which came forth the water of life (Num 20:10).

cf. O. Cullmann, *The Christology of the New Testament*, (London, 1959).

Newman, Cardinal John Henry

(1801–90)

The outstanding Christian figure in 19th century England; a Londoner who died in Birmingham. His life spanned the 19th century. Up to 1845, his Anglican period, he was establishing his profound understanding of the Fathers, in particular ↗Ignatius of Antioch from whom he learnt the deep significance of the sacramental system with the Eucharist and the bishop at the centre. From the works of ↗Athanasius he brought forward the vital certainty of the Incarnation and the consequent new creation in Christ. *The Parochial and Plain Sermons* are the fruit of that prolonged meditation, as also *The Arians of the Fourth Century*, with its considerations on the names of Christ; Son and Word and his favourite, Emmanuel (*cf.* its place in the *Dream of Gerontius* so many years later [1865]). The three years at Littlemore (1842–5), an austere retreat from the world, led to his conversion to the Catholic Church. The contrast between Littlemore and the Oratory of St Philip Neri at Edgbaston, Birmingham, is startling. St Philip, now his patron, was the 'fool for Christ', almost happy-go-lucky, out-going. It is said that in ordinary living Newman was always affable, not gloomy, almost frolicsome. Friendship was central to his life.

Since his youth Newman seems always to have been profoundly aware of God's presence. Conscience was the way God spoke to him and remained his ultimate basis for action (*cf. Letter to the Duke of Norfolk*). His piety was not 'enthusiastic', he had a horror of 'excitement' (the word he used for 'enthusiasm') in religion. Already in his Anglican days he was preaching frequent Communion.

Newman's spirituality is best seen in his life. He followed the invitation of Jesus to give up all by passing (when he left Oxford) into the camp of the despised remnant of the Catholic Church in England (the Italian mission). His sacrifices were not over. All his undertakings seemed to end in failure and ignomony; the failure of the Catholic University in Dublin, the debacle of his editorship of the *Rambler*, the abandoned plan for him to translate the Bible. In all these and others he showed restraint in public, not defending himself. But when the good name of the Church was attacked by Kingsley his defence was a masterpiece: the *Apologia pro vita sua*.

The Dream of Gerontius contains the quintessence of his spirituality, which was strongly Trinitarian, as was that of his beloved Fathers of the Church, personal almost in the manner of ↗Catherine of Genoa, and enshrined in the mediating Church of Christ, peopled with angels and saints. Life was a purgation leading to the ultimate Vision.

C.S. Dessain, *Newman, Spiritual Themes*, (Dublin, 1977). See also Newman's own works.

Night
An important and multiple symbol in the Christian life. Christians are the children of the Light and night is almost over (Rom 13:12). Christ is the Light that shines in the darkness (Jn 1:5). The image of light as faith in Christ, and darkness or night as unbelief, runs through the New Testament especially in the writings of ↗John. The imagery is also found in the Qumran documents. The Dark Night had become part of the language of prayer as early as Pseudo-↗Denis and standard since ↗John of the Cross; and now the jargon of the initiates. But there are many 'nights', not all of them of God; first, the physical night in which naught can be seen and men do shameful things (Eph 5:7 ff), though God sees even in the hidden crevices of the heart; the night in which we lose our way and do not see the shadow of the Beloved, nor even hear a whisper of his voice; then, that is, all spiritual things are lost to view and have become unreal. If this has been the result of sensuality, or pride, or anger, or any

of the deadly sins, then the ensuing darkness is not of God, except as punishment and warning. Even those on the way to God may fall into a darkness for lack of fervour, or failure to be rid of even some trivial matter. Only when the great storms and gusts of sin are spent and the soul is upon a peaceful sea does she sail into the Dark Night of faith, with not a glimmer of a star to guide.

Though ↗John of the Cross was writing for contemplatives his analysis holds for all, including the 'worldlings' trying to follow the Way. He describes two Nights, that of the senses and that of the spirit; but each is partly our own stripping, partly God taking a hand. These he calls active and passive. The one of the senses precedes that of the spirit. It is peculiar that he used the same stanzas of his poem the *Dark Night* as symbols for both experiences. The ones that concern many are the active; the passive referred to only the few. For quick reference the key place in John of the Cross' works are here given. He describes the active night of the senses in Bk. 1 of the *Ascent*: the active night of the spirit in Bks. 2 and 3. In the *Dark Night* (ch. 1. ss. 1–8) he recapitulates what he wrote in Bk. 1 of the *Ascent*; the rest of Bk. 1 is of the passive night of the senses. Bk. 2 is of the passive night of the spirit. John explains the plan in Bk. 1 (c. 1 ss. 1–3) of the *Ascent*. Can it be said that these experiences occur among those who have taken on an active apostolate? The answer is yes, but the experiences will be in a different mould and unfortunately often unrecognized.

Undeniably many a night comes from falling for the allurements of un-Christian pleasures. Many, however, having resisted or recovered, stand faithful to Christ. In early manhood and womanhood and in later life, they experience Dark Nights no less testing than those undergone by contemplatives – the young man alone in a great city, the young unmarried woman fearful of spinsterhood, battered on every side by temptations to sensuality, find prayer and sacraments and faith as tasteless as dry leather. All their old supports have dissolved. This is a true Dark Night. They must hold on like sailors at sea in a blinding storm. It will become tranquil. Then the abandoned wife or husband, whose life becomes senseless overnight and are tempted to despair, to drink. They too ask: is this what God does to those who have loved him? The faith has no more meaning than a stale newspaper. Yet faith is of the unseen; this life is not the meaning, it is the battle ground. Others, in middle age, have struggled all their lives against the current of public opinion, and now even those round them, including their children, abandon the faith; churchmen seem to have gone temporarily mad; the new liturgy is distasteful. All this builds up a powerful attack on faith. At the same time the mass media distort and magnify the differences and disturbances within the Church. These are all Dark Nights, and because they are dark, those within it *cannot see* either the sense of it all, nor where they are going. That is truly what is meant by blind faith, but not completely blind since they have the teaching of Christ and the example of so many before who have gone steadily forward along the same road.

Nicolas of Cusa (*1401–64*)
Christian humanist, ecumenist, mystic. Born at Cues on the Moselle, he very probably had his first education at Deventer with the Brothers of the Common Life; then, at 16, one year at the University of

Heidelberg, another at Padua and so on to Cologne (1425). He took his degree in Common Law and became a priest. Through the Cardinal-Legate, Giorano Orsini, to whom he was secretary, he became acquainted with the Italian humanists and then read Denis the Pseudo-Areopagite in the Greek. At this time he was hoping for the renewal of the Church through a general Council (see his *de Concordantia Catholica*, 1433), but the visible chaos of the Council of Basle finally turned his hopes towards the Papacy. For the rest of his life (from 1435) he remained its strong supporter. In 1437 he was sent as one of three envoys to Constantinople to bring the Emperor and the Patriarch with assisting bishops to the West for the Council of Florence. In Constantinople he studied the Koran in translation, determined to find a way of rapprochement with Islam. This resulted in his *Cribratio Alchoran* (1461). For ten years after his return (1438–48) he devoted his time to re-establishing unity between the Papacy and Germany, as Papal Legate in Germany. Only in 1452 did he take possession of his diocese of Brixen. He was continually harassed there by the Archduke Sigismund, and soon retired to Rome. But his link with a fervent Benedictine monastery in his diocese, that of Tegernsee, resulted in an interesting correspondence and a book he wrote to help them contemplate, *de Visione Dei*, which together with his *de Concordantia Catholica* is the most important of his literary works.

He was immensely well-read for his age, but he had a predilection for Plato and the Neo-Platonists, for Denis and for Augustine, and of course nearer home for Master Eckhart. God, for him, is the unknowable. To reach him we must go beyond the barrier of thought, beyond contradictions, to the darkness of faith, which is light. But he too learnt and wrote, 'God lets himself be known to one who loves'. In *The Vision of God* he has inspiring meditations on the part that Jesus plays in our search for and finding of God. He died at Todi in Italy.

J. Kosh, 'Nicolas of Cusa', an illuminating explanation of Nicolas's theological thinking in *N.C.E.*

Nicolas of Cusa, E.G. Salter (tr.), E. Underhill (intro.), *The Vision of God*, (London, 1928).

E. Vansteenberghe, *Le Cardinal Nicolas Cues; L'Action, La Pensée*, (Paris, 1920).

See also *D.T.C.*, XI, Pt. 1, 601 ff.

Nicolas von Flue, St (1417–87)
Brother Klaus, a hermit whose story is well documented. He was a son of a well-to-do Swiss farmer near Lake Lucerne. As a child he meditated regularly, at 16 he had a vision of a tower in the ravine of Ranft. Like others he was conscripted into the army and fought in the Zurich wars (1440–4) and the Thurgau war (1460). A companion reports that he 'protected the defeated enemy as best he could'. On one occasion he prevented the burning of the convent of Katherinental, where the enemy were hiding. He married, *circa* 1447, and had ten children; he was a respected citizen, councillor and judge. As the result of some unjust dealing to which he could not consent, he withdrew from public life in 1465, and two years later he carried out an old longing, to become a hermit. After some false starts he settled in the nearby ravine of Ranft. At first many opposed his venture, though not his wife, even though it was only three months and

a half before giving birth to their tenth child and fifth son. In 1469 he was visited by the local bishop who gave his approval to this strange way of living. Many began to come for advice and consolation including his wife, children and grand-children. They knew him as a holy man who never took any food, except the Holy Eucharist. This apparently lasted the full twenty years of his hermit life. From his youth he had fasted four days in the week. In 1481 the rural and urban Cantons were at loggerheads and in danger of war. Both sides came to Brother Klaus for advice. The Compromise of Stans was his proposal that both sides found just and accepted. He is venerated by both Catholics and Protestants. Note the withdrawal, the austerity, the prayer, the 'return' to the world at a spiritual level, by many people coming to him for help.

Articles in the encyclopedias and G.R. Lamb, *Brother Nicholas*, (New York, 1955). See also ↗*Hermits*.

Nilus of Sorsky, St
Born in 1433, died 1508, he is sometimes called St Nil Sorsky. Early he became a monk at the White Lake in the far north of Russia. In 1465 he set out for the East and visited Mount Athos and Palestine. He discovered from the monks of Mount Athos the prayer of the heart, the ↗Jesus Prayer. On his return to Russia he found that his monastery, which previously had been one of 'non-possessors', was accepting property. So he left and set up his own *laura* by the river Gorka. Companions joined him. His most important work is *The Tradition of Sketic Life*. It is the first major Russian mystical work. His monastery was planned on the Palestinian model, each monk living

in his own cell with a common chapel at the centre. The Liturgy would be solemnly celebrated only on Saturdays, and Sundays, and feast days, all the rest of the prayer was done in the cells. For each *laura* of twelve monks, there was to be one priest and one deacon. *The Tradition* is a short *Philocalia*, consisting of quotations from the ancient Fathers with his own comments.

S. Bolshakoff, *Russian Mystics* (London, 1977).

Nirvana
Both a Hindu and a Buddhist concept. In both it is the goal of existence; in both it necessitates the abandonment of all the superficial self; in both, at the highest level, it is in some way the absorption of the ephemeral self into the ultimate reality – whatever that is: the Buddha refused ever to say. ↗Atman is ↗Brahma. There are some sectors of both Hinduism and Buddhism which might qualify or even contradict this admittedly over-simplified presentation. Again, on the whole, the achievement of Nirvana is said to be no more than a process of taking thought, or self-help, especially in Buddhism which in its origin was a turning-away, among other things, from the old Hindu sacrificial pattern of salvation.

O

Obedience
From Latin *ob* and *audire*, 'to listen closely, intently, in a friendly way' (O.E.D.), reminiscent of the first words of St Benedict's Rule: '*Obsculta o fili*', 'listen my son'. Its primary meaning is: to carry out the command of another. In the

religious sphere its first meaning is: to obey God. As this act touches the deepest level of human activity, obedience of mind and heart, it is akin to love. Christ's teaching to his disciples was rooted also in obedience, summarized in the prayer, 'thy kingdom come, thy will be done'; in the saying that not those who say Lord, Lord, will enter the kingdom, but only those who do the will of his heavenly Father (*cf.* Mt 7:21). Mary at the moment of the Annunciation replied to the angel in obedient terms, 'may it be done to me according to thy word' (Lk 1:38). ⟋Paul in Romans expressed an important aspect when he wrote, that true worship is offering up our bodies as a living sacrifice, a worship of 'reasonable service', in which he links obedience with reasonableness and with sacrifice (Rom 12:1).

BLIND OBEDIENCE Some support seems to be given to this by ⟋Francis of Assisi, who says the friar should be like a corpse; so too by ⟋Ignatius, who in his letter to the Brethren at Coimbra actually uses the words 'blind obedience'. Today it is quite clear that the Church does not approve of that approach, i.e. unintelligent obedience. (It is not suggested that both the Franciscans and Jesuits were or are in disagreement with the Church's understanding.) In Vatican II's decree on religious life, superiors are encouraged to discuss with their community together or individually a matter of obedience that affects them personally or as a group. 'Let him (the superior) give the kind of leadership which will encourage religious to bring an *active* and *responsible* (my italics) obedience to the offices they shoulder and the activities they undertake. Therefore a superior should *listen* willingly to his subjects and encourage them to

make a personal contribution to the welfare of the community and of the Church' (n. 14). It goes on, however, to affirm that the superior's authority to decide what should be done and the doing of it, should not be impaired. Earlier the document says that members of communities should bring 'the resources of their minds and their wills' to bear on their lives (*ibid*) and that this is not to diminish obedience but to combine it with freedom, to enlarge it. It should be borne in mind that self-will can easily slip in when a subject religious begins to weigh the good and the bad of a decision; but misuse should not destroy good use; and better a reasonable service than a blind one. Best a loving service.

THE COUNSEL OF OBEDIENCE A teaching of Christ for those who seek earnestly for perfection. The counsel of obedience is not so easily grounded in Scripture as the other two, chastity (Mt 19:12) and poverty (Lk 10:25 ff), though it is there in the texts implicitly. Jesus encourages obedience by his own life and death and words. But does he encourage obedience to a human superior, to one not necessarily a member of the Church's hierarchy? It would at first sight seem not. On closer inspection the answer is yes. Obedience in religious Orders is first to the Rule; while the abbot, prior, guardian or superior, is the recognized interpreter of that Rule. The Rule itself is simply an expression, worked out by a holy man, of one among many lives lived in accordance with the life and teaching of Christ. Therefore by following a Rule, men and women are following Christ in a particular setting. Instead of taking their own, probably very imperfect, understanding of the way of perfection, they accept the deeper understanding of a great servant of God, ⟋Benedict, ↗Dominic, ↗Francis, ↗Ignatius. But, you will say, how do we know that these were in fact rightly guided in their inspirations? We do not, unless the Church examines and pronounces upon their Rules, and says, this is a sure way of following Christ and reaching holiness. This is precisely what the Church does, after due consideration, for the Rules of the major Orders in the Church.

OBEDIENCE AND CONSCIENCE
Today there can be no hesitation in saying that conscience is supreme, we must do what our consciences tell us. See the texts of Vatican II, e.g: 'Man has in his heart a law written by God. To obey it is the very dignity of man; according to it he will be judged. Conscience is the most secret core and sanctuary of a man.' (*Gaudium et Spes*, n. 16 also *Religious Freedom*, nn. 3, 13.) Man has no right to 'follow his conscience' without duly seeking all means to inform that conscience. Crass ignorance is no excuse for a false conscience; therefore he must consult the teaching of the Church. In cases of obedience in which a subject's view is opposed to that of the superior, the normal response is to obey, unless he thinks that to do so is morally wrong. ↗Benedict has a useful phrase in these cases, he should obey 'with a quiet mind'.

OBEDIENCE TO HUMAN AUTHORITY
Unconditional obedience can only be given to God since he is Truth. But how do we, in the religious sphere, know what God wants? There are several lines of approach. Here inevitably we enter somewhat controversial territory, and each reader must make his or her choice and bear with the writer. Each reader's answer will differ according to whether he or she is Orthodox, Catholic, Anglican, Lutheran, Calvinist, Methodist, Quaker and so on.

(i) The first and last test is conscience. In all circumstances it would be wrong to go against one's conscience, to turn away from what we consider, after mature consideration, is right, that is after having seriously examined all sides of the question. For example see in text of Vatican II, 'Man has in his heart a law written by God. To obey it is the very dignity of man; according to it he will be judged . . . Conscience is the most secret core and sanctuary of a man'. (*The Church in the Modern World*, n. 16. See also the Decree on *Religious Freedom*, nn. 3 and 13.)

(ii) Sacred Scripture is a guide to conscience, as it is held to be the very word of God.

(iii) Jesus' teaching and life are the quintessence of the Bible's teaching on obedience as on all else.

(iv) The Church as teacher and guardian of Scripture also helps us to know God's will, so as to obey it. The chief occasions of the Church's intervention would be, on disputed points, and by the Bishops gathered together in Council or the Pope in Rome using his authority as shepherd of the Flock.

OBEDIENCE OF JESUS Jesus saw his life as one continual obedience to his Father. 'Thy will be done' was a refrain in his speech. He only said what his Father wanted him to say, he saw his own death as an acceptance of the Divine Will. At the supreme moment Jesus said it was consummated, fulfilled (see especially Jn 10:17 and Lk 22:39–43). The 'Our Father' in its first part is a desire to carry out God's will on earth. ↗Paul expressed the meaning of Christ's life and death, in terms of obedience in Phil 2:6–8.

OBEDIENCE AND LAW Law is what is reasonable to do, and laid down as such. Therefore to obey such a law is to be reasonable. To be reasonable is to be free. To act from anything but what is reasonable is not to be free. It is reasonable to obey God, therefore obedience in the religious sense is an act of freedom.

But law can be considered simply as a law, regardless of its reasonableness; this is called legalism, and was condemned by Jesus when he condemned so strongly the Pharisees in their extreme views on ritual uncleanness, on work on the Sabbath Day, e.g. picking corn, doing miracles! Christians and especially persons in religious orders are prone to this weakness, idolizing rules. A rule can be obeyed simply because it is a rule, whereas it should be done because it is reasonable and/or the will of God in some way. Soeur ↗Thérèse in her *Little Way* advocated the careful practice of the smallest rule as this was the only way most could show their devoted love of God. But this has its dangers, especially legalism, rule for rule's sake; as was shown when, after Vatican II, so many good religious found it impossible to accept the little changes required for renewal.

OBEDIENCE AND LOVE To love is to conform, to unite one's being, mind and heart with the beloved. Obedience is to conform the heart (the will) with the beloved. Any other obedience – routine, military or fearful – is not religious obedience. Only loving obedience will serve. All religious obedience in ultimate analysis must be obedience to God and therefore an act of love for God.

Origen (*circa 185–circa 254*)
Born in Alexandria, child of fervent Christian parents in the centre of Hellenic and Jewish culture. His father Leonidas was martyred; Origen's mother only saved her son from the same fate on one occasion by hiding his clothes. At a very early age Origen was appointed teacher to the new Christians, whom he found often knowledgeable in Hellenic, Platonic philosophy; he therefore immersed himself in it, but only in order to penetrate deeper into Scripture. One of the greatest exegetes of all time, he established the allegorical interpretation. Living before theology had been stabilized, he explored many possibilities, but without committing himself; some of these theories were judged later heretical, especially in the form that his disciple, ↗Evagrius, gave them; and Origen was enveloped in the condemnation of the latter, particularly by the attacks of Jerome and finally in the Provincial Council of Constantinople (543). His works were destroyed in the East but they survived in part in the West. His influence, especially in spirituality, never ceased. He had believed that his life should conform with what he read in Scripture and with what he taught. Thus he practised intense asceticism, even, it is probable, to self-mutilation (which he regretted in his later life); he practised extreme poverty; he believed in solitude, not of place, as a hermit, but solitude of the heart, which he claimed could be practised in the market place or even in the theatre. He lived with his disciples in a quasi monastic manner, praying together, studying, and at meals reading from the Scriptures. His teaching and his life both pointed towards that explosion into the desert that occurred soon after his death. Having left Alexandria after a quarrel with its bishop, he settled at Caesarea in Palestine with his great library. In the Decian persecution he

suffered terrible tortures and died from their effects, a martyr in all but name. His was a spirituality of light, not of darkness; he saw man as the image of God, and with the *Logos* embedded in the centre of his soul; this had to be discovered by prayer and asceticism, by the acquiring of ↗*apatheia*, or custody of the heart. He saw the relationship of the soul with God as it is described in his commentary on the *Song of Songs* (*A.C.W.*), of which he was the first to treat as personal as well as between God and the Church. Again his work, *On Prayer*, is the first of its kind. Many of his ideas came into their own in the 12th century with the writings of ↗Bernard and ↗William of St Thierry, the former with his conferences on the *Song of Songs* and William of S. Thierry with his teaching on the image and presence of the *Logos*.

H. Crouzel in *Théologie de la vie monastique*, (Paris, 1961).

J. Daniélou, *Origen*, (London, 1955).

Eusebius of Caesarea, *The History of the Church*, (Harmondsworth, 1981), Bk. 6, ss. 1–3, 15–19, 23–6, 30–9.

R.A. Greer (tr.), *Origen*, (New York, 1979). Useful collection of Origen's ascetical writings with introduction and biblio.

Orthodox Spirituality
The Church in the East whose major centre is the Patriarchate of Constantinople, has a unique quality through preserving, seemingly intact, the spirituality of the Patristic age. Its centre is the liturgy, both the sign and the cause of unity; an attitude that reaches back to ↗Ignatius of Antioch (martyred *circa* 107). Thus the Christian's life springs from the divine liturgy: the readings of Scripture, the beautiful canticles, the solemn ceremonial. It is based on a theology, which, in simple terms, sees Christ as glorified Lord, who carries mankind up with him to heaven to share in the Divine life (a theology that ↗Irenaeus brought from the East to the West *circa* 200). The direction is Godwards, the end; and the means – the Passion and Death – are less stressed than in the West. This other-worldliness is also exemplified sublimely in the world-renouncing monastic tradition which culminates in the monasteries of ↗Mount Athos. Here the ancient contemplative way is expressed often in the ↗Jesus Prayer and the ↗Philocalia. For the Orthodox, the Church is not just an organization, not merely a hierarchy, nor is it simply the faithful, or the theologians, but all these in one, as a living unity in Christ (the Russians have a word: *Sobornost*), vivified by the Spirit. As the result of polemics with the West, perhaps, the devotion to the Spirit has been somewhat overlaid with theologizing, but one is aware of the deep devotion to and reliance on the guidance of the Holy Spirit in the Eastern Church. These are some of the characteristic glories; and today, in the ecumenical world we live in, it is to be expected that the riches of each Church will become the riches of all the others. This has already begun: thus the Eastern Fathers are beginning to be better known, a study of comparative liturgy is under way; those great Eastern feasts of Easter and Pentecost have received once again in the West their pre-eminence, as has also the Transfiguration. Likewise the eschatological sense is strong, especially the understanding of the Incarnation as a-becoming-man of the Son that we might become God-like. All have some-

thing to learn from Orthodox devotion to the Mother of God and to the saints, signs of God's great mercy and power. The ↗icons bring the reality of the saints in glory right into the Divine Mysteries and into the home.

S. Bulgakov, *The Orthodox Church*, (London, 1935). Very useful.

G.P. Fedotov, *A Treasury of Russian Spirituality*, (London, 1952).

J. Meyendorff, *L' Eglise orthodoxe hier et aujourd' hui*, (Paris, 1960).

J. Paine and N. Zemor (eds.), *A Bulgakov Anthology*, (London, 1976).

V. Soloviev, works, especially *Russia and the Universal Church*, translated 1948.

T. Ware, *Orthodoxy*, (Harmondsworth, 1963).

H. Zernov, *Eastern Christendom*, (London, 1961).

Orthodox Spirituality, by an Orthodox monk, (London, 1974).

Oxford Movement, The
Said to have begun with the sermon preached by John Keble (1792–1866) in the Oxford University church in 1833, called 'National Apostacy'. The occasion, the suppression of ten Irish bishoprics, symbolized the abandonment by the Church of England of her duty as the Church of the nation. The Anglican Church was as it were awakening from a long sleep. John ↗Wesley had drawn off the enthusiasts in the 18th century; the Liberals were corroding the Church from within. These men, Keble, Edward Bouverie Pusey, Professor of Hebrew, J.H. ↗Newman and others, were determined to stem that tide and to awaken their Church to the richness

of its ↗Caroline and Catholic heritage. The first results were *Tracts of the Times* (1833–41), culminating in *Tract 90* by Newman which seemed to prove that the Anglican Church believed what is the official teaching of the Church of Rome. The uproar was intense and Newman retired to Littlemore. It is not the purpose of this article to expound once more the progress of the movement, but rather to notice the spiritual effects. In the first place, and this superficial, the followers of the movement began to use Roman liturgical manners: vestments, candles, incense, statues. What this signified was a return to certain doctrines of the ancient Church, especially in Eucharistic worship, and in maintaining episcopal dignity as of apostolic origin. This led, through controversy, to a closer study of the Fathers of the Church, the translation of their works into English (*The Library of the Fathers* edited by Keble, Newman and Pusey and others) which, for the spiritual life of Christians in England, was an immense enrichment; for the Fathers are so close to Scripture, not so much for controversy (though sometimes) but for prayerful meditation on Scripture. This in its turn led to the deepening of the study of Scripture itself. The whole sacramental system of the ancient Church was made visible. In the case of John Henry Newman this revelation of what the early Church actually believed led to submission to the Catholic Church. Not so Keble and Pusey, who stood firm in the Anglican tradition. But the Romantic movement, with its idealization of the medieval scene, somehow became mingled with the Oxford Movement – partly through the insights of Richard Hurrell Froude (1803–36), an intimate friend of Newman and a historian. He died young, but his *Remains* (1838–9) caused a great stir, particularly his attack on the Reformers and the disclosure of his own very Romish pious practices. The *Apologia* (1864) of Newman gives a fascinating retrospective view of those bewildering times. In fact the Movement had incalculable importance, not only for the Anglican Church itself and the Roman Catholics in England but for the Non-conformists also. No one today is uninfluenced by the liturgical, Patristic and Scriptural movements that emanated from the Oxford of 1833–45. As the years passed the Anglican Church gradually, in part, flowered into a very Catholic life: frequent Eucharistic celebrations, even reservation of the Sacrament, the sacrament of Confession, the development of religious and monastic life both male and female, especially in the contemplative form: Benedictines, Franciscans and orders of its own invention. Roman Catholics and Anglicans can share the rich ancient and medieval heritage of the Church, particularly of the English mystics. Yet the two streams remain distinct, each being able still to enrich the other.

G. Battiscombe, *Life of John Keble*, 1963.

O. Chadwick (ed.), *The Mind of the Oxford Movement*, (Oxford, 1960). Collection of contemporary material.

C. Dawson, *The Spirit of the Oxford Movement*, (London, 1933).

J. Keble, *The Christian Year*, (1927). A collection of poems.

E.B. Pusey. Translation of *St Augustine's Confessions* and Intro., 1838.

G.W.E. Russell, *Life of Edward Bouverie Pusey*, 1907.

P

Pantheism

In its simplest expression means all is God. One stream of Hindu mysticism is frankly pantheistic and this would seem to be the meaning of a number of Upanishads and reminds one of nature mysticism (*cf.* Jean Jacques Rousseau). 'This infinite is below, it is above, it is to the west, to the east, to the north and to the south. Truly it is the whole universe. I am below, I am above, I am to the west (etc.) ... Truly I am the whole universe.' (*Changodya Upanishad*, vii, xxv, in R.C. Zaehner, *Hindu Scriptures*, London, 1966, p. 121). On the whole, Buddhism denies the abiding reality except the Atman or real Self which is not you or me, but the Ultimate, the *plenum void* beyond all thought. Here there seems to be the denial of the permanence of the human soul, the distinct entities that we are (*cf.* Christmas Humphreys, *Buddhism*, Harmondsworth, 1967, p. 16 and *passim*). The Jewish and Christian doctrine is different, since here God is known to have created all things, neither out of himself nor out of anything else. These have a true reality and the relationship between the Creator and the created is not one of absorption but one of love or union. Yet the experience of love on the psychological level tends to blur the distinction of the two and so even Christian mystics have inadvertently at times given the impression that the highest union is one of unity, even ↗John of the Cross, '*Amado con amada, / amada en el Amado transformada*' (sixth stanza of the *Dark Night*: 'The Lover with the beloved; the beloved transformed into the Lover'). Unless the Knower and the known, the Lover and the beloved are kept distinct, the true nature of union with God evaporates.

Pascal, Blaise (*1623–62*)
A layman, passionately concerned for renewal within the Church, a mathematician, natural scientist, a founder of modern French prose, mystic, associated with *le parti* of the Jansenists, but theologically not one. A tempestuous berater of laxity in morals, which he attributed to Jesuit writers, and so covered the whole Order with odium, unjustly. As a spiritual writer he is striking and profound. His 'memorial' is one of the few immediate descriptions of a religious mystical experience. It begins 23 November, lasting from about 10.30 to 12.30 at night: 'Fire – God of Abraham, God of Isaac, God of Jacob, not of the philosophers and the intellectuals (scientists). Certitude, certitude, feeling, joy, peace. God of Jesus Christ. Joy, joy, joy, tears of joy . . .'

'The Mystery of Jesus', another famous prayer, often included among the *Pensées*, contains such sentences as the following: 'Be consoled, you would not be seeking me, had you not already found me', and 'I was thinking of you during my agony; that and that other drop of blood I shed for you'.

Pascal the scientist wanted evidence; the experience of that night gave it him in his search for God. In this he approaches the Protestant apologetic. In the great unfinished Apology for Christianity, the fragments we call *Les Pensées*, Pascal provides a penetrating analysis of *divertissement*, how we avoid facing the ultimate realities; of the need to know by *le coeur*, which is not the sentimental heart but the Biblical 'heart' which is the deepest form of knowledge we have, that includes the workings of love. He backed away from the metaphysical proofs of God's existence because they did not have the power to move the heart.

L. C. Brunschvicg, *Les Pensées*, (Paris, 1900).

J. Chevalier, *Blaise Pascal*, (1922). Old, but the most sympathetic.

Blaise Pascal, Louis Lafuma (ed.) *Oeuvres Complètes*, (Paris, 1963).

Passion of Christ
The heart of the Christian life. It has been looked at from different angles in different periods. It was probably the first part of the Gospels to be written down. ↗Paul wrote that he came to preach Christ crucified (1 Cor 2:2). Jesus himself after the Resurrection was eager to explain the meaning of his Passion, a hideous sight and so difficult to accept by those early disciples and by us of all ages (Lk 24:25 ff). The secret of its meaning and power was enshrined in the Last Supper and in the ever-present Eucharist. Paul gives the Passion its deepest meaning in Phil 2. From the earliest times, Baptism (Rom 6:3), the Eucharist (1 Cor 11:26) and probably Confession (Jn 13:6 ff) were already seen as intimately linked to Christ's Passion. The early Christians, who were faced with the prospect of martyrdom, saw their own death as a conforming to the martyrdom of Christ on the Cross (*cf.* Phil 3:10); in their passions they were filling up what was wanting in the sufferings of Christ (Col 1:24). Not that Christ's sufferings were insufficient – they were infinite in power – but we are free to accept our redemption or not. This is our part, which the martyrs victoriously fulfilled, for example we could read the martyrdoms of ↗Ignatius and ↗Polycarp in this way. Yet in the early Church Christ's death and his Passion were rarely portrayed in art – as perhaps seeming too humiliating – but rather his glory. As the struggle

against Arianism progressed, the emphasis is quite correctly put on the glorified Christ, Son of God – but his humanity was less adverted to in its weakness and suffering, except for the revived interest in the holy Places and the sites of his Passion, inaugurated by St Helena and followed up by the mysterious Etheria from Spain. The Irish, long before ↗Bernard (d. 1153), who is said to have spread the devotion, were particularly devoted to Christ's Passion.

↗Anselm could theorize about the Passion, but it was left to Bernard to experience and express the impact of that suffering done on our behalf. Now appears that desire to share in Christ's sufferings, already deeply expressed by Ignatius of Antioch in his letters. Its climax came with ↗Francis of Assisi receiving the stigmata – had not the *crucified* Saviour spoken to him, telling him to restore his church? Now pilgrims in their thousands start going to the Holy Land; now appear the holy Shroud, the crown of thorns, the spear, Veronica's cloth. We find also the cloistered devotion to the Sacred Heart.

At the same time ↗Thomas is penning perhaps the finest little treatise on the Passion. (*S. Th.*, III, especially questions 46 and 48.) Thomas is not satisfied with sensibility but studies the causes and the effects. All Christ's life, he writes, was salvific but the Passion was needed to eliminate certain obstacles on men's part. Thus the Passion satisfied, certainly because it took the sufferings of us all, but more, it did enough (*satis fecit*) loving – what greater love can any man show than to give his life for those who do not love him – to make up for all our lack of love of God. His Passion faced both ways; the perfect Son, doing his Father's will; the perfect friend, 'provoking

us to love in return' – for men are so prone to selfishness. The Passion was needed for that.

As we approach the Reformation the emotional side becomes more pronounced; we see this in the art of the Passion especially in Spain and Germany. In the Low Countries the mystics begin to move more towards an abstract spirituality, leaving the contemplation of the humanity of Christ on one side. ↗Teresa (d. 1582) reacted strongly against this, so too ↗Ignatius and his whole Society. Likewise the French School, led by Cardinal ↗Bérulle and Olier. ↗Margaret Mary was in the line of the cloistered devotion to the Sacred Heart of the Middle Ages. The 18th century saw the rise of the Congregation of the Passion, founded by St ↗Paul of the Cross.

Today we distinguish between the facts of Christ's human life and their meaning. With ↗Thomas we see the Passion both as *cause* of our redemption and as the supreme *example* to us of love and meekness, of courage and hope; it is also the supreme *sign* of God's love for us, and an *incentive* to love him in return. But we would also include Christ's Resurrection as a constituent element in the redeeming act.

Passive Prayer

Called Contemplative, this has a bewildering variety of manifestations, due no doubt to the endless differences among men and women. When we are today faced with 'instant' mystical experience, it is welcome to find ↗John of the Cross declaring such experiences to be veritable obstacles to union with God at that level. In this he voices the tradition of Catholic mystics. The so-called Nights are precisely the process by which a man is weaned from all that is not God whether in the sensible or spiritual experiences associated with prayer. But John was writing for enclosed nuns of the Carmelite Order. This subject has a much wider implication. In different ways active persons, clerical, religious or lay are being led to depths of prayer that run parallel to that described by John. The following is a tentative approach.

Adolescents 'lose' their faith partly because many must find it again, some because the sensual appetites are temporarily so powerful that the spiritual is obscured. We are concerned with seasoned Christians who have struggled many years to live in Christ by the power of the Spirit. A time comes when what once appeared crystal clear, most attractive, inspiring, now is unreal, unattractive, irrelevant. Before proceeding, a warning is needed. Unawares, we grow imperceptibly lax; luxury, pride, or any other of the deadly sins could have re-entered the 'house'. If so, only one course can be proposed – begin again. But here we are taking the case of one or a pair for whom the old spiritual ways, and for no apparent fault of their own, have become dead. What is to be done? First, it must be believed that this is a deepening, a change of life, like passing from youth to middle age. Remember the simile of the cathedral with bright sunlight without, within at first utter darkness. With time the luminous beauty of the glass discloses itself. So, God will disclose himself, but not before we have passed from the bright daylight into a darkness. Secondly, the laity are beset with much positive challenge to the spiritual: materialism, the pleasures of this life, the urge for middle-aged comforts, the all-penetrating economic or political or social motivation of everyday living, these drain the soul of idealism.

Then, liturgy, once so attractive, has become a bore, and, even worse, a trial, our own prayers trite. The overpowering temptation is to give up. The old ways do not work any more.

So we need to try new ways, especially that of passivity. A dangerous word, because it implies doing nothing. Rather it is not attempting to rationalize what is going on, but to *rely* on the action of the Holy Spirit. In this we are reassured by the words of the Epistle to the Romans (ch. 8):

'Hope would not be hope at all if its objects were in view; how could a man still hope for something which he sees? And if we are hoping for something still unseen, then we need endurance to wait for it. Only, as before, the Spirit comes to the aid of our weakness: when we do not know what prayer to offer, to pray as we ought, the Spirit himself intercedes for us, with groans beyond all uttering: and God who can read our hearts, knows well what the Spirit's intent is; for indeed it is according to the mind of God that he makes intercession for the saints' (vv. 26, 27). Our part is to plead silently and remain attentively loving. We will be refreshed.

Traditionally Passive Contemplation comes after a period of illumination and insight but also deepest darkness, with trials innumerable, so that one lives by naked faith. There emerges a condition in which the soul knows itself to be held by God in a union so intimate as to make one suppose fusion or absorption, an embrace of God. This condition has varying degrees of permanence, these are sometimes described in terms of 'marriage'. The earlier stage is called ↗Espousals, the later mystical Marriage (*cf.* ↗Ruysbroeck and ↗John of the Cross). Nothing is easier to imagine than that warm emotional experiences in prayer are just this. But a Darkness of Night, a stripping of the self has to come first.

Words transferred from one language to another are deceptive. Passive does not mean in this context negative, inactive, but active as a receiver; we must be accepting with all our being, in faith, in love.

St Paul and Prayer
His conversion was rooted in a vision and in hearing a voice; he both saw and heard the Lord. The content of that experience was so rich, it filled his life; and after, he was taught by the living Christ. The ecstasy described in 2 Cor 12, it is presumed, was his own and, though concerned with ineffable experiences, he states they were *in* Christ. It is possible that the mystery referred to in Eph 1 is the revelation he received in that vision. Each of his epistles begins with a prayer, usually thanking God for all his blessings; at other times his prayer overflows into petition for his converts, as in Eph 1:17, and 3:1 – where he falls on his knees, note specially v. 14 ff. In Rom 8:26 he refers to a form of passive prayer in which the Spirit is active, praying in us, envisaging wordless prayer as directed by the Spirit of God. His very life was directed by the Spirit, a truly Spiritual life (which is what spiritual really signifies). His way of expressing it is 'in Christ', which he uses 164 times. As he got older this mystery loomed larger, especially in the Captivity epistles; there the theme of the Body and the Head or Source, are much developed.

For Paul the first move in our sanctification is always with God: he comes before (prevents), co-operates and completes, without at any time our remaining inactive, but so that to him be all the glory. The Cross was

also central to his prayer and spirituality. God's wisdom was our folly; to be nothing was to be wise. Christ humbled himself to dying on the Cross. But for Paul that was the beginning, since for him the Risen Christ was all in all; and the way to share his life was through the sacraments of Baptism and Eucharist. To live with him, we have to die with him first. Through sharing in the body of Christ, we share in his divinity and in the Sonship of Christ; we become co-heirs with him.

In Acts 16 we get the measure of Paul, the man of prayer. He and Silas at Philippi had been stripped and beaten and put in prison: 'At midnight Paul and Silas were at their prayers praising God'.

Peace of Mind
Translates ↗Cassian's *custodia cordis* and the Greek ↗*apatheia*, but with shifts of meaning. The last could have a sense of passionlessness, akin to Stoicism and even the Far Eastern turning away from all desire, (*cf.* the Buddhist ↗Four Holy Truths, the last of which is: 'If you wish to be free of all ills, be free of all desire'.) ↗Augustine wrote of all this in the *City of God* (Bk. 14, ch. 9). The *Bhagavad ↗Gita*, that most treasured of Hindu books, takes a less stringent view: not complete denial of life but non-attachment.

So too the Christian teaching, especially as according to Christian and Jewish truth all things and people were created by God and are good, even if that good is limited. Therefore the aim of the Christian is not the elimination of love but its control. Love is part of creation and is there to be used. Man's instability has made the just mean difficult to attain.

Pearl, the

Or *Pearl of the Gospel*, by an anonymous writer (1463–1540). Recently an edition of 1542 has been found with a preface by Nicolas van Esche. He writes that the authoress was a pious woman living in the world who died in 1540 at 77 years of age; possibly she was from Costerwijk in Brabant, perhaps a relation of St Peter Canisius, SJ. *The Pearl* belongs to the Rhino-Flemish mystical tradition with borrowings from ↗Ruysbroeck and ↗Tauler. She is the last writer of the period openly to mention ↗Eckhart. She follows Eckhart and Tauler in seeing the presence of God in the soul by his essence and by grace: God is always there; he is the life of the spirit, and the spirit the life of the soul, and God is always in the spirit, which is the image of God in the soul (Bk. 1, ch. 14).

'I believe that from eternity I was uncreated in your divine essence' (Bk. 2, ch. 4). We must eliminate all images, enter into the abyss of our soul, first transformed in Christ. Christ is the means, that is, he is passed beyond; he is in the way (Bk. 1, ch. 4). She writes of the superessential life in God. *The Pearl* was much read until 1620, going into many editions. ↗Francis of Sales thought it too much in the heights.

Latin translation, Cologne, 1545.

See also *H.C.S*, Vol. 2, pp. 434–5.

Pentecostal Movement

It aims at reviving the spirit of the ancient Church. The Spirit has many times broken through the hard crust of ecclesiastical routine in the past from the prophets of the apostolic Church to ↗Francis of Assisi, to John ↗Wesley, right up to our day. Pope John XXIII prayed before his Council assembled that it would bring a new Pentecost. In an unexpected way it did, though its leaders prefer to call it the Movement of Spiritual Renewal. In 1906 the Pentecostalists first caught the headlines in Los Angeles; in 1915 the 'Elim Foursquare Gospel Alliance' was formed, with ↗Baptism of the Spirit but not necessarily ↗Tongues. In 1924 'The Assemblies of God in Great Britain and Ireland' was formed; these did not require a manifestation of Tongues. All this was on the fringe of the more evangelical part of Protestantism. In 1966 at Duquesne University, Pittsburg, five Catholic members of that university, students and professors, became increasingly aware of the disparity between their lives and that described among the early Christians in Acts and the Letters of ↗Paul. They happened to read a remarkable book, *The Cross and the Switchblade* by a pastor, David Wilkerson, in which he described how, by the power of the Spirit and Baptism in the Spirit, he had converted confirmed drug addicts and gangsters. The five went to an Episcopalian minister, had themselves 'Baptized in the Spirit'; and this was followed by the usual manifestations of the Spirit, tongues and prophesying. Much the same at about the same time occurred at another Catholic university, Notre Dame in Indiana, near South Bend. Thus, *circa* 1970, this movement of the Spirit had penetrated – though not yet in very large numbers – both the Episcopal and Catholic Churches in North America and Britain and elsewhere. The Catholic hierarchy of the United States set up an Institute in Detroit to examine and guide the movement. But it must be emphasized that in the Church it is *not* an organization, and does not want to be, but simply a movement of the Spirit. This style of thing often turns into a new sect. In Africa, particularly in the South, over five thousand sects have hived off from the older Churches in the last fifty years, and another one thousand been formed by spontaneous generation.

What are the main characteristics of this phenomenon? (i) A belief that the Spirit is active in a Christian's life, if the Christian will allow him to be; (ii) An outward sign of this confidence is to be 'Baptized' in the Spirit by a laying on of hands by someone already a charismatic person and the praying of the community or group; (iii) At this point there often occur (and *de rigueur* among some Protestant Pentecostalists) certain manifestations of the Spirit, in particular the gift of tongues or ⁊healing or prophecy and any of those mentioned in the epistles of Paul (*cf.* particularly 1 Cor 12–14); (iv) It will be found that the life of this prayed-over person will be joyous in the Lord; (v) Usually holy Scripture becomes luminous and insights into its meaning frequent; (vi) It is said that a truly charismatic Catholic becomes more attached to the Sacraments (which he may even have ceased receiving before), to the faith and to obedience to the authorities in the Church. That is true, but to be guarded against is the ever-present danger of sectarianism, of setting up an élite group which cuts itself off from the common herd and considers itself the elect.

The fact is that by the sacrament of Baptism and that of Confirmation the Holy Spirit is given to every Christian. In that sense the whole Church is charismatic, since the greatest gift is the Spirit himself who dwells in our souls (Jn 14:26; Rom 5:5). What Christians often do not

manifest is a knowledge, a belief that this is so, and have instead a Pelagian reliance not on him but on themselves. Therefore this movement for all its dangers and exaggerations, has been a telling reminder to the whole Church that its life *is* the Spirit. Further, the young, who have not been attracted by the over-staid ancient structures, have been captivated by this free and happy way of being Christian.

K. McDonnel, OSB, 'Catholic Pentecostalism', in *Theol. Digest*, Spring, 1971 (St Louis).

L.J. Cardinal Suenens, *A New Pentecost?*, (London, 1975).

F.A. Sullivan, SJ, *The Pentecostal Movement*, (Rome, 1972).

Petition, Prayer of

Has recently, for superficial reasons, been dropped by some Christians. Moses, in the Old Testament was the outstanding intercessor for the People of God; he was forerunner of the sinless mediator, Christ. The Psalms too are filled with prayers of petition. In the new dispensation Jesus himself petitions the Father: 'He offered up prayers and entreaty, aloud and in silent tears, to the one who had the power to save him out of death' (Heb 5:7). He went into the desert to pray on his mission; he prayed before choosing his apostles; he prayed in the Garden, even to saying, 'Father, if you are willing, take the cup away from me' (Lk 22:42), and then the perfect acceptance: 'Let your will be done not mine'. It is not always noted that Jesus responded to many prayers of petition for material things. The miracles he did were not only signs, they were responses to prayer: the ⁊curing of the blind man, the raising of Lazarus are examples. He himself taught us to ask, and he promised we would receive. Mark puts it strongly: 'Anything you ask and pray for, believe that you have it already and it will be yours' (11:24). But ↗John in his first epistle is more cautious, he says that the Son of God listens to our prayers whenever they are in accordance with his will (1 Jn 5:14). This last would seem to lead us to a prayer of acceptance; but this is not entirely in accord with the spirit of the Gospel where Jesus often encourages us almost to pester the Father, as in the parable of the importunate widow, the story of the friend who comes late at night. We almost feel the purpose is to 'change God's mind'. There are two pertinent comments upon this. The first is ↗Thomas Aquinas: Prayer (*oratio*), he says, is not aimed to influence God's plan but to bring us ourselves to a right frame of mind, to accept his providence as the Creator and Guide of the universe. One who comes before God as a beggar is a truly humble man. Does that mean that our prayers have no effect on the course of events? As Karl Rahner says, that is the wrong question. When we lift a weight we are interrupting a lower law (of gravity) by a higher law of human energy. So too with God, his ways of acting are not ours, but they can include in their orbit our prayers. The Liturgy has followed the teaching of Christ. It is full of petitions, even in the Canon. There are Masses to avert war, famine, pestilence. The Church stands before God as a suppliant, the *Orante*.

Finally, Jesus said at the Last Supper, 'Whatever you ask for in my name I will do' (Jn 14:14).

Perfect

The name for those in the spiritual life who have reached a very close union with God and so of contemplation (*cf. S. Th.*, II, II, 24.9). It is a name for those in the ↗Unitive Way. The 'perfect' soul concentrates on God alone, not even on the illuminations such as occur in the condition of the proficients in the ↗Illuminative Way. But no matter how high the state, no one is perfect in this life. Nevertheless, in this state all, or nearly all, the action seems to come from the Holy Spirit; the creature must be absolutely receptive and alert to receive. This can only come about after a stripping naked of the self to a degree that ordinarily we cannot conceive. 'Unless the seed die . . .', 'He who loses his life shall find it' (Jn 12:24–5); 'Take up your cross and come follow me' (Mk 8:34). In this case it is not merely a giving up of wealth or even one's body, or human love; it is giving up the very central core of one's liberty, the self, to become self-less, open, given to God. To write or talk of this is easy, the accomplishment difficult in the extreme (*cf.* St John of the Cross, *The Spiritual Canticle*).

Philocalia

Title of a Greek compilation of extracts from the Eastern Fathers of the Church on spirituality and the Prayer of the Heart, the ↗Jesus Prayer. Its first printing was in Venice, 1782. The compilers were Macarius of Corinth (1731–1805) and the monk of Mount Athos, Nicodemus the Hagiorite. The title in Greek means Love of the Beautiful, or Beautiful Love. English versions so far are extracts from this great compilation (though the full version is in process of publication). The general theme is first the elimination of everything from without or from within the self that might militate against prayer or union with God. The second is the practice of silence or quiet concentration. The third is the practice of the ↗Jesus Prayer. Lastly there is some account of ↗Hesychasm. The book thus contains the quintessence of the Orthodox monastic tradition especially from Mount Sinai and ↗Mount Athos.

An anthology from the works of ↗Origen was also called *Philocalia*, compiled by ↗Basil and his friend ↗Gregory of Nazianzus between 358–9 (*cf. O.D.C.C.*).

G.E. Palmer, E. Kadloubovsky (tr.), *Writings from the Philocalia on Prayer of the Heart* (London, 1962). Translated from the Russian text *Dobrotolubiye*.

Pietism

A religious movement which sprang up as a reaction against the extreme aridity of Lutheran polemical thinking in the late-17th century and against the dead hand of rationalism in the 18th. It sat lightly by dogma except for an exclusive reliance on God for salvation and also a profound devotion to the humanity of Christ, his Sacred Heart and to him as the Lamb. A lack of intellectual content sometimes led to sentimentality. This loving zeal led not to the creation of another Church but to the spread of their ideas first on the mainland of Europe, then England, America and India. A group of Pietistical Moravians – the '*Unitas Fratrum*', an *ecclesiola in ecclesia* – had a profound effect on the ↗Wesley brothers. The missionary impetus given by the Pietists was an important element in the great surge of missionary endeavour in the Churches of the Reformation in the 19th century.

The three central figures were Philip Spener (1635–1705) who gave the inspiration for the founding of the University of Halle (1694); August Francke (1663–1727), his disciple who founded 'the Institutes', in particular the famous orphanage at Halle, and who started their mission at Tranquebar in southern India under the patronage of King Frederick of Denmark; the third was Lewis Count von Zinzendorf (1700–60), the resuscitator of the Moravian 'Church' in Saxony at Bethelsdorf on a hill called Hernhut.

G.R. Cragg, *The Church and the Age of Reason, 1648–1789*, (Harmondsworth, 1960).

R.A. Knox, *Enthusiasm, A Chapter in the History of Religion*, (Oxford, 1950).

Pilgrimage

An activity with complex origins and many levels of meaning, of great extension, being common to many religions – Christian, Jewish, Muslim, Hindu and Buddhist. A common factor seems to be: the desire to be in physical contact with the Divine, the supernatural, ultimate reality, by means of something associated with these: a sacred river, the Ganges; a holy person, a guru, a saint Simon Stylites; a sacred place, the Kaaba and the black stone at Mecca, the holy Places of Palestine.

In the Christian world the first pilgrimage was to Jerusalem and the Holy Land, in order to be where Christ had been, see what he had seen, be where he had been born, died and risen again. St Helena, mother of Constantine (4th century), gave this a great impetus by building churches over the holy places. The most detailed account from antiquity of such pilgrimage places is that of Etheria, a Spanish lady (abbess?) who visited them *circa* 400. Rome very soon ran the Holy Land close for popularity because of the bodies of SS Peter and Paul venerated there, and those of many other martyrs. In the Middle Ages each country had its shrines: St James of Compostela, the Madonna of Chartres, St Thomas of Canterbury and St Cuthbert of Durham. Many a pilgrimage was frivolous (*cf.* the account by Chaucer and the criticisms of Erasmus and More). But in the Middle Ages there was elaborated a profound symbolism; the works of the English mystics, e.g. ↗Hilton in the *Scale* and later Augustine ↗Baker in *Sancta Sophia* (Holy Wisdom). These places, especially Jerusalem, were symbols of the heavenly Jerusalem, and all this life where Christians had no abiding city was a pilgrimage to the City of heaven. Like the Israelite escaping out from Egypt for the promised land we are pilgrims on the earth seeking the heavenly Jerusalem. When a Christian goes to the Holy Land or to Rome, he is not merely a sightseer but someone who hopes, if only for a spell, to commune with the divine, and so stir himself to seek what is above. The Russian pilgrim sets out, not to return, but to find God *in* his pilgrimage.

H.F.M. Prescott, *Friar Felix at Large*, (New Haven, 1950). A 15th century Pilgrimage.

J. Wilkinson (tr.), *Egeria's Travels*, (London, 1971).

L. Zander, 'Le Pèlerinage', in *1054–1954: L'Eglise et les Eglises, études et travaux offerts à Dom Lambert Beauduin*, Vol 2 (Chevetogne, 1955), pp. 469–86.

See 'Pèlerinages' in *D.A.C.L.*, col. 40–116.

See also 'Pilgrimages' in *N.C.E.*

Plotinus (AD *205–70*)
Born at Lycopolis. In 244 he settled in Rome to teach. He had been influenced by Christian thought and like ↗Origen his contemporary had studied at Alexandria under Ammonius Saccas. His disciple Porphyry collected his writings and edited them as *Enneads*. Plotinus was a Neo-Platonist who created a religion from the thought of his Master, a religion of the alone with the Alone. It owes something to association with and opposition to Christianity (Porphyry had certainly been a Christian and so too possibly had Ammonius Saccas). But Plotinus, it is known, was interested in Far Eastern thought. He even went with the Emperor Gordian on a military expedition to Persia.

For Plotinus union with God (the Alone) can be attained by one's own unaided efforts, and it is an intellectual rather than a loving union. He also provides a method for attaining his goal, and it is akin to Christian ascetical practice as well as Eastern methods, i.e. purity of heart, recollection, putting aside all imaginings and thoughts, since 'the One cannot be any existing thing, but is prior to all existents'. It is impossible to pin down where the influence lies, between him and ↗Origen; though it is sure that they both influence later writers especially the Pseudo-↗Denis and ↗Augustine, and through them all subsequent writers on prayer.

From the point of view of Christian mysticism the Neo-Platonism of Plotinus and others tended to create a division between soul and body quite alien to the biblical tradition in which spirit and body are *one whole*, and it seemed to make the Incarnation and sacraments irrelevant, since the Neo-Platonic objective was to be *free of the body*, which was conceived of as a prison.

The confrontation on this point between Christian spirituality and the Neo-Platonic strain in Christian thought came in the ↗Hesychasm controversy, 'the writings of ↗Gregory Palamas'.

A.H. Armstrong, *The Architecture of the Intelligible Universe in the Philosophy of Plotinus*, (Cambridge University Press, 1940).

F. Copleston, sj, *A History of Philosophy*, Vol 1, pt 2, (London and New York, 1960) pp. 208–18.

S. Mackenna (tr.) and B.S. Page, P. Henry (intro.), *The Enneads*, (London, 1957).

Postures in prayer
Christ himself lay prostrate in the Garden of Olives to pray. Sometimes he stood, as he prayed before raising Lazarus from the dead. He prayed nailed to the cross; and so too many martyrs prayed as they were tortured. We know that St Paul 'fell on his knees' to pray for his Ephesian converts (Eph 3:14). A typical Christian posture, as described in ancient murals, is that of a figure standing with arms upraised: the *Orante*.

In general, Christians have specific 'stances' for different types of prayer – standing for a response to the challenge of faith, e.g. the Gospel, the Creed, also as a sign of respect and in memory of the Resurrection; kneeling or prostration are signs of abasement, humility and contrition. The raised arms are a sign of supplication; the bow of respect.

Christians have much to learn from the East, both Hindu and Buddhist in this matter. The Buddha himself at the moment of his enlightenment was seated in the Lotus position, that of meditation, with body relaxed, the breathing unimpeded. In the Zen discipline right posture is a pre-requisite, and the master paces up and down among the novices in time of meditation to see that they are seated correctly. (*cf.* ↗Yoga postures).

↗Ignatius, in the *Exercises* (it is significant that he calls the notes 'exercises') suggests that a prayer could be repeated in rhythm with one's regular breathing, which – whether he knew it or not – is standard eastern technique, and also common among the Orthodox. Yet he lays down no right posture but admits that even lying down could be a suitable one. What produces results is what concerns him.

Just as a restless mind or imagination in certain forms of prayer may be left to 'go their own way', and be ignored in deep contemplation, so the body in restless periods is better controlled by movement than by stillness. Thus ↗Francis of Sales often meditated pacing up and down. The Fathers of the Desert would keep their fingers occupied, while praying, making mats and unmaking them. Modern men and women, geared to activity, might find walking up and down a railway platform or rocking a baby to sleep more conducive to prayer than physical stillness. For all our planning, we must not forget that the Spirit blows where it will and when it will and how it will. We are not master.

Poverty and the Poor
In the ancient world before and at the time of Christ, poverty was considered an inevitable if unfortunate state of affairs. The Old Testament manifests several reactions to the fact. The Law of Moses and the Prophets are sensitive to justice being done to the poor, and to the tendency of the rich to take

advantage of their poverty (Ex 20:15 ff; Amos *passim*, e.g. 2:6 ff; Is 10:1 ff). The Psalms show a variety of attitudes, at first as above, also the thought that it could be a punishment for sin, riches being a sign of God's favour (Ps 1); later, after the Exile, 'poor' begins to mean the meek and humble and so those devoted to God and to whom God is devoted (Ps 22:26 and many others). The word *'anawin'* 'the poor', is rightly often translated meek and humble. The Wisdom books are sometimes harsh to the poor, *cf.* the Comforters and Job himself, who suggest his destitution is due to some hidden sins. But here also the demand for justice comes through. Thus by the time of the New Testament the meaning of 'poverty' and 'poor' is multiple. Mary in her *Magnificat*, at the beginning of the New Testament story, uses 'poor' in the sense of humble. But Christ in Mt 5:3: 'Blessed are the poor in spirit', certainly means the really poor but who are humble before God. Christ is more concerned in his teaching with the rich who are unjust, e.g. Dives and Zaccheus. But he identifies himself with the poor in his life, at Nazareth, in the public life and on the Cross. He requires that his disciples give up all to follow him. This was certainly the spirit of the very early Church in Jerusalem. Jesus wants his disciples to imitate him, who was 'meek and humble of heart'.

St James in his Epistle has the genuine Hebraic and Christian teaching on poverty and riches, with this difference: that he emphasizes the falsity of judging people by their wealth. He sees evils in the world as springing from the unruly desire for riches.

Today, those living in a wealthy country with an average income of perhaps twenty times that of a poor country (e.g. New Zealand compared with Tanzania, according to President Nyerere in 1973) have a personal obligation towards their fellow men living in such comparative poverty, and as members of a wealthy State they must urge both a reduction of expenditure on their own comfort and a plan for helping the Third World. There are also groups of very poor in our own midst (*cf. North, South*, the Brandt Report; Pope Paul VI, *Populorum Progressio*; ↗Social Justice).

Prayer
Here are given the main divisions of Christian prayer, for details see various articles.

(i) Prayer is *public*, and either official (↗Liturgy, ↗Eucharist, ↗Divine Office, Sacraments etc); or unofficial (e.g. shared prayer, the ↗Rosary, family prayers).

(ii) *Private* – this can be:
(a) *discursive*, meditation verbalized, if not vocalized,
(b) *transitional*: aspirations, silence, ↗Jesus prayer, simplicity or ↗recollection,
(c) *Contemplative*, which is active, prayer of ↗proficients,
(d) passive when illuminative prayer begins, with which are associated certain unessential phenomena: levitation, visions, ↗locutions, ecstasies, stigmata.
(e) Finally the ↗unitive prayer, called Espousals and then ↗mystical marriage.

There are a number of characteristic schools of prayer: the *logos*-centred, bridal mysticism, both of which stem from ↗Origen; then the *via negativa* stemming from ↗Gregory of Nyssa and ↗Evagrius; the

176 Prayer and the Old Testament

Christo-centric mysticism of which ↗Augustine and ↗Bérulle would be examples. There are those who stress the intellectual, i.e. the contemplation of truth, e.g. ↗Thomas Aquinas, and those who stress the will, ↗Bonaventure, Augustine ↗Baker, ↗Benet of Canfield. We distinguish schools of prayer: the patristic tradition; the Pseudo-↗Denis; the medieval monastic, the Rhino-Flemish; the medieval English, the Spanish, the French.

Prayer and the Old Testament

It has no treatise upon prayer, but its overall atmosphere is one of gratitude to God for his wonderful deeds, hope for the future and sorrow for man's ingratitude. Throughout the Old Testament may be found innumerable prayers of every kind, from the battle hymns of Moses and Deborah to the moving laments of the Psalms; prayers of gratitude, of sorrow, of praise and petition, even of vengeance – but these last have been eliminated from the Church's Hours. The *Song of Songs* has been used by Christian mystics – ↗Origen, ↗Bernard, ↗Teresa and others – to express the quintessence of the soul's relationship with God, one of intimate union in love.

The Psalms and the Canticles of the Old and New Testaments have a special attraction for the Christian as well as for the Jews, because they are in the first place prayers of a people, transcending the littleness of the individual. They cover almost every possible prayerful movement of the human heart. They are expressed with a sobriety and yet deep sentiment that do not pall. Besides, we believe that they are inspired by the very Spirit of God; and though some are reflected through a very primitive mind, there is scarcely one

that does not possess in its centre divine riches. They relate to a Personal God, not a nebulous Ground of Being; yet God is not trivialized, sentimentalized, but remains 'beyond', supreme, majestic. To express his love, the Old and New Testaments cannot but use the symbol of human love.

Presences of God

Not one but many. We do not make him present; we become aware of the fact. This is the first great step in the spiritual life and prayer. To practise this incessantly would be unwise. Even ↗John the Evangelist would relax to play with a dove; and he is reported to have said that the string must not always be kept taut for fear of tiring the bow.

God is present in his creatures as the Creator and Providence. Man senses this by the order in the universe, whether in a flower, a galaxy, an atom or ourselves. We recognize him in the beauty of the universe, in the power of the winds, waves, earthquakes, thunder, as Elijah did; we know his nearness within, symbolized too for Elijah by that sound of a gentle breeze. The other presences were as nothing compared with the interior one (1 Kgs 19:9–13). We are present to him as he knows us, as also he loves us. But the horrors, the wasted lives, the injustices, the successes of the wicked, all challenge these ideas of God's presence. By faith we know God is all-wise. Yet we can see no wisdom there. This is the true Dark Night for every Christian, as it was for Job – and though he had less reason than we for belief, since the idea of a future life was scarcely above the horizon of his mind, yet he believed. God is truly present in the world's Theatre of the Absurd, for we cannot expect to know the whole story. Has God made man his counsellor? If we dare to share Christ's Passion, he is there also.

God is present in history: he chose the Jews for a purpose; he has made himself known in every culture and civilization. God is known through the Old Testament as the Saviour, as one who loves and has mercy, as well as the just God. In the New Testament he made his presence yet more visible in the humanity of Jesus Christ. Now we have the revelation that God is not only present *in* his creation but present *to* men through the gift of his grace. We know that the Holy Trinity *dwells* in our hearts. Jesus promised to send the Spirit so to dwell.

God is present therefore in all succeeding generations, by his personal grace; he is present in the Church as such, the Body of Christ; in the Revelation enshrined in the Scriptures when we read them. He is present specially in the sacraments, and most clearly in the Eucharist. We can find Jesus in each other: wherever two or three are gathered in his name, he is there in the midst of them. But in no case do we *see* God himself. He remains the *mysterium tremendum*, until the vision of heaven. According to the Eastern Orthodox tradition of ↗Hesychasm God is present by his own very Light to those advanced in prayer and that Light is not only present but experienced. By themselves they reach to the ultimate.

God being by definition infinite has an infinite number of possible ways to be present to us. That they differ is not to be surprised at.

Priest, the

The person in religions who represents the people before God – God to the people, and found almost everywhere in the ancient world

from China to the Americas; among the primitives (e.g. Pygmies), the emperor-priest in China, the priestly caste in India, the Hebrew priesthood, all have this in common: that the priest represents others and that he offers a sacrifice. But *circa* 5th century BC, the complexity of sacrifices had obscured their true meaning. A reaction occurred, in India with the *Upanishads* and the rise of Buddhism, in the biblical world also with the rise of the prophets demanding not mere outward show but the humble and contrite heart. At the same time magic mingled with true sacrifice. Not surprising therefore that Jesus Christ, though the true Priest, never used that title of himself, nor referred explicitly to his death as a sacrifice. Looked at more narrowly his words however often point to that reality of which all other sacrifices were but the foreshadowings. He did not refuse the title of Lamb of God given him by ↗John the Baptist. He prophesied he would be put to death, a death that would be a ransom for many (Mt 20:28; Mk 10:45); he had likened himself to the shepherd who gives his life for his sheep (Jn 10:11 ff). At the Last Supper the words of Consecration are full of sacrificial terms: 'my body *given* for you (Lk), the cup of my blood *offered* (Mk, Mt, Lk), the reference to the New Covenant. It is the author of Hebrews who expounds the significance of all this, showing that Christ being both human and Divine can alone be the perfect priest and perfect sacrificial victim.

Nor is 'priest' used of any individual in the Church in the New Testament, only of the whole People of God, a fulfilment of Ex 19:6. The Greek word *presbyter* – from which our word priest comes – meant elder. The implication was that there was only one priesthood in the new dispensation, Christ himself; and since all are part of his Body, all share in various ways in his priesthood. All the People of God offer Christ in the Eucharist as well as themselves in him (*Constit. on the Liturgy* ch. 2. n. 48, Vatican II). In Catholic, Orthodox and Anglican theology the ordained priest shares this priesthood but over and above it he has the duty and the power to administer the sacraments and be the officiator at the Eucharist, alone having the power to bring Christ to the altar, with his bishop who has the fulness of the priesthood. He ministers to the Church the life of Christ (grace) by means of the sacraments, by interpreting holy Scripture (preaching), by his example. His is the ministerial, cultic, officiating priesthood, just as Christ's own was and is before the throne of God and in his living work for mankind.

Priestly Spirituality

The first duty of the priest is to follow Christ in proclaiming the Word, in bringing the Good News to all; this he does by celebrating the Eucharist, administering the sacraments, preaching, consoling, leading the People of God. But this being an engrossing, time-consuming task, seems to cut out traditional spiritual exercises. A tension has often arisen between what was thought to be spirituality and the activity of the apostolic life. Vatican II, in the Decree on the *Ministry and Life of Priests* (Ch. III), shows how this is a false tension, since the activity for the most part is prayer: the celebration of all the sacraments, and especially the holy Eucharist, recalls Christ's saving death and resurrection, draws down the grace of God upon people; reminds all of future glory. The

preparation for preaching the Word of God envelops the priest in Scripture, the very message of God himself; as he goes among the people he is meeting Christ among the poor, the sick and dying; he acts through the power of the Spirit in the love of Christ.

Of course the priest should also have his times of meditation and other spiritual exercises, but they cease to be separate from his work, which they fortify and which themselves are enriched by his apostolic experience. In them both, he becomes 'another' Christ, completely given in his life to others. In the case of a minister or priest of Christ who is celibate, this is a sign of dedication to Christ's cause and frees him from limiting ties that could impede where he went or what he did. On the other hand it must be admitted that ↗celibacy has its problems too.

Proficients

The traditional word for seekers after God who have passed through the stage of ↗Beginners (Purgative Way), having purged themselves of vices, and are now in the ↗Illuminative Way and positively seeking the life of virtue and especially charity. While beginners tend to pray by meditation, proficients at first pray more by acts of faith, hope and love, praise (affective prayer) and at times receive from God in those moments of quiet occasional insights (or illuminations and hence called the Illuminative Way).

Between the stage of Beginners and that of Proficients is the Active ↗Night of the Senses and of the Spirit, and one's prayer goes through a number of changes: the prayer of acts, that of silence or recollection, which is succeeded by the *prayer of quiet,* the beginning of what is sometimes called supernatural prayer, though from the point of view of the Christian all Christian prayer needs grace, all prayer already has that element of the supernatural. In the prayer of quiet however the Spirit begins to take a more prominent part. Today we are less ready to accept the validity in practice of these minute analyses of mental states. God may choose other methods.

To attempt to enter into this stage by one's own powers would be a serious mistake, and impossible to achieve. The signs that the time has come to pass this threshold are the following:

(i) The impossibility of meditating the old way; and this not because of any slackness in one's life.

(ii) One no longer craves for the delights of this world.

(iii) A desire to be with God even though often there is no sense of his presence.

These indications were written by ↗John of the Cross for enclosed Carmelites. What of men and women in the world? The first sign is the same for all. The second may be different. Those in the world while enjoying what God has given them, will be weaned from attachment to them. This will come by their own desire but also through God's providence when something or someone they love inordinately is taken away; and then they learn non-attachment. It is a time of great trial and could lead either to deepened faith or to unbelief.

Purgative Way, the
The way of beginners, who apply themselves to purging themselves of vices. All spiritual writers are agreed on this stage, and especially the great mystics themselves. A close union

with God can only be attained after a long period of self-denial unless God decides otherwise. In the East Buddhists might put it differently – the mirror has to be polished clean before the image can come through clear – but the message is the same: a moral life is presupposed for enlightenment.

The teaching of Christ is: 'If a man would come after me, let him deny himself and take up his cross and follow me' (Mk 8:34). Our world is self-indulgent because it has so much. Yet the cross is as accessible as ever, being essentially an abandonment of those basic disorders: pride, vanity, laziness, sexual excesses, drink, hatred, contempt, selfishness. None of this can be done except through the power of the Spirit. 'Who will save me from the body of this death? The grace of Jesus Christ our Lord' (Rom 7:24–5).

The normal kind of prayer for this stage is meditation on the life of Jesus, particularly on his Passion and Death, these being caused by our sins, and at the same time being the cause of our redemption. A regular daily period of prayer is essential. Daily attendance at Mass would be the best of all. A guide is also of the utmost assistance, and regular Confession. In the world a sense of loneliness in Christian living is so common, some association with other dedicated lay people or with a community of religious could be of great assistance. If one's only reading or intellectual 'intake' are the daily newspapers and television, the spiritual element could become atrophied; and therefore some spiritual reading is essential: *The Way,* or modern writers such as F.J. Sheed, Karl Rahner, Yves Congar, Henri de Lubac, Michael Hollings, Jock Dalrymple, would suit different tastes, or the ancient authors, not least the medieval English mystics,

↗Julian of Norwich, *The* ↗*Cloud* and others, but best of all the New Testament.

Q

Quakers

Now a respected name, originally given as a gibe in his lifetime to George Fox and his movement and fellowship to which he gave no name. By 1800 it was called the Society of Friends of the Truth. The 'Friends' are of peculiar interest today since the rise throughout the Christian world of the practice of shared prayer and of the Charismatic Movement. George Fox (1624–91) reacted strongly against the dogmatizing and the intolerance of his age and fell back upon the 'Inner Light', or personal guidance of the Spirit in all things. It gave him the certainty of having his sins forgiven; he therefore felt no need of Baptism. To define doctrines only divided people, therefore he would have no authoritative Church, no ritual, no sacrament. Everything, including Scripture, was subject to the 'Inner Light'.

The only 'liturgy' is a weekly prayer meeting in a bare room, silent unless someone is moved either to pray aloud or to prophesy; perhaps it might be that such or such a work should be undertaken. Good works and pacifism are prominent in the Friends' outlook.

George Fox himself made apostolic journeys to the Western hemisphere; but it was William Penn (1644–1718) who established the Friends in Pennsylvania.

R. Barclay, *Theologiae verae Christianae Apologia*, (1676).

H. Brinton, *Friends for 300 Years*, (London, 1953).

Quietism

Came into prominence with the condemnation by Pope Innocent XI in 1687 of ↗Molinos' teaching of complete passivity in prayer and indifference in moral matters; and came to an official end with the condemnation of Madame ↗Guyon in 1695 and in 1699 of a number of propositions from a work by Archbishop ↗Fénelon. The fundamental error of Molinos and Madame Guyon in the matter of prayer was to maintain that during it God does all and we should do absolutely nothing, not even acceptance. Then, in the matter of morals, Molinos claimed that provided the will was completely passive there could be no sins even if they were sins of the flesh. Quietism may sound remote and dated, yet it is very much among us today, if in somewhat different contexts. A number of prayerful people, doubtless misinterpreting the great ↗Zen masters, seem to approach their meditation with a completely negative reaction, instead of an alert attention to the Ultimate Reality. Likewise it is possible to be so 'relaxed' in the charismatic sense, as to feel, as the saying is, 'anything goes', which approximates to a modern form of antinomianism, that is disregard of all moral norms. It is easy for enthusiasts, perhaps inadvertently, to fall into one or other of these traps. On the other hand this anxiety over Quietism led to a backing-away from all mystical prayer, and many a holy man and woman has come under suspicion. Even a book of St Francis Borgia, SJ (1510–72) was condemned by the Inquisition, no doubt quite unjustly. Mystical or contemplative prayer has taken about two hundred years to recover from this cloud of suspicion.

R

Reconciliation

Proposed by the Holy See as a better word for the sacrament of Penance than either Penance or Confession. These two bring out only one aspect each, and both are the human elements, whereas the sacrament has three sides: the penitent, God himself and the community (the Church). Taking an insight from a parable, it is the compassionate Father who makes the first move and the decisive one. He moved forward to meet his wayward son when he was far off. The sacrament of Reconciliation is a bringing back of a Christian who has lived for himself and neither for God nor for his fellow men. Therefore he must turn back (conversion) and be reconciled both with God and with the community.

The old form of Confession has much to commend it: it is a personal act on the part of the penitent, and, without that, no reconciliation is possible; there is a personal act on God's part through the instrumentality of the priest. But the old form has its limitations; a danger of a mechanical, almost magical forgiveness, owing to the many coming to Confession in a row and the speed at which the sacrament is administered. There is little sign of the community element. Thus the Church is moving towards new forms: a communal penitential service followed by personal confession and personal absolution; and in special cases, when the concourse of people is great, a penitential service followed by general absolution; with the proviso that anyone who feels he has

committed a grave sin, must, as soon as convenient, make a private confession of that sin. Yet at the general absolution he will have been absolved. Nor can that be rescinded. If he fails to make his private confession, that is another matter, whose gravity must be measured by the wilfulness of the omission.

A much wider sense of Reconciliation covers all life: reconciliation between husband and wife; within a family, cousins, in-laws; within a community, within a nation, between nations. It must begin with the recognition of one's own part in the fault, humility; an attempt to restore charity and respect, a desire for the good of the other and a control of selfishness. These apply not only in private affairs, but in public: between classes and 'interests'; between nations, especially the rich and poor, and over ancient emnities. One begins by meeting, and so understanding the point of view of the 'other'; this will engender respect. Patience and generosity can bring peace.

The world today needs reconciliation and all the means to it, to a degree greater than ever before.

Redemption

One of the many names given for the reuniting of men with God, none of which can fully describe it. By 'redeem' we mean: God 'buys back' (Latin) us from the slavery of sin. This emphasizes God's initiative. Salvation brings out the change in us; we are made healthy, being sick before. Justification brings in the element of justice, since men had offended the justice of God and as they became unjust they need to be made just. All these are Pauline images, as also is the one named 're-capitulation' by ↗Irenaeus, bringing mankind back to its head or source, since ↗Paul sees the restoration as our being united with Christ, we the body, he the head, or source of its life, and so united through the humanity of Christ, to the divinity. An English word that brings out the same idea is atonement, which at first sight appears to mean taking the punishment, but etymologically signifies 'making one', at-one-ment.

It is ↗John who has treasured Christ's own words – or is it his own comment and insight? – 'God so *loved* the world as to send his own Son that those who believe in him might not be lost' (Jn 3:16). And in his first epistle again he centres his understanding of the great mystery on the truth that *God is love.* We approach nearest to an understanding not through our human sense of justice but through divine love. So also thought ↗Thomas Aquinas in Pt. III of the *Summa*, where he says that Christ saved us by satisfaction, not satisfying an inexorable judge but by showing enough love, in his dying in obedience to God's will, to make up for all our lack of love; and at the same time provoking us by his crucifixion to love in return on seeing so much love expended on our behalf (*cf.* q. 47.2 ad. 3; q. 48. 2. corpus; q. 49.1 corpus). Though Christ has won the victory, it has to be applied to each individual soul, and this can only be done, seeing that we are made free beings, by our acceptance, which is the continual struggle of the life of the Spirit in us. We can either remain enclosed within our selfishness, or strike out to the love of others and of God by giving ourselves to them.

Included in translation with the *Trinity, Incarnation, Redemption*, Hopkins and Richardson (ed. and tr.), St Anselm, 'Cur Deus Homo', (London, 1970).

St Athanasius, R.W. Thomson (ed. and tr.), *The Incarnation*, (Oxford, 1971).

M. D'Arcy, SJ, *Christ: Priest and Redeemer*, (London, 1928).

St Irenaeus, *On Heresies*.

Abbé L. Richard, J. Horn (tr.), *La Rédemption, The Mystery of the Redemption*, (Baltimore, 1965).

J. Rivière (tr.), *The Doctrine of the Atonement*, (London, 1909).

Resurrection of Christ, the

In the Apostolic preaching, not so much the climax of an apologetic, as the summit of the faith that they proclaimed. They themselves had seen the Lord; but, they were proclaiming, he had not only appeared to them, he was still alive among them, and for always. The central theme of their preaching, the Good News, was that through the resurrection of Christ we can be saved. Over and over again in the Acts the preaching returns to the risen Christ: 'God, then, raised up this man Jesus to life, and all of us are witnesses of that, . . . he has received from the Father the Holy Spirit, who was promised, and what you see and hear is the outpouring of that Spirit' (Acts 2:32–3). We must often translate 'Spirit' as 'life', and 'holy Spirit' as 'God's Life'. So, the Good News is not merely that Christ has risen but that by so doing we have the opportunity to share this Life. Even the most apologetic passage in the New Testament on the Resurrection (and the earliest by far), 1 Cor 15, though it speaks of as many as 500 being witnesses to the risen Christ, and many still alive to bear witness, does not pursue the argument with: and therefore you must believe, but: therefore we too shall share the resurrection. 'Christ has in fact been raised from the dead, the first-fruits of all who have fallen asleep' (v. 20). It is ↗Paul who brings all the strands together, showing that our resurrection comes through our being united to the risen Christ. Rom 6:8: 'We believe that having died with Christ we shall return to life with him', and later v. 11, 'dead to sin but alive for God *in* Christ'. The new life is Christ's very own. Jesus had said as much, as recorded in John: 'I *am* the resurrection and the life' (11:25). The Eucharistic feast must be understood in this context; by sharing in Christ's body and blood, we share his life. Again John: 'Unless you eat the flesh of the Son of Man and drink his blood you shall not have life in you' (6:53). But it is in Ephesians (ch. 1 and 2) that the full splendour of the mystery is displayed, a cosmic view in which mankind and the universe are restored in Christ. And in Phil 2, the hymn tells us why: because Jesus was obedient (loving the Father's will) even to the death on the cross, and so God raised him up. He has become fully Lord. Christ's resurrection, then, is our resurrection, our hope and already our life.

B. Davies, OP, 'The Resurrection and Christian Belief', in P. Burns and J. Cumming (eds.), *The Bible Now*, (London and New York, 1981).

cf. F.X. Durrwell, R. Sheed (tr.), *The Resurrection*, (London, 1960).

X. Léon-Dufour, *Resurrection and the Message of Easter*, (London, 1974).

Retreat
A withdrawal from the world into silence and prayer, for anything

from a day to a year or even more, usually for a week and under the guidance of a trained person. In the New Testament Jesus himself is shown to have withdrawn into the desert for 40 days in order to face his future work in accordance with the will of the Father. St Paul, after his conversion, also withdrew into the Arabian Desert, before re-emerging as the apostle of the Gentiles. In the 4th and 5th centuries the mass 'retreat' into the deserts of Egypt became the birth of monasticism within the Church. Arnold Toynbee, with a world view, sees this tendency of withdrawal and return as symptomatic of a deepening of the spirit. The modern retreat movement in the Catholic Church – and now in many Churches – had its remote origin in that withdrawal of St ↗Ignatius of Loyola to Manresa in 1522–3, an event which changed his whole life. The *Spiritual Exercises*, an outcome of that encounter with God, are very carefully arranged meditations and prayers on the spiritual life, starting with elimination of sin and ending in the decision to follow Christ more closely and a choice of a vocation. As time went on, this precise theme became less clear and was converted into different allied purposes. Today retreats are very popular as part of the general renewal programme of the Church. But there are also specialized retreats such as Marriage Encounters, when husband and wife open themselves up to each other in all honesty, not always easy after twenty years of married life.

Revelations, Private
Divine truths claimed to be revealed to private individuals. In these days of charismatic renewal private revelations are not a dead letter and need another gift, discernment of

spirits. Neither the recipient nor the Church can judge of a revelation from within, since even the Evil One can disguise himself as an angel of light, thus deceiving the recipient of the revelation, while the Church can only judge from what the person concerned says. Not even the holiness of the person is a guarantee, since holy people have been mistaken; nor can the 'unholiness' be a completely sure test, as God may make use of unworthy instruments, e.g. Balaam's ass and Caiaphas. Thus we are left with the *content* of the revelation that either conforms or not to already revealed truth. If it does not, it can be rejected out of hand. It may provide new material not in 'the deposit of faith'. This too can be rejected, since the age of new revelations is over: Christ is the last; only through him can anyone be saved. Thus the revelations of ↗Margaret Mary and ↗Bernadette are not new: ↗John spoke of the heart of Jesus and of Jesus's exceeding love. The whole Bible is full of what Our Lady said to Bernadette, namely that men should do penance.

The more profound the revelation or insight into the mysteries of God, the more difficult it becomes to express this in human language, resulting at times in some distortion of the message; besides, the simplicity and untheological background of the seer may be such also as to express the revelation in halting and over-visual terms. This may be true of the revelations granted at Fatima; leaving however intact the essential message.

↗Joan of Arc's case is peculiarly relevant here but also has peculiar elements: her revelations seem political and also military; the Church appears to have, on the one hand, condemned her to be burnt and on the other called her a saint.

Politics are rarely free of moral implications. For ↗Joan the intrusion of the English, though in one sense political, was a grave injustice to the whole French people. The only means for ejecting the English was by waging war, a means not considered at that time an intrinsic evil. There could be a just war. It was not the Church that condemned Joan, but only a time-serving Bishop Cauchon, in the pay of the English. When Joan appealed to the Pope, which she had a right to do, the reply was that he was too far away. Joan was declared a saint not because of her 'voices' but because of her heroic virtues: her sense of justice, love, her faith, her defence of her virginity.

Richard of St Victor (?–*circa 1173*)
Like his master, Hugh of St Victor, he was a canon regular of ↗Augustine in that house outside Paris, of which he became sub-Prior in 1159 and Prior in 1162. His major work is: *A Treatise on the Trinity*. His writings on spirituality are *Benjamin major* and *Benjamin minor* and a *Commentary on the Song of Songs*. His manner is still patristic and scarcely at all scholastic, 'the greatest theoretician of mysticism of the Middle Ages'. ↗Thomas, ↗Bonaventure, the Rhineland mystics used the structure of his thought here. He notes that contemplation (probably equivalent simply of prayer) is divisible according to what is its source. The first is purely human, gained by attention, and this is delightful. The second is divine and human, i.e. mixed, grace giving the human element wings and a deeper understanding. The third is divine, because here God, as it were, takes over and suspends the operations of the soul, producing an '*excessus*

mentis', i.e. an enlargement of spiritual insight resulting from divine charity.

F. Cayré, A.A, *Patrologie et Histoire de la théologie*, Vol II (Paris, 1936), pp. 437-45.

For full bibliography see Cross, *O.D.C.C.* and *D.T.C.* in the appropriate article.

Rolle, Richard (*circa 1300-49*)
Early English mystical writer, probably born at Thornton le Dale near Pickering, North Yorkshire, and died at Hampole, near Doncaster and probably of the Black Death. He studied at Oxford for three or four years, and had a sudden conversion to be a hermit. That he studied at Paris is not proved. He may have become a priest; he must have read much theology as his works are both orthodox and theologically accurate. He knew the works of ↗Augustine, ↗Bonaventure, ↗Richard of St Victor and Peter Lombard. He was in the tradition of the prophetic witness, freely criticizing clerics and monks, which got him into trouble. He therefore moved from Pickering to Richmond (Yorkshire) and finally near the Cistercian convent of Hampole. His works are voluminous in both Latin and English; the most famous and enlightening on his life and mystical experiences are *Melos Contemplativorum* and the *Incendium Amoris*. Among his devotional works: *Ego Dormio*, *The Commandment*, *The Form of Perfect Living*, which are more in tune with the mentality of ordinary Christian folk. According to Dom David Knowles (*The English Mystical Tradition*, London, 1961) his mystical experience of *calor* (heat) and *canor* (song) are on the lowest rung of the contemplative ladder, though Rolle himself thought there

was nothing higher or deeper. Rolle had a lasting devotion to the use of the Name of ↗Jesus, which he claimed was the source of his spiritual advance.

For his own account of his spiritual pilgrimage see especially *Incendium Amoris* xv. This has been translated as *The Fire of Love* by C. Wolters, 1972, in the Penguin series; it includes a short bibliography.

cf. Rolle's *Works*, edited by H.E. Allen, and *Pre-Reformation English Spirituality*, edited by James Walsh, sj (London, 1964).

Rosary
An old and popular devotion to Mary, especially in the Catholic Church. Its history is obscure, though already in the time of ↗Bernard (d. 1153) occurs the combination of the subject matter (the Joys of Mary) with the repetition of the ↗Hail Mary – though the latter in a very abbreviated form. The general shape of the devotion, as we know it, probably only goes back as far as the Carthusian, Dominic of Prussia (15th century) and the full Ave to just before the Reformation. For this tangled history see H. Thurston, sj (Old) article 'Rosary' in *E.C.* and *N.C.E.* and the article 'Rosaire' in D.T.C.; supplementary cols. 2902-11, by M.M. Gorce.

As a prayer the Rosary has great depth and flexibility for all its apparent simplicity, resembling in its purpose the ↗Jesus Prayer of the Orthodox Church. Thus its heart is not so much the reciting of regular prayers as the contemplation of the underlying mysteries, or basic incidents in the life and work of Jesus. The fifteen mysteries or groups of ten Aves, one Glory be to the Father and Our Father, are divided into three groups of five: the

Joyful mysteries are concerned with the Incarnation, the *Sorrowful mysteries* with the Passion and Death of Jesus, and the *Glorious mysteries* with his triumphal Resurrection, Ascension, the founding of the Church and the Glory of Mary and all the saints. So we find that in the Rosary we are following closely the liturgical year, as well as the Gospel itself; and that it agrees exactly in its contemplative side with the kerygma of the early Church, as exemplified in the famous hymn in Phil 2 where the Son stripped himself of his Godhead, became man; he went further, dying on a Cross; for this he was raised from the dead and glorified.

The Hail Mary's are not meant to be gabbled, nor on the other hand to be concentrated on word for word, but each rises to a climax in the word Jesus; so at each climax we are considering Jesus in each mystery in turn. In the Glory be to the Father etc., we find the typical ending that occurs in the Church's prayer, as in reciting the Psalms. In the Our Father is a fitting restart of each mystery, in which we put ourselves in the presence of the Father, who sent his divine Son, and who receives him back together with us (*cf.* the Encyclical, *Marialis cultus*, by Pope Paul VI, 2 February 1974).

Ruysbroeck, John of
One of the greatest mystics in the whole history of the Church. He was born at Ruysbroeck in 1293 and died at Groenendael in 1381. Aged 11 he joined his uncle John Hinckaert, canon of the cathedral of St Gudule, Brussels, and Francis of Coudenberg, a younger canon, where they lived austere and holy lives. John was ordained priest in 1317. At 50 he and his two companions withdrew to the hermitage of Groenendael in the

forest of Soignes, near Brussels (1343). The Prior of St Victor, Paris, accused them of Rule-lessness; they adopted that of ↗Augustine. ↗Gerhard Groote, founder of the Brethren of the Common Life, first visited them in 1374, and frequently thereafter. During those years at Groenendael Ruysbroeck wrote his major works:

(i) *The Spiritual Tabernacle* – somewhat fantastical.

(ii) *The Twelve points of True Faith.*

(iii) *The Book of the Four Temptations* (against egotism).

(iv) *The Book of the Kingdom of God's lover.*

(v) *The Adornment of the Spiritual Marriage* – (iv) and (v) are orderly descriptions of the mystical life's progress.

(vi) *The Mirror of Eternal Salvation* (1359) – for a novice nun.

(vii) *The Seven Cloisters* (1363) – for a now professed nun.

(viii) *The Seven Degrees of the Ladder* (1372) – the third of the trilogy with (iv) and (v).

(ix) *The Book of the Sparkling Stone* – edited by Evelyn Underhill, (London, 1915).

(x) *The Book of Supreme Truth* – a commentary on obscurities in (iv).

(xi) *The Twelve Beguines.*

Apart from his own experience his sources are chiefly, Augustine, the Pseudo-↗Denis, ↗Richard of St Victor, ↗Bernard, ↗Eckhart, ↗Suso, ↗Tauler. He is famous for his expressions of the mystery of God, for his descriptions of our union with that mystery and for his avoidance of any hint of pantheism. He is rarely read, therefore the following extracts are given: God is 'Simplicity; one-foldness, inaccessible height and fathomless depth; incomprehensible breadth and eternal length; a dim silence and a wild desert' (*The Spiritual Marriage*,

Bk. 2, ch. 37). Following ↗Eckhart he writes, (there is) 'a distinction and differentiation, according to our reason, between God and the Godhead, between action and rest. The fruitful nature of the Persons, of whom is the Trinity in unity and Unity in Trinity, ever worketh in a living differentiation.

'But the Simple Being of God, according to the nature thereof, is an eternal Rest of God and of all created things' (*Twelve Beguines*, ch. 1). He also writes of 'the Deep Quiet of God', 'An immeasurable flame of Love', 'the Fathomless Abyss that *is* the Being of God'. 'When we soar up above ourselves and become in our upward striving towards God so simple, that the naked Love in the Height can lay hold on us, there where Love cherishes Love, above all activity and all virtue (that is to say, in our Origin wherefrom we are spiritually born) – then we cease, and we and all that is our own die into God. And in that death we become hidden Sons of God, and find in ourselves a new life, and that is Eternal Life. If we would *taste* God, and feel in ourselves Eternal Life above all things, we must go forth into God with a faith that is far above our reason, and there dwell, simple, idle, without image, lifted up by love into the unwalled Barrenness of our intelligence. For when we go out from ourselves in love, and die to all observances in ignorance and darkness, then we are made complete and transfigured by the Eternal Word, Image of the Father . . . What we are, that we gaze at; and what we gaze at, that we are. For our thought, our life, our being, are lifted up in simplicity, and united with the Truth, that is God. Therefore in this simple gazing, we are oᵤe life and one spirit with God – and this I call the *seeing* life' (*The Sparkling Stone*, p. 171).

But this does not amount to the extinction of the human person: 'The iron does not become fire nor the fire iron; but each retaineth its substance and its nature. So likewise the spirit of man doth not become God, but is God-formed, and knoweth itself breadth and length and height and depth' (*The Twelve Beguines* ch. 14); or, 'No creature can either be or become holy to the point of losing its created nature and become God' (*The Book of Supreme Truth*). And, 'Love cannot be lazy, but would search through and through, and taste through and through, the fathomless kingdom that lives in her ground; and this hunger shall never be stilled' (*The Sparkling Stone*, ch. 9).

Trans: no. 11 by J. Francis, (London, 1913); nos. 5, 9, 10 by C.A.W. Dom, (London, 1916); no. 8 by P.S. Taylor, (London, 1944).

H. Pomerius, *De Origine Monasterii Viridisvallis una cum vita Joannis Rusbrochii*. 1420, completed.

See, for further bibliographical material, *O.D.C.C.*

S

Sacraments

As ↗Augustine wrote, these are sacred signs, that is signs of God's presence, of his action. For the ancients a sign was not a sign in place of something not there but in some way a sign that the thing or person signified was in a certain sense actually present. The greatest, the unique sign of God's power and love is Jesus among men, his humanity, the sign of the divinity. He said, 'he who sees me, sees the Father'. He came to do his Father's work, the saving of men, 'since God so loved the world as to send his only Son' (Jn 3:16). But Jesus' life on earth ended with the Ascension, and still his saving work has to go on. 'There is no other name under heaven by which men may be saved' (Acts 4:12). His saving death and resurrection are the cause of our redemption. Christ therefore instituted his Church, not merely as an organization working under his name; it was in a mysterious way to carry on his life, to share it, to be himself, his Body, to make him present under the sign. The Church is the great Sacrament of Christ's presence. The Church is the Body of Christ; it is the continued presence of Christ as Saviour in the world, so that all men in every age may come in contact with him and his saving power. The scandal is that the Church in its members is so often inadequately Christ-like. The Eucharistic meal is the means by which the Church shares ever more closely in the life of Christ through a sharing of his body and blood under the signs of bread and wine. Thus, just as Christ is the supreme sign of the Father, so the Church is the great sign of Christ himself and of his grace. Through the Church the graces of redemption flow in many channels. Of these, seven have with time been seen to be in a class apart, in some way instituted by Christ himself, if not explicitly at least in an implicit way. These are the seven sacraments. Each stands at a crucial moment in the Christian's life, from the first step of ⟋Baptism to the last, the Anointing of the sick, those moments when the Christian shares most intimately in the passion of Christ, his acceptance of our mortality. In every case it is no magical action; Christ is present in and through his Church and it is he who gives his grace.

E. Schillebeeckx, OP, *Christ the Sacrament*, (London and New York, 1963).

Sacred Heart, Devotion to
Reached a first world-wide climax when Pius IX in 1856 extended the feast to the universal Church, as an expression or symbol of devotion to the love Christ bears us. The heart is not the source of love but is affected by all forms of it: sensible, affective, spiritual, and in Christ's case – since he is both God and man – his divine love. His side was pierced and blood and water flowed (Jn 19:3387; *cf.* also 7:36–9). The early Fathers saw here the Church's beginning. However, neither Scripture nor the Fathers used 'heart' exactly in the sense of love, but as a symbol for the deepest central source of man's thought and volition. Though this scriptural meaning still persisted in the 17th century as in the *Pensée* of Pascal, 'Le coeur a ses raisons que la raison ne connaît pas' the modern devotion to the heart of Jesus had already invaded the Christian consciousness with Anselm (d. 1109), after him ⟋Bernard, with the *Vitis mystica* of ⟋Bonaventure, ⟋Albert the Great, ⟋Catherine of Siena, ⟋Julian of Norwich and especially the German Benedictine mystics, chief of whom was ⟋Gertrude of Helft. For these and their immediate successors – the Brethren of the Common Life, the Carthusians, and Abbot ⟋Blosius – it was a private devotion, but with ⟋Francis of Sales and John Eudes (d. 1680) the faithful became involved. St Margaret Mary (d. 1690) a member of Francis of Sales's new Visitation Order, provided dramatic intensity to its spread when her revelations and visions, which occurred at Paray le Monial between 1673 and 1675, were made known by her Jesuit guide St Claude de la

Colombière. She told how Jesus had said that he wanted men to remember his great love, to atone for the outrages done to it, especially against the Blessed Sacrament. There should be an hour's prayer each Friday to share his agony; every first Friday of each month holy Communion. All this was peculiarly appropriate in the late 17th century when Jansenism was drying up devotion to Communion and when the anguish of predestination and the possibility of being thus destined for hell gripped many people including ↗Luther and Francis of Sales himself, both caught at one time in the fear of damnation. When God's infinite, compassionate love was being forgotten, this devotion put Jesus's love once again in the forefront.

St John Eudes, founder of the Eudists congregation (d. 1680) gave the devotion a theological foundation. Pius XII by his encyclical, *Haurietis aquas*, 1956, spurred a group of specialists to produce a Scriptural, Patristic and Theological survey (A. Bea *et al.*, eds., *Cor Jesu*, 2 vols, Rome, 1959). They show the devotion 'latent' in early Saints and the Fathers. Since these show Christ's total humanity, therefore his heart like ours would be moved by every form of love, and thus be a suitable symbol for his human and divine love. The ultimate object of all devotions to Jesus is *Jesus himself*; the proximate object, here, is his heart as symbol of his human and divine love.

cf. Article by C.S. Moell, *N.C.E.*, (Vol. 12, pp. 818–20).

Sacrifice

An offering made to a deity, common to almost all religions but complex in meaning as well as multiple in form, from the honeycomb of the pygmies to the solemn (twice yearly) ritual of the old Chinese Emperors. The Jewish sacrifice is also complex: the holocaust, the peace offering, the expiatory offering, the thanksgiving sacrifice. Every sacrifice of the ancient world is a sign of a relationship between the worshippers and their god, though with the passing of time this is not always clear. In general it may be said that sacrifices signify praise, thanksgiving, sorrow for sin, pleadings for benefits, for forgiveness. The danger everywhere, particularly in Israel and in India, was to be satisfied with the symbol, the exterior act. Among the Jews it was the prophets who reacted strongly, reminding the people that it was the change of heart that counted: obedience, humility, a contrite heart (*cf.* 1 Sam 15:22; Ps 40:6; 50:14; 51:16; Hos 6:6). The last reads: 'What I want is love, not sacrifice; knowledge of God, not holocausts'.

Jesus shows peculiarly little interest in the old sacrifices, though he is meticulous about going up to Jerusalem for the feasts. In Mt 9:13 he quotes Hos 6:6 with approval. Thus, perhaps in order not to confuse his own sacrifice on Calvary with the rather exteriorized sacrifices of the Old Law, only very guardedly does he point to the fact that it is a sacrifice at all (*cf.* the wording of the Eucharist). This is significant for his followers, who also must be aware of the danger of making their sacrifice a merely ritual act. The ↗Eucharist is a rite but also a reality, exterior and interior; without the latter it would be devoid of true meaning. Christ's life was a 'living' sacrifice, because it was a continual conformity to the holy will of his Father, a life of obedience (Phil 2).

The ritual sacrifice is but the expression of that lived sacrifice. So the Christians worship God in a way that is 'worthy of thinking beings, by offering our living bodies as a holy sacrifice' (*cf.* Rom 12:1, also Heb 13:15f and 1 Pet 2:5).

St Augustine, *The City of God*, Bk. 10, chs. 5, 6, 10 (Harmondsworth, 1972).

R. P. Trille, *Les Pygmées de la forêt équatoriale*, (Paris, 1932).

R. de Vaux, OP, *The Sacrifices of the Old Testament*, (Cardiff, 1964).

Saints
The word originally meant simply holy, as God is holy, in fact given over to God. Christ said 'be perfect as your heavenly Father is perfect' (Mt 5:48; *cf.* Lev 19:2 – 'Be holy, for I, the Lord your God am holy'). For a Christian the perfect following of Christ was considered the centre of holiness. St Paul repeatedly calls his converts saints (1 Cor 1:1); to the Romans he says, 'called to be saints' (1:7). Those who died like Christ as witnesses to the truth, as martyrs (Greek for witness) were acclaimed by the People of God as holy. When the first age of martyrdom was over with the Peace of Constantine (313), others were considered witnesses by *living*. A Confessor, therefore, is one who confessed (professed) his faith by *living* perfectly. In the East St Antony was such a one and in the West St Martin, monk and Bishop of Tours (d. *circa* 397).

In the early Church no official method existed for proclaiming anyone a saint. *Vox populi*, the voice of the people, was sufficient. With time it became clear that this was not an entirely satisfactory method. Then local bishops authorized veneration (of a local holy person) in the liturgy. Only in the 12th century under Pope Alexander III did the Roman See declare that all canonizations had to be done in Rome. The present procedure began in 1634. Later, Pope Benedict XIV (1740–58) established the norms of sainthood in terms of heroic virtue. The miracles and visions of the person concerned are not part of the procedure. Canonization does not make anyone a saint, it simply is a process by which the Catholic Church examines someone's life to see whether it really was saintly and therefore worthy of imitation. However, no saint is perfect, and indeed it may be that the struggles they have had to become perfect are, for the rest of us, more interesting and useful than the almost unreal picture one sometimes receives of the final product. From the point of view of praying, saints are objects of veneration, in the same way as we venerate some noble person we know. In the liturgy we thank God and praise him for manifesting his power and love in them. The Catholic tradition is to ask the saints to help us along the way by their prayers to God for us. Just as Mary asked Jesus a favour at Cana she can still do so now. We are all so *one* in the Body of Christ that we are involved in each other's well-being just as Christ is himself. How this is so we can leave to God. The earliest example of the cult of saints in the Church is that of St Polycarp's martyrdom (*circa* 155).

Vatican II *Constitution on the Church*, c. 5.

Pope Benedict XIV, *Treatise on Heroic Virtue, a Portion of the Beatification and Canonization of the Servants of God*, 3 vols, (London, 1850).

Saints, Devotion to the. An excellent historical summary in *O.D.C.C.*

Sanctity
A Christian term to express the goal of the human being in its relationship with God. Sanctification implies that this is a work of God; and, as holiness (*sanctitas*) is an attribute of God, it is not something that can be acquired by man's own powers. For Christians the ultimate is not this cosmos, but Beyond, a union with the source of this cosmos, utterly mysterious, infinite in all degrees, and beyond infinity. By Revelation we know that God has a life within, of Three in One, that God is *Logos*, ultimate truth, *agape*, ultimate Love. We know that he is as a Father and so we are his sons, sharing in the Sonship of Christ his Son. Thus holiness or sanctity is first a transformation of us into a likeness of the Godhead, through the redeeming work of Christ in the sacrament of Baptism by which we die with Christ and rise in him, to become co-heirs in his kingdom, which is a life of union with the Holy Trinity, far beyond and above any union, however marvellous it may be – and surely is – of ourselves with the ultimate reality of this universe. There, all connected with it, is supernatural, that is ↗grace.

For a Christian, sanctity does not require a denial of this material universe, since he knows it was created by God and that he saw that it was good; indeed it shows forth God's perfection, and it is there for our use. Man's abuse of God's gifts is not a reason for complete rejection.

In the experience of union with God that Christian saints have described, often the wording implies a complete loss of consciousness of their own personality at the height of the experience of God. But in no case, not even that of Meister ↗Eckhart, does it imply that the existence of the mystic has been completely absorbed into the Godhead any more than if one ceases to think of a loved one, does the loved one cease to exist, or a mechanic absorbed in the machine, himself cease to exist because he has ceased to be aware of himself. These are two distinct levels of being, the psychological and ontological.

Scripture
The foundation of the spiritual life, as interpreted in disputed cases by Tradition. It is God's message to his People, and as such has something of a sacramental character, the very reading of it is a grace and penetrates the heart unless an obstacle is interposed. As the Holy Spirit guided the writers, so he will enlighten the readers. The early Church had no other reading; the Fathers of the Desert lived by it, so too all the great saints in the history of the Church. The liturgy is replete with Scripture. Yet since the invention of printing, the excess of books and of books on the Bible, a danger exists of reading only the commentaries and not the book itself. Besides, scholarly reading is not spiritual reading. To read the Bible is to receive a personal message from God; for it is not the printed words – black lines on white paper – that constitute the message, the revelation, but those same signs read and understood, that is: what God reveals to each one who reads.

It is easy for the modern Christian to misread the Bible, taking it all as historical matter in the modern sense of historical, whereas it is all a description of God's ways with man, his loving mercy and man's waywardness. Some of it has an historical substratum, some is imaginative writing (the Book of Job, the Song of Songs). The message is God's relationship with men. Thus there is a literal sense, the one God first meant, embedded in an historical narrative or dressed in a story, e.g. that of Jonah. This sense is sometimes prophetic, as when it refers to Christ himself or his Church, the New People of God. The New Testament is full of texts of the Old 'fulfilled' in the New. Much of the Old Testament may be applied to the Christian life: the Song of Songs, the prayers of the Psalms, the story of Exodus. The reader should let the Spirit guide him in the interpretation of any particular text.

Lectio divina – or divine reading – should not be done hurriedly, but in a meditative frame of mind, relishing each phrase, so as to extract the spiritual honey. The Fathers of the Desert would take one phrase or sentence and repeat it through the day and even longer. There is no reason why moderns should not do the same. In the *Dogmatic Constitution on Revelation* the Fathers of Vatican II remind the faithful that to read Scripture is to know Jesus Christ; and that we do it prayerfully 'so that God and man may talk together' (n. 25).

God's saving plan is laid out in the Old Testament when he chose a People to be the vehicle of his promise; their story is strangely and wonderfully fulfilled in the New: a new People is chosen – the whole world of those who believe – and a new Covenant made, with a new Sacrifice to seal it; a new promised land, heaven itself; a new law written not on tablets of stone but on those of the heart, a law of love; mediated by a greater than Moses, by the Son of God himself. The Christian reader can see the *mirabilia Dei*, the marvellous deeds of God, in the Old as wonderful in themselves, but he sees them also as heralding even more stupendous wonders in the New.

Thus there are also various applied senses of Scripture. It can be applied to the individual Christian, as when we apply the words of Peter to ourselves 'Depart from me, Lord, for I am a sinful man'; or a situation such as Simon of Cyrene helping Jesus to carry the Cross.

It can be applied to the Church as a whole, as when we interpret the passage of the Chosen People through the Desert, led by Moses, as the Church (the New People of God) passing through this life, led by Jesus, on their way to the Ultimate Promised Land, heaven.

It can be applied to heaven, e.g. the joys of love as expressed in the *Song of Songs*.

(I mention only two so as to encourage the actual reading of the Bible.)

J.L. McKenzie, sj, *A Dictionary of the Bible*, (New York and London, 1965).

Old Testament and New Testament Reading Guide, (Collegeville, Min.).

Scruples

Or scrupulosity: an intractible disease, for disease it is. But the patient has this peculiar symptom that he does not, apparently, desire to be cured. In the moral area a scruple is a fear that some action is a serious sin when clearly to everyone else it is not so. Perhaps we are justified in going a little deeper than the symptom and saying that what lies behind is a deep fear of God's avenging Justice. More doubtful but perhaps useful at times, the scrupulous fear comes from identifying this harsh God-figure with a harsh father-image of early childhood. But there could be other hidden causes, and perhaps the commonest, as scruples often centre on sexual temptations, is a faulty conscience. A child has an instinct that some sexual behaviour or experiences are wrong, but as these experiences are often involuntary or partially so, he gets confused. Have I sinned or not? He does not have the instrument to give him certainty, namely that a sin must come from full knowledge and full acceptance and for it to be serious it has to be serious in itself. Yet even this approach is insufficient. The person is entangled in the search for human perfection under the all-seeing eye of God, whereas in the Christian dispensation it is not perfection God demands – as was thought by some pharisees – but a complete trust in the *mercy* of God. The story of ↗Thérèse of Lisieux is instructive in this since she extricated herself, or was extricated by casting herself not on an assurance of her own sinlessness but on God's infinite loving mercy.

The confessor or spiritual director has a difficult task. He should try to elicit obedience from the sufferer, so that the latter relies on his confessor's judgement and not his own. But in the long run this cannot build up assurance. The confessor needs to be patient, reasonable and firm, refusing to go over the same ground again and again. He can point out that the matter is insignificant, that knowledge was insufficient for serious sin, etc. He must persuade that the great devotion is *trust* in God and the acceptance of one's sinfulness.

It is now recognized that scrupulosity, the incapability of coming to a decision as to what is right to do, this agonizing, need not be religious in character. It is probable that a religious scruple is nothing more than a natural scrupulosity which has been given religious colouring and what the sufferer needs is a mind doctor. It appears that religious scrupulosity is on the wane, now that ecclesiastical legalism is no longer acceptable.

See 'Scrupulosity' in *N.C.E.*

Senses of Scripture

Inspired Scripture is a unique sort of writing since its authorship is shared by the human author and God. When we talk of the 'senses' of Scripture we mean the ways in which we understand what God intended to communicate by the text, and which might therefore be more than the human author knows. This division of authorship gives rise to the division of the senses of Scripture into 'literal' and 'spiritual'.

The meaning consciously intended by the human author is called the *literal* sense, even when he chooses to express himself in metaphor or other figures of speech (e.g. 'All flesh is grass' – Is. 40:6). But St Thomas says: 'The mind of the prophet is a defective instrument . . . even true prophets do not know all that the Holy Spirit intends in the things seen, said or done by them' (*S. Th.*, IIa–IIae, 173, 4). The deeper, more complete meaning which is unknown to the human author we call the *spiritual* sense. It can be brought to light, not by individual whim and ingenuity, but only by a later, more explicit prophecy or by subsequent events.

There is a kind of spiritual sense called the 'sensus plenior' or 'fuller sense' which is distinguished from the other kinds by the fact that it depends always on an extension or deepening of the sense of the words themselves, rather than of their general meaning or content. So, for example, when Zechariah says,

'They will look on the one whom they have pierced' (Zech 12:10) he was not consciously describing the details of the crucifixion of Jesus, but this later event reveals the fuller sense of the prophet's words.

The *moral* (or tropological), *allegorical* and *anagogical* senses are all spiritual and require some explanation. The *moral* sense is an interpretation of a scriptural subject, person or event which teaches right conduct. For instance, the need for gathering up the manna early in the morning (Ex 16:21) is, according to Wisdom 16:28, a sign that we should rise early to praise the Lord.

The *allegorical* sense is also called the 'typical' sense because it works chiefly by seeing earlier scriptural persons or events as being 'types' or prefigurings of the life of Christ, his Church on earth, its teaching, the sacraments and so on. So the manna in the desert is a 'type' of the Eucharist; the Paschal Lamb and the Cornerstone rejected by the builders (Ps 118:22) are both 'types' of Christ.

The *anagogical* sense concerns the Church triumphant, the second coming and its results. So, when Isaiah describes the restoration of Jerusalem (4:2–6, 54:11–14) we can understand it in terms of the last judgement and the establishment of the New Jerusalem as described in Revelation (21:9–27).

The spiritual senses are not opposed to or extra to the literal sense; they are always an extension of it or a deepening of its significance. Some historical critics would deny that there is any sense other than the literal, while some other exegetes, notably Origen and the Alexandrians, tended to be less interested in the literal sense. But the Old Testament is a preparation for the New Testament both historically and theologically, and it is unfortunate therefore to lose sight of one or the other.

None of these senses of Scripture, however, should be confused with 'accommodation' which is the use of a scriptural text as a literary allusion, applying it to an unrelated subject. Accommodation can be a perfectly proper use of Scripture, and is often used in the liturgy, but since it is a meaning intended neither by God nor by the human author it cannot be a true sense of scripture.

Sensible Devotion

A common phrase descriptive of a certain kind of prayer in the writings of 17th-century spiritual writers. 'Sensible' means, in this context 'of the senses' and 'devotion' is the prayer of the heart directed towards God. It is presupposed that all the emotions and senses are available to aid the soul to rise to God. If, for example, the Passion of Christ is the subject of the prayer, the tender emotions of compassion and sorrow will arise, which should lead to repentance and a turning away from sin. This is all to the good. There are two dangers, the first the failure of the appropriate emotions to be roused with the consequent feeling that the prayer was a failure too; the second danger is to take the emotional experience for prayer, which it is not. For prayer is essentially in the will. We must not turn the emotional experience into an idol nor should we give up praying if the emotions cease to function. All we can conclude in this situation is that we cannot pray that way any more and must find another way, perhaps that of the 'naked will', one of faith only.

In this connection see ↗Dark Night, Augustine ↗Baker, Gertrude ↗More. Also ↗John of the Cross, *Canticle* stanza 18, also *Ascent*, Bk. I, c. 7:5.

Sensuality

A tendency to take delight in sense pleasures, often used in a derogatory sense. Sense pleasures were made by God together with the rest of the human make-up, and he saw that it was very good (*cf.* Gen 1:31). Sin has upset the balance but not to the extent of making such pleasures in themselves sinful. They extend from the delight in a Bach chorale to the orgasm of sexual love; which all have their place, and all can be exaggerated. Because of the unity of the human psyche there is a close link between both sense delights among themselves and between them and the delights of the spirit. Thus both ↗John of the Cross and ↗Teresa point out that an intense love for God in prayer may induce, quite unwanted, a reaction of pleasure in the passions. They both say: ignore this (*cf.* Dark Night, Bk. 1, ch. 4 and St Teresa's Letters No. 173, sect. 10 in *B.A.C.*).

Sensuality, disassociated from altruistic love, and practised entirely for self, experience proves, leads to a drying up of an attraction for things spiritual and a loss of faith. On the other hand, in married love where the one gives himself or herself for the sake of the other, sensuality does not degenerate into selfishness but is an aid to the wholeness of true love.

Sergius, St (*circa 1314–92*)

Was of noble origin but lived all his childhood and youth in peasant style with his parents at Radonezh, about 50 miles north of Moscow. He was no student, could scarcely read or write until visited by a stranger, a holy man, who miraculously helped him. Even so he never once preached nor did he write any treatise on the spiritual life. At the age of 20, both his parents having died, he and his elder brother penetrated into the deep forest to live together in seclusion. They built a chapel to the Life-giving Holy Trinity. Stephen, the brother, soon found the conditions too austere: the wild beasts, the impenetrable forest, lack of food, the silence; and left to join a monastery. For years Sergius was alone. Like St ↗Antony of the Desert he won the victory over the natural man. Disciples gathered and against his will he found himself their superior: this is the beginning of the monastery that still exists, a few miles from Moscow, now called the Monastery of the Holy Trinity at Zagorsk. It was the new beginning of monastic life in Russia after the Mongol invasions, and it is St Sergius' first claim to fame. But his monastic ideal was also new in some ways. He and his monks were in touch with Mount Athos and the Patriarch of Constantinople and the ↗Hesychast movement. Sergius' prayer it seems was of a mystical character. His style of spirituality has remained typical of Russian life: based on profound humility and prayer. Even as abbot, Sergius wore the meanest of clothes; he would never command, only persuade, and if repulsed, not press. On one occasion when his disciples rebelled against the Rule, he simply withdrew. After four years the community implored him to return, which he did. The Rule was akin to St ↗Basil's and had affinities with that of St ↗Benedict. In his life-time the monastery of the Holy Trinity made forty foundations, and soon after his death another fifty. Here again was an innovation. These monasteries were 'outreaches' of Russian culture eastwards. The peasants followed the monks, as they have followed the monks in our day in southern Tanzania.

Unexpectedly, he is found at least four times mediating in the strife of quarrelsome Russian princes, at the request of Alexius, Metropolitan of Moscow. The climax of his activities in political affairs came during the invasion by the Tartars in 1380. Prince Dmitri was unsure as to the possibility of resistance. He visited St Sergius, who firmly told him to fight and trust in God. In a message on the day of the battle he repeated his assurance. Dmitri defeated the horde of 400,000 Tartars on the field of Kulikovo (1380). Sergius became the national hero for Russia from that moment, and of all its saints the most popular. He died at the Holy Trinity monastery in 1392. St Sergius was at the rebirth of his nation as one of the founders of its spirituality, establishing one kind of monastic life; as the ultimate source of the expansion of the nation, as the symbol of resistance to tyranny.

S. Bolshakoff, *Russian Mystics*, (London, 1977).

St Epiphanius, *The Life of St Sergius.* Abridgement in G.P. Fedotov's excellent *A Treasury of Russian Spirituality*, (London, 1952).

N. Zernov, *St Sergius, Builder of Russia*, (London, 1939).

Shared Prayer

The opposite of prayer in private or in isolation. It is common to many religions, religion being both personal and communitarian. Among Christians it is as old as Christianity. Jesus said, say '*our* Father', not 'my Father'. In St Paul's Church at Corinth we find an early account of shared prayer (*cf.* 1 Cor 12–14), including speaking with tongues and with prophecy. The former Paul tried to control, since tongues he thought were useless for a group without an interpreter. The aim he said of shared prayer was 'the common good' (14:26). Perhaps because of the unruliness of these manifestations, shared prayer, except in a formal manner with singing of psalms and hymns and readings, in general went out of use. It came back strongly at the Reformation and particularly with the Society of Friends or ↗Quakers, who preferred shared prayer in silence unless the Spirit moved one to speak.

In this century shared prayer has once again become a normal form of praying, especially in the ecumenical field, where it has done much to break down barriers at the level of mutual respect and love through the action of the Spirit. It also has proved a help for 'beginners' in their personal prayer.

The manner of it is unstructured, but generally speaking begins with a reading of Scripture or a hymn, followed by silence until the Spirit moves one to pray aloud. These silences could last five, ten or twenty minutes. It seems that the most natural manner is to begin with praise and thanksgiving to God for all and every blessing, and towards the end of the session to conclude with petition. Though usually no time limit is set, it is advisable in each meeting for the leader to aim at a specific time to bring the meeting to a close. So it is useful to have a leader, though one who leads as little as possible, since here the Spirit is expected to guide. Obstacles to a good meeting are: one of the participants preaching to others under the disguise of a prayer; a breaking in with very personal prayer on a sequence of prayers that seems to be being led by the Spirit.

If the meeting is ecumenical, each group may find the other's manner up to a point uncongenial; and there is no need to imitate for instance groaning or clapping, since these peculiarities may be extrinsic 'baggage'. On the other hand a coldness and reserve and a prayer seeming to lack warmth could be inhibiting for others. Slowly we learn what is good from others and what can be ignored.

Silence

In private life can be golden, when it denotes sympathy too deep for words and love more intimate than any speech; but it can be more deadly than the most venomous phrase, and contribute to total separation, a death to love, a breakdown in communication. There is a bitter silence, a sweet silent acceptance, a silence of patient waiting for enlightenment. The music of silence has every mood – a gift, a weapon.

In public life, when to speak and when to keep silent is a grave question, the answer depending not only on the injustice present but also on the usefulness of protest, not to oneself but to those oppressed. A man in public office has a greater duty to bear witness to truth and justice than the private citizen; but in democracies we are all public officers, we share in the govern-ment. Private protest is the first step, unless such a move would simply alert the evil-doers – often the government – who would take action to silence the protesters. A public protest needs to have some prospect of succeeding and par-ticularly not a likelihood of worse evils following – as in the case of Pope Pius XII, had he publicly berated Hitler, in no mood to listen but rather to find an excuse for further barbarities. The harm that would come to oneself should not weigh against the good, pro-portionately greater, that would come to others, should one protest. But the prophetic mantle has not

been placed on all our shoulders; we should pray that we be strong enough to bear, as Christ did, the ill treatment that comes from witnessing to the truth. ↗Thomas More is an exemplary case of when to speak and when to remain silent. But we must never do what is itself evil, for example the silent protest of suicide – that good may come of it.

Silence in prayer, is a receptivity to God's inspirations, an acceptance of his will, even in what appears unjust, i.e. keeping a silent mind, as Job learnt, 'I had better lay my finger on my lips. I have spoken once . . . I will not speak again' (40:34) . . . The prayer of ↗Simplicity is one of silent attention and expectation, a silencing of all the faculties, a turning away from the world of sense and discursive reasoning – as ↗Augustine and Monica did at Ostia – to be aware of the presence of God. This is the justification for the positive silence of the contemplative orders. In itself silence is negative; for a deeper communication it is supremely positive. Silence in the religious and contemplative context is for listening to God.

Simplicity, Prayer of

It has many names: recollection, prayer of simple regard, loving attention. It stands at the threshold of the prayer of Quiet in which a form of passive prayer begins; whereas here the soul makes an effort to still all the faculties so as to remain in the presence of God, without words or discursive reasoning. Its duration is short, at most five minutes, ↗thought ↗Teresa. She herself for years prayed with a book handy; ↗Francis of Sales advised a correspondent always to prepare a subject for prayer, even should the prayer of simplicity be possible, it being an unstable condition. Indications for its practice are: a difficulty in mediating, an attraction towards a simplification of prayer. There is no method in this form of prayer but many ways: a loving gaze on God, a slow repetition of a phrase or word (*cf.* ↗ *The Cloud*), a contemplation of a mystery of the Faith. It is important not to do violence to oneself; a peaceful approach is essential.

In life many situations arise, of delight, of intense sorrow, or disappointment, of confusion. The total abandonment to God's Holy Will without words – which seem useless anyway – is a perfect form of prayer. It will be God who will inspire us with suitable thoughts, courses of action, attitudes to take up.

Sin

In a Christian context, this is the refusal to obey God's will. It can only exist where there is freedom and a conscious wilful going against God's plan. In certain psychological states, what appears on the surface as sin is a compulsion from the subconscious. But experience shows and Scripture tells us that sin exists; dark forces may be at work, but we experience a measure of freedom and we know that we have gone against what is right, willingly. Scripture, put simply, is the story of man's sin and God's infinite mercy.

It would be foolish to deny that man, as he emerges from materiality, from a 'beastly' state, is subject to a physical process of trial and error; in so far as this is not willed, it is no sin; foolish also to deny that man makes mistakes, and given more information he will correct his error, as Buddhist teaching emphasizes; but a residue still persists when a man is not in ignorance, but knowingly does what he should not. There is a sense in which a sin can be seen as a breaking of a law, of nature or even a Divine Law, a legal misdemeanour; here again we are not at the deepest level. The Old Testament seemed to see sin in this dimension, yet examined more closely the Covenant or agreement was one of a 'marriage', therefore one not merely of law but of love. Finally, it is true that, in many sins, we offend humanity; but there are others in which we know that we have offended against a higher will, when we offend against truth, even if it hurts no one.

In the Biblical sense a sin is a breakdown of love. God is love and he has shown that he loves us to an unimaginable degree, exemplified in Christ's life and death as well as in the parable of the Prodigal Son, more rightly styled that of the Merciful Father. Sin is a failure to respond in love to the way God wants things to be. This we know from our reason, from revelation and from the inexorable thing we call ↗ conscience.

Conscience is the ultimate arbiter over right and wrong. It is embedded at the deepest level. It can be enriched, strengthened; it can be profoundly shaken, even to madness.

It seems impossible that we should choose consciously, wilfully as an alternative a lesser good in place of the infinite Good who is God. Darkness is the symbol of sin and evil, and rightly because in a mysterious way it is possible for man to know and yet hide knowledge from himself, so that he does that which he knows he should not do (*cf.* Rom 7:19). We do not see God in this life, if we did we would never sin, as God is the All-Good. We only know *of* God, while good things of this world are tangible and compelling.

Social Justice

An attempt to apply to groups – families, classes, unions, territories or nations – the standards of justice that are taken for granted between individuals. In the 19th century most felt enough was done for the under-privileged if they were helped out of charity. This complacency was shattered by socialist writers and revolutionaries, headed by Karl Marx, and in the Christian world particularly by the German bishop Ketteler and by the encyclicals of Leo XIII, beginning with *Rerum Novarum* (1891). Not only individuals but *groups* have a right to a share in the world's goods which they do not now have. We are accustomed today to the idea of a Third World which is precisely in this way under-privileged. The United Nations has issued a statement on *The Rights of Men*; this included not only economic rights but also the basic liberties: of speech, of writing, of fair trial, of movement, etc.

As we live in a politically and economically divided world, it is thought impossible to have an overall plan for world justice. Even so, this does not excuse anyone from attempting what is within the possible. This can be effected either by private enterprise or by governmental aid, even inter-governmental aid. Private enterprise is often impotent before the avarice of government officials in the receiving countries; help from governments or the United Nations has suffered from planning too big. Besides it is important not to be deceived by words – Aid is not aid if it has to be paid back with interest, or if it has 'tabs' attached, by which the receiving country has to buy goods at high prices from the loaning country.

It seems that nothing effective will be achieved unless there is a change of heart, in which selfishness truly gives way to a massive desire to help others less fortunate than oneself. Meanwhile the Third World gropes lamely forward with increasing population and diminishing returns per head.

W. Brandt and others. *North, South, a programme for survival*, (London, 1980).

Pope Paul VI, *Populorum Progressio*.

E.F. Schumacher, *Small is Beautiful*, (London, 1974).

The Song of Songs

Has been the inspiration of many in the prayer-life of the Church from ↗Origen's *commentary* in the 3rd century to ↗John of the Cross' *Spiritual Canticle* in the 16th. The most famous commentary is the conferences given by ↗Bernard of Clairvaux to his monks (and polished up in Latin for the general public). In itself the *Song of Songs* would appear to be either a sequence of love poems of an erotic character, or erotic love poetry turned to a divine purpose, *vuelto a lo divino* as ↗John of the Cross called one of his poems; or poems of divine love expressed in that literary form, God's love for his Chosen People, so understood by Jewish commentators from the earliest times. They can be interpreted as referring to the Church, or the individual soul (*cf.* ↗Origen). The heights of mystical experience are impossible to express adequately in human language, but of all imagery that of human love seems to the mystic – especially ↗Ruysbroeck – the least unsatisfactory.

Origen on *The Song of Songs*, in *A.C.W.*

St Bernard, *Conferences on the Song of Songs* (vol I. Spencer, Mass., 1970; vol II. London, 1974).

Soul

A word used to translate the biblical Hebrew word *nepeš* and the biblical Greek word *psyche*. But 'soul' also translates the Greek word *psyche* as used in ancient Greek secular writings. The secular Greek meaning of *psyche* is very different from the meaning of the same word *psyche* in the Old and New Testament. On the other hand, the biblical use of the two words *nepeš* and *psyche* is almost identical in the Old and New Testament. This difference of meaning between the secular use and the biblical one is extremely important for the meaning of the word 'soul' in English translation, as it is obviously easy to slip into a secular Greek understanding of it when reading holy Scripture.

The ancient Greek secular meaning of *psyche* (soul) is that of a distinct spiritual entity that might not be linked with a human body. If it was so linked, then the Greeks considered it, as it were, imprisoned in the body, and their aim was to liberate the soul from that enslavement. This is particularly true of the disciples of Plato called Neo-Platonists. But once ↗Gnosticism began to infiltrate into the Christian world, its use of 'soul' was even more alien because, for Gnosticism, almost always, the body was considered positively evil as was all the material world. The purpose of gnostic asceticism was to be rid of the body; not so the purpose of the Christian ascetics, who wanted to control the body by the spirit and, even more, to share in the sufferings of Christ.

The meaning, therefore, of *nepeš* and *psyche* as found in the Bible is of great importance. 'Soul', as translating *nepeš* and *psyche* in the Bible, signifies that underlying spiritual and immortal *principle* of each human being and principle of all his activities, in fact it is the totality of the living conscious being with all his activities. It means the self, the person (Gen 49:6; Ps 6:4; Jer 38:16), its activities: hunger (Ps 107:9), thirst (Ps 42:4); the emotions: hatred (Is 1:14), sorrow (Gen 42:21; Job 3:20); occasionally thinking (Prov 19:2). Sometimes these words, *nepeš* and *psyche*, translated by 'soul' could simply mean I, you, he, she. As J.L. McKenzie says, in psychological terms, we could say that *nepeš* and *psyche* in the Bible could mean the *ego*. For the Bible the body is not something bad, to be rid of, but something positively good (Gen 1:31, God saw that all he made was good). Only if the body has this value as being an intrinsic part of this totality, the 'soul' or the self (*psyche/nepeš*) have the Incarnation, the Passion, the Resurrection their profound significance. Here too perhaps is the great divide between the religion of Christ and much religion of the Far East: the real abiding value of human beings and our openness to union with the God who draws us towards a kind of deification. By grace this totality which is the human being is raised to a new state of union with God, soul and body.

J.L. McKenzie, article 'Soul', in *Dictionary of the Bible*, (London, 1965).

Spiritual Direction

See Direction, ↗Ignatius.

Spiritual Ecumenism

Ecumenism in which praying alone or together plays a major part. It is for all, whereas much ecumenism is above the heads of the ordinary faithful. All can pray for unity among Christians, and should do so, since no amount of discussion or shared activity can succeed without a renewal of heart at the level of humble pleading with God. This prayer is a daily activity; the Canons of the Mass all have reference to the unity we long for and which will come through the working of the Holy Spirit. This spiritual ecumenism can also take the form of shared prayer with those of other Churches, in each others' homes. The French Abbé Couturier who coined the phrase was a promoter of the Unity Octave, ending on the feast of the Conversion of St Paul. He did not invent it; this distinction belongs to Fr Paul Wattson, who founded the Franciscans of the Atonement. This world-wide week of prayer should not be the be-all and end-all of spiritual ecumenism but only its beginning.

Spirituality

The ways in which Christians at different times and in different situations have followed the guidance of the Spirit of Christ in their lives. It can be said, therefore, to be the life and *history of the Church* at its deepest level. Such a study would have to examine the spirituality of the Early Church, that of the martyrs; the Church of the Fathers; the spirituality of the Desert; that of the Dark Ages, the rise of devotion to saints and the 'withdrawal' of Christ to a distant heaven; the spirituality of the Middle Ages, its clericalization, the monastic orders, the spirituality of the people, Christ's humanity, pilgrimages, indulgences; the spirituality of the Reformation, of the Counter-Reformation; the flowering of mysticism

and the apostolic spirit; Orthodox, Anglican and Protestant spiritualities; the dying embers of the 18th century, ⁊Pietism and ⁊Wesley; the Romantic spirituality of the 19th century; our own age, the spirituality of Scripture, of ecumenism, of the liturgy. Or the spirituality of the Church could be studied from the point of view of *groups of people*: the laity, the clergy, the religious, urban society, agricultural society. It will certainly be studied in the future in relation to *various cultures*: the Eastern Churches, the Western; Christ in Hinduism, among Buddhists, in Africa, in post-Marxist society. Or it could be examined under such headings as: the place of the love of god, the love of neighbour, good works, the apostolic spirit, asceticism, its liturgy, its interiority or legalism, the place of the mind and the heart, etc. Further, the *spirituality of an age or group* or of an individual is intimately *connected with prayer*; thus the kinds of prayer will give a clear indication of the depth of the life of the Spirit: liturgical prayer, the sacraments, Divine Office; private prayer, the place of Christ and his Passion; devotion to the Eucharist, to Mary. It would even be possible to find a typical French or Irish or English spirituality, but here the cross-fertilization is so considerable throughout the centuries that it might prove to be more stylized than real. Nevertheless there are salient features in the Christian life of most peoples, e.g. the austerity of the Irish, their devotion to the Passion, their apostolic zeal. Spirituality varies from culture to culture. Spirituality therefore is the application of doctrinal, moral and especially ascetical principles, to particular ways of Christian living. Vatican II recognizes this by speaking for example of lay spirituality and of missionary spirituality being different from one another and different again from that of contemplative religious (for laity *cf. Lumen Gentium*, nn. 39–42; for missionaries, *Ad Gentes*, nn. 24–6). This insight could be extended. There must be a spirituality for housewives, for soldiers, politicians, lawyers, shop-keepers, doctors, nurses, professors, students, artists, factory workers. Some of this has been worked out, as in the case of the Young Christian Workers and among *Opus Dei* members. Slowly spiritualities for different cultures are being evolved, which however can only be successfully done in stages; first the missionary gives what he has; this will in due time be transmuted into an indigenous spirituality by the local peoples, not different in essence, but certainly in dress and stress from the Mother culture and not least in the liturgy.

Finally it must be emphasized that all 'spiritualities' whether of individuals or groups – religious orders, nations – all share the same basic elements; the differences are those of emphasis, and are often substantial.

M. Ward (ed.), *The English Way*, (London, 1933).

Bremond.

See also 'Spirituality' in *Sacramentum Mundi*, Vol. 5.

See ↗Lay Spirituality.

Spirituality of the Catholic Revival

That of the 16th and 17th centuries, or the Counter Reformation, a misnomer if is meant any change in the basic principles of the Christian approach to God through the Church and Scriptures and Sacra-

ments; but if it means a special emphasis, special methods of applying the age-old means of holiness, then that spirituality existed. What are these characteristics?:

(i) A combative spirit, out to convert, to refute, to establish the kingdom of Christ throughout the world. (ii) An emphasis on devotions; or practices, e.g. on Confession, on the Rosary, on veneration of the Blessed Sacrament in all its forms: Benediction, processions, Forty Hours; devotion to saints, especially to Mary, carried to great extremes; an almost blind obedience to authority, from the spiritual director to the Pope. But above all an intense devotion to the person of Jesus Christ; and to frequent Holy Communion, but this was short-lived.

For the first time the laity were being given intellectual training in the numerous schools for the well-born; possible as a by-product of the invention of printing. But theology was taught more as an apologetic exercise than as an understanding of the word of God. This has remained with us up to this century, when the Biblical revival is restoring a true balance.

Systematic prayer and regular retreats became features of lay life. ↗Ignatius and ↗Francis of Sales, who owes much to the Jesuits, popularized meditation beyond the confines of religious houses. Mystical prayer began to flourish, but with the scare of ↗Quietism, and other deviations, it was almost completely suffocated, to revive only in our own day.

We must not think that only Jesuits were active in this revival; the Observants (e.g. ↗Peter of Alcantara); the ↗Augustinians (↗Luis of León); Dominicans (↗Luis of Granada); the Oratorians, begun by ↗Philip Neri; ↗Vincent de Paul with his retreats and missions; the great bishops, Giberti of Verona, St Charles Borromeo, to mention only a few; all contributed something to the climate of opinion which created a distinctive spirituality.

L. Cognet, *Post-Reformation Spirituality*, (London and New York, 1959).

Spiritual Reading
Called in the Middle Ages ↗*Lectio divina*, in the early Church and still in the Catholic and the Orthodox Churches is enshrined in the divine liturgy, where normally it would be the word of God proclaimed and commented upon. Justin in the 2nd century already writes, describing the Eucharist, of the reading of 'the memoirs of the apostles'. With the passage of time, naturally enough, were added the reading of the Acts of the martyrs and the writings of famous bishops, such as Clement of Rome's letter to the Church in Corinth. In the monastic world ↗*Lectio divina* has always been a daily occupation of monks for whom besides the above, the works of ↗Cassian and of ↗Augustine and ↗Gregory the Great were favourites. This reading is not just storing up information, it is a way of stirring the heart for prayer.

Since the Reformation, much reading of the lives of the saints, and of devotional writings has taken the place of Scripture, though today, happily, Scripture has returned to favour. Yet it would be a pity if the reading of the lives of saints ceased, as these holy people give us an insight into the way that the Spirit can work in human lives, and lives *nearer to us in time and customs* than those of the Old and New Testaments. Disfavour has come upon this genre because the writers have been unrealistic, making plaster saints of men and women who, though imbued with the Spirit of Christ, were of flesh and blood, and had their faults, and these faults are among the most interesting elements of holy people.

J. Leclercq, *The Love of Learning and the Desire for God*, (London, 1974).

D. Rees (ed.), *Consider your Call*, (London, 1980).

Stigmata
Reproductions of Christ's wounds appearing on the bodies of holy people, especially the wounds of his hands and feet, and even of wounds caused by the crown of thorns. Normally these phenomena occur with women, though there are two famous examples among men, those of ↗Francis of Assisi (the first ever recorded) and of Padre Pio (d. 1972); they also occur in unspiritual and even deranged persons. It would appear that the human psyche has a two-way action, of body on mind and imagination, and of mind and imagination on the body. Thus even symptoms of illness may occur without any bodily cause. Therefore it is not unreasonable to suppose that intense compassion for the physical side of Christ's sufferings could produce an 'echo' of them in the person meditating upon them. Such a supposition does not exclude the possibility of a miraculous intervention causing these stigmata in a particular case. But miracles – as Ockham wrote – must not be multiplied. In any case stigmata are not a matter of faith, nor are they a certain sign of sanctity in the one who has received them.

H.C. Graef, *Theresa Neumann*, (Cork, 1950).

H. Thurston, SJ, J.H. Crehan (ed.), *The Physical Phenomena of Mysticism*, (London, 1952).

Stirrings

The word used by the author of *The ↗Cloud of Unknowing* for that beginning of prayer, deeper than words, which may come from the saying of a word, such as 'God' or 'Love', and is the beginning of contemplation: (*cf.* 'Lift up thy heart with a meek stirring of love' (ch. 7) also ch. 4.) Modern versions sometimes change 'stirring' to 'impulse'.

Sufism

From *sufi* (the woollen garb of the Muslim monks), Sufism is, according to Prof Arberry, the mystical movement of an uncompromising Monotheism (p. 4). Thus in Islamic mysticism there is no worship of Muhammed or of any other prophet, only of Allah. However, if the message of God is complete in the Koran, this presents a difficulty to the mystic (who expects a direct relationship with God) as there can be no further revelation, and so how can the Sufi claim or even desire to have a direct relationship with God? But they reply that as God did speak to his prophets, so they long to hear his voice also. They find in the Koran the pregnant phrase, 'He (Allah) loves them, and they love Him' (51:59). God was concerned to love men, and this sufficed for the Sufis, to launch into the unknown.

Sufism, somewhat like the rise of early Christian monasticism, began with a wave of extreme asceticism, a revulsion from the world, a reaction against the luxury of a worldly successful Islam in conquered lands. This was followed by an approach to God in love and in some cases in undisguised pantheism or absorption into God. Among the greatest Islamic mystics are the following: al Muhasibi (the founder), Al Harith b. Asad, Dhu' I-Nun the Egyptian, Abu Yazid the Persian, the thinker al-Junaid of Baghdad, and supreme among them al ↗Hallaj who was crucified. Then Rabi'a the woman mystic of Basra, and Jalal al-Din Rumi, the poet. ↗Al-Ghazzali (11th century) provided Sufism with a philosophical and religious ground.

The Muslim mystics had the inestimable advantage of growing to maturity in a world already rich in mystical experience, Christian, Neo-Platonic and Eastern. There can be little doubt that these Sufi mystics were in touch with their Christian counterparts in their monasteries – Muhammed himself had been well received by Christian monks – and that they were also aware of the mystical speculations of India.

A.J. Arberry, *Sufism, an Account of the Mystics of Islam*, (London, 1950).

A.J. Arberry, *Discourses of Rumi*, (London, 1975).

L. Gardet, *Mohammedanism*, (London and New York, 1961).

H.A.R. Gibb and J.H. Kramers (eds.), *The Shorter Encyclopedia of Islam*, (1960).

J. Kritzeck and R.B. Winder, *The World of Islam*, (New York, 1960).

R.A. Nicholson, *Rumi, poet and mystic*, (London, 1950).

Suso, Bl Henry (*1295–1366*)

Born at Constance and died at Ulm. He was a faithful disciple of ↗Eckhart whom he knew at Cologne and like him was a Dominican. From the age of 18 he called himself a Servant of the Eternal Wisdom. He was more of a director of souls and a preacher than a professor. His writings are a simplified and orthodox interpretation of ↗Eckhart's teaching. We are in God before creation, which presence is in the mind of God, in his essence. Though he wrote of our unification with God, he is at pains to explain that this is not identification; we still remain creaturely. It is a union in the essence of our soul, which he called the 'birth of God' or the 'birth of Christ'. His thought is more Christo-centric than Eckhart's, being influenced by the devotional stream from ↗Bernard. Suso, and Eckhart before him, together with that other Dominican John ↗Tauler, have this in common: that they emphasise God as present in the very essence of the soul, not merely in our powers; and this presence Christians should endeavour to be aware of and live by. He was beatified by Gregory XVI in 1831.

J.M. Clark, *The Great German Mystics*, (Oxford, 1949).

J.M. Clark (ed. and tr.), *The Little Book of Truth, The Little Book of Eternal Wisdom*, (New York, 1953).

Sr A. Edwards (tr.), *The Exemplar, Life and Writings of Bl. Henry Suso*, OP, 2 vols (Dubuque, Ill., 1962).

Symbol
See ↗Images and Icons.

Symeon the New Theologian, St
(949–1022)
Monk and mystic of importance in the Orthodox tradition. At first he joined the Studios monastery in Constantinople and almost idolized his director. Soon he went to St Mamas monastery nearby, of which he became abbot. As some of his teachings were not acceptable to the authorities of the Church of his day he was exiled to Asia Minor, but was soon recalled on certain conditions. Almost immediately, however, he returned to Asia Minor and founded a monastery there. His writings include catechetical discourses, hymns, sayings ('chapters'), letters. These have survived only in modern Greek and in Latin translations. On the Eucharist and the Holy Spirit he is profound but the application of his insights would seem on occasion unorthodox.

Baptism and the Eucharist cause and increase the deification of the Christian. But this, he wrote, must be experienced, otherwise it has not happened. The soul is still a cadaver or corpse. The two recognized signs that the sacrament has taken are: that the recipient feels the presence of the uncreated grace in the soul – with no hint of pantheism; the other an experience of divine Light. In this Symeon prepares the way for the Hesychiast movement. This presence of the Spirit of God gives the recipient a kind of knowledge of revelation akin to Scripture itself and he needs no teacher.

Bishops and priests, he says, do not experience this grace, nor claim to, therefore they are 'dead' Christians. It is the monks who have it and so are the true ministers of the sacraments. By their vows they have had a kind of second Baptism. It is not surprising that the hierarchy, feeling threatened, took appropriate action against Symeon. When his director died he took into his own hands the promotion of his 'cause' as a saint, putting up statues in the church, composing a liturgy in his honour. This was the last straw.

A careful examination of the case is to be found in an article by J. Gouillard in Vol. XIV, Pt II of *D.T.C.*, 2941–59. See also B. Koivocheine, 'The Brother-Loving Poor Man, the Mystical Autobiography of St Symeon the New Theologian', in *Christian East*, N.S. ii (1953–4).

See, for further bibliography, 'Simeon' in *O.D.C.C.*

T

Tauler, John (*1300–61*)
Born at Strasburg, where he died. He joined the Dominican Order in 1315, studied at Paris, became an attractive preacher and was noted and revered for his heroic care of the sick during the Black Death. At Basle he was acquainted with the 'Friends of God'. In his teaching he is the third of the great trio: ↗Eckhart, ↗Suso and himself, nor does his admiration for Eckhart, whose doctrine he distils into simple homely terms for his lay audiences, make him anything but completely orthodox. Christ plays a larger part in his teaching than he does in Eckhart. Much has been attributed to him, mostly by others, but enough is genuine to provide a clear view of his doctrine. God is in the centre of our souls; we must get in touch with him by humility and prayer; this will lead us to greater charity, which he says is more important than any mystic state.

Tauler and Suso were friends of ↗Ruysbroeck and influenced him greatly. Tauler also influenced ↗John of the Cross but in a work that contained writings of Eckhart and of ↗Harphius, masquerading under Tauler's 'safe' name, in the Latin translation of his works by Surius printed in Cologne in 1549. The *Opera Omnia* were also edited by

Surius and also printed in Cologne in 1603.

J.M. Clark, *The Great German Mystics*, (Oxford, 1949).

V. Rev. W. Elliott (tr.), (Washington, D.C., 1911).

Teilhard de Chardin, Pierre
(*1881–1955*)
Both scientist and theologian. He was born and reared in the Massif Central of France at Sarcenat near Clermont. From an early age the rock formations of the Auvergne enthralled him. After a Jesuit schooling he joined the Society in 1899, but before priesthood (1911) he was sent to Cairo for four years (1905–8). In the First World War he was a *brancardier* and often carried the Blessed Sacrament on his person. In 1922 he received a Doctorate in science from the University of Paris. His superiors were anxious about the hold he had upon the young with his original ideas on evolution, and packed him off to China where he remained off and on for thirty years, returning to France in 1946. He had played a leading part in the expedition of unearthing the remains of primitive man near Peking; he had made extensive geological excursions into the interior, particularly to the Ordo desert; he had found time in China to write his major work, *The Phenomenon of Man*. But he was cut off from intercourse with minds of his own calibre and interests on which to try out his novel theories. No sooner back in France than he had his first heart attack. In 1951 he was elected a member of the *Académie des Sciences*. Still only allowed to publish his purely scientific work, he was sent to New York. After a short visit back to Paris he had his second heart

attack on Easter Sunday, 1955 and died. It was his lay friends, who, after his death, published all his works. The Roman authorities remained anxious, without however actually condemning his works. The reason for their anxiety was perhaps primarily the looseness of his expression on delicate areas and because he was writing in terms of an apologetic to non-believers while they were thinking in terms of a full scholastic theology. He rarely mentioned grace, Original Sin, The Redemption, Adam. The outline of his tentative synthesis between the evolutionary theories of modern science and the Christian religion can be stated very roughly as follows: Palaeontology and Anthropology point to a remarkable evolution from rocks to living beings, from living beings (the biosphere) to conscious beings and from there to thinking beings (noosphere) by an ever more complex process of unification. Man is the summit of this development. But man, being intelligent and free, can now direct this evolution as he wills. The only way in which this could carry forward rather than destroy what has already been achieved, would be man's subjection to the Christ, both divine and human, the Christ of the universe, the cosmic Christ, and so in union with him reach God's goal, not only Man but the universe in Christ also, that is, the Omega point which will be reached when Christ is All in all. Some Scriptural support for this 'vision' can be found in the following: Col 1:6–20; 2:9,10; Rom 8:18–20; 1 Cor 15:28; Eph 1:10; 2 Pet 3:13; Rev 4:11.

Two other works deserve special mention, *The Divine Milieu*, in which Teilhard propounds a positive, not a detached, attitude towards creation. Man by his work co-operates with Christ in the building-

up of the universe in Christ. The second is a meditation on his offering of the cosmos, with Christ to the Father, as he stood in the desolation and silence of the Ordo desert: *The Mass on the World.*

Teilhard de Chardin, *Hymn to the Universe*, (London, 1965). (This contains *The Mass on the World*).

The Divine Milieu, (London, 1964).

The Phenomenon of Man, (London, 1959).

C. Cuénot, *Teilhard de Chardin, A Biographical Study*, (London, 1965).

H. de Lubac, SJ, *The Faith of Teilhard de Chardin*, (London, 1965).

R. Speaight, *Teilhard de Chardin, A Biography*, (London, 1967).

Teresa of Avila, St (*1515–82*) Carmelite Foundress, mystic, writer and doctor of the Church. She was born in Avila and died in Alba de Tormes. She was of a pious family; her paternal grandfather was a 'converso' from Judaism and having reverted, was pardoned on doing penance. Her writings are so intimately associated with her life that the two must be presented together. Aged 12 she became infatuated with novels of chivalry and filled with romantic longings. Her mother died in 1528 and in 1531 her father put her to board with the Augustinian nuns. On the way there her hermit uncle gave her ↗Jerome's letters to read; these turned her mind towards a religious vocation. She ran away from home in 1535, to the Carmel of the Encarnación outside Avila. In 1539, having ruined her health for life by excessive mortifications, she returned home for a cure; this nearly killed her. She was in a coffin for three days ready for burial. She revived, though she was paralysed, until 1542, when cured by St Joseph, for whom ever after she had great devotion. Her return to the convent was a period of worldliness, as she, a young nun, was given too much liberty in the parlour; her prayer became dry but she persisted. God was showing that contemplative prayer was his doing.

From this time on, her prayer became mysterious to herself, with her being unable to use discursive reasoning, with the experiencing of locutions and intellectual visions. Apart from a Jesuit, P. Diego de Cetina, her advisers said these things were of the devil.

In 1556-7 she experienced a profound conversion as she prayed before a portrayal of Christ covered with wounds ('un imagen ... de Cristo muy llagado', *Life* 9.1). Almost 20 years of her religious life had passed.

She claimed she did not find an understanding confessor for 20 years; in fact she was blessed with the arrival in 1557, of Francis Borgia, SJ, who for the time reassured her, then in 1560 ↗Peter of Alcantara came, a Franciscan; he likewise reassured her. Meanwhile she was writing out accounts of her prayer experiences for her various confessors; these accounts finally became the Autobiography, *La Vida*; the version we know was written in 1562 and revised in 1564 for John of Avila, who approved it only in 1568. It has a unique limpid description of the various stages of prayer that she experienced, from dryness through recollection and the prayer of quiet to the highest union with God.

Meanwhile in 1562, with the utmost difficulty, she founded her first convent of the 'Reform', San José in Avila. There during quiet months she wrote for her nuns another masterpiece, a simple ver-

sion of the ways of prayer without the autobiographical elements, *The Way of Perfection*. This too had several versions, particularly that of 1569 in a less familiar style, printed in 1583, a faithful copy of the 1569 version. In 1566 she wrote the first version of her *Meditations on the Song of Songs* (final version 1574), and though an order came to burn it *circa* 1580, fortunately a number of copies survived. In 1567, when she was making her first foundation outside Avila, at Medina del Campo, she met her faithful disciple and friend, the Carmelite we know as ↗John of the Cross. He then agreed to join the Reform, he aged 25 and she 52.

Her life is now one long series of journeys, founding new Carmels and wrestling with the reform of her old convent of the Incarnation. Fr Jerome Ripalda ordered her to write a history of her foundations, 1573. This most human book she began (chs. 1-9) and put down; told by P. Gracián to proceed with it (1574), she completed chs. 10-29. She reached ch. 27 and the end, so she thought in 1579. But there were still more foundations before her death, the last in Burgos. So *The Foundations* stretch out from 1573-82.

A great storm broke over the Reform in 1577, stirred up by those in the Order who saw no good reason for the Reform. Both John of the Cross and P. Gracián were imprisoned. The former destroyed all Teresa's letters to him; thus, though we have over 400 of her letters, not one survives to her best friend. These letters are among the most human documents ever written. During this troubled period she wrote with utmost calm another masterpiece, *Las Moradas*, or *The Mansions of the Interior Castle* (June and November, 1577), also for P. Gracián, since he had never seen the

Vida which was now in the hands of the Inquisition; this work is a mature statement of her teaching on prayer, with some modifications and enlargements on what she had written in her *Autobiography* and the *Way of Perfection.*

Teresa combined the highest lights of mystical prayer with an extraordinary capacity for practical government. Her advice on prayer is also practical. She is strongly against what she calls the 'Northern School' which leaves aside the sacred Humanity of Christ; this she thinks lacking in humility. We should begin with the Humanity. In the choice of a confessor or ↗ director she advises a learned before a pious man, since with learning one may know of the states of prayer even if one has not experienced them oneself. Her descriptions of the degrees of prayer have been of inestimable use to many, especially of those stages between meditation and the illuminative way.

Santa Teresa de Jesus, Obras Completas, intro. and notes, E. de la Madre de Dios, O.C.D. and O. Steggink, O. Carm., (Madrid², 1967), in *B.A.C.*

In English the safest guide is E. Allison Peers, *Mother of Carmel*, (1945). Also his translation of her *Works*, (London, 1946), is sound.

Theodosius of Petchersk, St (?–*1074*)
Born at Vasilev, near Kiev in Russia. We have a unique contemporary biography by a monk, Nestor. The family soon moved to Kursk and, on his father's early demise, the boy's redoubtable mother took command. Even as a child Theodosius was devoted to the poor, worked with the peasants in the fields, exchanged his fine clothes for their ragged ones. One day he set off secretly for Jerusalem to be where Jesus had lived. Enraged, his mother caught up with him and beat him till *she* was exhausted. The next time he left home was to become a monk; he sought out St Antony of the Caves in a hillside by Kiev. Despite his mother he held firm. St Antony's spirit was one of extreme asceticism in the style of the Syrian hermits. When he moved away for greater seclusion, the many disciples who had gathered, before very long, chose Theodosius as their spiritual leader. His way was not Antony's. In 1062 he and his monks left the caves to inhabit some buildings nearby which Theodosius had had built. He thus turned a *skete* (*laura*) into a group of cenobites, or monks living a common life. He went further, as He chose the Rule of the famous monastery established by the Consul Studios (*circa* 463) at Constantinople, whose Abbot Theodore (759–826) had composed a Rule which was grounded on the spirit of St ↗ Basil and had close kinship with the Rule of St ↗ Benedict in the West, one of moderation, order and community life. Theodosius' monastery still kept the name of the Monastery of the Caves, and his own life was very austere by our standards. He never slept lying down, but in a chair. In spite of acting the superior, he was always the first to cut the wood, grind the corn, carry the water. Though he was befriended by princes, with them he was stern, while humble with the poor. Every day he celebrated the Sacred Mysteries (the Eucharist). He was so gentle that a fugitive monk was always received back. This leniency caused discipline to slip. But on one point he was firm: poverty, even to the burning of surplus food if there were no poor about.

After his death an inevitable reversal of policy followed, that is, back to the extreme asceticism of St Antony. The tension between the moderation of Basil and Theodore the Studite and the eremitical ideals of an Antony always remained in Russian monasticism as elsewhere.

A shortened version of Nestor's biography is to be found in G.P. Fedotov, *A Treasury of Russian Spirituality*, (London, 1952).

Thérèse of Lisieux, St (*1873–97*)

Born at Alençon, and died a Carmelite nun at the Lisieux Carmel where she had been a nun since the age of 15. Canonized in 1925, she never experienced visions or ecstasies such as had her namesake of Avila. In what did her outstanding holiness consist? She was abnormally normal for a saint. Hers was the 'Little Way' which opened the road to God for innumerable little people. Her message was total oblation but in the little things of daily life – and life is mostly little things even for the great; and they count in the eyes of God if done or accepted for love of him. She saw that it is the intention, the motive that matters most. It would be easy to become obsessed with the actual doing of the little things, and forget the motive, and so slip into a modern form of phariseeism or legalism.

The heroism of her sanctity was unobtrusive but real. Probably the old Prioress was not such a tartar as legend would have it. But Thérèse's father, whose mental instability grew steadily worse, was a true source of anguish. It is clear from her Autobiography – *The Story of a Soul* – that her spiritual insight went through four stages of development. At first she was almost obsessed with the fear of having committed mortal

sins – she regained peace through a confessor telling her she had not. It would have been more Christian simply to have appealed to the mercy of God. Next she thought perfection was in doing little things perfectly. Here again she had limited insight, and only towards the end (The Third Stage) does she throw herself on the infinite mercy of God, quoting the passage from Isaiah: 'even should a mother cast off the child at her breast, I, God, would not cast off thee' (Is 49:15). Then finally, as her death approached, she was brought to utter darkness, a darkness of naked faith, and so great that she could even say she did not believe. Yet she clung on and died with a word of love on her lips.

The best translation of her *Story of a Soul* is that by R.A. Knox which uses the restored text of the M.S.S. (London, 1958).

R. Laurentin, *Ste Thérèse de Lisieux*, (Paris, 1973), for a summary of modern studies on the subject.

A. Combes has made a number of studies which have brought to light much hitherto unknown material.

Thomas à Kempis (*circa 1380–1471*)

Born in the Low Countries. He was educated at Deventer, the centre of the Brethren of the Common Life and therefore of the ↗Devotio Moderna, just as Erasmus was to be some years later. In 1399 he became a Canon Regular at Agnietenberg, a daughter house of Windesheim. There he lived all the rest of his life, a life of prayer, study and writing. His one official position was that of novice master.

Today his authorship of the ↗*Imitation of Christ* is generally accepted. Its spirit is anti-intellectual, understandably so in his age of excessive subtleties, which were beloved of the decadent Scholastics of the late Middle Ages. It also contrasts with the works of ↗Eckhart and ↗Suso and ↗Ruysbroeck, being more restrained and less mystical. In the early books the emphasis is on virtuous living; in the fourth book he treats of Holy Communion.

Thomas à Kempis takes a gloomy view of the world, for which he has been censured by modern writers. The world of pre-Reformation Europe perhaps deserved his strictures. It is worthy of note that many saints have been devoted to the *Imitation*, including ↗Ignatius of Loyola and ↗Thérèse of Lisieux. Yet he should be read with caution and the beginner reminded that the Christian is 'for others'.

Thomas wrote much, including biographies of his brethren and meditations on the New Testament.

L. Sherley-Price (tr.), (Harmondsworth, 1952).

Thomas Aquinas, St (*1255–74*)
Born at Roccasecca in southern Italy, and died at the Cistercian monastery of Fossanuova while on his way to the Council of Lyons. He is the greatest luminary of the Dominican order and the Common Doctor of the universal Church; his teacher was ↗Albert the Great; he taught at the universities of Cologne, Paris, Rome and Naples. His greatest work – though incomplete at his death – is the *Summa Theologica*, of which a simpler version is his *Compendium*. His defence of the faith chiefly against Moslem thinkers is the *Summa contra Gentiles*. The commentaries on Scripture are still valuable, e.g. that on ↗John's Gospel, on Romans and his little commentary on the *Magnificat*. Here

we are only concerned with his influence on the spiritual life.

Thomas was not afraid to apply his reason to the utmost on the data of Revelation, to elucidate, coordinate and deepen the understanding of the latter. His penetration of the meaning of creation made of him a great Christian humanist, never falling into the error of supposing that either men or the rest of creation were in themselves evil, but that they are essentially good. Grace was for him the restoration of all in Christ; his theology of contemplation and the vision of God was based on the nature of grace, which he saw as the transformation of the human soul into a likeness of God, and it becoming thus able to have friendship, mutual knowledge and love with God (*cf. S. Th.*, Ia, IIae, qq. 109, 110, 111). Grace adds a new presence of God in the soul, as the object of love (*S. Th.*, Ia, q. 8. a. 3). The Sacraments he saw as effectively making present the saving power of Christ's Passion and Death and Resurrection.

Thomas recognized three stages in the spiritual life: those of – beginners (*incipients*), proficients and the ↗perfect. This distinction is related to that of the purgative, illuminative and unitive ways – but these he did not use. The latter refer more to forms of prayer, the former to the practice of virtues. The beginners' chief occupation (*studium*) is to avoid vice, that of the proficient to acquire virtue, that of the perfect, to love. Note that Thomas is not for eliminating the passions but would have them used for good ends (*S. Th.*, Ia, IIae, q. 24 a. 3 ad 1).

He saw the ultimate end of man – beatitude – as the vision of God, which we already have in a glass darkly through the gift of wisdom. This begins in desire for beatitude and ends in the love of God in the beatific vision of heaven. Thomas therefore was no mere intellectual, a mere Christianizing Aristotelian, but a lover of God, the Triune. As he was dying he was commenting on the *Song of Songs*: the love of the Lover and the Beloved (*cf. Life* by William of Tocco, ch. 57); and in the final vision did he not write, 'I can write no more, for the things revealed to me are so exalted, that all I have taught and written up to now seem to me to be almost valueless' (*ibid*. ch. 47). On another occasion, near the end, the Lord said to him: 'Thomas, you have written well of me. What would you have as reward from me for your labours?' and he replied: 'Lord, nothing, only yourself' (*ibid.*, ch. 34). Thomas knew that in ultimate analysis God himself is beyond our comprehension, and that we need to contemplate him in silence, not because we cannot say anything or because we are completely ignorant of him, but because he infinitely exceeds our understanding. (Com. De Trinitate de Boethio, q.2.a.1. ad 6).

Though the style of Thomas's *Summa Theologica* is old-fashioned and unattractive to modern readers, it would be a pity if this prevented its perusal; its riches are immense; e.g. the little treatises on grace, on each of the virtues, on the Passion of Christ, to mention a few. The English Dominicans have completed a new translation into English.

St Thomas Aquinas, *Summa Theologica*, Latin and English, with notes. Gen. Ed., Thomas Gilby, OP, (London, 1963 ff).

F.C. Copleston, SJ, *Aquinas*, (Harmondsworth, 1955).

E. Gilson, *The Christian Philosophy of St Thomas Aquinas*, (London, 1957).

P. Rousselot, SJ, *The Intellectualism of St Thomas* (tr., London, 1935).

J.A. Weisheipl, OP, *Friar Thomas d'Aquino, his Life, Thoughts and Works*, (New York, 1974).

K. Foster, OP, *The Life of Saint Thomas Aquinas*, (London, 1959). Biographical documents, translated and edited with an introduction.

Tongues, The Gift of
The New Testament seems to know of two kinds of tongues, one described in Acts 2:4–11 where the apostles speak in tongues unknown to themselves but recognized by their hearers from many countries; another which sounds like tongues or languages but may be merely babble, in 1 Cor. 12:10,28 and ch. 14 *passim*. St Paul is, to say the least, cautious about this gift, though he claims himself to be proficient at it (*ibid.*, 14:18). He implies that 'tongues' can be turned on or off at will, since he lays down rules that it is better not so to speak, if no one can interpret them, and in any case only one person should speak at a time and never more than two or three at one session (*ibid.*, 14:27–8). Not against tongues, he would have them used only for the edification of the church (*ibid.*, 14:4); he puts tongues on the lowest rung of gifts, way below prophecy, and urges all to seek the higher gifts, especially the gift of love (*ibid.*, 13:1 ff). It has been claimed in our time that this gift of tongues liberates one from the servitude of reason. St Paul on the contrary says this: 'If I use a strange tongue when I pray, my spirit is praying but my mind reaps no advantage from it ... I mean to use mind as well as spirit when I offer prayer' (*ibid.*, 14:14f).

In the modern Pentecostal or Charismatic Movement the gift of tongues has an important rôle. Often it is expected to be induced by the ↗Baptism of the Spirit – more accurately called a prayer for the coming of the Spirit. And this is often the case, though not always. Some would then consider that the 'Baptism' has not 'taken'. This gift has an element of abandonment of self, to allow the Spirit to act; and this seems good, as modern man is very self-opinionated. Such phrases as 'let go' or 'relax' are heard at charismatic prayer meetings, meaning: allow the Spirit to act. This is good also but always within limits, in particular within the limits of what is true and seemly. There is always the danger that the 'spirit' taking over is evil disguised as an 'angel of light' as the past has not infrequently shown. It will be obvious to all that great discernment is required at this point, and one may prudently ask 'which spirit'? (See ↗Discernment of spirits).

Though one needs to be prudent, it is an undoubted experience of very many that this gift has made prayer a much more real and personal activity, especially in churches where praying was little more than the repetition of ready-made prayers. There is here a deeper level of consciousness than words and it may well be that by the speech mechanism being 'automatically' occupied, one is made aware of this deeper level.

Transcendence
A word used to describe how God is beyond all categories of being. For some centuries the Western Church's spirituality has been concentrated on the humanity of Christ. The supporters of this approach to God have excellent reasons. As Jesus said: 'He who sees me sees the Father'. Yet God in himself is the hidden God, the transcendent One, found neither in the whirlwind, nor in the earthquake. This Western simplification was not always so. The writings of ↗Gregory of Nyssa and of the Pseudo-↗Denis, of the early English mystics, of Master ↗Eckhart and of ↗John of the Cross bear witness to a firm grasp of the other aspect, the transcendence of God.

Transforming Union
A phrase used to describe a high state of prayer in which the human soul is so close to God that it is transformed into a special God-likeness. ↗John of the Cross expresses it as best he can thus: 'He (God) raises the soul most sublimely and informs her, that she may breathe in God the same breath of love that the Father breathes in the Son and the Son in the Father, which is the same Holy Spirit (breath) that they breathe into her in the said transformation . . . This for the soul is . . . so high a glory that . . . it cannot be described by mortal tongue.' (*Spiritual Canticle*, st. 38.2, tr. E. Allison Peers). But he carefully says in section 4 that this does not mean that the soul is one in essence with the Father, but by 'union of love'.

Tranquillity
A quality of soul which is rooted in conformity to the Divine Will. The mind of man, like a dog on a leash, leaps this way and that with a troubled heart. Restlessness in spiritual matters comes from a lack of trust in the all-guiding hand of God. The endless procession of things to be done, which make up life, causes lack of peace, since the energy for the doing of them gets out of hand; this needs controlling, limiting, for all its value. The second type of happening that causes unrest

is an exterior calamity: death, tragedy, financial disasters, family break-up. The life seems unjust, irrational. Prayer seems impossible, useless. Yet a Christian, though blind to God's intentions in the matter, in desolation can still say: thy will be done, if not with joy at least with acceptance and so a deep peace.

Trials

Far from being obstacles to the spiritual life, trials are among the chief means of advancement. They are of many kinds: exterior – persecution – or interior – sickness, dryness, ↗accidie. None from a Christian point of view but can lead to greater union with God, for all are at least permitted by God and for our good. In the prayer life itself trials come, often called Dark Nights – of the senses and of the spirit. Sometimes, unthinkingly, lay Christians suppose these are only for contemplative, enclosed religious. A man in the world, but dedicated to seeking God in all he does, will often in his own way experience desolations especially of faith in which his only prayer appears to be a blind groping in the dark, of pure faith and wordless union with God.

Trials may be borne in a spirit of revolt; they may be accepted with forced resignation as unavoidable; or with a willing acceptance as a condition sent by God in his inscrutable wisdom.

Not infrequently this 'wisdom of God' appears to the human mind to be illogical, almost cruel. At this point the Christian can only hold on with blind faith. Of course all human means should be taken to be rid of such trials as in the cases of an illness, or of violence. But what has to be borne, can be with God's grace. As ↗Paul wrote, God would not try anyone beyond his strength. 'My grace is sufficient for you' (2 Cor 12:9). See also Heb 11:32–40; 12:13.

Trinitarian Spirituality

Characteristic of Christians, because their spiritual life is essentially related to the three Persons, Father, son and Holy Spirit. Prayer in the liturgy and in ancient times is usually to the Father, through the Son and in the power of the Spirit. Though Origen, in his zeal for the unity of God, pressed that Christians should always pray to the Father, neither he nor others in practice always did so, because they rightly sensed that Christ and the Spirit being equally God with the Father, each should be praised and thanked and petitioned as much as the others. In practice it would be possible to pray to God without being conscious of approaching any one of the Three but globally God.

By the gift of sanctifying ↗grace the Christian receives a new life, namely a sharing in the very Life of God. The Life of God, in so far as we have been granted a glimpse, especially through the New Testament is one of mutual knowledge and love within the Holy Trinity. It is this Life we already share. The mutual knowledge is muted, for us, in this mortal life as it comes to us under the veil of faith, darkly. But by the gifts of the Holy Spirit – especially Wisdom, Understanding and Knowledge – the cloud, though not lifted, becomes luminous, on condition that we truly die to self. The ↗Hesychast movement is of great interest in this regard. The other side of the Divine Life is mutual love. God is Love. We are not in this life inhibited from loving though we may be from seeing God; ↗Augustine showed, in the final part of his *City of God*, that when we pass from this life to the next with the help of divine grace, we shall share in the divine Life of Love and of vision as we shall see God face to face (Bk. 22, ch. 30).

U

Unitive Way

As the word 'unitive' implies, the characteristic of this spiritual condition is a special union between the soul and God, so much so that at times it seems as though distinction between the two has melted away – but this is only seeming; though most Hindu and Buddhist tradition would say it had. In the Christian tradition, though at times the experience may be expressed in such a way as to seem to imply an absolute one-ing, yet in each case, if the writings of these authors is fully studied, they prove to safeguard the truth that the ultimate distinction remains between the essence of God and the essence of the soul – particularly ↗Eckhart and ↗John of the Cross.

The form of prayer that accompanies this Way leaves the person who prays apparently completely passive except for a strong clinging or attention to God. All the action seems to come from God's side, he being like a harpist plucking the strings, making them reverberate. No word need or can be uttered any more than it need be between lovers. God fills now the mind, now the heart with himself, so that the self seems to be swallowed up, non-existent, in the infinity of truth and love. This appears to have the lastingness of marriage, but with suffering (*cf.* St Teresa, *Interior Castle*, 5th Mansion, chs. 1 and 2; 7th Mansion, ch. 3).

V

Victorines

A group of theologians from the house of Canons Regular at the Abbey of St Victor. The most influential ones in the 12th century were ↗Hugh and ↗Richard of St Victor. St Victor at that time was the house of studies founded by William of Champeaux (*circa* 1070–1121) at Paris for the Canons Regular of ↗Augustine in the 12th century. Originally St Victor's had been an abbey of monks.

Virginity

The condition of one, male or female, who has not had sexual intercourse. From a merely physical point of view alone this has no spiritual significance, for such a virgin could be lusting in the heart; whereas a virgin who was, say, raped by soldiers against her will would still remain spiritually a virgin.

In Christian parlance virginity usually includes both the physical and spiritual elements. (For reasons see ↗Chastity). Note that both Jesus and Mary were virgins, this alone is a weighty argument in favour. In our time it is seen preferable to think in terms of a vow of chastity, leaving the past behind, and looking to the future.

See ↗Celibacy.

Visions

Are of many kinds: objective, subjective, visual, imaginative, intellectual, and are not much esteemed by the highest authorities, in particular by ↗John of the Cross, on the grounds that the devil can disguise himself even as an angel of light. The only type of vision, he claims, free from this 'interference' would be intellectual insights.

Nevertheless visions have played a considerable part in the lives of characters in the Old and New Testaments and in that of many saints. Abraham himself entertained God and two assistants to a meal. Mary had a vision of an angel and so on. Visionaries in modern times tend to be women, perhaps being more imaginatively receptive. The Church gives no special credence to such visions or to what is said, except in so far as all this conforms to divine revelation, of which she is the custodian. The visions that St Margaret Mary had of Jesus and his ↗Sacred Heart for example brought to the notice of the faithful the neglected truth of Christ's infinite compassion for sinners.

Visions sometimes have a core of truth but are wrapped in the imagery and 'mythology' of the seer; these two have to be separated; an example would be the visions of hell experienced by the children of Fatima.

Vocation
In the Biblical sense, this is a call from God to carry out his will. In the Old Testament Abraham, Moses, Samuel and the Prophets, especially Isaiah (ch. 6) and Jeremiah (ch. 1), were called for a particular mission. In the New Testament Mary's vocation was to be the Mother of the Saviour. Jesus had no call since he always knew and was attentive to the divine will. The Father at his Baptism did not say 'You will be', but 'You *are* my beloved Son'.

The apostles were all called by Jesus, even Paul, he out of due time (1 Cor 15:8). All Christians also have been called to follow the Way (Acts 9:2), to be holy, that is saints (Eph 4:1). In that sense all Christians have the same baptismal vocation, yet the Spirit who binds them all into one Body of Christ gives each different gifts, and these modify the vocation of each (1 Cor 12:4–13). The Church too is called as a whole, the very words '*ecclesia*' or 'synagogue' mean those who are called. But all Christians find themselves in a particular situation: Europeans, Asians, Americans, Africans; they may be rich or poor, intelligent or skilful or neither; their health may be poor or good. To a certain extent these and other circumstances determine the vocation that God wants each to fulfil. A vocation depends also on opportunities available as well as on one's leanings.

The priestly and religious vocations have this in common that their ways of life of their very nature are structured for assisting the coming of the Kingdom either through apostolic activities or in prayer and penance. But there are innumerable degrees of activity and prayerfulness between what are sometimes called (and rather confusingly) the active and contemplative ways of life, as though there were only two. All must pray, all must be apostolic, but in different proportions.

The great sacrament of Marriage is the entrance into yet another vocation; it too requiring very careful thought and prayer before being engaged upon. Today it is particularly urgent to examine the spiritualities of the many lay vocations and what particular virtues are needed in for instance the life of a lawyer, a doctor, a businessman, farmer, housewife, or husband, to name only a few.

von Hügel, Baron Friedrich
(1852–1925)
A European by upbringing, he was well acquainted with German philosophy and theology. He added an historical dimension and a special

interest in the mystical tradition, as witnesses to the existence of God. At that time the mystics were almost forgotten. From the age of 15 his home was London and he married an English woman, Lady Mary Herbert. The Abbé ↗Huvelin of Paris became his friend and guide, and he made frequent visits to the Continent. In 1905 he founded the London Society for the Study of Religion. He chose a congenial subject for his studies in the life of St ↗Catherine of Genoa: a lay woman, of the 15th century, married, one of the greatest of the Church's mystics yet at the same time, for all her raptures and fastings, a most practical person, nursing and managing a large hospital in her native city of Genoa.

This research confirmed him in one of his basic convictions, that the greatest of the mystics were among the most human and most integrated of the human race. His studies bore fruit in *The Mystical Element of Religion as Studied in St Catherine of Genoa and her Friends* (London, 1908).

The deepening and purifying of his spirit came about through a conflict of loyalties in the religious sphere; loyalty to the Church in its teaching and disciplinary activities – he remained an obedient son though allowing himself much freedom of expression; loyalty to his own intellectual conscience – he maintained his intellectual integrity; loyalty to his friends in the struggle of that generation – who fared less compassionately than he did. He never abandoned them.

M. de la Bédoyère, *Life of Baron von Hügel*, (London, 1951).

G. Greene (ed.), *Letters from Baron Von Hügel to a Niece*, (London, 1928). See also his *Selected Letters 1896–1924*

and B. Holland (ed.), *Memoir*, (London, 1972).

Fr. von Hügel, *Essays and Addresses on the Philosophy of Religion*, (London, first and second series, 1926 and 1938).

W

Ways or Degrees of Prayer and the Spiritual Life

Terminology is important. The following is a simple guide:

ORIGEN (d. *circa* 254) speaks of beginners, proficients, perfect (in equivalent terms).

CASSIAN (d. 435) writes of beginners (who have good will), of proficients (who are virtuous) and the perfect (whose prayer is love) (*cf. Conferences* 9:15 and 10:6, 7).

GREGORY OF NYSSA (d. *circa* 395) in his *Life of Moses* introduces into mystical writing the symbol of the Cloud (which hides God on Mount Sinai).

THE PSEUDO-DENIS (*circa* 500) writes of purgation, illumination and union (*cf. Heavenly Hierarchy* 10 and *Ecclesiastical Hierarchy* 6). He also introduces the Cloud. By this time there is another distinction: the active and the contemplative lives, the former meaning the elimination of vices (and this could be the first stage in a hermit's life), the latter referring to the withdrawal from all things to find God in the soul.

AUGUSTINE (d. 430) also used this distinction in the modern sense, of people whose life is active and those who withdraw to live a life of prayer (*cf. City of God*, 19:19). But he adds the 'mixed life', thus 'the life of leisure, the life of action and the combination of the two' (*cf. City of God*, ed. Knowles, p. 880).

HUGH OF ST VICTOR (d. 1141) had his own terminology: meditation, speculation, possession.

THOMAS AQUINAS (d. 1274) integrates the two in strands: beginners – purgative way; proficients – illuminative way; and perfect – unitive way (*S. Th.*, IIa, IIae, q. 24, 9), without using the word 'purgative', etc.

JOHN OF THE CROSS (d. 1591) accepts this terminology.

TERESA OF AVILA (d. 1582) has her own divisions and not always consistently. Over the years, experience made her modify her earlier writings. (i) The *Autobiography* uses the image of watering a garden (the soul) – a very Spanish image – according to *four* methods: (a) with a bucket pulled up from a well by hand; (b) with a water-wheel and windlass, less laborious; (c) with a stream irrigating the garden; (d) with rain from heaven. The first is meditation, fighting distractions; the second is the state of recollection, of prayer of quiet, in which the will is firm, the other faculties restless; in the third, God has become the gardener; all the faculties are asleep to the world and can turn only to God; the fourth is the union of all the faculties with God. This lasts for a short time, at most half an hour (*Life* chs. 11. 14–16, 18, 20). (ii) *The Way of Perfection* (chs. 27–42) is an exquisite commentary on the Lord's prayer – she here distinguishes the prayer of quiet from that of recollection. (iii) *The Interior Castle*: in the Soul are many mansions (i.e. rooms): the first is humility; the second, the practice of prayer; the third, meditation and a virtuous life. The first way of watering corresponds to the first three mansions (and is the purgative way). The fourth mansion is the start of supernatural prayer, i.e. the prayer of quiet (i.e. second method of watering); here the faculties of the soul are quiescent. The prayer of recollection precedes this and according to St Teresa is the first step in supernatural contemplative prayer. The fifth mansion (i.e. the third method of watering) is the prayer of union or spiritual betrothal; God takes possession, an unforgettable experience but brief (*cf.* the silkworm becoming a butterfly). The sixth mansion (*cf.* Dark Night of the Spirit, of St John on the Cross), locutions and visions. The seventh is the spiritual marriage, dazzling light – permanent peace, '*para siempre*'. Greater space has been given to Teresa because she is rightly more read than the others, but also is at times more confusing.

Many other divisions have in recent times been suggested, besides these classical ones. It has been rightly seen that the major division is at the point where the action of God becomes more noticeable than the action of the soul, i.e. during the transitional period of the illuminative way; and the first stages of this are the most critical, as the person is at a loss to know whether he should stay quiet or revert to being active in praying. A few rules may be in place:

(i) With Teresa and Francis of Sales, always prepare something to pray about, 'not presuming on God giving his special favours.

(ii) Any other prayer has, in fact, become impossible, for example words and images seem obstacles.

(iii) All other interests, besides God and his work, have ceased to attract.

(iv) The person now longs to be alone with God, and finds peace therein.

These last three are in *The Ascent of St John* (Bk. 2:13). When the river has been crossed, it remains to follow the guiding of the Spirit, and not delay on the road, not seeking anything other than God, who is found by faith and love.

Beginners, proficients, perfect describe rather the degree of virtue in each stage; *purgative, illuminative, unitive,* more the degree of union with God.

See ↗Apophatic way.

Weil, Simone (*1909–43*)
French philosopher and spiritual writer of partially Jewish extraction, but not of Jewish religion or practice. At school she came under the powerful influence of Emile Chartier Alain, with his emphasis on the will. As a young woman, wanting to identify herself with the workers, she became a factory worker for a time (1934–5) and also associated herself with the communists of the day. During the Second World War she escaped with her family from France and went to the United States, but feeling guilty in not sharing the sufferings and famine of her friends and race, she returned to England. There she fell ill and refused to eat enough partly because she wished to share the want of her compatriots. This caused her death.

It was on reading the poem by Herbert entitled 'Love' that she had a mystical experience, in which she knew that Jesus was beside her and that he was God incarnate, a belief she never abandoned. This made her passionately interested in the Catholic Church and for a long time she wanted to be baptized. The obstacle was her conviction about other religions, notably Buddhism and her certainty that other religious 'heroes' were incarnations of God. Further she could not accept the God of the Old Testament whom she thought cruel, and so considered herself a kind of Marcionist, or latter-day Gnostic, Marcion having repudiated the Old Testament for the same reason. Her esteem for the idea of the Catholic Church remained, but a professed member she never became. Her sincerity, the depth of her researches, the living out her convictions no matter how painful to herself, make her a heroine for her generation and after.

Emma Cranford (tr.), *Gravity and Grace*, (London, 1972).

J.B. Perrin and G. Thibon, *Simone Weil as we knew her*, (London, 1953).

J.B. Perrin, *Waiting for God*, (New York, 1959).

S. Petrement, *Simone Weil, A Life*, (London, 1977).

Richard Rees (ed. and tr.), *Seventy Letters*, (London, 1965).

Richard Rees (ed. and tr.), *On Science, Necessity and the Love of God*, (New York, 1968).

Wesley, John (*1703–91*)
A Lincolnshire man, fifteenth son of an Anglican parson, he went to Oxford with his brother Charles. There they founded what was called derisively 'the holy club'. Three hours a day they spent in pious exercises. They rose at 4 a.m. They visited the sick. Yet John was offered a fellowship at Lincoln College, and acted also as curate in the Anglican Church. Dissatisfied, seeking greater dedication, he went to America. On board ship and on arrival in Georgia he was in contact with Moravian missionaries – i.e. disciples of the fervently emotional Count von Zinzendorf – himself a

disciple of the Pietist movement that had swept Germany. Wesley, back in England, attended one of their meetings and there in 1738 he was 'converted', he felt that Christ had saved him. 'I felt that I did trust in Christ, Christ alone, for salvation' (*Journal*).

From that time till his death he gave himself to spreading the Good News of Salvation. The Church of England disliked this enthusiasm. He therefore preached in the open. Thousands, tens of thousands, came to listen and believe. He was another St Francis in 18th century dress. Sadly, though he d:d not wish it, the Anglican Church cut him and his followers off from communion. The cause: his ordaining of some to the episcopate and priesthood for his followers in America. His own theology on grace was not Calvinist but traditional, he laid special stress on salvation, on the Eucharist, on the human personality of Christ, on faith. But also he stressed the need for personal religion, for prayer, for meeting to share the Bible, for good works. The simple people were thirsty for God, those herded into factories or down the mines. Wesley showed the way to a missionary Church, and the following century, in Protestantism, this became the hall-mark of the true Christian, preaching the Word from Ghana to India to China.

N. Curnock (ed.), *Journals, 1735–1790*, 8 vols, (London, 1909–16).

G. R. Cragg, *The Church and the Age of Reason*, (Harmondsworth, 1970). For general background.

J. Pudney, *John Wesley and his World*, (London, 1979).

William of St Thierry

Born at Liège about 1085 and died in the Cistercian monastery of Signy

1148. An intimate friend of St Bernard, they once, while both exceedingly ill, shared a hut at Clairvaux and discoursed the while on the *Song of Songs*. William in youth (perhaps at Laon) became aware of the Eastern Fathers and their teaching on prayer: ↗Origen, St ↗Gregory of Nyssa and the Pseudo-↗Denis. He became the bridge between East and West in this matter. First a monk of St Nicaise, then abbot of St Thierry, finally simple monk of Signy, he there came in contact with the newly-founded Carthusian monastery of Mont Dieu near Rheims. To the Carthusians there he wrote the little treatise on the spiritual life which Mabillon felicitously named, the *Golden Epistle*. He was the author of other spiritual works, *On the Nature and Dignity of Love*, the *Mirror of Faith*, *On Contemplation*, *Exposition on the Song of Songs*. He saw love as leading to knowledge of God. He went further: *amor ipse intellectus est*, to love is itself to know. He is writing of the love for God at its perfection; love then is a kind of knowledge. *Amor* is an inclination towards God; *dilectio* is an adherence to God, *charitas* is enjoyment of God. At this point the *Spirit* takes over our spirit, and the Spirit being both love and knowledge of Father for Son and Son for Father, we share not only in the love within the Trinity but also in their knowledge. We are in a sense deified.

'Yet humble and enlightened love attains to a more certain perception of it (i.e. God's life) than any effort of the reason to grasp it by thought; and it is always better than it is thought to be. Yet it is better thought than spoken of' (*The Golden Epistle*, s. 294, p. 104; but see also *S. Th.*, IIa, IIae, q. 23, art. 2 of Aquinas).

T. Berkeley (tr.), J.M. Déchanet

(ed.), *The Golden Epistle*, (Spencer, Mass., 1971).

J.M. Déchanet, *William of St Thierry, the Man and his Work*, (Spencer, Mass., 1972).

Y

Yoga
A most ancient far Eastern form of discipline of mind and body to reach the ultimate reality. In the Hindu tradition (in India) there are two kinds of Yoga, one the Classical which is concerned with control of all our members in order to set the soul free to attain ultimate awareness, the Raji or Royal Yoga. The other is also concerned with control but its aim is 'magical', that is, to acquire certain supra-normal powers, e.g. levitation. This is the Hatha Yoga. (For a critical view of the more esoterical aspects of this see *The Lotus and the Robot* by A. Koestler, London, 1960.)

The basic controls are as follows, and, as will be evident, have relevance to Christian meditation as possible technical aids:

(i) Counsels, compare the commandments of God in the Old Testament.

(ii) Discipline – ascetical practices, virtuous living, e.g. serenity.

(iii) Posture (see ↗Yoga postures).

(iv) Breath control, compare some eastern Christian practices.

(v) Withdrawal of the senses, similar to Recollection in Christian asceticism.

(vi) Concentration – and fixing attention on a single point.

(vii) Meditation.

(viii) Contemplation, that is total absorption in the object (*samadhi*), an identity with the object.

The final stage (viii) is not, as it stands, compatible with Christian revelation, but may be more a statement of what is experienced than of an ontological reality, more especially as the Hindu mind does not normally think in terms of essences but rather in that of experience. There is much here from which Christians could learn in the technique of recollection.

See B. Griffiths, OSB, 'Yoga', in *N.C.E.*

Yoga Postures
Or *Asana*, are postures of the body, practised in Eastern religions, which, by bracing or refreshing the whole body, influence the whole man and so aid meditation. Their number is very great. Among the chief are:

STANDING POSTURES 1. The obeissance; 2. The tree;

HORIZONTAL POSTURES 3. The snake; 4. The bent bow; 5. The dolphin;

KNEELING POSTURES 6. The (full) backward bend; 7. The folded leaf;

SITTING POSTURES 8. The back stretch; 9. Reintegration, the perfect posture (the lotus);

INVERTED POSTURES 10. The candle; 11. The plough; 12. The pole;

POSTURE OF RELAXATION i.e. flat on one's back.

Each of these postures is linked with controlled breathing (*pranayama*). If practised *with discretion*, and best under an experienced guru, they produce physical well-being, promote calm relaxation for meditation and energy for virtuous action. The generally applied form of yoga is a sitting position which is both relaxed and yet steady, so that the practitioner can remain still to meditate for long periods without discomfort.

J.M. Déchanet, osb, *Christian Yoga*, (London and New York, 1960).

J.M. Déchanet, osb, *Yoga in Ten Lessons*, (London and New York, 1965).

Z

Zen

By origin a Buddhist method for reaching *satori*, enlightenment or ultimately Nirvana. It originated in China in the 7th century but we know it today as a Japanese phenomenon which has adherents throughout the Western world. In China it developed into two schools, which schools came over to Japan *circa* 1200. There they are called the Rinzai school and the Soto school. They are both techniques for facilitating the experience of *satori* or enlightenment. The Soto method is a gradual elimination through meditation of all that can impede enlightenment. Rinzai's method is in a sense no method, but a use of shock tactics, to eliminate the last obstacle, 'thinking', by presenting to the novice some apparently incomprehensible statement called mondo, or ↗koans. A *mondo* is a dialogue between master and disciple, a *koan* is often only the unexpected, disconcerting concluding remark of the master. This state of beyond-reasoning is of the essence of Zen; it is clear that some forms of Christian prayer resemble this, though not self-induced, when the condition becomes enlightenment rather than reasoning. In recent centuries this break with reason has been called 'the ligature' when reasoning is no longer possible. Christian masters however normally teach, not so much to aim at this condition, as to make way for it if God desires one so to pray. Christian masters of the spiritual life do not esteem any less the Scriptures since these are both a stimulus and a safeguard in such obscure regions of the Way. Both traditions, Zen and Christian, declare that this suspension of reasoning can be of inestimable value and both declare that we must get down also to ordinary living during this life, in the light of the wonder of these experiences. Of course there still remain differences that may be important for a just judgement of Zen. But Zen certainly has penetrated deeply into the nature of meditation and beyond. The Christian's aim or goal is not primarily enlightenment in *this* life but in *the next*. Zen can be this also.

H.M. Enomiya-Lassalle, *Zen, Way to Enlightenment*, (London, 1966).

A. Graham, *Zen Catholicism*, (London, 1964).

A. Graham, *Conversations: Christian and Buddhist*, (New York, 1968).

C. Humphrey, *Zen*, (London, 1962).

D.T. Suzuki, *Essays in Zen Buddhism*, 3 series, (London, from 1927).